Organizational Management

Systems and Process

Earl F. Lundgren
University of Missouri, Columbia

Canfield Press ⽊ San Francisco
A Department of Harper & Row, Publishers, Inc.
New York   Evanston   London

Editing: Linda Purrington
Text and cover design: Joseph di Chiarro
Cover photograph: Elihu Blotnick, BBM Associates
Line illustration: Carl Brown

Organizational Management
Systems and Process

Library of Congress Cataloging in Publication Data

Lundgren, Earl F.
    Organizational management: systems and process.

    1. Industrial management. I. Title.
HD31.L78   658.4   73–21940
ISBN 0–06–385355–8

74 75 76 77   10 9 8 7 6 5 4 3 2

To Georgianna, Esther, Andrew, Diane,
Christopher, and Augustina

Preface

The challenge in writing a book on management rests in the need to systematically pull together several theoretical approaches to the study and practice of management. The challenge is met by providing a comprehensive coverage of those decisions managers must make to run an organization and the associated knowledge necessary to decision-making efficiency and effectiveness. The three major theoretical management models—classical, behavioral, and management science—contribute to an understanding of organizational management whenever and wherever necessary. And because the practice of management is eclectic in its selection of the best managerial methods from among diverse alternatives, this management text will also be eclectic.

Since one cannot prescribe for every specific managerial situation, however, the text must also provide a general, noneclectic understanding of the theories underlying the several management decision areas. Thus theory will help to bridge the gaps left by a necessarily eclectic approach.

This book has been prepared with the two- and four-year undergraduate college student in mind. It should, therefore, be helpful to anyone with little or no previous knowledge of organizational management.

The book contains five parts divided into sixteen chapters. Part I introduces the basic concepts of organization and management, relates theory to practice, and reviews the development of theory up to the present time. An overview of management practice is provided in chapter 1, a brief history of management in chapter 2, and coverage of modern theory in chapter 3.

Part II introduces some of the knowledge a manager should have in order to understand the decision-making process and to make effective decisions in the various management decision areas. Chapter 4 describes behavioral aspects of decision making as well as introducing some of the quantitative tools that help in decision making. Chapter 5 stresses the importance of information to decision making.

Part III deals directly with the three important management decision areas: planning, controlling, and organizing. Chapter 6 discusses types of plans and the planning process. Chapter 7 stresses the importance of control systems, while chapters 8 and 9 describe the various organizational structures and the impact of structure on behavior.

Part IV sets forth the importance of knowledge about people and their behavior to organizational success. Chapter 10 describes facets of people management and development. Chapter 11 relates the individual to the organization, while chapter 12 relates the group to the organization. Chapter 13 integrates the previous chapters with a discussion of leadership.

Part V closes the book with an analysis of operations management in chapter 14; a discussion of a theory of organizational growth and of problems associated with change in chapter 15; and in chapter 16, a look at some of the issues and challenges facing business organizations today and in the future.

I gratefully acknowledge the help of several individuals in the preparation of this text. My colleagues at the University of Missouri, Columbia read and commented on several of the chapters. M. Gene Newport, University of Alabama in Birmingham, and Thomas J. Nolan, Los Angeles Pierce College, made many valuable suggestions for improvement.

My thanks to Debbie Woodward for typing the manuscript and my special appreciation to my wife, Georgia, for her constant encouragement.

Contents

Part IV Working with People

Part V   The Job and the Challenge

Introduction

I

The Practice of Management

1

All about us, every day, we see the practice of management. It may be on a lofty scale, involving the management of entire nations, or it may be on a smaller scale, such as the management of a household or of a corner newsstand. All of us manage something—our personal careers, our finances, our homes. And some of us have had experience at managing groups and organizations as well. Management, in one form or another, is required in all areas of life and has been developing since man began.

In the formal study of management, however, the intimate relationship between management and the complex organization concerns us more than, for example, managing our personal affairs in the routine of life. This formal study is fascinating, because the management of large, complex organizations often is tense, creative, and exciting. We can catch a hint of this excitement just by reading advertisements—competing airline ads, for example.

In the business world, competition among companies is often keen and intense. We have all watched companies competing to become number one in an industry—Schlitz battling to wrest leadership away from Anheuser-Busch in brewing and Ford going all-out to match the profitability of General Motors. These battles royal command public attention; but there are also hundreds and thousands of other companies and organizations that daily pit their managerial talents against each other as they strive to survive, grow, and prosper. The formal study of business management takes us behind the scenes in this gripping drama.

Good management is vital to success, and there is great demand for top-flight managerial talent. Organizations spend vast amounts of time, energy, and money searching for outstanding managers who can lead the way to organizational success. The road to managerial success is challenging and difficult, and the rewards are proportionately great.

This book is an introduction to the study of management—a guide to learning about the managerial job and what a manager must know and do in order to meet the challenges facing him. A considerable body of knowledge about management has built up over the past hundred years. This knowledge and the application of it will be the focus of our attention.

The Complex Organization

Organizations today grow large and complex very rapidly. Governments, businesses, hospitals, volunteer organizations, and others reveal an intricacy today that would have confounded the casual observer a few years back. Technological development is the primary reason for this organizational growth and intricacy. Complex products—the automobile, computer, television, aircraft—force complexity on the organizations that manufacture these products. Sophisticated communications and data-processing methods facilitate the development of farflung enterprises and the employment of thousands of people. Advances in one specialized area of activity—travel in space, for example—often lead to new product developments that spawn entirely new industries. Developments in compact space foods have been transferred to the manufacture of foods for campers, mountain climbers, and storage in survival kits. Camera, toy, razor, and toothbrush manufacturers have successfully applied the newest battery technologies in their products.

And the process continues. Some people feel that if organizations exceed a certain size, these organizations lose effectiveness and may topple, like overgrown, clumsy giants. But no limit on size has been established by experience. And although we often complain about bureaucratic labyrinths, most organizations today are more responsive to the consumer than ever before. These organizations retain flexibility and growth potential through good management. Let us examine some of the challenges to management that complex organizations present.

What Is an Organization?

An organization is a system, and *a system is composed of elements or subsystems so interrelated and integrated that they form a whole that displays unique attributes.*[1] A system of this description, however, could be biological in nature, requiring no conscious direction to make it work. So we have to elevate our relatively simple system to a new and higher level—to the level of a social system or the level of a human organization.

On this plane, we include people as a subsystem, and we include so many people that constant face-to-face personal interaction is impossible. In other words, the system or organization is complex. If the number of people were low enough to allow constant face-to-face interaction, we would call the set of people a *group*. Using this standard of personal contact, the differentiation between a group and an organization would occur at from fifteen to twenty people. This sliding figure is derived from management experience.

Another important subsystem we add is management practice or the management process—what management must do to direct the organization as a whole toward the achievement of established goals. To summarize, then, *an organization is a complex system, which includes as subsystems: (1) management, to interrelate and integrate through appropriate linking processes all the elements of the system in a manner designed to achieve the organizational objectives, and (2) a sufficient number of people so that constant face-to-face interaction is impossible.*

All subsystems are vital to the successful functioning of an organization, but if one were to be chosen as "more equal than the others," it would be management. Without management, an organization soon declines to a state of chaos and disintegration. With management, it comes alive and achieves. Figure 1–1 illustrates the organization as a system, showing some of the possible subsystems and the interactions among them.

What Is Management?

Management can be and is defined in different ways. For example: "The process of managing consists in getting things done for, with, and through people. Therefore, knowledge about managing must break down into two categories: (1) knowledge about the things to be done, the work, and (2) knowledge about the people who do the work."[2] Also: "Management is the planning, organizing, directing, and controlling of the enterprise's operations so that organization objectives can be achieved economically and effectively."[3]

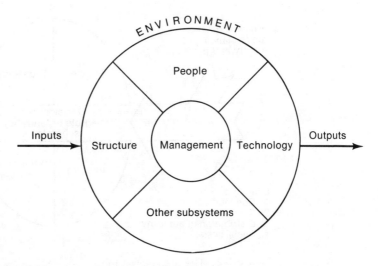

Figure 1–1 The organization as a system

We can begin our definition of management by stating that it is the application of knowledge to reality through decision making. This definition means, in part, that management must make decisions about all aspects of the organization, including the setting of goals, choosing ways to achieve the goals, deciding what sort of formal structure to have, determining how best to provide day-to-day leadership, and planning how to integrate all subsystems into a unified whole.

The knowledge and understanding that management must possess includes knowing the subsystems of an organization, knowing the tools that can aid in decision making, understanding how people behave as individuals and in groups, and understanding how different types of formal structures work. And these are only a few of the decisions that must be made and represent a small part of the knowledge and understanding that management should command.

A Formal Definition *Management, then, is a force that, through decision making based on knowledge and understanding, interrelates and integrates, via appropriate linking processes, all the elements of the organizational system in a manner designed to achieve the organizational objectives* (figure 1–2).

Notice that this definition says nothing about the quality of management and whether it will make the organization effective. That depends on the depth and breadth of knowledge and understanding that management commands and the skill with which

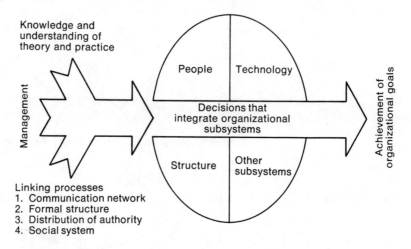

Figure 1–2 The managerial job

management applies the knowledge. The skill, knowledge, and understanding that management has will be drawn largely from personal experience and from study of the classical, behaviorial, and quantitative approaches to management and to organizations. These three approaches will be explained in chapter 2.

The linking processes mentioned in the formal definition include an organization's communication network, its formal structure, its distribution of authority, and its social system. Some of these linking processes are more easy to control than others. Ordering person *A* to report to person *B* on Monday morning at 8:00 A.M. for a job assignment is an example of formal structuring as a linking process that is relatively easy to control. We will try to indicate throughout the book how much difficulty management might find in using linking processes to integrate the various subsystems of an organization.

Management, Organization, and Synergy

A favorable result of the management–organization link is called *synergy*. This term means that when all the organizational subsystems work together under the guidance of management, the total system produces an impact greater than the sum of all individual parts. This total impact is the synergistic effect.

Synergy is a phenomenon common in nature (in many biological systems, for example), and it is a phenomenon of human organizations, too. Synergy is the reason why a school is more than a long list of students and teachers and administrators; it is the reason why an organization of these people makes a functioning school. *Synergy* helps define *organization*. Explicitly recognizing the synergistic effect of an organization, the effect of being greater as a whole than the sum of its parts, and then trying to increase that effect are made easier by thinking of an organization as a system and by working with it as such.

Having begun our study by defining management and organization, we now have a foundation for looking at management practice. In subsequent chapters, we will consider separately the various management activities of planning, organizing, controlling, and leading. First, let us consider the general question of whether management practice is a science or an art.

Management: Science or Art?

Management is an art in that skill is required of the manager, but the quality of the art depends on the manager's skill in using the scientific theory, data, and technique of management. Harold Koontz has described this relationship quite well:

Managing is an art, but so are engineering, medicine, accounting, and baseball. For art is the application of knowledge to reality with the view to accomplishing some concrete results.... As can be readily recognized, the best art arises where the artist possesses a store of organized and applicable knowledge and understands how to apply it to reality.

Thus engineers have long understood that the best designers are those who are well grounded in the underlying sciences and who have an ability to conceptualize a problem in the light of goals sought and the further ability to design a solution to the problem to accomplish goals at the lowest system cost.

The same can be said of the task of managing. As an art, there is every reason to believe that it will succeed best if the practitioner has a store of applicable and organized knowledge to serve him. This knowledge, when organized, is science. When it is organized in such a way as to serve practice best, it becomes a truly operational science.[4]

Experience Adapts Knowledge

If art in management is the application of management knowledge to reality, then experience, repetition, and practice should help make that application skillful and effective. For example, problem finding and opportunity finding are as important to the manager as problem solving. But whereas problem-solving methods may be taught in formal education programs, skill in problem finding and opportunity finding more frequently develops through experience. J. S. Livingston, a writer for the *Harvard Business Review,* comments on this point: "Managers who lack the skill needed to find those opportunities that will yield the greatest results, not uncommonly spend their time doing the wrong things. But opportunity-finding skill, like problem-finding skill, must be acquired through direct personal experience on the job."[5] Experience does count and must be acquired along with fact learning by anyone striving to be an effective manager (figure 1–3).

Talent and Study

Are some managers *naturals?* If by natural management, we mean the ability to successfully manage in all circumstances without benefit of the available, formal body of knowledge, the answer probably is no. Of course, there are many successful managers whose only training was acquired in the school of hard knocks. And experience can be a great teacher. But twenty years of experience can also mean one year of experience repeated twenty times over without any real development. So while the manager who has only experience to guide him may be quite successful in one particular business or at one point in time, he might fall flat on his face if he tried to manage in another situation or at some other time. He has no scientific foundation to complement his experience. Theory helps to make application of experience flexible and adaptable.

The great entrepreneurs in our own business history demonstrated a flair for starting a business and achieving great organizational success—up to a point. It often happened that when their organizations reached a certain size and age, their entrepreneurial talents were no longer appropriate. An approach to management was needed that would better meet the demands of a relatively mature company as opposed to a young and rapidly growing one.

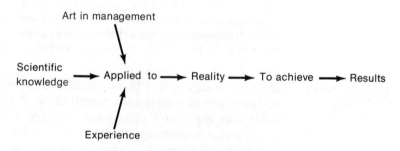

Figure 1–3 The practice of management

For example, both John D. Rockefeller and Henry Ford were remarkably successful entrepreneurs; yet both had to move aside as their organizations matured. Perhaps the best example of this necessary shift in leadership shows up in the early history of General Motors. The GM president until 1920 was Will Durant, a brilliant, innovative individual who guided the company's fortunes through the wild early years of the automobile industry. However, as is typical of many empire builders, Durant exercised a personal control that hindered rather than helped as the company grew. As GM became larger and more complex, it was impractical for one man to personally oversee every detail of the company's operations. What GM needed by 1920 was someone who could consolidate what the company already had, laying a foundation for future growth. Such a person would have to delegate much of his authority, set up an appropriate organizational structure, institute effective planning and control systems, and decentralize operations so that top management would be free from minor decision problems. The man who brought this kind of managerial talent to GM was Alfred P. Sloan, Jr. He replaced Durant in 1920 and provided effective leadership for the following three decades. During that time, of course, GM developed into the gigantic corporation with which we are all familiar today.

Business historian S. M. Davis says much the same thing: that the organization builders who followed the Rockefellers, Fords, and Durants were "men who systematically and explicitly set about defining organizational relationships and structures." Davis adds that, "The functions which the early owner-mangers had performed personally on a day-to-day basis became the subject of rational scrutiny and of strategic policy formulation. Moreover, organization structures were specifically devised to help administrators implement new growth strategies."[6]

The individual who has the natural ability to manage even one kind of organization under varying conditions is, at the very least, unusual. It is true that some persons have a greater aptitude than others for the art of managing—for the skill required to apply learned knowledge. But even for these talented individuals, managerial success requires knowledge and experience in order to transform talent and motivation into an acceptable level of skill. Even after these elements have been welded together, most managers are likely to encounter some difficulty in transferring from one managerial role to another. The role of initiator is very different from that of consolidator, and different skills, experiences, and knowledges are required.

How universal are the principles and theory of management? Can we transfer management know-how from one organization to another, from one country to another, or from one organization at a given point in time to that same organization at a later time? Koontz suggests that when the proper separation is made between art and science in managing, it is possible to assert the universality and transferability of the science part of management—the body of knowledge that underlies all management action.[7]

Hence, if one speaks of the transfer of American managerial know-how to another country, the science of management—the basic concepts, theory, and principles—may be transferred. But the practice, the art, the application of theory to reality, must be modified and adapted to the new cultural environment—that is, the economic, technological, social, political, and ethical milieu of the country. Only then will the practice of management have a chance to be acceptable and successful in the new environment.

But separating out the basic fundamentals of management from the practice of management is easier said than done. In the field of comparative management, many studies contribute to an understanding of management in differing environments, but few studies, if any, effectively separate the science of management from the art.

Likewise, the same problem that plagued Will Durant of General Motors has also afflicted many American companies in recent years as they have tried to set up operations in other countries. Their failure to adapt the practice of management to another country's culture has sometimes aroused resentment and even alienation from the American approach. In response to these experiences American organizations are becoming more sophisticated and are realizing that American practices and techniques can seldom be transferred to another culture without adaptation. Theoretically the science of management is universal and transferable. The problem lies in precisely defining the science so that a transfer of essential knowlege and theory can be made.

Management Philosophy

Every organization has a unique pattern by which its various elements are integrated, and management philosophy predominantly shapes that pattern. The attitudes and values of top management shape the management philosophy, which is the product of both conscious deliberation and unconscious evolution over time.

For example, the management of a given company may decide, at a given point in time, to be more venturesome than before—to get involved in new projects, to institute a profit-sharing plan, or to change from a centralized to a decentralized operation. If the new programs are successful and the philosophy becomes known outside the organization, the company will tend to attract other managers with similar attitudes and values. As new managers are hired and promoted, some of the criteria for advancement may well be agreement with the current philosophy. In this way, the philosophy will be reinforced and probably will continue to evolve organically in the direction established by managerial decision.

According to an old proverb, you cannot argue with success; by the same token, nothing will destroy a management philosophy more quickly than failure. If one philosophy fails, a brand-new philosophy most likely will be the order of the day—deliberately chosen to avoid past mistakes and to help assure future success. The institution of a new philosophy is often aided by the hiring of a new management team—complete with attitudes and values to match the new philosophy.

So *management philosophy is a general guide that determines how an organization will be run and that affects every facet of its operation.* If, for some reason, fact and philosophy do not correspond, there can be trouble. For example, if top management is dedicated to highly centralized control and authority while the organization has a formal structure set up for a decentralized operation, lower-level managers are likely to be frustrated and angry by what they will perceive as excessive control from above. If they do, efficiency may plunge and continue at a low level as long as top management and lower-level managers are working at cross-purposes. Eventually informal adjustments may improve the situation, but improvement would take place more rapidly if either the philosophy were changed or the structure were modified to accommodate the philosophy. Most successful organizations seem to prove this point in that their philosophies and practices agree with and reinforce each other.

Theory and Philosophy

What is the relationship between theory and philosophy in management? For one thing, values held by managers will lead them to choose alternatives they consider desirable and to reject those they consider undesirable. These choices are prescriptive; they are courses of action that establish, set forth, or prescribe what management feels is appropriate behavior and proper states of affairs.

Scientific findings and theory, on the other hand, are generally descriptive; they help to explain for the manager what will happen for each of the alternatives available. Therefore, in choosing among alternative courses of action:

> ... it would help the manager to know (1) the consequences of his choice and (2) the alternatives from which he might choose. This is where scientific findings and theory come into play. It is the role of the scientist, through investigation, to describe (rather than prescribe) the consequences of certain actions, and the means of attaining prescribed ends. Accurate description and explanation of phenomena make it possible to predict the consequences of actions. Although a manager is not expected to be a scientist, he does need an appreciation of the role that scientific study plays in the development of an integrated and useful management philosophy.[8]

In making his decisions, a manager cannot act as though his organization were a world in itself. He must act knowing that the decisions he makes have an impact on the environment outside the organization, and that the environment in turn will modify decisions made within the organization. In recognition of this interaction, management must run the organization on an open-system basis. The values held by management and incorporated into management philosophy must be flexible enough to permit adaptations to the real external world.

The Organization as an Open System

An analysis of systems shows that there are open systems and closed systems. A *closed system* is a self-contained unit, isolated from its external environment. On the other hand, an *open system* "recognizes the existence of aspects of its external environment which affect the system and are in turn affected by the system."[9] Modern theory assumes the organization to be, and therefore speaks of the organization as, an open system.

Setting limits to a system or subsystem is often a matter of accommodation to purpose. For example, a research study of a purchasing department may regard the rest of the organization outside the purchasing department as part of the external environment. A broad view of an organization, however, may enclose customers, suppliers, and distributors within the boundaries of the organizational system. The system boundaries are fluid, depending on the purpose for their location; but when we deal with an organization as a unitary whole, the government, stockholders, customers, suppliers, and distributors are usually placed outside the system and considered part of the external environment (figure 1–4).

Maintaining System Equilibrium An important characteristic of an organization is its constant effort to maintain stability. Changes both within the organization and in its environment may threaten the smooth operation of an organization and its ability to achieve organizational goals. This threatened disruption or potential chaos in an organization is a continuing phenomenon and is called *entropy*, a word borrowed from the field of physics, where it describes the continual tendency toward randomness, disorder, or chaos in a system.

In a closed system, there is no possibility of energy or material input from the environment. Such a system inevitably moves toward a static equilibrium or condition in which it can no longer function, since functioning implies a dynamic state as opposed to a static one. A clock or engine is a closed system. From the moment a closed system, such as a clock, is completed, entropy sets in. The system can be repaired, of course, but it has no capacity for repairing itself.

The characteristic of capacity for self-repair is reserved to the open system. A human body is an open system. It continuously

Figure 1–4 The organization as an open system

adjusts to the environment. If the weather is hot, the body activates its cooling mechanism; if the weather is cold, the body responds to conserve heat. When the body is injured or sick, it immediately reacts to heal the injury or to fight the disease. Eventually, of course, the body can no longer respond, and it ceases to live. To this extent the human body is also a closed system. Whether or not a system is considered closed depends on the scope of one's inquiry. For example, in physics, the question of whether or not the universe itself is a closed system is now under heavy debate.

Classification of Systems and Equilibrium The natures of systems vary considerably from each other, and therefore in general systems theory a threefold classification has been found useful. One class consists of physical or mechanical systems that are closed; the second consists of biological systems that are open; and the third consists of human and social systems that are open. Organizations fall into the third classification.

This classification of organizations is significant, since a social system can exist indefinitely, while open biological systems die and physical or mechanical systems, being closed, must eventually succumb to entropy and cease to function. Through constant interaction with and through the receipt of resources and information from the environment, the social system can survive as long as the environment is favorable.

All open systems can resist entropy and continue to survive through interaction with the environment and the achievement of an equilibrium condition called *homeostasis*. This stable condition is dynamic rather than static and requires constant adaptation to the environment. It is a characteristic of biological systems, which must finally die, and of social systems.

The Challenge to Management The fact that an organization is an open social system suggests one basic criterion for defining the task of management. Management must control the elements leading to homeostasis in order to maintain a dynamic equilibrium and to assure the survival of the organization. This means that management must acquire adequate resources and accurate information so that necessary internal adjustments of subsystems can be made in response to environmental changes. In more specific terms, the business organization, for example, must be able to predict market fluctuations and make the necessary internal adjustments to meet customer demand.

Many companies also attempt to influence the environment and to create demand for new products or newly styled products. But whether one is trying to influence or is simply reacting to the environment, the importance of accurate information cannot be overstated. To get this information, management must establish an adequate *feedback* system.

Feedback is a common phenomenon. The home thermostat for heating is one example. The thermostat monitors temperature in the house, and when it gets too cold, the thermostat sends a message, by triggering apparatus, to the furnace to send more heat. Feedback involves the measurement of variance about some norm—the measurement of temperature variance about a norm of 72 degrees Fahrenheit, for example (figure 1–5). All states not centered at the norm are registered as plus or minus states compared to the norm.

Similarly, the business organization must have feedback—information about what is going on in the world. Norms can be any measures the company chooses: share of the market, last year's level of sales, customer complaints, and so on. With information about its share of the market, for example, the company can make whatever adjustments are necessary to keep it at or close to the established norm. Naturally, most activity will be generated when share of the market falls below the norm—that is, when we receive negative feedback. Positive feedback produces happiness but provides little motivation for change. While many norms, such as a desired maximum level of customer complaints, may remain constant for many years, other norms pertaining to

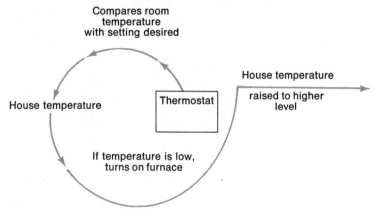

Figure 1–5 Feedback

such areas as sales volume should constantly increase in order to stay abreast or ahead of inflation and competition. Thus, feedback and adequate resources, both received from the environment, are necessary for management to make the adjustments and generate the outputs that will help the organization maintain its homeostatic condition.

Another important consideration for management is the speed of adaptation. If an organization reacts too quickly to external input, the internal balance among subsystems may be disturbed. Reacting too slowly may throw the whole system out of kilter with the environment. Even when the speed of adaptation is just right, some stress and strain is bound to occur. The organization must find ways of maintaining internal harmony while constantly striving for compatibility with the environment.

A related problem is the mode or manner of adaptation. If adaptation is handled clumsily, without regard for human feelings, relationships inside the system may be upset, cancelling out the original good intent of bringing the organization in line with the environment. How adaptation is handled is the responsibility of management, of course; and since adaptation of internal affairs to external affairs is so vital to the life of the organization, and since these affairs are so complex, the management of them is also bound to be very complex.

Levels of Management Responsibility

We have been speaking of management as though it were a homogeneous whole, as though all managers in an organization had the same responsibilities. In complex organizations, however, managers at different levels have different responsibilities.

There are three easily identified management levels in most complex organizations: top management, middle management, and operating management (figure 1–6). The top level usually comprises the chief executive officer, vice presidents, and top staff officers. The middle level embraces a wide variety of titles: production supervisor, sales manager, purchasing agent, chief accountant, advertising manager, and many others. The operating level encompasses foremen, branch managers, section chiefs, and others.

Titles are deceptive, of course, although they do give an indication of the nature of a job. But the real definition of a job lies in the duties. At the top level, managers confront great uncertainty and spend much of their time dealing with environmental influences.

TOP MANAGEMENT	
	Deals with environmental forces
	Plans, organizes, controls
	Provides overall leadership
MIDDLE MANAGEMENT	
	Coordinates inputs, production, and outputs
	Acts as intermediary between top and operating management
OPERATING MANAGEMENT	
	Gets the work done

Figure 1–6   Management levels

The openness of the open system is most critical at this level. Top executives must interpret information and establish resource plans that will assure the organization's dynamic equilibrium.

Top managers try to reduce uncertainties about the environment by setting up information systems and by planning. These managers must also structure the organization so that its components are properly integrated and must provide the overall leadership necessary to the achievement of goals. Moreover, at the same time uncertainty reduction is going on, top management must assure organizational flexibility so that continued adaptation to the environment is possible. Top-level management orchestrates the conflict between internal stability and external change. They establish homeostasis as a defense against entropy.

Middle Management   A prime responsibility at the middle-management level is the coordination of resource inputs so that the operating level can effectively produce goods and/or services. The distribution of output—the volumes of sales for the different kinds and styles of products and services that an organization markets—must also be integrated with the transformation of inputs to outputs. In other words, production managers, for example, must know when to produce and how much to produce of specific products. To achieve this integration requires close cooperation between middle-management production and marketing people. They will naturally work under guidance from top management as to the overall emphases given to market segments. Middle management must do the detailed distribution of resources within the organization—again following general guidelines from top management.

In many instances, the job really is that of intermediary between top management and operating management. The long-range plans of top management must be converted to intermediate-range plans for the operating department. If internal restructuring or process changes are necessary to meet environmental demands, the job of making the change falls to middle management. There is more routine at this level than at the top level and more concern for ensuring internal coordination and efficiency than for relating organizational activities to the environment.

Operating Management

At the level of operating management we get down to the most concrete, detailed aspects of the organizational task. Here the intermediate plans of middle management are translated into short-range operating plans. The operating managers often find themselves involved in routine, day-to-day production.

Depending on the type of organization, operating management may include a great variety of personnel. In addition to factory production foremen and straw bosses, there may be university professors, scientists in a research lab, and stewards in a trade union. Although these people are not physically producing goods and although their work may be technical, they are still carrying on the business of their organizations and, as such, are included at the level of operating management. The diversity of their jobs helps to define the job of operating management too.

Interdependence of Management Levels

While the three levels of management have different responsibilities, no level can operate independently of the others. To ensure organizational success, they must recognize their interdependence as a function of ongoing activity. All three levels are part of the managerial system and of the total organizational system. As such, their actions and decisions must be interrelated and integrated so that organizational goals may be achieved.

This completes our initial view of management practice. Before moving on to other perspectives, however, we should set the conceptual scheme that will guide our study throughout the book.

Our Conceptual Framework

Having completed an initial overview of management practice, we can now set up a conceptual scheme to guide further study. Our formal definition of management contains the essence of the conceptual framework; that is, we define management as decision making based on knowledge and understanding. In the various areas of management activity, therefore, we will indicate the decisions that management must make and the knowledge it must have to make effective decisions. A common thread throughout will be the interrelatedness of decisions that is required to move all integrated elements of the organizational system along the path to success.

As figure 1–7 shows, management uses a variety of tools to integrate all the organizational subsystems. Furthermore, man-

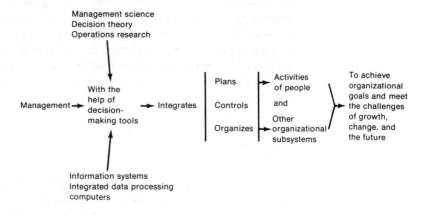

HOW MANAGEMENT OPERATES

CORRESPONDING ORGANIZATION OF THE BOOK

Part I	Part II	Part III	Part IV	Part V
Introduction	Decision Theory	Management Decision Areas	Working with People	The Job and the Challenge

Chapters	Chapters	Chapters	Chapters	Chapters
1. The Practice of Management	4. Deciding How to Decide	6. Planning	10. Managing and Developing People	14. Operations Management
2. Historical Perspectives	5. Managing Information	7. Control	11. The Individual and the Organization	15. Organizational Growth, Change, and Development
3. Modern Theory		8. Variations on Organization Structure	12. The Group and the Organization	16. Current and Future Issues
		9. Structure and Behavior	13. Leadership	

Figure 1–7 Organizational management and the conceptual framework of the book

agement integrates subsystems primarily through the planning, organizing, and controlling of the linking processes. All of this managerial activity, of course, aims at the setting and achievement of organizational goals and the preparation of the organization to meet future challenges.

As figure 1–7 also shows, we will cover all of these topics in later chapters. The material presented will be both descriptive and prescriptive. We will try to describe how various forces, many of them unplanned and unanticipated, modify what management would like to do. We will prescribe how management must recognize these forces and cope with them—must try to predict problems and try to provide for as many contingencies as possible. Both in describing and then in prescribing, we will be drawing on three approaches to the study of organizations and management: classical theory, behavioral theory, and management science. The overall approach will be eclectic: for each problem we consider, we will draw on whichever theory will explain for the manager, as he makes decisions, the courses of action open to him and the consequences of each.

Summary

In this first chapter, we have examined the nature of management and of organization and have offered an overview of management practice. We have suggested that management is an art and that the quality of management depends heavily on the acquisition and maintenance of a scientific body of knowledge. The artistic element in management is the application of knowledge to reality with the intention of achieving certain concrete results.

Experience is valuable in the development of a successful manager, but experience alone probably will limit a manager to developing skill in only one particular, familiar situation. It is extremely doubtful that there are very many born managers who need neither experience nor theoretical study. The best combination for success is formal education in the science of management, modified by experience in the field.

There has been controversy over the transferability of management principles from one situation to another. We suggested that the science component of management may be transferred but that the practice or art component must be adapted to local conditions. Adapting management philosophy or maintaining openness in philosophy is important in the process of transfer. Every organization develops a philosophy, which is usually heavily influenced by the attitudes and values of top management. This philosophy is a general guide for the organization and affects every facet of its operation. Managers should combine the results of scientific studies with their own value systems in developing a management philosophy for their organizations.

An organization is an open system. The organization interacts constantly with its environment and must adjust to environmental changes in order to maintain a dynamic equilibrium (homeostasis). Otherwise, a natural tendency toward disorder (entropy) will develop unchecked, and the organization will eventually cease to function. This analysis is of great importance to understanding the job of management.

Responsibility for analyzing the environment and for making long-range plans to anticipate changes or to influence the environment lies with top management. Middle management is charged with coordinating all internal subsystems and processes and with acting as intermediary between top management and operating management.

The third level of management, operating management, sees to accomplishment of the organizational task. In other words, it organizes and leads the work chosen and facilitated by the other two levels. Operating managers may be foremen and section chiefs or technical and professional people such as professors and scientists. Although the three levels of management have different responsibilities, they are not independent. They must recognize and emphasize their interdependence to assure a coordinated effort for organizational success.

Management Profile

Henry Ford I

Throughout the book, we will present a management profile. In some instances, the men chosen for these profiles will be practitioners, while others will be known mainly for their contributions to theory. These personal sketches of individual contributors are intended to broaden the historical context, to contrast and compare past and current management theory and practice, and to provide enjoyable educational experiences.

Our first subject, Henry Ford, was not a typical manager—perhaps not even a very good one if considered as a model for management today. Nonetheless he made his mark as a daring and innovative entrepreneur and manufacturer during the early part of this century. Ford was tremendously successful in the rough-and-tumble world of car manufacturing and certainly must be classified as a contributor to modern manufacturing management because of the many innovations he introduced.

A New Car for $500 Ford was a believer in price competition and was eminently successful in following this philosophy for over twenty years—until 1927. His manufacturing innovations enabled him to sell the Model T Ford for less than any other car on the market. In 1913, with the installation and operation of the first automobile assembly line, Ford produced 250,000 cars and was thus able to price one model at only $500. His innovations accelerated product turnover, and the profit he realized helped him cut prices competitively.

Although Ford was responsible for many advances in metallurgy, machine tooling, and manufacturing routines, he did not believe in changing car models from year to year, as manufacturers now do to stimulate the market. He produced the same car, the Model T, from 1908 to 1927. Furthermore, he is reputed to have said that customers could have any color car they wanted as long as it was black. Today color supply and variation are used to appeal to buyers. The Model T was preceded by models A, B, C, F, K, N, R, and S; and the Model A label was revived in 1928 when Ford was finally forced by competition to redesign the Model T.

His Own Man

Ford did not like bankers and therefore tried to finance all expansion from retained earnings, but by 1917 he was compelled to sell stock to raise additional capital. Then, when the stockbrokers sued to compel payment of dividends, for which there were ample funds, Ford determined to buy back all the outstanding stock. He did just that, and thus the Ford Company became the biggest privately owned company in the history of business. That record size still stands.

Ford was a strong and contradictory personality. He was interested in the welfare of his workers as he perceived it. He created a sensation in 1915 by paying his workers $5 per day and including them in a profit-sharing plan when the average manufacturing wage was $11 per week. But he was strongly anti-union and fought unionization bitterly until 1941, when he was finally forced by his workers to negotiate with the United Automobile Workers.

Ford ran a paternalistic shop, feeling that he knew best about everything affecting the company and the workers, and he had little tolerance for exhibitions of independence among his employees. One man whom Ford weeded out for displaying independence was William S. Knudsen, who went on to make Chevrolet into Ford's chief competitor for many years.

Not satisfied with just making cars, Ford also integrated his supply sources by investing in coal and iron mines, forests, glass-making plants, steel, railroads, cargo ships, and a rubber plantation in Brazil. He was also interested in developing village industries—small plants on streams offering water power. He wanted to take the industry to the country, where he planned to use farm labor during agriculture's slack winter season. And during World War I, Ford chartered a peace ship on which he sailed to Europe in an effort to see the German Kaiser and end the war, a gesture that reveals his grand scale of thought, if not his humility.

Ford's Contributions to Management

Although we would not choose him as a model for management today, Ford did contribute many innovations to manufacturing industries: standardized processes and products, integrated supply industries, the building of assembly plants at dispersed locations (to facilitate distribution as well as supply), and the organization of manufacturing around continuous line-to-line assembly of product components. All of his successful competitors, including Knudsen and Chevrolet, adopted Ford's techniques of manufacture. He also understood the importance of mechanical service, and had sent factory-trained mechanics out in the field by the second year of his company's existence. Ford was thus ahead of his time in many areas, and his frequently unrealistic attitudes and actions do not diminish his importance in the history of management.

Discussion Questions

1. What is the relationship between theory and practice in management?

2. What is your view on large, complex organizations? Do you feel some organizations are too large to be effective?

3. What is the central characteristic used for classifying an organization, and what implications does this characteristic have for analyzing the job of management?

4. Can you think of any outstanding managers who had little or no formal education in management? Is it possible for experience to serve as a kind of formal education? If so, what kind of experience would serve in this way?

5. We say that the fundamentals of problem solving can be formally taught but that problem-solving skills develop primarily through experience. Is this statement true, and if so, why is it true?

6. Can you think of any business organizations with a conservative management philosophy? Of any with a daring management philosophy? How important is philosophy to success, and how are they interrelated?

7. An organization is an open system and must interact with its environment. Give examples of a business being influenced by government actions and also of a business attempting to influence government actions. Explain how these concrete examples describe the behavior of an open system.

8. Suppose that a company makes a decision to substitute aluminum for steel in a component part of its product. What factors probably have contributed to this decision? At what managerial level would this decision most likely be made? Can you cite other related decisions that would then be made at the various organizational levels?

9. Suppose that Company *A* finds out that its competitor, Company *B*, has lowered its price on a major product that they both produce. Should *A* immediately lower its price, responding competitively? What factors might *A* want to consider before following *B*'s lead? Include in your answer a consideration of such a decision as related to homeostasis.

References

1. *See* H. L. Timms, *Introduction to Operations Management* (Homewood, Ill.: Richard D. Irwin, 1967), p. 84, for a more complete definition of *system*.

2. E. F. Urwick, "Papers in the Science of Administration," *Academy of Management Journal*, 13 (1970): 365.

3. E. B. Flippo, *Management: A Behavioral Approach* (Boston: Allyn & Bacon, 1966), p. 4.

4. H. Koontz, "A Model for Analyzing the Universality and Transferability of Management," *Academy of Management Journal*, 12 (1969): 420.

5. J. S. Livingston, "Myth of the Well-Educated Manager," *Harvard Business Review*, 49 (1971): 84.

6. S. M. Davis, "U. S. versus Latin American Business and Culture," *Harvard Business Review*, 47 (1969): 93.

7. Koontz, p. 422.

8. A. C. Filley and House, R. J., *Managerial Processes and Organizational Behavior* (Glenview, Ill.: Scott, Foresman, 1969), p. 26.

9. R. W. Millman, "Some Unsettled Questions in Organization Theory," *Academy of Management Journal*, 7 (1964):194.

Suggested Readings

Drucker, P. *The Practice of Management*. New York: Harper & Row, 1954.

Koontz, H. "A Model for Analyzing the Universality and Transferability of Management." *Academy of Management Journal*, 12 (1969): 415–429.

Litterer, J. A., ed. *Organizations: Systems, Control, and Adaptation*. Vol. 2, 2d ed. New York: John Wiley, 1969, pp. 1–264.

Rock Valley College - ERC

Historical Perspectives

2

It is important to study past managerial practice in order to set modern practice and theory against a historical perspective. As we develop a historical perspective, we will see that there have been tremendous advances in certain areas of management while in others progress has been exceedingly slow.

History of Productive Systems

Where we set the beginning of management in history is purely a matter of choice. We might, for example, start with Neanderthal man. Some 50,000 years ago, these squat, powerful people had leaders who directed food gathering, who determined where and how the people would live, and who managed social interactions. We can cite many such examples from ancient history, showing the long line of management development.

For example, pyramids have impressed tourists for thousands of years. The Egyptian pyramid of Khufu alone required twenty years of construction by 100,000 workers. The workers moved 2,300,000 blocks of stone, each weighing two and one-half tons. Obviously, such an immense job required management —planning, organizing, and coordinating. From Egypt, the Roman Empire, and China to pre-Columbian Mexico, there are examples of management practice. Some Aztec managers even practiced a form of social responsibility, thus predating our concern with it by 500 years. Aztec merchants sponsored religious banquets and public religious celebrations that were free to the general populace.

From the fall of the Roman Empire in A.D. 476 to around 1450, Europe went through what is commonly referred to as the Middle Ages. This period witnessed the development of the feudal system. The king owned all the land, parceling out portions to high-ranking lords in exchange for their military and financial support. The lords in turn allowed persons of lesser rank to live on and work part of the land in exchange for a share of the crops and/or taxes. Occupying the lowest rank in this pyramid arrangement was the serf, who received protection and sustenance, and was born into hereditary attachment to one or another lord or sublord.

There was virtually no opportunity for a serf to become a lord or a lord a king. People were born into their jobs—the sons of a serf became serfs, while the sons of kings became kings or high-ranking lords. Serfs and high-ranking individuals were also bound to areas of land. This total absence of upward and horizontal mobility inspired little individual motivation and a lack of common interest among all the participants toward making the total organization work. Such a rigid system could not flourish in today's socioeconomic environment.

Long before 1450, events took place that would eventually spell the end of feudalism, the emergence of different methods of agricultural management, and new systems for the manufacture of goods. Over a tortuous route, these events finally would culminate in the factory system. We know, of course, that management is and has always been required in all types of organizations, but most of the presently applicable changes in management practice and research occurred first in manufacturing organizations. Therefore, it will help to trace the development of the factory system through two antecedent systems—handicraft and cottage—both of which developed from feudal times.

Emergence of the
Factory System

With the growth of towns in the Middle Ages and with an increasing demand for goods that agricultural manors could not supply, the opportunity arose for the development of crafts and craftsmen. At the same time, with improvements in agriculture, farmlands gradually were diverted more to use as pastureland, and fewer serfs or farmhands were required to work the manors.

Under these changing conditions, more serfs began to learn skills in various crafts. Eventually, some of them were able to buy or in some other way establish their freedom from the feudal lord. These craftsmen could work in towns as carpenters, shoemakers, blacksmiths, and in other crafts, and they could charge for their services just as many independent craftsmen still do today.

As business grew, some craftsmen began to hire helpers, and soon a structured arrangement developed—the handicraft system. Those who were fully skilled and who owned their shops were considered master craftsmen, while those who had completed apprenticeships but who still worked for others were considered journeymen. On the lowest rung of the ladder were the apprentices, learning to be journeymen and dreaming of being master craftsmen.

Organizing the Crafts The masters soon began to seek some protection for themselves and their advantageous positions. They were successful in their search, organizing powerful craft guilds around the various levels of skill. The guilds strengthened the hierarchy of master, journeyman, and apprentice and also regulated hours of work, wages, prices, number of apprentices, and sales territories.

Many guilds also provided fraternal benefits in the case of death, sickness, or disability and thus proved to be forerunners of modern organizations and practices in these areas. Guilds reached the peak of their power around 1400, when they frequently controlled municipal governments and advanced their own commercial interests at the expense of others in the community.

Decline of the Guilds Shortly after 1400, the guilds began to decline in power. Three factors were involved in the decline. First, growing trade and transportation began to overwhelm the guild's tight control of local markets as goods were brought in from other areas—including foreign countries. Second, the initiation of power use and the growing necessity for powered machinery raised capital requirements and made it more difficult for individual journeymen to set up shop as master craftsmen and to own their own businesses. Third, the new machines created new jobs and new divisions of labor, which in turn led to new guilds and helped to weaken the old trichotomy of master, journeyman, and apprentice. These three factors reduced the upward mobility of journeymen and apprentices and provided the base for a permanent wage-earning class in the manufacturing industry.

The Cottage System The transitional form of manufacture between the handicraft and the factory systems was the cottage system. Arising some time in the fifteenth century and continuing until about 1700, the cottage system was characterized by the delivery of raw materials to the homes or cottages of workers where family members used hand tools to fashion the materials into in-

the French and English Utopian communities, these conditions and this type of management predominated during the eighteenth and nineteenth centuries.

Scientific Management

In 1878, an intense young man who had been forced to drop out of college because of illness went to work for the Midvale Steel Works in Philadelphia as a common laborer. This was how Frederick W. Taylor launched his fascinating career as pioneer in the development of scientific management. Advancing from laborer through a series of jobs at the factory, Taylor became the chief engineer of Midvale by 1889.

In his various jobs at Midvale, Taylor observed what he considered to be shortcomings of factory operations:

He saw, for example, that management had no clear concept of worker-management responsibilities; that virtually no effective work standards were applied; that no incentive was used to improve labor's performance; that systematic soldiering existed on every hand; that managerial decisions were based on hunch, intuition, past experience, or rule-of-thumb evaluations; that virtually no overall studies were made to incorporate a total-flow concept of work among departments; that workers were ineptly placed at tasks for which they had little or no ability or aptitude; and, finally, that management apparently disregarded the obvious truth that excellence in performance and operation would mean a reward to both management and labor.[1]

Taylor has been portrayed as a cold, calculating individual whose only interest in workers was to obtain more production from them through various clever schemes. It is true that he was interested in increasing production and efficiency, but he also displayed remarkable insight into the behavior of workers.

For example, Taylor observed that workers at Midvale engaged in systematic soldiering—that is, pretending to work or loafing. He pointed out a reason for this behavior in *The Principles of Scientific Management:* that workers who soldiered often were not acting out of innate laziness. Rather, they were reacting to management actions. If management, for example, cut a piece rate when management felt that the workers were beginning to make too much money, the workers would react by vowing never to overextend themselves again. Hence there would be soldiering, for there was no motivation for hard labor.

The Right Tool for the Job

Taylor's work with a gang of shovelers at the Bethlehem Steel Works illustrates his approach. He observed that the men worked hard and that there was no loafing. He also observed that they shoveled different kinds of material throughout the day, from very light to very heavy materials such as iron ore. And they used the same kind of shovel all the time, even though their shovel loads varied from four pounds to thirty-eight pounds.

Taylor hypothesized that there must be an ideal load for a shovel that would maximize production and minimize fatigue. He began to experiment by selecting two of the best workers and varying the loads on their shovels as they worked away at various materials. He kept track of many possibly significant items relating to the work, but his most important finding was that the greatest productivity occurred when the shovel load was 21½ pounds. To implement this finding, shovels of various sizes were provided for different materials, larger shovels for light materials and smaller shovels for heavy materials.

In this and other experiments, Taylor demonstrated the importance of standard methods of working, output quotas, wage incentives, regulated rest periods, and of the proper selection and training of workers for each type of job. His success is indicated by the fact that the shoveling experiment findings, when implemented, resulted in an increase in production of over 300 percent, an increase in pay for the workers, and a reduction in unit costs of over 50 percent.

The Overall Principles

All through his work, Taylor advocated the substitution of scientific methods for rule-of-thumb methods. The scientific method, as he practiced it, focused on careful observation, experimentation, and measurement—all intended to find the best way of doing a task. He modified this prescription in his writings by warning that scientific management in itself was "not any efficiency device, not a device of any kind of securing efficiency; nor is it any bunch or group of efficiency devices."[2]

Taylor was trying to look beyond mere techniques: beyond piecework systems, incentive bonus systems, time studies, motion studies, and all the other techniques for increasing efficiency. He said the techniques were mere adjuncts to scientific management; that while scientific investigation was necessary to assure the establishment of equitable methods, procedures, and work loads, the most important component of success was the recognition by all parties that cooperation rather than discord was the only means by which the full fruits of production could be achieved.

This was the complete mental revolution that Taylor felt scientific management required. Full cooperation in working together and in using scientific methods would provide the greatest return to management, to the foremen, and to the workers. Taylor believed that if the principles of scientific management were applied to the simplest individual acts as well as to the work of the great corporations, the results would be truly astounding. The fundamental principles that he developed are as follows:

1. Managers should develop a scientific method for each element of a man's work to replace the old rule-of-thumb method.

2. Managers should scientifically select and then train, teach, and develop the workmen.

3. Management should cooperate with the workers to insure that the work being done is in accordance with the principles of the scientific method that has been developed.

4. There should be an equal division of the work and responsibility between management and the workmen. Management should take over all the work for which they are better fitted, such as planning, which in the past had been largely accomplished by the workmen.

Taylor had trouble getting his message across to management. Meanwhile labor criticized him for alleged speedup attempts. Taylor, on the other hand, claimed that he was not opposed to labor unions but that there would be no need for labor to organize if management and labor both adopted the principles of scientific management.

He presented many papers at meetings of professional societies and groups, but his audience often failed to grasp and appreciate the significance of his concepts. In 1910, the American Society of Mechanical Engineers shelved a paper by Taylor on the grounds that the membership was not interested in "papers of this sort and there was nothing new in it."[3] The paper later became famous under the title *The Principles of Scientific Management*.

Finally, starting in 1911 with hearings by the Interstate Commerce Commission over a rate increase requested by the railroads, Taylor's ideas began to receive national publicity. Testifying at the hearings, he declared that if the railroads would adopt his methods, not only would a rate increase be unnecessary but the railroads could improve their profits at the current rates.

Startled, Congress ordered an investigation of scientific management. Instead of finding vindication for his espousal of a rational, scientific approach, however, Taylor tasted only bitterness as he believed his testimony had been distorted and misrepresented.

The Efficiency Experts In the years following the Congressional hearings, many so-called efficiency experts helped preserve the public image of their mission as cold and calculating by concentrating solely on the physical aspects of jobs, ignoring worker needs and attitudes. Even more damaging to the cause were the charlatans who, in the name of scientific management but with little or no training, presumed to consult with industry on methods of increasing efficiency.

Despite all the confusion and misunderstanding that plagued Taylor's work before and after his death, the fact remains that he made a great and solid contribution. He and others identified with the movement—Henry Gantt, Frank and Lillian Gilbreth, Henry R. Towne, and Harrington Emerson—advocated and justified research and experimentation, planning, training, the setting of standards for operations, controls for checking results against standards, and cooperation between management and workers.

By World War I, the initial momentum of scientific management had run down. While the techniques—motion and time study, fatigue studies, incentive plans—and the philosophy are still widely applied, particularly at the shop level, we now realize that the means to high productivity and job satisfaction are far more complex than Taylor envisioned as a result of his mental revolution.

At about the time that the pioneers of scientific management were literally dying off—Taylor in 1915, Gantt in 1919, and Gilbreth in 1925—yet another theory about management and organization was developing. This theory has been labeled *classical administrative, traditional,* or just plain *classical* theory. It was and is a rather formal and rigid conceptualization of management and organization. For those readers unfamiliar with the steps involved in building a theory, the basic dimensions of theory, and research techniques, we recommend reading the notes on theory in the appendix at the end of this chapter before reading the next section.

Dimensions of Classical Theory

Where scientific management focused on the shop operation, primarily at the foreman and operator levels, classical theory was concerned with administration of the whole organization. Classical theorists sought to design the ideal organization structure and assumed that if such a structure were achieved, management's job would be a relatively simple, impersonal, and rational one of coordinating all elements of the organization toward the accomplishment of stated objectives. Of the many principles encompassed in classical doctrine, there are four key pillars: (1) a division of labor, (2) scalar and functional processes, (3) a logical relationship of functions in structure, and (4) a span of control.[4] Let us begin with a brief working description of each of these principles now, although we will consider them, along with other classical principles, in greater detail later.

Division of Labor

A division of labor permits the specialization of knowledge or skill and is presumed to result in greater efficiency (up to certain limits). A division of labor is accomplished by breaking down a job into its component parts and by having as many people as necessary working on the job, each one doing a component part of the total. Such specialization is justified by at least three reasons.

First, it may be physically impossible for one person to perform all the necessary tasks by him- or herself. Second, no one person can know in detail everything necessary to the job. Third, division of labor can result in greater efficiency because of the use of specialized machinery requiring skill that workers may acquire when limited to a single task. For example, assembling an automobile is much more efficient when many workers each do a small, specialized task than if one person does everything.

Scalar and Functional Processes

Classical theory conceptualized the organization in the form of a pyramid, with the president or chairman at the pinnacle and members of lesser rank composing the bulk of the pyramid in increasing numbers until the bottom or operative level is reached, where the greatest number of workers are located. Now, if you were to draw lines between the president and his vice presidents, between the vice presidents and the next lower rank, and so on, you would have an illustration of the scalar principle, since the lines you have drawn divide the organization into authority levels. Figure 2–1 illustrates this point.

The higher the level in the organization, then, the more authority that attaches to the job. The *scalar chain* is the line of authority flowing from the top person down through the organization and representing the process of authority assignment and authority exercise throughout the organizational hierarchy.

The functional process is really specialization because it prescribes that each person will have a definite function to perform. Naturally, several persons may perform one function, but sales,

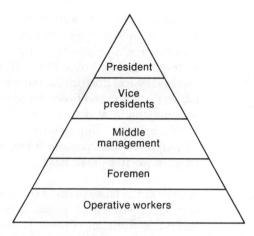

Figure 2–1 The scalar principle

for example, will be separated from purchasing and other functions, and the other functions will be similarly specialized. Vertical lines could be drawn, as in figure 2–2, to illustrate the functional process.

In its strict application, the salesman will only sell, the purchasing agent will only purchase, the manufacturing specialist will work only on production, and so on. The types of functions performed depend, of course, on the type of organization and its objectives—a church, for example, will have a different structure from a business because the two organizations have different functions and goals.

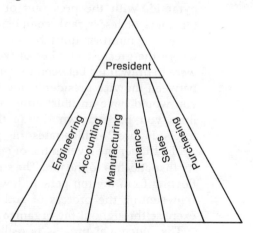

Figure 2–2 The functional process

Logical Relationship of Functions

For the pyramid structure to operate successfully, the various organizational functions must relate to one another in a logical pattern. Similar functions on one level are grouped together and are referred to one boss. On the next higher level similar groups are again grouped for reference and accountability to one boss. This pattern continues up the pyramid in a process that is also called *departmentation*.

The success of this structuring hinges to a large extent on the effective delegation of authority, or to use the classical terminology, on the effective implementation of the scalar chain. Until a job is properly defined in terms of its content and functional relationships, authority cannot be delegated appropriately. Structuring and definition are interdependent: functions must be logically related and defined before correct delegation is possible; and without effective delegation of authority, proper structuring may be largely ineffective.

Span of Control

The phrase *span of control* has to do with the number of people that one boss can effectively supervise. Generally, as a job becomes more routine and simplified, the span of control for persons in that job can become broader. For example, the span of control at the executive level may be from five to eight persons, but a foreman in the shop may be able to supervise as many as thirty workers. The span of control also has an impact on the shape of the organizational structure—a wide span throughout can reduce the number of scalar levels, giving the pyramid structure a relatively flat profile when diagrammed, while a narrow span will increase the number of levels and result in a taller, narrower structure (figure 2–3). Classical management theory has tried to determine carefully the spans of control at all levels that will best advance overall organizational efficiency.

The Roots of Classical Theory

The development of classical theory was largely deductive; that is, the flow of logic was from the general to the specific, and its prescriptions were and are stated in the form of basic principles. The first full statement of classical theory was made by writers, such as James D. Mooney and Alan C. Reiley, who based their deductions or principles on their experiences and on their studies of other organizations, notably the Catholic Church and the military. For many years, these organizations have operated with the type of structure and the methods now reflected in classical theory. They do not conform in every respect to the theory, particularly

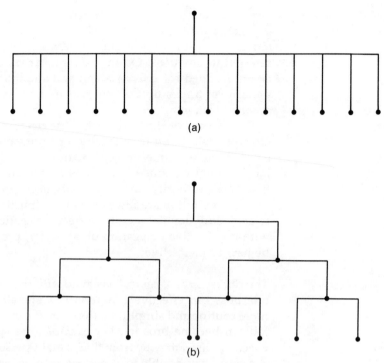

(a)

(b)

Figure 2–3 Span of control and organization profile: (a) wide span with two scalar levels, (b) narrow span with four scalar levels

today, but the nineteenth-century Catholic Church and the Prussian Army of the same period can be thought of as prototype models for classical theory.

As one might expect from such models, classical theory tends to be authoritarian and undemocratic. The historical image of these models is one of impersonality, rationality, and strict adherence to rules and regulations, and the management theory derived from these models leaves the twentieth-century student with an impression of rigidity and inflexibility. Classical theory assumes people will act in a rational manner and will be motivated by money alone to put forth their best efforts. It further assumes that the organization needs to be concerned only with the formal and official acts of its members as opposed to informal acts. Finally, the principles of classical theory are presumed to be universal; that is, they can be applied in any organization, regardless of its nature and location. In view of all this, it is not surprising that the classical model has often been called a machine model; it is, in fact, mechanical in many ways.

The Value of Classical Theory

Does classical theory have any value for the modern organization? Much of it does appear out-of-date in light of modern research findings, but some portions are still important and still deserve attention. For example, organizational studies continue to be made on span of control; the scalar and functional process patterns still provide the basis for most organizational structures; and division of labor is widely practiced and studied.

An awareness has developed, however, that management cannot apply many if not all of its principles in the rigid manner that the theory suggests. The major faults of classical theory lie in what it fails to say, in its lack of specificity, and in its inability to handle the unanticipated consequences of having people in an organization, who do not always act predictably, particularly in an organization more voluntary in nature than church or army. Furthermore, since the authors of the classical doctrine based their conclusions on their personal experiences and on their studies of other organizations, namely, the Catholic Church and the military, the theory was not developed and tested scientifically. In fact, a number of years ago, one modern writer, H. A. Simon, shocked the classical theorists by stating that the principles were nothing but "proverbs," meaning that they had never been tested to show their validity.[5]

Nonetheless, there is much in classical theory that is retained in a developing synthesis of management theories. What is retained no longer is stated in the form in which it was stated around 1930, for example, but is being modified by the knowledge gained through research.

The Bureaucratic Model

Closely allied to classical theory is the bureaucratic model. For most people, the word *bureaucracy* conjures up visions of large, complex government agencies where red tape makes it practically impossible to get anything done. Almost everyone has personal experiences to offer in support of this image.

But for the most part, a student dealing with management theory should not attach any value judgment to the word *bureaucracy*. The bureaucratic form of organization may be either good or bad, depending on how it is managed. A bureaucracy may be large or small, complex or simple, although the usual connotation is a large, complex organization. For our purposes, a bureaucracy will mean a relatively formal and impersonal model of organization and management, a theory that reflects many of the principles of classical theory. It may apply to either the public or the private organizational model; and, like most models, it is seldom found in a pure form.

The "Ideal Type" of Organization

Bureaucracy was first described as a generalized "ideal type" of organization structure by Max Weber, a German sociologist, in his book *The Theory of Social and Economic Organization* (1921). Weber's studies of organization theory and the development of capitalism are still considered first-rate; they provide the take-off point for nearly all sociological studies in these areas.

When Weber developed his model of bureaucracy, he did not intend it to be a model for a real organization. Rather he intended it to be a conceptual tool—a strictly logical, rational organizational design that could serve as a standard of comparison or as a skeleton for the development of structure for an actual organization. The ideal model of bureaucracy, as Weber conceived it, has several definite characteristics:

1. *Emphasis on form.* Its first, most cited, and most general feature has to do with its emphasis on form of organization. The other features illustrate this emphasis on form.

2. *The concept of hierarchy.* The organization follows the principle of hierarchy, with each lower office under the control and supervision of a higher one.

3. *Specialization of task.* Incumbents are chosen on the basis of merit and ability to perform specialized aspects of a total operation.

4. *A specified sphere of competence.* This flows from the previous point. It suggests that the relationships between the various specializations should be clearly understood and observed in practice. In a sense the use of job descriptions in many American organizations is a practical application of this requirement.

5. *Established norms of conduct.* There should be as little as possible in the organization that is unpredictable. Policies should be enunciated and the individual actors within the organization should see that these policies are implemented.

6. *Records.* Administrative acts, decisions, and rules should be recorded as a means of insuring predictability of performance within the bureaucracy.[6]

Weber emphasized professionalism in the bureaucracy, believing the system could not work effectively unless it were staffed by highly competent and specialized people. Selection for jobs would be rational, of course, based on tests, examinations, or degrees and diplomas certifying technical competence. The workers in such a bureaucracy would be subject to authority only with respect to their impersonal, official obligations. While on the job, they would be expected to carry out their duties within the prescribed limits of clear-cut systematic controls and discipline.

A real-life approximation of Weber's model would suffer the same problems as an organization constructed according to the principles of classical theory. Its impersonality and rationality would not permit competitive leadership, or perhaps even survival, in a dynamic environment. Its mechanical modus operandi and its disregard of human behavior patterns would stifle the creativity and flexibility so needed in the modern, successful organization. In this era of rapid change, the strict bureaucratic form is, in short, dysfunctional. It doesn't work.

The "ideal type" of bureaucratic structure occupies one end of the continuum that measures organization structure from highly rigid and rational to loose and flexible (figure 2–4). As such, however, the bureaucratic model forms a useful point of reference for studies dealing with organizations and their structures. For this reason, Weber's definitive work on the bureaucratic form was a great contribution to subsequent empirical research.

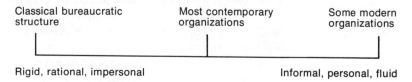

Figure 2–4 A continuum of organization structure

Summary

In this chapter we have briefly traced management history through the formation of the factory system. We have seen that the scientific management theory was the first systematic approach to the study of management problems, although it concentrated on the shop level to the relative exclusion of top-level problems. Its principal exponent, Frederick W. Taylor, during his lifetime was unable to convince management fully of the merit of scientific management although the value of his work has since been recognized.

We have also reviewed classical theory for both its historical context and substantive contributions. Key pillars of classical thought are (1) a division of labor, (2) scalar and functional processes, (3) a logical relationship between functions in structure, and (4) a span of control.

The bureaucratic model is conceptually similar to classical theory in its pyramid framework, rationalism, and mechanistic approach to human interactive behavior. Modern management syntheses reject the prescribed rigidity and accept the described organizational structure of classical and bureaucratic theories. It is important for any student of management to have an understanding of the historical significance of the major principles of classical theory and its related model, bureaucracy, for classical theory is one of the major schools of thought supporting contemporary management theory.

Management Profile

Frank Gilbreth

Frank Gilbreth was a member of the small band of men associated with the development of scientific management. In 1886, he passed up an opportunity to attend the Massachusetts Institute of Technology, deciding instead to take a job as apprentice bricklayer with a Boston construction company. On this job he improved bricklaying techniques so that production increased from 120 to 360 bricks per man-hour.

Within a few years he advanced to become general superintendent and in 1895 started his own construction company. Successful from the start, Gilbreth eventually built factories, dams, canals, and mills all over the world. He invented a new method for waterproofing basements, a new type of concrete mixer, and new types of conveyors, and became the first manager ever to use a cost-plus-a-fixed-sum contract.

Gilbreth left the construction business in 1911 and established a consulting firm in industrial engineering. With the help of his wife, Lillian, he pioneered in the use of motion pictures to study work and to break jobs down into minute elemental parts that they called *Therbligs* (*Gilbreth* spelled backward with the *th* transposed). By analyzing the Therbligs and their various combinations, refined and detailed motion studies could be accomplished.

In addition, the Gilbreths were interested in the employee as an individual whose productivity depended on attitude, opportunity, and physical environment as much as on the use of correct methods and ideal equipment. They were interested in studies of fatigue and training and even did studies, in their home, of bathing, brushing teeth, and touch-typing—using their children as subjects.

And they had an ample supply of subjects in their twelve children. The whole family was the subject first of a book and then, many years later, of a movie—*Cheaper by the Dozen*. The interest and intensity of the man are measured by his own family, and also serve as a characterization of the pioneer management analysts with whom he was associated.

Appendix

Notes on Theory

Management and organization theory forms the foundation for the content of this book. The theory has been developing for years and still is far from complete. Inputs come from diverse fields—psychology, sociology, anthropology, economics, political science, and mathematics—and from the practical experience of managers. Therefore, management and organization theory is initially eclectic; it draws from many sources and is gradually evolving into a cohesive and defined field of its own.

A theory is the end result of a search for generalization and is a plausible or scientifically acceptable general principle offered to explain phenomena. So a theory explains and/or predicts; the more precise a theory is and the broader its scope, the better the theory.

Building a Theory　An idea may occur as a flash of insight or, more likely, as the result of hard digging in existing facts and theories. For example, research results often suggest extensions of work already done or suggest a different approach to a particular problem. When we find an idea that has potential for theory development, we then state certain assumptions and hypotheses in preparation for testing the idea.

Assumptions specify the circumstances and conditions under which the theory might be true or valid, so that others may test the idea under the same conditions and so that any extraneous circumstances that might cause the predicted behavior are excluded as much as possible. A hypothesis is a tentative theory that embodies the original idea and that makes a prediction about the behavior of the phenomenon under study. If testing fails to disprove the hypothesis, the prediction ceases to be considered a hypothesis and is now considered a theory. If repeated testing fails to disprove the theory, we may be able to consider the prediction a law.

Several important dimensions of theory include descriptions of whether the theory is: (1) inductive or deductive, (2) microcosmic or macrocosmic, (3) descriptive or prescriptive, and (4) static or dynamic. We will explain the meaning of these terms below.

Inductive or Deductive Inductive theory emphasizes the flow of logic from the specific to the general and tests hypotheses on the basis of empirical data. An inductive theory often speaks of tendencies or probabilities that reflect the confidence limits established by statistical testing of the data.

For example, in election years various pollsters randomly sample a number of persons around the country and ask their preferences on political candidates. Usually using a sample of about 1,500 people, the pollster will generalize his findings to the entire country and perhaps say that Candidate A has 52 percent support from the electorate, Candidate B has 35 percent, while 13 percent remain undecided. Statistical testing may indicate a 5 percent chance that his findings are wrong, but such testing also enables the pollster to indicate 95 percent confidence in his results. Hence the pollster uses empirical data from a tiny fraction of the total population to predict national election results. This is induction, or the inductive method, the generalization from the specific.

Deductive theory is characterized by a logic that flows from the general to the specific. It is generally derived from a study of cause-and-effect relationships, must be internally consistent, and is often stated in a schematic or symbolic form such as a mathematical model.

To illustrate the deductive approach to the development of theory, assume that we wish to develop a model to predict the results of a specific presidential election. To do this, we might analyze all previous presidential elections to attempt a determination of factors that caused the various candidates to be elected. After identifying certain factors, we might even be able to quantify them and build a mathematical model. Using the model, then, we would make a specific prediction on a particular election—thus moving from a general logic to a specific conclusion.

Microcosmic or Macrocosmic A microcosmic theory is concerned with the unit or units that are part of some larger structure, while the macrocosmic approach centers on the larger structure and its total environment. In management and organization, micro theory concentrates on the individual or work group as a model of the whole, while macro theory encompasses the entire organization first and then moves to the smaller units within it.

Descriptive or Prescriptive   Descriptive theory (also called positive theory) explains a phenomenon. Prescriptive theory (also called normative theory) states what a phenomenon should be, on the basis of logical and/or empirical evidence, and also offers an explanation for the phenomenon.

Static or Dynamic   Static theory has no dynamic time dimension; that is, conceptually, the phenomena under study occur at a frozen point in time. It tends to deal with simple relationships and has limited scope, precision, and usefulness, since it applies to only one moment and does not describe or explain changes over a period of time.

Dynamic theory allows more variables to function than does static theory, and its explanations encompass more complex interrelationships. These complexities usually defy simple cause-and-effect statements. Dynamic theory is difficult to develop, but it can be more useful than static theory in explanation and prediction.

These definitions of theory dimensions should not be construed as pairs of complete opposites. It should be evident that in theory as well as in practice each extreme partakes of the other. For example, induction can be found in all deduction if the latter is traced back to its source. Where possible as we go along, examples of theory dimensions will be pointed out.

Research Methods   We will now consider three basic types of research methods that can be used in the building of theory. The reader will note that we speak of levels of rigor in the discussion of methods. A research method that is more rigorous than another is not necessarily better. A level of rigor has to do with the degree to which a given research method is free from the subjective bias of the researcher. A high level of rigor involves little researcher bias while a low level of rigor is at least subject to bias. A careful researcher using a method with a low level of rigor, however, will try hard not to allow his own biases to influence the research results. The methods we will look at are the case study, the field survey, and the laboratory experiment.

The Case Study   Examining the characteristics of a single unit typifies the case study approach. The unit may be an individual, group, part of an organization, or the organization itself. Case studies seldom can be repeated and therefore provide a limited base for generalization. Hence, the case study is limited in its usefulness—its prime virtue perhaps being the exposure of an area for other more rigorous research.

The Field Survey More rigorous than a case study, the field survey generates data via interviews, questionnaires, observations, or via a combination of these three. Statistical analysis then tests for significance of the findings. While a field survey may test hypotheses, the sample surveyed is seldom random, and this again severely limits generalization.

The Laboratory Experiment Most rigorous of the research methods, laboratory experimentation controls variables in order to isolate and verify cause-and-effect relationships. The researcher manipulates independent variables to observe and measure the response of dependent variables. Greater generalization is possible than with case studies or field surveys because the exact conditions are known under which the experiment occurred.

Controlled field experimentation is also possible, and it satisfies the requirement implicit in the objection that lab experimentation does not correspond to real-world conditions. Seldom used prior to 1950 for organizational research, because methods of controlling human variables had not developed, lab experimentation is quite common today.

The Usefulness of Management Theory Management theory is vital to effective managerial action. Most management theory is descriptive and therefore is relatively helpful in showing managers the consequences of alternative courses of action. To be completely reliable, however, management theory should conform even more strictly to criteria for scientific acceptability; that is, it should be supported by empirical evidence, be capable of verification by others, and have sufficient generalization to be useful.

But in many instances, management theory as a body of knowledge does not stand up to these criteria. A portion of management theory has been derived deductively and based on a priori propositions—assumptions that certain phenomena are universally true and that they provide a causative structure that makes possible the prediction of effects. Classical theory makes the most a priori assumptions of all management theories. Nonetheless, deductively derived theory can be instructive provided that its logical consistency is not mistaken for reality, which was too often the case with classical theory.

In addition, some of the empirical evidence we have is not susceptible to much generalization and is quite frequently subject to inconsistency—different studies provoke different conclusions with respect to the same phenomenon. These conflicts merely reflect the imprecise state of management theory, particularly the fact that there is no unifying theory to which everyone subscribes.

It is natural for theory to develop thus, however: through both inductive and deductive methods and through the reconciliation of conflicting findings by intellectual synthesis or by additional research.

These shortcomings do not destroy the usefulness of management theory by any means. Research studies covering certain phenomena have been repeated many times and they offer quite reliable guides for action to the practicing manager. As in all sciences, it is necessary to draw on theory to describe what happens in management and organization and, in certain instances, to prescribe what should be done.

It is particularly useful to have some knowledge of theory dimensions, since they enable us to characterize differing theories briefly and clearly. For example, scientific management theory is microscopic because it focuses on the foreman and operator at the shop level, while classical theory is macroscopic because it concerns itself with administration of the total organization. Also, classical theory is deductive, whereas scientific management is inductive. And both theories are similar in being static and prescriptive. These examples show the usefulness of terminology that permits the reduction of broad philosophies into one or two words.

Organization Theory or Management Theory

One last note on terminology will help to clarify discussion. The terms *management theory* and *organization theory* are often used interchangeably, although many writers often confine *organization theory* to explanation of and prescriptions for organization structure. We use *management theory*, on the other hand, to explain and prescribe (improve) the managerial job. Hence, organization theory is one part of management theory and forms a portion of the total body of knowledge that managers apply to their real-life situations.

Discussion Questions

1. Can you name examples of handicraft and cottage systems that still exist today? How can these systems in certain cases continue to survive alongside the most modern factories?

2. Do you believe that Taylor's ideas on scientific management should be applied in a modern business organization? Why or why not?

3. Where scientific management focused on the shop operation, classical theory concerned itself with the administration of the whole organization. How did the development of management theory benefit from the macroscopic emphasis of classical theory?

4. Division of labor has often resulted in great efficiency. Can you suggest instances where division of labor is or might be carried too far, and would revert to inefficiency? Why might this inefficiency come about?

5. Suppose that you are a boss and that for some reason you want to increase your span of control. What steps can you take to do this? Is there any limit to the span of control? If so what is it, and why does it occur?

6. Why has the word *bureaucracy* acquired a bad image among many people? What is that image? Can you cite any instances where a bureaucracy has worked well?

7. How many characteristics of the "ideal type" of bureaucracy do you suppose would be found in a modern corporation such as the Ford Motor Company?

References

1. C. S. George, Jr., *The History of Management Thought* (Englewood Cliffs, N. J.: Prentice-Hall, 1968), p. 87.

2. F. W. Taylor, "What is Scientific Management?" in *Classics in Management*, H. F. Merrill, ed. (New York: American Management Association, 1960), p. 77.

3. S. Haber, *Efficiency and Uplift* (Chicago: University of Chicago Press, 1964), p. 18.

4. W. G. Scott, "Organization Theory: An Overview and an Appraisal," *Academy of Management Journal*, 4 (1961): 9.

5. H. A. Simon, "The Proverbs of Administration," *Public Administration Review*, 6 (1946): 53–57.

6. J. M. Pfiffner and Sherwood, F. P., *Administrative Organization* (Englewood Cliffs, N. J.: Prentice-Hall, 1960), pp. 56–57.

Suggested Readings

Cochran, T. C., and Miler, W. *The Age of Enterprise*. New York: Macmillan, 1960.

Filley, A. C., and House, R. J. *Managerial Process and Organizational Behavior*. Glenview, Ill.: Scott, Foresman, 1969, pp. 25–55.

Gerth, H. H., and Mills, C. Wright, trs. *From Max Weber: Essays in Sociology*. New York: Oxford University Press, 1946.

Merrill, H. F., ed. *Classics in Management.* New York: American Management Association, 1960.

Merton, R. K., et al., eds. *Reader in Bureaucracy.* Glencoe, Ill.: Free Press, 1952.

Mooney, J. D., and Reiley, A. C. *Onward Industry.* New York: Harper & Row, 1931.

Wren, D. A. *The Evolution of Management Thought.* New York: Ronald Press, 1972.

Modern Theory

3

Perhaps the most exciting development in management theory was the discovery not only that there are human beings in organizations but also that they often behave in the most unpredictable ways. This realization eventually led to the establishment of a major new approach to the study of management and organization—the behavioral science approach. Behavioral science began about fifty years ago with the human relations movement or with the development of neoclassical theory, as it is sometimes called.

Human Relations

Sprawling over several city blocks in Chicago, the Hawthorne plant of the Western Electric Company has manufactured telephone parts and equipment for decades. Starting in the late 1920s, it was the scene of some dramatic experiments conducted by Elton Mayo, Fritz Roethlisberger, William Dickson, and others. The initial purpose of the experiments was to investigate the reactions and possible changes in attitudes of groups under varying conditions.

The first experiment was a rather simple one, intended to find the relationships between the quality and quantity of illumination and the efficiency of the workers. The workers were divided into two groups: (1) the test group, which was to work under lights of different intensities, and (2) the control group, which was to work under lighting that remained constant. The experimenters assumed that the better the light the greater the output would be.

As the intensity of illumination was increased for the test group, production did go up—but it went up the same amount for the control group! Mayo and his colleagues were surprised, but they went on with the experiment. Next the amount of light was decreased, but production continued to climb; and it climbed for the control group too. This result was clearly not what the experimenters had expected. The intensity of illumination was then continually decreased; but not until the light was equivalent to that of ordinary moonlight was there any decline in the output rate.

Needless to say, the researchers were puzzled; and in a masterful understatement, Roethlisberger announced that nothing positive had been learned about the relation between illumination and industrial efficiency. The experiment was a classic example of trying to deal with a human situation in nonhuman terms. No data on people were collected; the experimenters only manipulated electric bulbs and plotted average output curves. Seeking answers to the mystery, they planned a new and more ambitious project.

Relay Assembly Test Room In this new experiment, a group of six girls was placed in a separate room where their conditions of work could be carefully controlled, where their output could be measured, and where they could be closely observed. Each girl's job was to assemble small devices called *relays*, each relay using thirty-five separate parts. As each girl finished a relay, it was dropped into a chute and counted. First the experimenters decided to introduce at specified time intervals different changes in working conditions to see what effect these innovations had on output.

Records were kept on factors such as temperature and humidity; the kind and amount of food each girl had for breakfast, lunch, and dinner; and the number of hours each girl slept at night. These records were only for measurement of base conditions. Output went up, but the researchers could find no single correlation of enough statistical significance to explain any relationships between physical circumstances and variations in production.

The Hawthorne Effect Pushing doggedly ahead, Mayo and his colleagues next introduced more improvements: different days off, varying rest periods, and shorter hours. These trials went on for many months, and as conditions of work gradually improved, output also improved. At last the research team felt they had strong evidence in favor of their current hypothesis: that fatigue was the major factor limiting output. Now came the crucial test. After improving conditions for a year and a half, they took every improvement away from the girls and restored conditions to what they had been when the experiments began. They expected, of course, that output would drop, but, without rest pauses, without hot lunches, and working a forty-eight hour week, the girls reached an all-time high in output! Stuart Chase humorously describes what happened:

The staff [Mayo and his colleagues] swooned at their desks. They thought they were returning the girls to the original conditions of the experiment, but they found that the original conditions had gone forever. The experiment had changed under them, and the group they now had was not the group they had started with. Because of some mysterious X which had thrust itself into the experiment, this group of six girls was pouring 25 per cent more relays into the chutes, though working arrangements were precisely like those at the beginning of the test.

What was this X? The research staff pulled themselves together and began looking for it. They conferred, argued, studied, and presently they found it. It wasn't in the physical production end of the factory at all. It was in the girls themselves. It was an attitude, the way the girls now felt about their work and their group. By segregating them into a little world of their own, by asking their help and cooperation, the investigators had given the young women a new sense of their own value. Their whole attitude changed from that of separate cogs in a machine to that of a congenial team helping the company solve a significant problem.

They had found stability, a place where they belonged, and work whose purpose they could clearly see. And so they worked faster and better than they ever had in their lives. The two functions of a factory had joined into one harmonious whole.[1]

Hence the group itself became important to the experiment. Feeling part of a team and consulting with the researchers about the changes to be made, the girls developed pride in their work, in themselves, and in one another. The planned experimental innovations were not found to be particularly important, and cumulative fatigue was not shown to be present at any time. The impact of the girls' behavior on the outcome of the experiments has often been called the *Hawthorne effect*. From the standpoint of good research, the Hawthorne effect is undesirable, since it precludes control of experimental conditions and contaminates research results. Experimenters working with human beings are now aware of the effect and try to exclude it from their research work. The results of the relay assembly experiment intrigued the research team, and they decided to conduct another experiment in order to learn more about this fascinating group process.

The Bank-Wiring Experiment

In the next experiment, the observation room contained fourteen workmen representing three occupational groups—wiremen, soldermen, and inspectors. All were working on bank wiring. These men were on a group piecework incentive plan. Classical theory would have predicted that the men would be interested in keeping total output at a maximum and that the faster workers would put pressure on the slower ones to improve their efficiency. But the research team learned that the group set its own standard for production and did not necessarily try to increase output. For a worker to be accepted as a member of the group, he had to act in accordance with the standards of the group. Therefore, output was actually a form of social behavior.

Particularly interesting were the names given to those workers who violated the norms of the group. A worker who turned out too much work was termed a *rate buster*, while one who turned out too little was a *chiseler*. A *squealer* was a worker who would tell the supervisor something detrimental about a fellow worker. In addition, a worker should not be too officious; that is, if you were an inspector, you should not pull rank. These findings contradicted the concept of human economic behavior in classical theory, for the lure of higher wages apparently was less important to the workers than were social acceptance and security in the group.

The initial assumption in the Hawthorne experiments was that a certain physical change would bring about a desired response in accordance with classical theory. That, for example, providing better light would improve productivity while decreasing illumination would decrease output. To illustrate:

$$\text{change} \longrightarrow \text{response}$$

However, the Hawthorne studies showed that workers' response to a change can only be understood in terms of their attitudes or sentiments; that is, in terms of how they interpret the change and in terms of the meaning that the change has for them:

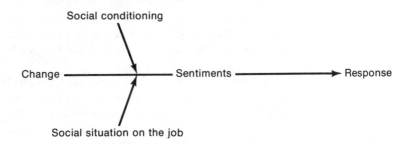

The way a worker interprets a particular change depends upon his social conditioning or the sentiments (values, hopes, and fears) that he brings to the work situation from his family and other group associations away from the job. It also depends on his social situation at work, where the worker does not act as an isolated unit but acts as a member of a group that strongly conditions attitudes and actions. From this point of view, the behavior of no one person in an organization can be regarded as motivated strictly by economic or logical (from the viewpoint of the organization) considerations. For example, a child who is a tattletale is strongly condemned by his brothers and sisters and by classmates in school, and he is socially conditioned not to behave this way at work.

As the studies indicated, over time the work group manifested a high degree of stability, with member roles and status rather strictly prescribed. In many cases workers would act to protect their position in the group rather than to help management achieve higher productivity through some technical change. They also sacrificed economic gain to social acceptance. That people can act in what seems to be a totally illogical manner still amazes many managers. But the workers' ingrained fears of exploitation, handed down from father to son and derived perhaps from the old sweatshop conditions, go far to explain their attitudes and sentiments.

Popularity and Misapplication

Human relations theory became immensely popular in the years following World War II. A wave of consultants, some of them self-anointed experts in human relations, flooded industry. They made sweeping promises of vast productivity increases and happy work forces. Following their recommendations, business executives spent hours memorizing the first names of all their workers. Birthday cards were sent, bowling teams organized, picnics held, and so on.

But the basic premise for all this activity was wrong: the premise that a happy work force is necessarily a productive work force. When management finally realized their mistake, many managers and companies committed yet another error in their disillusion. They totally rejected human relations as well as the bowling teams and picnics.

A Saner View   Over the years management has gained a better understanding of human relations and of the whole behavioral approach. Most companies are now quite willing to consult with an expert in the behavioral sciences or to have such a person on their own staffs. Managers understand, for example, that while it is undoubtedly desirable to have happy workers, their happiness does not guarantee high production. As two of the original Hawthorne researchers, Roethlisberger and Dickson, suggested in their famous book *Management and the Worker*,[2] management should seek a balance between morale and efficiency in order to reach the highest levels possible for both productivity and worker cooperation.

In summary, the Hawthorne studies and human relations theory had a tremendous impact on management and organization theory. The classical concept of economic man, that man is wholly dedicated to increasing his income and his share of the world's material goods, was demolished. Man was shown to be capable of nonrational behavior. The power of the individual and the group to seriously affect the success of an enterprise was convincingly demonstrated. Finally, the human relations movement functioned as a trailblazer for a more general application of behavioral theories.

Modern Management Theory

There is no single, grand theory of management, no total explanation and analysis, but the three schools of thought that we have described—classical, behavioral, and management science— dominate the field. In addition, other schools can and have been identified. One modern writer, Harold Koontz, suggests as many as six major schools of management theory.[3]

Management theory is, of course, quite young in comparison to other fields, such as physics, in which theory development may be traced back hundreds or even thousands of years. Management theory is not even old enough for everyone to agree on its vocabulary usage. This is one of the reasons Koontz gives for the confusion. Other problems he mentions are failure to understand formal principles, inability or unwillingness of management theorists to understand each other, and differences in the definition of management as a body of knowledge.

There are, however, some fairly definite things we can say about modern management theory. For one thing, most writers date its beginning at about 1950. At that time, on the foundations that human relations and classical theory had established, a whole new wave of interest in management theory was generated. Over the intervening years, many new studies have been undertaken, most of them to collect data, and much new knowledge has been developed.

The new wave has not yet resulted in a grand theory, but it represents the sort of activity that can lead to one. General theory develops gradually. The development of a general management theory requires a convergence of our three schools of theory and no doubt will proceed in a rather irregular way.

The Complementary Natures of Existing Approaches

Convergence still lies in the future. But the fact that the classical, behavioral, and management science approaches complement one another is promising. Each approach makes a contribution toward explaining the areas of concern in management theory:

> Theories of management are all essentially similar in one respect. They all involve consideration of three basic areas: (a) the nature and purpose of the business firm; (b) the contribution the manager can and should make, given the nature of the business organization, to the accomplishment of its objectives; and (c) the tools and techniques which best serve the manager in making a contribution.[4]

Knowledge about the basic areas can not be considered reliable until the full power of all three major schools of thought is brought to bear. And the recent widespread application of the systems approach, which we will discuss later in this chapter, would not be fruitful if we omitted any one major element of theory. Increased complexity is, of course, one result of combining theories. But we are dealing with complex organizations, so simple explanations are not enough.

The Behavioral Science Approach

The behavioral science approach is an extension of human relations theory, but it is a new approach to the study of management and organization. Human relations theory still conformed to classical theory—hence its other name, neoclassical theory. Behavioral science, however, is quite different from classical theory. The behavioral approach suggests that the physical and emotional needs of people compose the foundation for organization. Organizations may arise spontaneously from the association of people who have mutually supportive needs, interests, or goals. In addition, behavioral science draws on psychology, sociology, social psychology, and anthropology. It directs attention toward the organization as a whole as well as considers the behavior of individuals and groups inside the organization.

From psychology, we learn about individual personality—how people regulate behavior in trying to satisfy their needs—and about the many influences that affect our thinking. Psychology is a complex study because each person is unique and confronts conflicts within himself as well as with others. This knowledge helps management to study motivation, learning, attitudes, and leadership.

Social psychology directs attention to the interactions between individuals and between individuals and groups. Since individuals in organizations are constantly interacting with other individuals and with groups, these relationships directly affect the organization and are of great interest to management. Management would like to know the results of various kinds of interactions and would also like to influence these interactions.

Sociology provides us with information about groups and the formal organization. Both formal and informal groups form within organizations and exercise tremendous influence on the behavior of their members. Management is interested in the nature and effect of this influence. For example, how do groups affect productivity? What is a group's impact on member attitudes? Answers to such questions help managers understand the group process and may suggest ways to encourage the positive impact of groups on the organization.

As organizations expand into foreign countries, anthropology becomes increasingly important. People behave differently in different cultures. Managerial style must change from one environment to another. Organizations today take great pains to make sure they are in tune with other cultures in which they are operating.

Since the Hawthorne research studies, there have been hundreds of studies that have tremendously increased our knowledge about human behavior in organizations. These studies are enriched by progress in the related fields of social science. A more detailed discussion of behavioral science will show how knowledge gathered from various fields is applied to the study of management.

Research Approaches in Behavioral Science The behavioral approach has been largely empirical in its investigations, using experiments and observations made under controlled conditions to accumulate knowledge. Researchers have been trying to find out what variables specifically determine behavior. Behavior appears to be determined by at least two conditions. The first consists of environmental variables that affect behavior. For example, someone receives an award at a banquet and responds with a short speech to express pleasure and appreciation—his behavior is affected in an expected way. The second condition relates to physical and emotional states and activities within the individual. These states and activities may make a person behave in an unexpected way. For example, the individual receiving the award at the banquet may respond with an angry speech instead of one expressing pleasure. Since both internal and external causes exist for an individual's behavior, research has developed two approaches to determining motivation. Behavioral research draws on psychology to explain what goes on inside an individual, and on other social sciences to explain external motivation.

Management would like to better understand the internal mechanisms governing behavior. Such an understanding could help many people be more satisfied in their jobs. So far, however, environmental variables governing behavior are better understood and more controllable than internal variables. Management can affect desired behavior by granting larger salary increases for superior performance, for example. Of course, most situations are more complex and require more complex changes in behavior, particularly when dealing with groups and with whole organizations. One can see that if in addition management seeks to understand and affect individual internal motivation, a great deal of behavioral research must underlie decisions and actions.

The Contribution of Behavioral Research   Most behavioral research results are descriptive in nature. Their great contribution to managerial decision making consists of the help they provide in predicting the consequences of alternative courses of action. This kind of prediction requires management to understand the relationships between varying sets of circumstances and patterns of behavior produced by these circumstances.

For example, suppose that a manager is well-liked by his subordinates, has a well-defined task to perform, and has the benefit of formal organizational power behind him. These conditions certainly appear favorable to effective leadership, but the manager still might wonder what particular leadership style would be best in the light of his subordinates' reactions. He could be a very positive and forceful leader; he could allow his subordinates to participate in his decision making; he could allow his subordinates to initiate and carry on their own activities; or he could lead in any one of several other ways.

Behavioral science research can indicate the consequences of the various possible leadership styles, given the circumstances. The manager can then consider these consequences in relation to his own talents and inclinations. He will be able to make a more appropriate choice than would otherwise be possible. In this specific case, research results suggest that a positive and directive leadership approach would be best. His subordinates are ready to be directed; and leadership will tend to be most effective where style is adapted to expectations. If his subordinates were rebellious, the same manager might choose to involve them in their own leadership, thus diverting their hostility to authority.

There are thousands of situations with behavioral implications that may confront a manager. Research results will not always suggest an answer to every problem that arises. But behavioral science is increasingly able to help management in decision making. Behavioral science helps us predict, with greater confidence than ever before, what will happen as a result of given managerial actions.

Behavioral science findings apply equally well to businesses, hospitals, governments at all levels, and other organizations. Therefore there is no need to develop a separate body of knowledge for each organizational type.

Management Science Behavioral science and management science comprise the two modern approaches to the study of management and organization. Quantitative tools are the hallmark of management science. It emphasizes effective planning, controlling, and decision making. Miller and Starr offer the following description of management science:

> Management science differs from Taylor's scientific management in many ways. It is not primarily concerned with production tasks and efficiency of men and machines. Rather, it views efficiency as a secondary achievement which should follow adequate planning. Both good and poor decisions can be implemented in an efficient way. A company can manufacture a high-quality product at minimum cost, but the product might not be the best choice for the company's objectives.
>
> Management science is concerned with both short- and long-range planning. It attempts to establish whatever relationships exist between an organization's objectives and its resources. In this way, it cuts across the traditional areas of management. Such crossing boundaries characterizes management science, which is *problem oriented....*
>
> Similarly, management science neither avoids nor overlooks the effects of behavioral problems, even though such problems cannot always be formulated or solved. Management science is essentially quantitative, although if important problems cannot be quantified they may be handled qualitatively. Whether quantitative or qualitative methods are applied, operations research is used to produce rational decisions and logical plans of action.[5]

Operations research is the vehicle by which management science goals are met. It uses scientific, mathematical, and/or logical means to structure and resolve planning problems. During World War II, when operations research was first used, teams of scientist were able to generate enough tactical information through mathematical calculations to significantly increase the effectiveness of Britain's defense against enemy bombers and submarines. Information on the number of fighter planes needed to intercept a given bomber force and on the proper depth for the explosion of depth charges helped Britain to use its limited resources more effectively.

Since the war, a number of new techniques in operations research have been developed, some of which will be covered in chapter 4. In recent years operations research teams have included personnel from a variety of fields—mathematics, the physical sciences, industrial engineering, economics, psychology, and sociology. Operations research has grown into sophisticated maturity and is capable of handling many problems that were literally insoluble a few years back.

Decision Theory Decision theory is the heart of management science. It is concerned primarily with how to assist people and organizations in making decisions; in planning; and, naturally, how to improve decision making. Operations research techniques are used to implement decision theory; operations research can be partially defined as "applied decision theory."

Decision theory also plays an important role in the study of management. The management analysts Shull, Delbecq, and Cummings list three points of interest for decision theory in the management process:

1. As a conceptual vantage point for the development of models to gain insight and improve the administrator's decisions as he operates as a responsible agent within the total administrative system;

2. As a conceptual framework for understanding, influencing, and predicting interaction between other actors holding positions in the organization; and

3. As a first approximation for understanding the organization as a system manifesting decisions in its struggle for survival and growth within a dynamic and competitive environment.[6]

Decision theory thus provides a means of understanding the organization and the multiple interactions that occur within it and therefore provides a means of improving managerial decision making.

The behavioral science approach tends to be descriptive, explaining how and why people act the way they do. The management science approach, on the other hand, has tended to be more prescriptive. It frequently indicates what *ought* to be done; for example, what decision should be made under given circumstances. Decision theory and management science are being used to complement each other in gaining understanding of how people interact in organizations and of the organization as a system, as well as in explaining and improving the decision-making process.

The Systems Approach

The systems approach is an integrative approach. In management theory, the systems approach tries to integrate or combine the various elements of the behavioral science, management science, and classical approaches into a cohesive whole. A complete definition of *system* will establish a basis for our discussion of the systems approach:

A system is a set of elements so interrelated and integrated that the whole displays unique attributes. This definition implies that to understand the cause of the attributes of a system one must understand the interrelationships of the elements, called *subsystems*, and how they are integrated. If one were to cause a change in the interrelationships of the elements and thereby bring about a different integration, one would expect the system to display different attributes.[7]

In management theory, then, the problem is to discover the system elements, or subsystems, and how they are integrated into a whole. While generalization for differing organizations may be possible, particularly with regard to the subsystems, the interrelationships and style of integration of the subsystems may be different. That is, each organization or whole may be unique in the way similar elements are put together. The systems approach is a vital step toward the development of a grand management theory, which would permit total generalization, complete explanation for organizational phenomena.

In chapter 1, we identified organizational subsystems as management, people, structure, and technology. Other writers list different sets of subsystems, depending on their viewpoints and how comprehensive they desire to be. Equally important subsystems are the linking processes available to management as it strives to integrate organizational subsystems into a cohesive whole. These processes include communication, social interaction, decision making, the distribution of authority, the development of organizational roles for people, and the establishment of and agreement on goals. Figure 3–1 illustrates organizational subsystems and their linking processes.

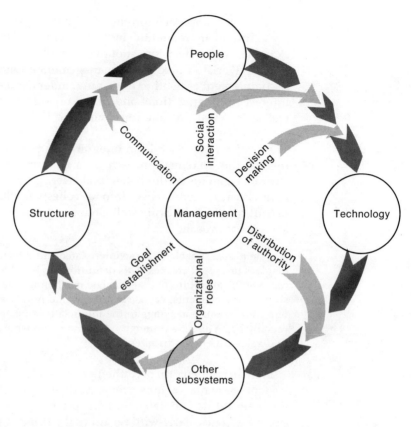

Figure 3–1 Organizational subsystems and their linking processes

All the linking processes work simultaneously, of course. A convenient way to think of these processes in operation is as a series of overlays superimposed on the organizational system (figure 3–2). For example, two subsystems such as management and workers may be linked by communication processes. The result is complex; but even though the links and style of linking may differ from one organization to another, the linking processes may be the same. If one could pin down the exact nature of the processes as well as identify the appropriate organizational subsystems, given certain common goals for all organizations, one could make broad generalizations not only about *what* happens in organizations but about *how* and *why*.

Different organizations have widely varying goals, of course, although continued existence and/or growth are goals shared by most organizations. Regardless of differing goals, however, the systems approach suggests ideas that any organization can apply.

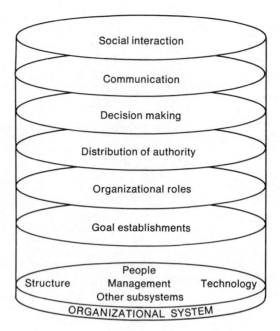

Figure 3–2 Linking processes as overlays

For example, the organization as a system contains management and people as major subsystems. Within these broad categories there are further breakdowns by types of jobs and functions. There is, therefore, a great diversity of interests within the system. An organization should shape its goals in a way that enables these diverse interests to realize their own aspirations through achievement of the common goals.

In other words, there should be an overall, unified goal as well as a hierarchy of goals for each separate subsystem. Management's job is to coordinate efforts to meet the individual challenges so that the overall goal is achieved. Conflict among individual, specific goals should be at a minimum so that achievement of one does not make another difficult or impossible. Building such a goal structure is difficult but necessary to successfully implement a systems approach.

Once a satisfactory goal structure has been established the managerial job moves on to activate and integrate all system components toward goal achievement. These components include people, technology, and structure; and in a specific type of organization, such as a business, also include such functional areas as purchasing, production, sales, and finance. Management develops the necessary coordination through planning, controlling, and or-

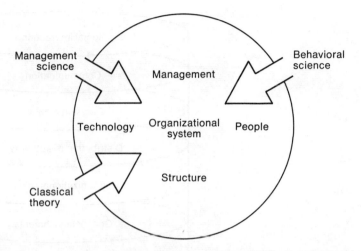

Figure 3–3 Theoretical approaches to the study of management and organization

ganizing activities, and by effectively using the available linking processes.

The systems approach has been valuable as an integrating mechanism. It is also a meaningful way to study management and organization. The systems approach involves integration of the behavioral science, management science, and classical approaches

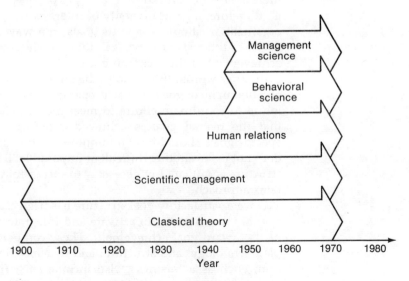

Figure 3–4 Development of management thought

into a cohesive whole. Thus we can use the systems approach on at least two levels. First, we recognize that the organization is a goal-oriented system composed of various subsystems and linking processes. Second, we attempt to systematically integrate the several theoretical approaches in our study of the organization system (figure 3–3). Figure 3–4 illustrates the chronological development of these various schools of management thought.

Summary

Human relations or neoclassical management theory began with the Hawthorne studies in 1930. While classical theory was quite inflexible and regarded man as little more than a rational automaton, human relations emphasized the importance of the individual to organizational success. The Hawthorne studies also showed that individuals and groups could act in ways that classical theory would consider nonrational.

Human relations theory was a springboard for the first of two modern approaches to management theory—behavioral science. The behavioral approach suggests that the physical and emotional needs of people form the foundation for organization. Behavioral science depends heavily on experimentation to accumulate knowledge about behavior. It draws ideas and concepts from the disciplines of psychology, sociology, social psychology, and anthropology.

The second major modern approach is management science, which emphasizes planning and decision making, and which relies on operations research in applying concepts. Operations research is a general method that employs scientific, mathematical, and/or logical means to structure and resolve planning problems. Operations research is carried out by teams whose members bring the findings of mathematics, the physical sciences, engineering, economics, psychology, and sociology to bear on a particular operations problem.

The systems approach offers a highly effective way to study and explain what happens in organizations. A system encompasses all elements of an organization, including management, plus the interrelationships and style of integration that creates a unique whole. The systems approach also integrates the major theoretical approaches to management, drawing on each to explain the whole organization and to prescribe for organizational success.

Henri Fayol

Some of the most valuable contributions to the development of management thought have come from practicing managers such as the classical theorist Henri Fayol. Born in France in 1841, he joined the S. A. Commentry-Fourchambault Company in 1860 as a mining engineer. By 1888, he was promoted to managing director. Unfortunately this was like being promoted to captain of a sinking ship, for the company was on the verge of bankruptcy.

Undaunted, Fayol set to work. By 1918, when he retired, the company was sound in every way, including financially. In 1914, Fayol was ready to publish the product of his years of experience, thought, and study. It would eventually establish his reputation as the father of classical management theory. But World War I interfered and until 1916 delayed publication of his now famous book, *Administration Industrielle et Generale (General and Industrial Administration,* tr. Constance Storrs [London: Pitman, 1949]).

The delay was most unfortunate for Fayol, because in those intervening two years Frederick Taylor's ideas on scientific management were receiving an enthusiastic reception in France and throughout the rest of Europe. The French in particular were so impressed with the speed of American troops in constructing bridges, docks, and roads that every efficient operation was labeled *Taylorism.* Georges Clemenceau, then French Minister of War, even ordered all plants under his control to study and apply Taylor's principles of scientific management.[8]

However, French managers soon began to study Fayol and apply his principles, and his work was widely acclaimed, although it was many years before his ideas became generally known in the United States. Unlike Taylor, Fayol studied management and organization from the top down; for this reason he is classified as a classical theorist. He felt that management was the most important organizational activity, and he divided it into five elements: (1) planning, (2) organizing, (3) commanding, (4) coordinating, and (5) controlling.

These five divisions still describe the management process. In this book, for example, we are specifically concerned with planning, organizing, leading (command), and controlling; and coordinating threads its way through many chapters. Fayol developed many principles to apply in management, and he believed that these principles could apply in many other situations, including the home. He was dismayed that only technical knowledge and skills were taught in schools and urged that the development of managerial ability also be part of the curriculum.

Thus Henri Fayol wrote the first comprehensive theory of management. His contribution was outstanding, and his basic concepts still find expression in the most up-to-date management books. Fayol's development from working manager to management theorist serves as a model for the development of theory from practical experience.

Discussion Questions

1. Human relations theory helped to explain many events in organizational life at the same time that it greatly complicated management theory development. Can you explain this apparent contradiction?

2. Think of a group of which you are or have been an active member. Based on your experience, in what ways would you say group membership modifies attitudes and behavior? How would you assess the overall impact of group membership on individuality?

3. Why does the behavioral science approach to the study of management offer greater potential for explanation and understanding organizational behavior than human relations theory?

4. Do you believe we will ever be able to precisely explain why people act as they do or to precisely predict behavior? Give reasons for your answer.

5. Do you think that management science would be more valuable to the president of a corporation or to a middle-management person such as a production supervisor? Why?

6. It seems quite logical to many people to think of an organization as a system. Are there any specific circumstances, however, under which a chief executive might not run his organization using a systems approach?

7. Do you think practicing managers have more to offer to theory development than purely academic management theorists? What are your reasons for your answer?

References

1. S. Chase, *Men at Work* (New York: Harcourt, Brace & World, 1941), pp. 21–22.

2. F. J. Roethlisberger and W. J. Dickson, *Management and the Worker* (Cambridge: Harvard University Press, 1939), p. 569.

3. H. Koontz, "The Management Theory Jungle," *Academy of Management Journal*, 4 (1961): 174–188.

4. O. Behling, "Unification of Management Theory: A Pessimistic View," *Business Perspectives*, 3 (1967): 5.

5. D. W. Miller and M. K. Starr, *The Structure of Human Decisions* (Englewood Cliffs, N.J.: Prentice-Hall, 1967), p. 10.

6. F. A. Shull, Jr.; A. L. Delbecq; and L. L. Cummings, *Organizational Decision Making* (New York: McGraw-Hill, 1970), p. 6.

7. H. L. Timms, *Introduction to Operations Management* (Homewood, Ill.: Richard D. Irwin, 1967), p. 84.

8. C. S. George, Jr., *The History of Management Thought* (Englewood Cliffs, N.J.: Prentice-Hall, 1968), p. 107.

Suggested Readings

1. Ackoff, R. L., and Sasieni, M. W. *Fundamentals of Operations Research*. New York: John Wiley, 1968.

2. Gibson, J. L.; Ivancevich, J. M.; and Donnelly, J. H., Jr. *Organizations: Structure, Processes, Behavior*. Dallas: Business Publications, 1973.

3. Johnson, R. A.; Kast, F. E.; and Rosenzweig, J. E. *The Theory and Management of Systems*. New York: McGraw-Hill, 1973.

4. Kast, F. E., and Rosenzweig, J. E. *Contingency Views of Organization and Management*. Chicago: Science Research Associates, 1973.

5. Roethlisberger, F. J., and Dickson, W. J. *Management and the Worker*. Cambridge: Harvard University Press, 1939.

Case Problem for Chapters 1, 2, and 3

Admiral Airlines*

When Samuel McDonald became president of Admiral Airlines, he was the fourth individual to hold that post in a decade. Of the three previous presidents, the first had been the founder, the second a financial expert, and the third an operating man. McDonald, former chief executive in a competing airline, faced the job of revitalizing Admiral and bringing it up to the level of prosperity enjoyed by the industry. To quote a position paper prepared by Admiral's board of directors, "This airline is slowly dying, and it

*From *Management Strategy and Tactics* by John G. Hutchinson. Copyright © 1971 by Holt, Rinehart and Winston, Inc. Reprinted by permission of Holt, Rinehart and Winston, Inc.

will die more rapidly unless it gets a transfusion of new blood. Survival depends on new men, new approaches and new techniques." The board felt that McDonald possessed the skill, experience, and judgment needed to bring about Admiral's recovery.

Recent History

Some of the problems plaguing the new president of Admiral Airlines had deep roots. For thirty years Admiral had been under the control of Merriwether Dunlap, a former Navy pilot described by one colleague as "a real entrepreneur in the classic sense." Dunlap was considered by many to be a strong, dominant person with colossal confidence in his own skills and abilities. He was a controversial individual, respected by some colleagues and feared by others. A former Admiral executive had once called him "the last of the pure SOBs." Upon hearing this comment, Dunlap retorted, "He seems to know a lot more than he did when he worked for Admiral."

The basic philosophy guiding Admiral Airlines during Dunlap's reign was that low-cost transportation was the key to profits and success. To Dunlap, extras not related to rapid, economical movement of passengers were unnecessary frills. He once remarked to a gathering of his top executives, "We'll load passengers like cattle if we have to: we must never forget to keep costs down." Another of Dunlap's favorite phrases was framed on the wall of his office. It reminded everyone to "Watch the pennies and the dollars will take care of themselves."

In his final years as president of Admiral, Dunlap became more and more concerned with the importance of cutting costs. He frequently walked around corporate headquarters flicking off lights not in use. He saved string and paper clips and personally developed a filter to strain and reuse oil formerly discarded in maintenance operations. As Dunlap grew older, even some of his most loyal followers began to feel his attitude toward cost cutting was becoming something of an obsession. One result of his continual pressure on costs was that many passenger service operations were so understaffed they could not adequately satisfy the customers. Whenever priorities were issued by Dunlap, machinery and equipment rated well above customer satisfaction. Passengers began to resent their treatment at the hands of Admiral's overworked employees. The firms's public image began to suffer, and employee morale dropped. At one point, Admiral and Eastern airlines were the two leading airlines in terms of complaints handled by the Civil Aeronautics Board. Admiral passengers often remarked that if they had any other choice, they would take it rather than fly Admiral.

In one area, however, Admiral did have an adequate, competent staff: pilots and aircraft crews were well-trained. When the jet age came to commercial aviation, Admiral moved quickly into training its pilots on commercial jets. Like Howard Hughes of TWA, Dunlap wanted good pilots, trained to fly all available aircraft. Unlike TWA, however, Admiral purchased jets long before its route structure had the volume to make their use economical. Thus, Admiral's seating capacity was far in excess of customer demand, and in some seasons the company suffered losses even on its most lucrative routes. On some routes, losses were incurred in all seasons.

Route Structure

At least some of Admiral's problems could be traced to its route structure. Although Admiral had a number of long and intermediate hauls, short hauls constituted the bulk of its business. In addition to being uneconomical for jet aircraft, many of these hauls were too competitive to yield reasonable profits. Admiral was not as big as such transcontinental carriers as United Airlines, TWA, Eastern Airlines, and American Airlines, but its sales were somewhat higher than local service airlines such as Trans Texas, Lake Central, Mohawk, and Allegheny. Admiral was thus an intermediate-size carrier in the same size class as National and Delta Airlines.

Admiral's main offices in Chicago were the hub of a system that fanned out in several directions. On its north–south routes, Admiral flew in competition with Delta and American Airlines to cities such as St. Louis, Kansas City, Memphis, New Orleans, Dallas, and Houston. Admiral also serviced a route to Seattle via Denver in which Northwest, Continental, and United Airlines were direct competitors. Admiral's Cleveland–Detroit–New York (Newark) route also operated in the face of strong competition from United, American, TWA, and Northwest. In addition, Admiral flew directly to several Caribbean Islands. These routes were largely noncompetitive, although several other airlines also serviced them to a limited extent.

In general, Admiral's routes were plagued by high operating costs. Terminal facilities in many cities were expensive, and waiting time for landing and takeoff was generally long and costly. Since many of its routes had spirited competition for the passenger dollar, Admiral's handling costs per passenger were above the national average. Although service to the Caribbean was profitable in season, it was run well below capacity for the remainder of the year. Like several other lines whose revenues were affected by seasonal factors, Admiral often had difficulty filling planes in the off season to the average break-even point of 45.8

percent of seating capacity. In the off season, for example, Admiral's planes commonly flew with only 25 to 30 percent of seating capacity filled.

Although the markets served by Admiral were potentially profitable, the line's inability to fill existing seating capacity made profits dwindle. Even with the advent of smaller, low-cost jets, Admiral had to cope with the problems of competition. On its most competitive lines, for example, Admiral's revenue per passenger mile was only 5.8 cents, one of the lowest in the industry (see table 1). The route structure was thus viewed by Admiral's management both as a potential strength and as an actual weakness.

Recent Management Changes

In the mid-fifties, Admiral suffered a series of low-profit years. Pressure arose from stockholders to check the downward flow of profits, but no action was taken until President Dunlap himself decided to step down. When Dunlap resigned to become chairman of the board, his hand-picked replacement was Stanton Tillingham.

Tillingham was as much unlike Dunlap as possible. His selection caused some surprise in the industry, since his training, temperament, and orientation were quite different from those of his predecessor. Tillingham's training had been in finance and marketing at one of the nation's better business schools. Although his basic orientation reflected his financial background, he felt the main focus of the airline should be on passenger service, not operations. He was firmly behind programs designed to improve the quality of passenger service, and he advocated such frills as champagne flights and deluxe dinner menus.

After a short time, it became apparent to insiders that Dunlap and Tillingham had too many personality problems to make an effective management team. Their personal differences were further accentuated by major clashes in philosophies, economics, and technologies. Dunlap continually second-guessed Tillingham, overruled plans he presented to the board of directors, and generally frustrated him in every possible manner. The board soon realized that either or both men would have to go before Admiral could return to profitable levels of operation. Before the board was forced to make a decision, Tillingham resigned, releasing a series of bitter public statements that caused great concern both within the company and throughout the industry.

Tillingham's successor as president was Horace Leggatt, a graduate engineer who had once been interested in patents and who had become an amateur authority on patent law. He had returned to school, taken his law degree, and was generally known

Table 1 Yardsticks of performance for airlines

	Growth (Six-Year Compounded Rate)		Profitability (Five-Year Average)								
	Sales	Common equity per share	Group ranking	Return on equity	Cash flow to equity	Operating profit margin	Group ranking	Earnings gain	Pretax profit margin*	Group ranking
Delta	16.3%	20.0%	1 Western	11.2%	41.2%	21.7%	1 Eastern	†	†	1
Western	16.7	15.9	2 Delta	12.2	39.4	22.6	2 Continental	210.3	9.0	2
Northwest	12.6	15.1	3 Continental	8.4	43.1	24.0	3 Northwest	143.4	14.7	3
National	14.9	9.8	4 Northwest	9.3	37.8	25.4	4 Braniff	156.9	6.1	4
Continental	18.1	9.1	5 Pan American	9.3	41.2	20.2	5 Trans World	111.0	7.6	5
Pan American	10.8	10.8	6 National	10.6	35.7	20.5	6 United	136.7	4.9	6
American	8.5	9.7	7 Trans World	7.7	62.1	16.4	7 National	70.0	5.2	7
United	13.7	6.5	8 American	7.1	33.9	17.2	8 American	100.0	4.3	8
				5.9	34.0	16.3	9			
Trans World	11.5	4.7	9 United	5.1	34.9	16.1	10 Delta	43.9	2.6	9
			Braniff	4.7	21.8	13.3	11 Pan American	37.1	0.6	10
Eastern	7.5	−7.8	11 Eastern	d	**	9.2	12 Western	32.9	0.5	11
Industry median	12.6	9.7	Industry median	8.4	37.8	20.2	Industry median	111.0	5.2	

*Gain or loss in percentage points
†From a deficit to a profit
**Not comparable
d Deficit

Source: Forbes Magazine, January 1, 1966, p. 82.

in the Chicago area as a rather outstanding engineer–lawyer. Leggatt, who had been with Admiral some fifteen years prior to assuming the presidency, had been hired and trained by Dunlap. The majority of the board felt, however, that Leggatt had enough of a progressive viewpoint to bring about changes needed to restore Admiral to a profitable operating position. His technical background was expected to be valuable in ironing out some of the operating difficulties Admiral faced, and the Board felt that his steady temperament would act as a balance on Dunlap's attempts to dominate operations. In short, he was considered the kind of person who could keep Admiral "on course" while instituting some much-needed changes.

After Leggatt had been in office for only a few months, several board members charged that he was reluctant to make any real changes without first gaining Dunlap's concurrence. Furthermore, it became apparent to these individuals that Leggatt's strongest suit was maintenance and cost reduction, not passenger service. And since profits continued to fall, a majority of the board began to feel the service problem had to be dealt with before the airline would obtain a satisfactory level of profits. After only one year in office, the board (with Dunlap's lone dissenting vote) asked Leggatt to resign. Leggatt did so immediately and joined another airline as vice president in charge of operations. Leggatt's departure caused no repetition of the furor or bitterness generated by Tillingham's resignation. In fact, those who knew him well felt certain Leggatt was happy to get back into the operations end of the business.

When Leggatt resigned, several board members recognized that few, if any, substantial changes could be initiated as long as Dunlap maintained an active influence over operating policies. These individuals asked Dunlap to resign "for the good of the company." Dunlap reacted by instituting action to have this group of directors removed. Dunlap solicited support for their ouster from several stockholders and touched off a rather flamboyant and bitter proxy fight. When news of this controversy reached the press, what had begun as an internal policy dispute became a public circus.

After the struggle for control had dragged on for almost a year, an outside group attempted to gain control of the board. The threat of possibly losing control to outsiders forced board members to unify, and Dunlap was pressured to resign. When Dunlap realized that a majority of the board favored his resignation, he stepped down for "reasons of health." Following the announcement of his resignation Dunlap was quoted in a newspaper column as stating,

"I was victim of these damned Eastern bankers and these pussyfooting pantywaists now running Admiral." In his official public statement, however, Dunlap stated, "This airline needs new blood and new ideas. It's time for the old timers like me to step down and let the young men have a chance to run the show."

McDonald's Presidency

When McDonald was first asked about his availability for the presidency of Admiral Airlines, his reaction was guarded. But several weeks later, when the offer was repeated, McDonald agreed to meet with two board members and a representative of a banking firm to discuss the terms and conditions required to attract him to Admiral Airlines. After several meetings, the liaison group agreed to McDonald's set of personal and financial conditions. McDonald also stressed that he had no interest in the job under any conditions if Dunlap was to have any influence over the company. McDonald stated that he did not want Dunlap's advice as "either an operating executive or as any kind of consultant to management." In addition, he asked for a two-year contract and a clear mandate to make any changes he deemed feasible without board interference. A majority of the board informally agreed to these rigid conditions. After Dunlap stepped down from the board, McDonald agreed to take over as Admiral's chief executive.

McDonald's first step as president of Admiral Airlines was to assess the current state of the company's operations and finances (see table 2). He spent several weeks talking to key executives and reviewing internal operating data. His initial evaluation was that Admiral needed strengthening in every major area of operation. To determine the extent and nature of some weaker areas, he hired a nationally known consulting firm to render a confidential report on passenger service and employee attitudes toward company policies. He also engaged another firm to analyze the struc-

Table 2 Admiral Airlines five-year operating data (in millions)

Year	Passenger Revenue First Class	Coach	Total Operating Revenue	Operating Expense	Net Income
1965	33.3	29.3	68.6	74.8	(2.9)
1966	23.4	33.4	63.7	70.4	(6.9)
1967	24.0	56.1	89.8	83.4	4.3
1968	22.8	76.1	109.4	97.0	6.2
1969	25.1	85.9	121.5	104.4	7.8

ture and functions of the various departments. Both reports seconded his own estimates that Admiral was in need of a major program of revitalization.

As a first step in his revitalization program, McDonald hired new vice presidents for finance, operations, and marketing. He also created a long-range planning department and brought in a member of the management consulting team to head this new group. After a brief period of orientation, McDonald asked the newly hired executives to look into the company in much the same way he had. The basic points outlined in their preliminary investigation indicated:

1. There were too few skilled or well-trained management people in the company.
2. Maintenance costs were excessively high in all phases of operation.
3. Equipment was obsolete in many cases. The greatest difficulty appeared to be in those routes where new short-range jets had not yet been purchased.
4. The company posture toward unions had left a legacy of hardship, and several of the skilled craft unions seemed to be on the verge of strike actions.
5. The company had an exceptionally poor public image because of the poor service given customers in past years.
6. The route structure needed some revision and revitalization. In particular, it was recommended that the company attempt to get a Chicago–Miami run to strengthen its north–south route structure.
7. The airline had a reputation of not running on time. This problem caused additional passenger complaints, since missed connections normally resulted from late operations.
8. Sources of cash for new equipment were limited because profits had been low in years when other companies had made substantial improvement in earnings.
9. Facilities such as hangars, terminals, and so on were archaic in many cases. Even new facilities had been designed poorly and were in need of expansion and/or replacement.
10. The sales force had been trained inadequately and had not exploited all available markets. Concepts such as package deals and special promotional tie-ins had not been tried even on special flights such as those serving the Caribbean.
11. The company had no formal training programs, and personnel knew very little about the company's goals, objectives, and aims.
12. The company had an extremely low profit per passenger mile, and very little information was available on the relative profitability of the various routes.
13. The conditions outlined in points one through twelve had been in effect for a number of years and seemed likely to continue unless positive actions were taken.

After reviewing this list of difficulties, McDonald set about preparing an order of priority to guide the group's actions. He felt that one urgent problem revolved around whether the company should promote mass transportation at low cost or emphasize more luxurious accommodations at a higher fare. He explained that this conflict should be resolved first, since many of the company's future objectives and goals depended on the results of deliberations on this point. He also felt that this problem had to be solved by the group before they could make any inroads on other complex problems.

McDonald knew that Charles Kenley, vice president of operations, and William Chaucus, vice president of long-range planning, favored mass transportation, so he asked them to prepare a report supporting a mass transportation, low-fare policy. Phillip Jordan, vice president of finance, and Kendall Barth, vice president of marketing, were asked to analyze the luxury service, higher-fare market of which they had been vocal advocates. McDonald felt that they would welcome the chance to expound their particular viewpoint. Because of the crucial import of the time factor, McDonald requested a preliminary report in two weeks.

All four men knew that McDonald had once coined the phrase, "Welcome aboard the world's finest airline," which had been used in advertising by his former employer. McDonald admitted his preference for quality over quantity, but said, "Though I've taken the quality route in the past, I'm willing to change my mind if circumstances dictate some other policy, so don't let this influence your recommendations."

The Committee Reports

At the end of a two-week period, the groups met to review the mass-versus-luxury transportation options. McDonald noted that the session was principally for information and discussion and that questions and criticisms should be open and freewheeling. He did say, however, that following this open meeting, the issue should be resolved "at the earliest possible time."

Charles Kenley spoke first for the study group reporting on the advantages of mass transportation. Kenley maintained that no basic changes in policy were needed to institute a mass-transportation concept. He reported that economy-class passengers currently provided 92 percent of Admiral's annual receipts and that a change to mass transport policy would require only slight modifications designed to "pare luxuries to the bone." He emphasized that passengers should not be herded like cattle but insisted that frills were costly and unsound. He argued that the coming of supersonic transports (SSTs) would require passenger loads of several hundred people to ensure a breakeven operation, since the estimated cost of each SST was in the order of $20–25 million. Kenley reported that domestic airlines were planning to purchase up to 400 SSTs, with expected delivery set for 1977. This SST delivery schedule would move back to 1972 or 1973 if the French supersonic transport, the Concorde, was developed on schedule. Kenley felt that Admiral would be forced to purchase the Concorde if competitors elected to operate the French version of the SST.

The main point in Kenley's presentation was that low fares were needed in order to increase the volume of passenger traffic. He held that high cost was the main deterrent to greater public use of air travel, now that the safety issue had been resolved. He cited how volume had risen and indicated that certain airlines regularly flew over one billion passenger miles during peak months. Kenley stated that an even greater volume would be needed to operate supersonic transports profitably. He indicated that the load factor problem was even more critical on short trips, which more and more people were making by car. He felt that Admiral's profits on short hauls would remain unsatisfactory until airlines could compete directly with autos on a cost–time basis.

Kenley cited two examples where a policy of low-cost transportation had proven to be profitable. First, he related how Mohawk Airlines had been profitable on its short-haul no-frills runs in the northeast. He next pointed out how the Eastern Airlines shuttle between New York, Boston, and Washington showed that low-cost travel could boost the number of passengers. Kenley conceded that the Eastern concept of the plane waiting for the passenger, rather than the passenger waiting for the plane, had been one reason that passengers had accepted the shuttle, but he insisted that its real success was due to its low price. In his opinion, the shuttle concept was the only way for a short-haul airline to operate profitably.

In closing, Kenley offered a series of cost-and-revenue projections showing the estimated results of his suggested policy changes (see table 3). These projections were described in detail by Chaucus. All data showed that substantial long-run improvements in earnings would accrue to Admiral if Kenley's recommendations were adopted.

Jordan began his presentation by stating that although Kenley's approach had been thorough, its premises were basically unsound. He made the point that it was far more important for Admiral to change its past image as a penny-pincher than to develop

Table 3 Admiral Airlines five-year forecast (in millions)*

Year	Passenger Revenue First Class	Coach	Total Operating Revenue	Operating Expense	Net Income
1970	26.3	93.7	135.9	111.8	11.8
1971	27.1	107.9	150.1	125.9	13.3
1972	28.9	120.1	163.7	132.4	15.5
1973	30.3	130.3	177.2	139.0	18.2
1974	35.4	145.2	200.1	146.0	27.1

*Kenley's data

the mass transport approach advocated by Kenley and Chaucus. His main thesis was that businessmen comprised a majority of airline passengers and that they knew a great deal about what to expect and what to demand in passenger service and comforts (see table 4). Jordan felt that businessmen were far too sophisticated to be fooled by insincere gimmicks and that the cattlecar image would have to be erased before they would fly Admiral instead of competing airlines.

One example he invoked to prove his point was the competition between Western Airlines, Pacific Southwestern Airlines, and United Airlines on the San Francisco–Los Angeles run. Pacific Southwest first offered a fare of $13.50 on a Lockheed Electra. Western then attempted to compete by offering a fare of $11.43 on a DC–6B piston-powered aircraft. Businessmen stayed on Pacific Southwest because they made the trip half an hour sooner on the Electras than on the DC–6Bs. United Airlines, which had been running a poor third to Pacific and Western, hopped into the lead by placing a Boeing 707 jet on the run with a fare of $14.50. Jordan

Table 4 Admiral Airlines five-year forecast (in millions)*

Year	Passenger Revenue First Class	Coach	Total Operating Revenue	Operating Expense	Net Income
1970	30.7	93.7	140.4	115.0	17.0
1971	35.8	105.1	115.0	132.0	11.5
1972	38.5	115.0	170.5	140.0	15.3
1973	45.5	135.1	195.0	148.0	23.7
1974	50.1	150.5	220.0	156.0	33.0

*Jordan's data

reported that all three airlines eventually instituted Boeing 727 jet service at a $13.50 rate; but United Airlines, which had moved into jets first, remained in first position. The lesson, said Jordan, was quite clear: the first-place airline is the one which offers first-class service without regard to price. To back up his example, he noted that a daily United Airlines flight from Hartford to Chicago, which carried first-class passengers only, had run at close to 100 percent capacity on most days, even though its fare was considerably higher than those of its competitors. According to Jordan, the use of a Caravelle (which was considered to be a luxury aircraft by many travelers) on this run enhanced its prestige and built up its popularity. He also mentioned in passing American Airline's "red-carpet service" and indicated how specialty flights such as the "Club 21" had been very successful operations.

Jordan's basic concept was that the airlines were selling a seat in motion, not just running a mass-carting operation. He agreed that economical operation was good, but insisted that Admiral's image could not be changed by cutting costs. Volume, he said, could never be obtained in the future unless the company could forge a new image. It was, in his opinion, "important not to spend foolishly, but to spend on the right things—namely, passenger service." He refuted Kenley' statements about Eastern Airline's shuttle, claiming that the shuttle had never been as prosperous as some believed. His parting shot on this point was that "Admiral has enough marginal operations without risking our future on shuttle-type ventures we're not sure of." Jordan also commented that he could not see how Kenley's points about the shuttle business related to the purchase of supersonic transports, since no SSTs would be used in the short-haul operations most likely for shuttle service.

At the close of the presentations, McDonald complimented both groups on the thoroughness of their reports and suggested that a week's moratorium be declared prior to making any action decisions. At the close of the meeting, McDonald returned alone to his office. As he thought about the meeting, two phrases kept running through his mind. The first was Dunlap's credo, "Take care of the pennies and the dollars will take care of themselves." The second was Jordan's advice "to spend on the right things, namely, passenger service."

What should Mr. McDonald do at this point? Suggest a step-by-step program to help him make a choice and carry it out.

Decision Theory

II

Deciding How to Decide

4

Our study of management is guided by the decisions that managers must make and the knowledge they need to make decisions. First we need to gain a common understanding of decision making, and then we need to see how decisions are made in organizations and how they should be made.

Everyone makes decisions, of course. We constantly choose from among alternatives in order to pursue a goal. A woman may decide to read a book to further her career. A man may decide to grow a beard to avoid shaving every morning. In each instance, there was probably more involved than the moment when the decision was actually made—to read the book or grow the beard—even though the individual may not have been totally aware of the series of steps he or she went through in the decision-making process. For example, let's listen to the man as he explains why he decided to grow a beard: "Every morning it's the same old thing. You know, stand in front of the mirror, lather up, scrape away the stubble. It gets tiresome. I'd like to get away from it—at least for a while. I know my boss won't like it, but it won't be forever. I'll shave it off in a few months. Besides, lots of guys have beards today. It's the thing to do. So what's the harm? My boss might even like it after a while."

Now what, really, has the man done? First of all, he has identified a problem—the monotony and inconvenience of shaving every morning. In so doing, he has also established a goal and criterion for making a decision. His goal could be interpreted as one of simplifying his life, eliminating one of the little chores that would normally accompany the routine of daily living. This would also establish his criterion—to base the selection of an available alternative on whether life is made a little bit easier, a trifle less routine. In the simplest sense, his alternatives are to continue shaving every day or to grow a beard. In evaluating the situation, he perceives quickly that growing a beard is the alternative that is most likely to simplify his daily life.

The solution seems easy, but another criterion has popped up. Will his boss like the beard? Apparently not, but he decides to go ahead anyway, confirming his decision in stating that it can do no harm and that his boss perhaps will learn to accept his beard after it has been around for a while.

This simple decision situation contains all the elements of much more complex decision processes. We have covered all the steps, and they are summarized in the following list:

1. Establish goals. Identify problems and criteria.
2. Establish the available alternatives and the consequences of each one.
3. Evaluate the alternatives in light of the criteria.
4. Select the best course of action—one that solves the problems and attains the goal.

The process sounds simple. But as you might expect, it is not simple. Like most other aspects of management, decision making tends to get quite complex and difficult. For example, before one even starts to make management decisions, he should decide how those decisions are going to be made; that is, what decision-making techniques and methods he will use for what kinds of decisions. Techniques and methods are the focus of this chapter. By the end of the chapter, several alternatives will have been offered and some decisions made about how to make decisions in organizations.

Rational Man and Decision Making

The classical theory of management assumed that man was motivated predominantly by economic incentives—a man would work harder given the opportunity to make more money. The "economic man" concept also prevailed in early decision-making theory. Within this context, economic man was presumed to act in a rational manner when faced with a decision-making situation. The assumptions for this rational behavior were: (1) that a man had complete knowledge of all the alternatives available to him, and knew the consequences of each, in any given situation; (2) that he had the ability to order preferences according to his own hierarchy of values; and (3) that he had the ability to choose the alternative for him. Money was usually used as the measure of value for the decision maker. It was considered only natural that a man would want to work harder if he could maximize the return of money by so doing.

But these assumptions are difficult for a man to achieve in real life. Just by looking at the first assumption—that a man has knowledge of all available alternatives and their consequences in any given decision situation—we can see how impossible it would be to fulfill these requirements in most circumstances. For example, if one were trying to decide whether to go to work on a Monday after a big weekend, there might appear to be just two available alternatives—to go to work or not to go to work. However, it is also possible to go to work for a half day only, or to go for the whole day and not do anything. And there probably are other alternatives available.

Furthermore, how can one possibly perceive all the consequences of alternative future actions? Not going to work may result in missing an important assignment or even in missing a chance for a promotion. Not staying home may be a mistake if the person is functioning poorly and may face an unexpected conference with a superior. The possible combinations of alternatives and consequences are overwhelming. At this point, one begins to suspect that people really cannot make decisions in this way and that classical theory was unrealistic in its assumptions. We will try to find a more realistic description of how people and organizations really make decisions. The writings of Herbert Simon, particularly his book *Administrative Behavior*,[1] provide a good source of modern decision-making theory, and will serve as a foundation for our discussion.

A Behavioral Description of Decision Making

Instead of using the economic man of classical theory to explain decision making, Simon used what he termed the *administrative man*. And he sought to *describe* what happens in the decision-making process rather than to *prescribe* what should occur. The concept of *administrative man* is opposed to classical theory. The classical standard of rationality cannot be achieved in practice because we lack knowledge about all factors that may affect our decision and because we usually see only a few of all possible alternatives. And since consequences are always in the future, we can only imagine what values to attach to them, and therefore, our predictions must be quite imperfect. So the classical standard of rationality, termed *objective rationality* by Simon, is beyond our means. These limitations, which we find difficult to overcome, are described by yet another of his phrases: *bounded rationality*.

What, then, can we do in decision-making situations? Given our limited capacities, we cannot maximize in an objectively rational way; that is, we cannot decide on what is "...in fact ...the correct behavior for maximizing given values in a given situation."[2] According to Simon, when faced with a problem requiring a decision, we search for alternatives until we find one that is satisfactory—one that meets and satisfies our own subjective standards. Once a satisfactory alternative or solution is found, the search for additional alternatives may cease or may be carried on simply to confirm our initial choice.[3] In the latter instance, the initial choice may be a satisfactory alternative, but we may also consider it the best course of action. That is, while the alternative is satisfactory, we are anxious because we are not completely convinced of the rightness of the satisfactory alternative. Hence, we may keep searching for new alternatives until we find another one that is acceptable. This confirms that the best we can do is find alternatives that are "just acceptable" or "just satisfactory." The search may be continued in this way because the final decision-making activities may be terribly difficult and anxiety-producing. Hence, we need to reduce our anxiety by confirming that no better alternatives exist and that our initial choice or most favored course of action really should be implemented. The final decision process, therefore, may be one of decision confirmation rather than one of seeking complete satisfaction. Simon has devised a term to describe this process. He says that when an individual attempts to make a decision by searching for satisfactory alternatives, the individual is attempting to *satisfice*.

There still remains the question of how one decides what is satisfactory. Simon suggests that satisfaction is determined by *level of aspiration*. We aspire to a given level of success or attainment that is determined by our previous successes and failures and by our ability to find or not find satisfactory alternatives. If we have experienced achievement in a related area in the past and if we have little difficulty in finding satisfactory alternatives, our level of aspiration rises. Conversely, it will fall as failure occurs and satisfactory alternatives are scarce or nonexistent. The level of aspiration appears to adjust upward faster than downward. In addition, the level of aspiration may be affected by what is anticipated in the future. The environment may provide cues that tell us to raise or lower our level of aspiration. The cues are outside our personal experience but can be incorporated into a total picture of our alternatives.

This description of behavior in decision-making situations defines what Simon calls *subjective rationality:* a decision is subjectively rational if "... it maximizes attainment relative to the actual knowledge of the subject."[4] The following incident may illustrate some of the concepts we have just described.

The Marriage

Stanley had wanted for some time to settle down and get married. But he felt he had not been successful at dating. The girls he most wanted to date didn't seem very excited by him. As a matter of fact, rejections had far outnumbered acceptances. Nonetheless, he actively engaged in the search process, dating as much as possible to find girls whom he considered satisfactory alternatives. One day Stanley borrowed some new hair tonic and observed how attentive some formerly haughty girls were. He also observed that other men who used this hair tonic were dating girls that he himself wanted to date.

If he used the new hair tonic, Stanley reasoned, no doubt he could expect better results. So Stanley raised his level of aspiration. Soon he discovered a satisfactory alternative, a girl he would like to marry. (He knew he couldn't optimize, couldn't find the single best girl for him, because it would take years to date every eligible girl in the world.)

But Stanley worried. How could he be sure that the girl he had found was the best he could do? So he continued searching (dating). He found another satisfactory alternative and another. But he could not seem to do better than the first satisfactory alternative or his most favored girl. So he confirmed his original choice, reduced his anxiety, proposed, and was accepted. Stanley was happy with his decision because he knew he had been subjectively rational and had made the best search and decision, given the actual knowledge he had.

Rationality—A Postscript

An integral part of every decision process is some sort of ordering of preferences. As individuals, we often decide matters on the basis of what we prefer, and the values we hold determine those preferences. A single person has many values, of course, and they are not all operative in any given decision situation. At one time the value for money may be overriding, while in another situation the value for safety and security may be most important. And even our loyalty to a single value such as money may not be constant over time but may change as the amount of money we possess changes. The concept of value measurement in decision making is called *utility*. It is entirely subjective, but it provides a way to measure success when some objective measure is not available or does not take subjective values into account.

For example, an individual may decide to live on a mountaintop, forego gainful employment, and live off the land. Others exclaim that he is crazy, irrational. But money apparently has little value for him; he has a very low utility for money. However, he has a high utility for other values—solitude, perhaps, or independence and simplicity as a lifestyle. For him, at least, the decision to live on a mountain is rational. It enables him to fulfill his own beliefs and attain his own objectives.

Hence, decision-activated behavior can be considered rational if the decision maximizes success according to what the individual knows and if the success relates to a goal set by the individual on the basis of his own values. Absolute amounts of money, a natural or objective measure, actually provide little or no indication of how successful he has been in reaching his goals. A complete measure must include a measure of his utility for money and what money may buy, as well as for other factors that may enter into his decision.

Let us consider utility in its simplest application. If you have a million dollars, you may not care to work very hard to earn one extra dollar. On the other hand, if you are broke and hungry, you will probably be willing to work very hard to earn a dollar. Your utility for money varies with your circumstances and can change over time. Or it may be that you have little utility for money no matter what the circumstances, perhaps because you can grow food or trade for your material necessities. Realistically, of course, if buying food is the only way to get it, utility for money, the medium of purchase, is going to be high—even if only temporarily.

Organizational Decision Making

So far we have talked about decision making in terms of the individual. Our primary interest, of course, is in the decision making done by members of organizations for their organizations—with primary emphasis on managerial decision making. Everything we have discussed thus far is equally applicable to management and organizations, for the organization basically is "... an extension of individuals making choices and behaving on the basis of their understanding of their environment and their needs."[5]

Decision making involves problems, however, which are heightened in an organization because it is a complex system with interrelated subsystems. Actions that organizations take to maximize or optimize the attainment of goals for one subsystem may make success difficult or impossible for another subsystem or for the total system.

For example, the sales division of a company may desire to maximize the total dollar volume of sales. They discover that the way to meet this goal is to push hard on one particular product. However, overemphasizing sales of that one product may well saddle the manufacturing division with a specialized production they are not equipped to handle. The result can be excessive costs and delays for that one product, neglect of other products, and a general failure for the company as well as for the manufacturing division.

The problem of goal attainment for the subsystems of an organization is particularly acute because all the subsystems are interdependent. What one subsystem does often affects one or more of the other subsystems. It is important for management to integrate decision making throughout the organization so that the total effort is founded on a high degree of coordination and cooperation. Seldom is complete success possible nor is the struggle for it usually made. Instead, organizations seek to satisfice or to obtain the best possible solution short of absolute success, given their limited capabilities and given the values prescribed by organizational philosophies. The best possible suboptimization for the organization usually means that its subsystems will also have to suboptimize—settle for less than absolute success.

Constraints on Decisions

In addition to the difficulties that interdependence makes in achieving a satisfactory suboptimization for the organization, there are other constraints that limit the decision-making process. We use the term *bounded discretion* to describe these constraints. In other words, there are certain social controls that limit our freedom in making decisions. These include legal restrictions, moral and ethical norms, formal policies and rules, and unofficial social norms. These controls do not apply equally to individuals and to organizations. Social norms are more likely to influence individuals than organizations. Competition, for example, may be much more overt between organizations than between individuals. Two persons competing for a promotion may observe an informal social norm not to be obvious about it. They may even feel compelled not to talk about it. Organizations, on the other hand, advertise quite freely and often even identify their competition when comparing products. Legal restrictions, however, apply more uniformly to both organizations and individuals. For example, neither may legally evade taxes in order to maximize income.

All the constraints involved in bounded discretion are restrictive to some degree, however. They define the boundaries of a residual discretionary area where acceptable choices of action can be made. The boundaries of the discretionary area not only include acceptable choices but also, at the same time, exclude certain decisions that might otherwise prove advantageous.[6] Figure 4–1 illustrates the concept.

Decisions by Trial and Error

People often develop a stereotyped image of how a businessman makes decisions. For example: subordinates hand the executive a complex problem that has defied their best efforts to solve it. After a few moments of concentrated thought, he begins issuing orders and instructions that are precise and detailed, and that solve the problem immediately. This image is perhaps one that managers dream about but rarely achieve in practice. Decision making and problem solving are extremely complex, and people make mistakes when they deal with complex issues.

Another fallacy is that a well-run organization has all subsystems revved up and operating at levels that will unerringly achieve organizational goals. Actually, one subsystem tends to move ahead at one time, another at another time, and so on—while the remainder are relatively static. This sort of uneven progress is due to the organization being an open system. Changes in the environment also cause changes in the organization. Imbalances occur and goals must be redefined or completely changed to fit new situations.

Figure 4–1 Bounded discretion in decision making*

*F. A. Shull, Jr., A. L. Delbecq, and L. L. Cummings, *Organizational Decision Making* (New York: McGraw-Hill, 1970), p. 19.

There is evidence that organizational progress is better if management does not attempt to decide all aspects of organizational problems or to achieve a permanent balance within the organization and between the organization and its environment.[7] This may be so because it is so extremely difficult for people to accurately perceive the future in all its complexity—including the future impacts of environmental changes on the organization. Better decisions may be made, from the total organizational viewpoint, if the basis for decision making remains relatively local, confined to those aspects of the problem that are predictable to some degree. Moderately unbalanced growth can foster greater progress than an attempt at balanced growth, because the imbalance fosters flexibility. Furthermore: "Simultaneous development of all subsystems and their early integration into a single plan may lead the policy maker into the illusion that the system is actually complete. Thus he may be less alert to possible further elaborations."[8] The argument in favor of reserving some decisions is largely in accord with Simon's explanations of bounded rationality and satisficing behavior.

While no open system is ever finally complete, the ideal, of course, would be to simultaneously make all the required decisions in order to completely rebalance a system every time a change occurred. This ideal cannot be realized because we lack the requisite knowledge and capability; that is, we cannot optimize for the entire organization. The ideal should not be discarded, however, since it serves as a useful, if somewhat abstract, standard for measuring decision-making scope.

Ill-Structured Problems   One of the principal reasons we cannot make simultaneous decisions for all subsystems within a total system is that most decision problems, particularly at top levels of management, are ill-structured. The following is an apt description:

Ill-structured problems . . . are those in which the alternative courses of action are not clear and tend to branch and multiply as the analysis proceeds. Often this type of problem is characterized by risk and uncertainty, while the well-structured types are not so characterized. In highly ill-structured problems, the analyst often does not really know how to proceed. Accordingly, he resorts to trial and error, probing until he makes a discovery or discerns a clue that points the way to the next trial. Discoveries and clues are remembered, stored in memory to combine with each other, and, through the mysterious processes of creative thinking such as incubation and illumination, the analyst discerns the ultimate meaningful alternatives.[9]

So risk and uncertainty characterize ill-structured problems. A classification of decision problems thus suggests four categories: decision problems under conditions of (1) certainty, (2) risk, (3) uncertainty, and (4) conflict or competition.

Decision making under certainty must deal with one or more alternatives but with only one *state of nature*. A state of nature is any uncontrollable variable that affects the outcomes of alternatives. Suppose you were going to sell Christmas trees, and out of all the possible demand amounts you might expect to encounter, somehow you knew you could sell exactly 1,000 trees. Your decision would be simple: buy 1,000 trees for resale (assuming they are all in good condition). You would have other alternatives—you could buy more or less than 1,000—but it would be foolish to buy anything but the exact amount you knew you could sell. The decision sounds simple, but in many instances it may be far from easy to reach a decision under certainty. If you had to arrange nine activities into a unified sequence that would incur the least cost, there are 362,880 possible arrangements that you might have to ascertain. Fortunately, computational methods often can reduce this kind of job to manageable size.

In decision making under risk, there are two or more alternatives and two or more states of nature, but the probability of occurrence of each state of nature is still known. If you are flipping coins with someone, you know the probability of a head or a tail is 50 percent. You have the alternative of betting or not betting; if you bet, you at least know you should not give odds to your opponent, given known probabilities for the states of nature.

In decision making under uncertainty, there are again two or more alternatives and two or more states of nature; but the probability of occurrence of each state of nature is not known. A difficult decision problem? Yes, and most practical organizational problems are of this ill-structured, uncertain variety. The situation is not hopeless, however. There is a way to deal with most uncertain cases. Even though we do not know the exact probability of some event happening, usually there is enough information so that we can make a pretty fair estimate. For example, if we were thinking about introducing a new product, we might want to know the probability of selling 10,000 units in the first year. We could ask experienced marketing persons, we could look at the experience of similar products in the past, and/or we could make some market tests in certain locations. On the basis of accumulated information, we could then develop subjective probabilities for various levels of output: let us say 5,000, 10,000 and 20,000 units.

What we have done is to convert the uncertain case to a case under risk, and we can proceed on that basis. Most business problems fall into this category of *partial information*—somewhere between a true risk situation with known probabilities (flipping a coin) and a true uncertain case (where there is no information at all on which to estimate probabilities).

In the fourth situation covering decision making, competition, the opponent(s) is assumed to operate in a rational manner. As in a game, if there are two competitors, the assumption of rationality makes their selection of strategies predictable. As a result, the outcome of the game can also be predicted. The concept of game theory will be more fully explored later in this chapter.

The Heuristic Approach Because most practical problems are ill-structured and involve only partial information, we use a heuristic approach to reach decisions. *Heuristic* means *seeking to discover*. In ill-structured problems, efforts are often on a trial-and-error basis. By trial and error we discover clues that lead to further trials and finally to a decision. To see how the heuristic process works, let us reconstruct our mental image of the organization as a system.

Recall that the organizational system has numerous subsystems. We named a few, such as management, other members, technology, and environment. Numerous other subsystems could be identified. For our present purposes, we will include the functional subsystems of a business such as production, sales, and finance; and the hierarchical subsystems such as top management, middle management, supervisory management, and operative workers. Our basic premise is that decisions made within any subsystem may affect not only the total system but every other subsystem within the total. Because of this overall effect on the system, decisions must be made with great care in order to avoid excessive suboptimization throughout the system.

To begin, each subsystem, each hierarchical level and each functional area, will have its own objective—called a subobjective, if the overall organizational goals are considered *objectives*. Furthermore, the organization will probably have multiple overall objectives, as will at least some of the subsystems. It is important that all of the objectives mesh properly and are appropriately related. Each subobjective should mesh properly with subobjectives of other subsystems and with higher-level objectives.

If the objective of an airline is to get an airplane safely from point A to point B within certain time constraints, then one subobjective of the maintenance department is to see that the airplane is in the safest possible operating condition. A subobjective of the scheduling department will be to see that the airplane leaves on time and arrives on time. And the subobjectives of maintenance and scheduling must mesh so the airplane is ready to leave when it is supposed to.

"The hierarchy of objectives is *not* a consequence of a hierarchy of management with its various levels ... The single manager of a very small organization would face the same set of hierarchical problems in solving the more complex problems of his organization."[10] Hence, the small organization as well as the large operates with a hierarchy of objectives in order to handle the very complex problems that are daily confronted.

Working Through the Subproblems Having a hierarchy of objectives also establishes a hierarchy of problems and subproblems as defined by the objectives. Once the objectives and problems are structured and decision criteria are disseminated and known, organizational decision making can begin. Subproblems are solved first, the sequence of attack being determined by the interrelationships of the subproblems. The initial subproblem solutions may be far from correct, since there is no way of knowing at this point exactly how each minor decision will fit into the solution of all subproblems or the final total decision.

When the first sequence of solutions is completed, another sequence may be begun. In certain situations the cycle may be repeated endlessly. In other cases, where a one-time decision is being made, there may be a time limit to the number of sequences or cycles that can be accomplished.

An example of continual cycling could be an operation like cattle raising where year after year decisions must be made about when to switch the cattle to different ranges, when to ship cattle to market, and how many and which ones should be kept for breeding purposes. On the other hand, perhaps a one-time decision is being made by a company about whether to bring a new product on the market. There may be a time constraint here since other companies may also be considering the same or a similar product. Waiting too long could allow others to gain a market dominance that could not be overcome. Therefore, there would be a limit on the number of cycles the company could go through in their decision-making process on the new product.

Cycles, or *iterations*, are important because each one moves the final decision closer to a satisfactory suboptimization. Each cycle should be a series of successive approximations, with each one improving the subproblem solutions in relation to the big problem and to the primary, overriding objective. This heuristic process also acknowledges, as we have discussed before, that it is not possible, given the present state of the art, to simultaneously solve all subproblems and achieve a balanced organizational condition that could be expected to last for a long time.

We now have an approximate description of how many decisions are made in organizations. The process is heuristic; it proceeds by trial-and-error methods to reach as effective decisions as are possible, given the constraints of time, knowledge, and money. We should emphasize again the interrelatedness of all organizational subsystems concerning decision making. For example, if a top-level decision has been made to produce a new product, this action is immediately translated into a problem for the manufacturing department of how to produce the new product. In turn, the decisions made by manufacturing will affect top management in its decisions about when to introduce the product, how much to charge for it, and how best to advertise and sell it. Other subsystems such as sales and purchasing will also be affected by the decisions that manufacturing and top management make. Figure 4–2 illustrates this heuristic decision-making process.

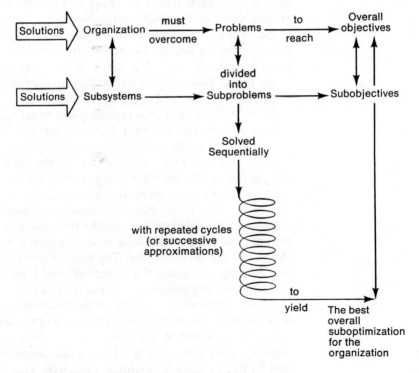

Figure 4–2 The heuristic decision-making process

We were descriptive in discussing the heuristic approach to decision making. Now we are going to be prescriptive as we study quantitative methods in decision making. This means we are going to suggest how decisions *ought* to be made in certain situations in order to come up with the *best* or *optimal* solution. Quantitative methodological tools are aids to decision making and often do yield optimal solutions, but they are limited to certain applications that are usually defined by hierarchical level and functional division.

Management science techniques find their greatest application in the technical or operating subsystem of a business organization. At this level, it is assumed that decisions are made within a closed system. The question that should be asked, perhaps, is whether making decisions in a closed system model at the operating level destroys the worth of the decisions. The answer is that, in certain instances, excluding environmental factors when making decisions at the operating level may have no impact on the efficacy of the decisions. In other instances, subsystem decisions may be optimized by using the closed system model, but seriously suboptimized within the broader organizational context. In the author's opinion, the assumption of a closed system at the operating level in order to use some portion of the available quantitative techniques is not a serious drawback, although interrelationships with other subsystems and the total system must constantly be kept in mind.

The Tools

We said earlier that an individual's decision could be considered rational if it moved the individual closer to his objective, even though others might view the values underlying his objective and decision as being odd or irrational. In other words, we may regard his *choice* as rational, but may at the same time label the *process* by which he arrived at his decision as less than rational if it was not accomplished in a scientific manner. Similarly, the heuristic approach to decision making is usually viewed as less rational than the scientific method of analysis. The heuristic process may combine rough judgments and intuitions with the rationality of the scientific method.

The scientific method encompasses the tools or techniques used in quantitative analysis for decision making, and it is commonly accepted as being a rational approach. It is formal, systematic, and based on logic and reason. The scientific method requires the user to:

1. Observe the problem situation, establishing an objective for decision making.
2. Build a hypothesis that explains the relationship of all relevant factors in the problem to each other and to the objective.
3. Test and revise the hypothesis until it serves as an appropriate model of the problem situation.
4. Develop the decision rule.
5. Apply the decision rule.[11]

Constructing a model is an integral part of the scientific method and of all the techniques used in quantitative analysis. Development of a model is particularly important in those cases where only partial information exists, because a characterization of the relationships between alternatives and outcomes is necessary to a reasoned solution. "This characterization which is called a *model* includes only what are believed to be the important features of the relationship. Both perfect knowledge and complete ignorance are unlikely cases and therefore, the vast majority of decision problems fall within this category."[12]

Suppose that we are in the business of manufacturing vacuum cleaners, and we find that we are slowly losing the share of the market that we have held for several years. A market survey tells us that our vacuum cleaner is not as attractive or as convenient to use as competitive models. To solve this problem, one of our goals becomes that of designing a more attractive and more convenient cleaner. If we state the problem in the form of a model, it could appear as follows: $x = f(y, z)$.

X represents a more competitive vacuum cleaner that will help reclaim our share of the market, y is for attractiveness or appearance, and z is for convenience. What our equation or model states is that being more competitive depends in part at least upon the attractiveness and convenience of the vacuum cleaner. In other words, x is a function of y and z. Attractiveness (y) and convenience (z) are the independent variables. Being more competitive (x) is the dependent variable.

Fortunately in this case, both y and z are controllable variables; that is, we can manipulate them in order to influence x. In some decision problems, uncontrollable independent variables complicate matters and make it more difficult to reach a decision. We could quantify the model by assigning numerical weights to each of the independent variables—attractiveness and convenience. The assignment might be done on a scale from one to ten, for example, with ten representing the most attractiveness and the greatest convenience. We could also define a standard of acceptance as a sum of the ratings of the independent variables, fifteen for example, and that precludes acceptance if either of the ratings falls below six. We could have the ratings done by persons within our organization, although having a consulting firm do them would probably be more reliable.

The decision rule, then, would be: to accept a new design, y plus z must be equal to or greater than 15 (using a scale from one to ten for each variable) and neither y nor z can receive a rating of five or less. If, for example, attractiveness (y) were given a rating of eight and convenience (z) a rating of seven, the sum of the ratings would be fifteen and the new design would be accepted. If y were rated ten and z five, the new design would be rejected since z has been rated below six.

We would want to test the model and the rating system before actual use. We might do this by rating the best competitive products and comparing those ratings to the requirements of our decision rule. If it appears the decision rule is too easy or too harsh, it can be adjusted accordingly—assuming the same individuals will continue to do all the ratings.

In developing a model, one is abstracting from reality and making simplifying assumptions. When applying the decision, then, one must be careful not to depend completely on the simplifying assumptions of the model. Factors that could not be abstracted into the model must be brought back in when the decision rule is being applied. Judgments must be made as to the impact of these factors on the objective, which is, in this case, becoming more competitive by having a more attractive and convenient vacuum cleaner. For example, we may have concluded that price could not be incorporated into the model. We must make a judgment, then, on whether the projected price of the vacuum cleaner, given the new design features, will help or hinder our desire to be more competitive. The cost of the new design might be higher than anticipated, forcing a high retail price that will be noncompetitive and making us finally decide on some other course of action. We could seek another acceptable design, we could attempt to change our manufacturing methods to lower costs, or we might discontinue the vacuum cleaner line completely.

The point is that no matter how carefully a model is constructed, the model alone usually will not yield a final answer. Factors omitted from the model must be returned to the decision problem and must be considered. In the vacuum cleaner example, setting a minimum criterion of 15 is no absolute guarantee of success even if the projected price of each unit is acceptable. There will also be some factor of probability associated with such a minimum criterion—perhaps that there would still only be a 75 percent chance of being more competitive if the criterion were to be equaled or exceeded.

The model we have just used is a symbolic model. It is one of three general model types:

1. An *iconic* model pictorially or visually represents certain aspects of a system (as does a photograph or model airplane).
2. An *analogue* model employs one set of properties to represent some other set of properties which the system being studied possesses (for example, for certain purposes, the flow of water through pipes may be taken as an analogue of the flow of electricity in wires).
3. A *symbolic* model uses symbols to designate properties of the system under study (by means of a mathematical equation or set of such equations).[13]

The specific tools that we will now discuss all use symbolic models. We shall be quite brief in describing the various techniques of quantitative analysis, for we intend only to familiarize the reader with the terms and the general areas of application. To do more, to give the reader a real appreciation of how the techniques are used and of their value, would require far more extensive treatment. More material on management science and quantitative analysis is listed in the suggested readings at the end of the chapter.

Simulation   As a technique simulation is broadly applicable and is often used where a precise mathematical model cannot define the real-life situation. Simulation employs models to test hypotheses. A familiar example is the iconic model of an airplane in a wind tunnel as a model for testing design characteristics under simulated flight conditions. There are many applications for iconic models in simulated testing.

An approach to simulation relevant to many business decision problems is the "Monte Carlo" approach, which uses a probabilistic model to help in the selection of alternatives. "A *probabilistic* model enables us to say only that certain states will *probably* result, given certain initial conditions. That is, given such and such conditions, a probabilistic model enables us to deduce a probability distribution for possible subsequent states."[14] For example, suppose we were trying to determine the number of checkout counters to have in a new supermarket and could develop some probabilities about the number of customers during various hours of the day, perhaps by using market research data and information from other stores. We could plug the probabilities into our simulation model and reach a decision that should effectively handle customer demand and minimize the risk of either under- or over-building checkout counters.

In a simple application, we might first determine the expected demand for checkout counters during various periods of the day from what appear to be comparable stores and from projected sales data on expected number of customers and sales per customer for our own store. We could compute demand for checkout counters on the basis of fifteen-minute periods spread over a fifteen-hour day when the store is open. If we also figure each checkout counter can handle ten customers in a fifteen-minute period, then our data might indicate a demand for two checkout counters during three fifteen-minute periods in a day, for three counters during five periods, and so on. Table 4–1 shows the demand for checkout counters along with a percentage breakdown of the demand.

The data we developed in table 4–1 describe a situation that we hope will also characterize our own store. To use the Monte Carlo technique, we would randomly sample our data which enables us to simulate actual operation of the store on a daily basis. We would want to do enough sampling to simulate operations for several days or weeks. In this simple application, extended simulation

Table 4–1 Projected demand for checkout counters during one day

Number of checkout counters needed to meet all possible demands	Demand* stated in terms of 15-minute periods throughout a 15-hour day	Percent of the total of 60 15-minute periods throughout a 15-hour day	Cumulative distribution of individual percent figures
2	3	5%	5%
3	5	9	14
4	11	18	32
5	20	33	65
6	12	20	85
7	7	12	97
8	2	3	100
	60	100%	

*This column states the number of demand periods for a given number of checkout counters. For example, from line 1 there are three 15-minute periods during the 15-hour day when there will be a demand for two checkout counters. From line 2 there will be five 15-minute periods or a total of 75 minutes during the day when there will be a demand for three checkout counters.

will yield a distribution identical to the one in our basic data (table 4–1). This will happen because we are only using one set of data and continued sampling brings the sampling information closer and closer to the original data. Accepting this aspect of our case, we can refer back to the column entitled cumulative distribution in table 4–1 for a suggestion on what to do about the checkout counters.

We see that for 15 percent (100 percent less 85 percent) of the working day, or for two and one-quarter hours there is a demand for seven or eight checkout counters. But there is a demand for eight checkout counters for only three percent of the day or for thirty minutes. Our decision on the number of checkout counters will depend in large part, then, on how willing we are to have customers wait. If we do not want any waiting, we will have eight checkout counters. If we are willing to have customers endure some waiting throughout thirty minutes of the fifteen-hour day, we will have seven counters. If we are willing to have waiting throughout two and one-quarter hours during the working day, we will have only six counters.

Other factors will affect our decision. If we want to have an image of a store offering the very best in service, we will want to minimize waiting as much as possible. If we want to emphasize low prices, we will carry this theme over to our investment in checkout counters, expecting customers to be willing to wait at times in order to take advantage of low prices. If we expect business to increase substantially in the years following the store opening, we may allot space in the store to add checkout counters as needed.

We have simplified the example of the checkout counters to illustrate the use of probabilities in the Monte Carlo method. We showed how Monte Carlo simulation would be used and then indicated it would not be necessary in this simple case. However, if we were to make our example more realistic, Monte Carlo simulation would be necessary. There are other probabilities that we should consider. What are the probabilities that we will be able to staff the checkout counters whenever necessary? This will depend on employee absenteeism, tardiness, and temporarily being tied up with other work. What are probabilities on the number of customers that one clerk can handle at a checkout counter during a fifteen-minute period? We said ten customers, but this could vary depending on the size of the customer's order and the skill of the checkout clerk. What are the probabilities on the number of customers shopping at varying times throughout the day? We can generate these probabilities from the past experiences of other comparable stores.

Using all of these sets of probabilities, we could now do a true Monte Carlo simulation of several days of business. We would set up each data set in a manner similar to that in table 4–1. By doing random sampling from each data set, we could simulate each fifteen-minute period of a day for, let us say, seven days. Thus we would be able to take into account the probabilities of (1) checkout counters being available; (2) number of customers taken care of in a fifteen-minute period; and (3) the number of customers likely to be shopping at the store at a given time. For this problem or more complicated Monte Carlo simulations, computer programmers can prepare the data for rapid simulation and quick answers.

One type of simulation you may have already tried is *business gaming*. Participants take the roles of managers, make decisions within the context of the business model, and receive feedback on the effects of their decisions. Many business games today are programmed on computers to handle greater complexity and to thus make the games more interesting. Large complex models have been built to simulate the operations of an entire company and even the economy of the nation. In the simulation process, the inputs to the model are varied and the results of variations observed to see what combinations of inputs yield the best results. It is an if–then proposition; that is, *"If* we do this, *then* what happens?"* These large complex models, of course, require the use of computers. Simulation is heuristic in nature and helps solve ill-structured problems under risk and uncertainty.

Linear Programming   Here is a powerful tool that has many applications. It is deterministic and solves problems under certainty; that is, with one state of nature and two or more alternatives. "A model is said to be *deterministic* if it enables us to say that certain states or results are certain to follow, given certain initial conditions. Thus, a deterministic model is a cause-and-effect explanation—certain conditions cause the subsequent state."[15] In linear programming, the initial conditions or state of nature often are in the form of cost figures, profit margins, and certain constraints. A simple, typical problem may involve how many units of two products to produce, given the profit margins on the products and manufacturing limitations.

For example, suppose you were making two products—*A* and *B*. The profit margin on *A* is $8 while on *B* it is $10. Furthermore, each product must first be machined on a lathe and then polished. The available hours on the lathes total 240 in a given time period, while there are 200 hours available on the polishing machines. Product A requires 4 hours on a lathe and 12 hours of polishing to be finished, and product B needs 10 hours of lathe time and 5 hours of polishing. Given these initial conditions, you are wondering what would be the best or optimal number of units of each product to produce to maximize profits, assuming you could sell as much of either A or B as you could make. Through linear programming, we can say (predict) that a certain state will result—the optimal state. We structure the problem as follows:

Objective function: $8A + 10B$ = maximum profit

Constraints: $4A + 12B \leq 240$ hours of lathe time

$10A + 5B \leq 200$ hours of polishing time

Of course, in this simple case, it would be easy to solve the simultaneous constraint equations and obtain the best answer, but a graphical analysis perhaps is more instructive.

Note that in figure 4–3 the two constraint lines for lathes and polishing enclose a shaded area. This is called the *feasible area* because it defines the total number of units of A and/or B that can be produced; that is, no more than 20 units of either A or B alone

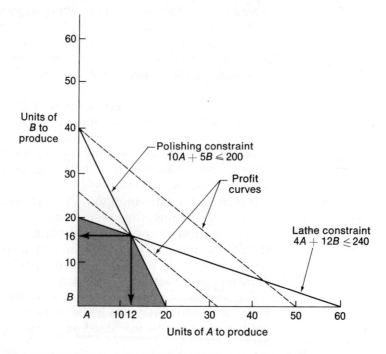

Figure 4–3   Graphic analysis of linear programming problem

can be produced, although lesser amounts of both in combination can be made. Now we have also plotted our objective function or profit line in two different locations to illustrate where it just touches the outermost point of the feasible area. At this point, it shows that 12 units of *A* and 16 units of *B* is the best combination to produce. Plugging these results into the formula for our objective function, we find the maximum we can make to be $256. Producing *A* or *B* alone or any other combination of *A* or *B* will not do as well.

A two-dimensional problem like this is quite easy to solve and obviously does not require a sophisticated computational routine. However, if you had ten products and fifteen constraints, the result would not be so obvious and certainly could not be graphed. But linear programming, through a repetitive computational routine called the *Simplex method*, will still yield the optimal answer, even in complex problems. Referring to figure 4–3 again, the Simplex method starts with an initial solution at the origin and then goes from point to point on the boundary of the feasible area until the optimal solution is reached. This optimum is indicated in the final iteration of the Simplex method. Fortunately, since the Simplex method takes so long when done by hand, computers easily handle linear programming.

An important advantage of linear programming is the ability to vary some initial conditions and then determine the impact on maximizing profit or minimizing cost without having to rework the whole problem. This valuable modification of the original, optimal solution is achieved through sensitivity analysis. In our illustration, a manager could quickly tell through sensitivity analysis what would happen to the profit if he relaxed the lathe constraint and provided, for example, 300 hours of lathe time instead of 240. Sensitivity analysis, like linear programming, is most valuable in complex situations.

Applications for linear programming include the following: (1) allocating limited resources (such as lathes and polishing equipment) to two or more products; (2) assigning men to machines, or branch warehouses to factories (the latter is a problem in routing and is a special application of linear programming called the *transportation problem*); and (3) mixing problems, such as a refinery might face in blending ingredients for gasoline and other petroleum products.

Dynamic Programming This type of programming is less well-defined than linear programming and, as the adjective *dynamic* suggests, it deals with a sequence of decisions through time. Depending on the problem involved, dynamic programming uses either a deterministic model or a probabilistic model. Hence, it may apply over a range from a relatively well-structured problem to an ill-structured one.

The three basic steps in dynamic programming are:

1. The total problem is divided into a number of subproblems.
2. Working backward from the natural end of the problem, each subproblem is solved in turn.
3. After each subproblem is solved, the answer is recorded, and the payoff (profit, cost, and so on) from that stage on to the end of the problem is also recorded.[16]

After working backward through the problem by the above procedure, the choice of the best alternative from those available is simply determined as the one with the biggest payoff. If you had five decisions to make over five successive months, you could apply dynamic programming to solve your last decision first. Then you could work backward to the first to determine your best course of action.

There is also a relationship between the maximum return at one stage and the maximum return at the next stage, and this is known as the *general recurrence relation*. The general recurrence relation must be determined to solve a dynamic programming problem.

Although the basic concepts of dynamic programming are present in every dynamic programming formulation and solution, the actual numerical procedures used for solution may vary widely. For this reason, no prepared computer library program or code exists for the solution of dynamic programming problems comparable to well-known computer codes for solving linear programming problems. In fact, a dynamic programming problem is not nearly so well-defined as a linear programming problem; all one knows is that decision stages are present, a state variable exists, and recurrence relations have been recorded. The complexity of the recurrence relations determines in large part whether the dynamic programming problem is easy to solve, hard to solve, or impossible to solve.[17]

Network Techniques There are several varieties of network techniques, all of which aid in planning, scheduling, and controlling. The best known probably is Project Evaluation and Review Technique, or PERT. Conceived by the Navy and the Lockheed Aircraft Company for development of the Polaris missile, PERT has been accepted for many different one-of-a-kind projects—such as shipbuilding, construction projects, and major equipment overhauls.

Among the key concepts of PERT is the idea that planning and scheduling should be separated—that it is necessary first to plan and define objectives and then to allocate and schedule the resources available to meet these plans. It has been found that among the numerous interrelated activities that make up a complex project, only a small number of the operations control or limit the completion time of the total job. Detecting these and concentrating on their performance allows true *management by exception* [so called because the characteristic process is one of successively eliminating the noncontrolling factors in decision making].[18]

In preparing a PERT diagram, it is essential to determine which activities must precede and follow other activities and which activities can occur concurrently. A completed network diagram will indicate if some activities have "slack" time, where some delay in completion of the task can be tolerated. It will also show the *critical path* or the particular sequence of events through the network where there is no slack time and which defines the minimum amount of time required to complete the entire project. Figure 4–4 shows a simplified PERT diagram for preparing instant coffee.

Network techniques usually handle cases under risk and uncertainty that may, however, be relatively well-structured in terms of

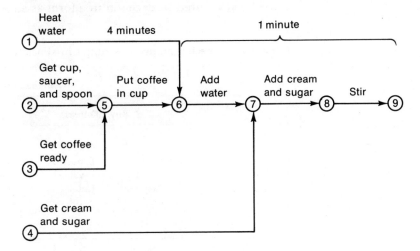

Critical Path is ①—⑥—⑦—⑧—⑨ This is the minimum time necessary to prepare a cup of coffee.

Arrows indicate *activities*, while circles show *events*, which mark the beginning or end of an activity. Usually all activities in a PERT diagram show the time required for completion.

Figure 4–4 PERT diagram for making instant coffee

some required sequence of activities. They tend to be heuristic in nature and generally offer a probability of achieving a specific target date for completion rather than an absolute guarantee.

Statistical Decision Theory Dealing for the most part with ill-structured problems under risk and uncertainty, statistical decision theory provides a heuristic approach to problem solution. The manager faced with several alternative courses of action will attempt to estimate as best he can the probability of each alternative actually happening. Then he combines these probabilities with the expected consequences of each possible event and compares the projected outcomes. From a rational viewpoint, he should choose the alternative that most likely will yield the greatest gain.

For example, imagine again that you plan on selling Christmas trees. You estimate that there is a 60 percent chance of selling 100 trees and a 40 percent chance of selling 200 trees. You can buy either 100 or 200 trees at $2 each, and your selling price is $10 per tree. You lose the $2 purchase price on each tree that is not sold. To determine your best expected value or profit, you could set up the problem in tabular form as shown in table 4–2. The same problem could be structured in decision tree form as shown in figure 4–5.

Table 4–2 Expected profits on selling Christmas trees

		Alternatives			
		Buy 100 trees		**Buy 200 trees**	
(1)	(2)	(3)	(4)	(5)	(6)
State of nature or event	Probability	Conditional value 100 trees sold × $8	Expected value Col. 2 × col. 3	Conditional value (trees sold × $8) less (trees not sold × $2)	Expected value Col. 2 × col. 5
Sell 100 trees	60%	$800	$480	$600	$360
Sell 200 trees	40%	$800*	$320	$1,600	$640
Expected monetary value			$800		$1,000**

*Only 100 trees can be sold as only 100 were purchased.
**Best alternative.

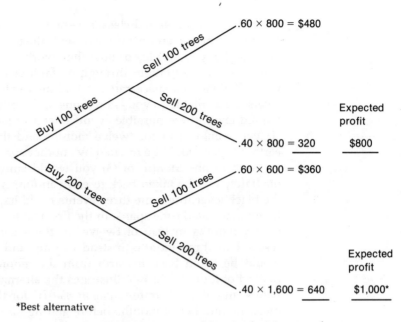

.60 × 800 = $480

.40 × 800 = 320   Expected profit

$800

.60 × 600 = $360

.40 × 1,600 = 640   Expected profit

$1,000*

*Best alternative

Figure 4–5 The Christmas tree problem in decision-tree form

This procedure, shown in both forms, is known as the *Bayes decision rule* and is commonly used in statistical decision making.

Now, you may feel your probability estimates on sales are unreliable. If so, you may wonder if a sample might give you more accurate information (assuming a sample could somehow be taken in this case). Statistical decision theory also offers methods to determine the value of additional information through sampling and, therefore, whether it would be worthwhile to take a sample with respect to the increased value (accuracy) afforded the probability estimates. Decision trees, incidentally, are an excellent aid to planning and decision making since they picture so well the available alternatives with their associated probabilities and outcomes. However, they get visually complex and therefore conceptually cumbersome if there are many alternatives or if the decision problem runs on through several sequences of events.

Decision Techniques for Total Ignorance As suggested earlier, making decisions under uncertainty or in total ignorance of the probabilities for the occurrence of various states of nature is quite rare. Usually some information is available to the decision maker so he can solve his problem as though it were a case of decision making under risk; that is, where the probabilities for the states of nature are known—as in the 50 percent probability for a head or a tail on a coin flip. Nonetheless, several techniques have been suggested for the uncertain case. We will illustrate just one of them here to give you an idea of how they work.

Imagine this situation: through no fault of your own, you find yourself alone in a spacecraft orbiting the earth. Only two control levers are available to you—a red one and a black one. If you pull the red lever, three possible events (states of nature) could occur: (1) you would orbit for twelve months and then land safely on earth; (2) you would be rescued by another spacecraft and be back on earth in one month; or (3) you would land on the moon immediately and be taken back to earth in four months. If you pull the black lever, the same three events could happen but with different associated time spans. In the first instance, you would orbit for six months instead of twelve; in the second, you would be rescued in three months instead of one; and in the third, you would be taken back to earth from the moon in eight months instead of four. Table 4–3 illustrates the alternatives and states of nature and also illustrates a *payoff matrix*, for the payoffs (in this case, the number of months before getting back to earth) are displayed in the cells or intersections of the alternatives and states of nature.

Now you have absolutely no idea which event will occur when you pull either the red or the black lever, but one of the techniques for uncertainty—in our case we will use what is known as the *minimax technique*—can suggest an answer. In the minimax technique, the decision maker determines the worst possible outcome for each alternative and then selects the alternative that minimizes the maximum loss, cost, or time before getting back to earth. For the alternative of pulling the red lever, the worst possible outcome is twelve months before getting back to earth, while for the black lever, it is eight months. Following the minimax procedure, then,

Table 4–3 Payoff matrix for "lost-in-space" problem

	States of nature		
Alternatives	Orbit—then land on earth	Orbit—then rescue by another spacecraft	Land on moon—then return to earth
Pull red lever	12 months	1 month	4 months
Pull black lever	6 months	3 months	8 months

Table 4-4 Application of minimax rule to "lost-in-space" problem

Alternatives	States of nature 1	2	3	Maximum of the row
Pull red lever	12	1	4	12
Pull black lever	6	3	8	8

you would elect to pull the black lever, for this *minimizes the maximum* time you might be away from earth. Table 4–4 shows the application of the minimax procedure.

The minimax procedure is pessimistic, for it concentrates on the worst possible outcomes and avoidance of the worst thing that could happen. Other techniques tend to be optimistic, while some are neutral. The techniques for the uncertain case have found little practical application and remain predominantly of academic interest, so we will not expand our discussion of them.

Game Theory While baseball, football, and other games have their special theories for winning success, the game theory we will discuss finds its application in particular kinds of competitive situations that may involve business organizations or nations as well as sporting events. The situation is one of conflict, where the gains of one party usually are at the expense of the other party or parties. Yet the nature of the game is such that all parties find it advantageous to reach some agreement rather than not to agree at all, and they will cooperate (act rationally) to achieve this end. The mathematics of game theory yields the agreement or solution that will be most satisfactory to all concerned parties. The analysis of and the mathematics for modern game theory were developed principally by von Neumann and Morgenstern and explained in their book *Theory of Games and Economic Behavior*.[19] The fact that the book was published in 1944 indicates that game theory, like the other quantitative techniques in decision theory, is of fairly recent vintage.

The simplest example of game theory is the two-person zero-sum game. Matching pennies is a game of this type, for the winnings of one party are the losses of the other, and the total winnings (including negative winnings or losses) add to zero for every play of the game. Every two-person zero-sum game has a unique minimax solution. The minimax procedure has the same interpretation here as it did under the case of uncertainty, but here we are assuming that both opponents are using the minimax strategy. Actually, if one opponent uses the minimax strategy, it will be to the advantage of the other opponent also to use the minimax strategy. And since in game theory we assume that our opponent is acting rationally, if we choose a minimax strategy, we also expect him to do so.

Furthermore, the unique minimax solution is a desirable one, so the opponents will end up using minimax strategies even if they start out with something else. Consider the following payoff matrix for two persons in a zero-sum game (table 4–5).

Assume you are opponent A and that the figures in the payoff matrix represent arbitrarily quantified gains to you and losses to your opponent. In using the minimax strategy, your opponent, B, will want to minimize his maximum loss; hence he will choose the lesser of the maximum losses, 8 and 10, from each of his possible strategies (as indicated by the arrow in table 4–5). You, on the other hand, in applying the minimax strategy, will want to *maximize* your *minimum* gain; hence you will select the greater of the minimums from each of the two strategies available to you. The selection of strategy 1 by opponent B, and the selection of strategy 1 by yourself, A, thus identifies the unique solution to the game or the *saddle* point of the game. The numerical value of the amount at the saddle point, eight, also is the winning *value* of the game.

In playing the game, then, you will always win eight. If you doubt this, try experimenting with other strategies for both A and B and see if you do not always come back to strategy 1 for both

Table 4–5 Payoff matrix for a two-person zero sum game

A chooses the maximum minimum gain, 6.

B chooses the minimum maximum loss, 8.

opponents. And in case the idea of one party always gaining with the other party always losing sounds unrealistic, think of the collective bargaining situation involving unions and management. The union is bargaining for a constant maximum possible gain, while the company is striving to minimize the maximum possible cost. Of course, you will not always be on the winning or gaining side. What position you play depends on the circumstances.

Game theory goes beyond the two-person zero-sum game to nonzero-sum games and other modifications that require fairly difficult mathematical treatment to solve. Yet despite its adaptability, game theory has enjoyed only limited practical application. Nevertheless, it remains an important conceptual tool in many situations.

Summary

Decision making is much more than an instant in time during which a decision is made. A study of decision making shows it to be a process starting with the setting of a goal and ending with the selection of a best course of action.

Organizational and individual decision making almost always falls short of objective rationality, but it does achieve subjective rationality through satisficing. If an individual or organization makes a decision according to his or its own values and goals, that decision may be considered rational from the viewpoint of the individual or organization, even though outsiders might consider the decision to be peculiar or quite irrational. Some decision-making methods tend to be more rational than others; management science techniques are generally considered more scientific and hence more rational than heuristic, trial-and-error methods.

Organizations must generally be content to achieve subjective rationality in their decision making. They search for alternatives until they find and confirm a satisfactory one, which is usually determined by their level of aspiration. The level of aspiration in turn depends on past successes and failures as well as on anticipations for the future.

Decision making for the organization as a whole is generally heuristic in nature, proceeding by trial and error and by successive approximation toward the best possible overall suboptimization. No model will perfectly solve all subsystem problems at once. Instead, throughout the decision-making process, constant attention must be given to the coordination of all the interdependent subsystems as first one and then another subsystem reaches decisions. Furthermore, all decisions must be made within the constraints of legal restrictions, moral and ethical norms, formal policies and rules, and unofficial social norms.

Decision problems are categorized as being under certainty, risk, or uncertainty. The pure cases of risk and uncertainty are rare. Most organizational decision problems fall in the category of what might be called *partial information,* meaning that enough information is available to take them out of the case of uncertainty and to treat them as though they were under risk. Problems under risk and uncertainty tend to be ill-structured, while those under certainty are well-structured.

At some points in the heuristic decision-making process of the organization—usually at the technical or operational level of the organization—it is possible to use quantitative analysis. Some major techniques and their applications are: the use of models, simulation, linear programming, dynamic programming, network techniques, statistical decision theory, methods for uncertainty, and game theory.

Deciding how to decide, then, means choosing the proper decision tool or method for a given problem. For the entire organization, there is not much choice: the heuristic method is the only available approach. There can be a wide variance between a systematic approach such as we have attempted to describe and a hit-and-miss effort. Management must choose the right quantitative tools in order to solve problems effectively. Deciding how to decide should always precede the problem-solving decision-making process. And lastly, choosing the proper decision tool or method for making effective decisions requires a good knowledge of decision theory.

Management Profile

Chester I. Barnard

Chester I. Barnard pioneered the ideas that an executive is predominantly a communications center and that an organization is a system of decision making. Barnard was a practicing executive by vocation and not a scholar. A self-made man, Barnard worked on a farm as a boy; supported himself at prep school as a janitor for the school chapel, and earned his living at Harvard by tuning pianos and leading a dance band. Impatient with crusty academic rules, he left Harvard without a degree at the end of three years and went to work for the American Telephone and Telegraph Company. In 1927, at the age of 40, he was promoted to the presidency of New Jersey Bell Telephone Company.

In 1938, his now classic *The Functions of the Executive* was published. The book included exciting and important new ideas on informal organization, authority, and decision making and proved a fountainhead of thought for later writers in the field. In addition to stressing the management function as a system of communication, Barnard emphasized the importance of offering organizational inducements to members in order to gain and assure their contributions. He suggested that a required balance between inducements and contributions would support the system of interactions characterizing any organization.

Barnard's ideas on authority surely must have startled management theorists at the time, who were predominantly classical, for he conceived of authority as being accepted by subordinates as their choice rather than as being imposed on them from a superior organizational position. Carried to its extreme, this would mean that there would be no authority if organization members chose to reject it. This idea is certainly a far cry from classical theory and the Weberian ideal bureaucratic form.

Barnard also said that one executive function was to carefully define the purposes and goals of an organization, which is an important part of any decision-making process. Establishing communications, securing a balance between inducements and contributions, and carefully defining goals are his main contributions to analysis of executive functions.

Like many successful synthesists, Barnard was a well-rounded person. His interests were not confined to the logical analysis of organizations and management. An accomplished pianist, he was president of the Bach Society of New Jersey. At various times, he also was a director of the National Probation Association, an assistant to the Secretary of the Treasury, a consultant to the United Nations Atomic Energy Commission, and president of the Rockefeller Foundation. Barnard died in 1961, leaving a valuable legacy of management theory derived from his successful experience in a variety of enterprises.

Discussion Questions

1. In the incident "The Marriage," what was the environmental event that gave Stanley a cue that he should raise his level of aspiration?

Can you think of cues in your own experience that may have caused you to raise or lower your level of aspiration?

2. In "The Marriage," would it have been possible in any way for Stanley to achieve objective rationality? In a decision situation, is it ever possible to be objectively rational? Explain your answer.

3. Mr. Smith, Mr. Jones, and Mr. Brown all live five miles from work. Mr. Smith drives to work, Mr. Jones takes the bus, and Mr. Brown walks. Are any or all them acting rationally? Explain.

4. While organizational and individual decision making have many similarities, organizations do run into problems that do not affect the individual very much. What are some of these problems and why are they more serious for organizations?

5. With all of our theoretical knowledge and computerized capabilities, why is it still not possible to keep an organization and its subsystems always in a perfect state of balance? Would it be advisable to keep them in balance if it were possible?

6. Most organizational decision problems are characterized by sufficient information to convert the uncertain case to one of risk. Can you describe any instances where there would be true uncertainty?

7. What is the relationship between successive approximations and suboptimization? Do individuals ever go through a series of successive approximations in their decision making? If so, describe a possible decision and process.

8. Management science techniques have their greatest application at the operating level of an organization. Why is this so? Can you describe instances where these techniques would be operative at the top managerial level?

9. Build a model of your future career, for buying a car, for cooking a dinner, or for describing a successful trip.

10. Illustrate a PERT network for making coffee and boiling an egg, for preparing a complete lunch, for making the arrangements for a party, or for remodeling a kitchen.

References

1. H. A. Simon, *Administrative Behavior*, 2d ed. (New York: The Free Press, 1957).

2. *Ibid.*, p. 76.

3. *See* A. C. Filley and R. J. House, *Managerial Process and Organizational Behavior* (Glenview, Ill.: Scott, Foresman, 1969), pp. 118–120, for a more complete discussion on the termination of search activities.

4. Simon, p. 76.

5. J. M. Pfiffner and F. P. Sherwood, *Administrative Organization* (Englewood Cliffs, N.J.: Prentice-Hall, 1960), p. 386.

6. F. A. Shull, Jr.; A. L. Delbecq; and L. L. Cummings, *Organizational Decision Making* (New York: McGraw-Hill, 1970), pp. 18–19.

7. Filley and House, pp. 101–104.

8. Filley and House, p. 102.

9. H. L. Timms, *Introduction to Operations Management* (Homewood, Ill.: Richard D. Irwin, 1967), p. 68.

10. *Ibid.*, p. 56.

11. *Ibid.*, p. 71.

12. H. E. Thompson, "Management Decisions in Perspective," in W. E. Schlender; W. G. Scott; and A. C. Filley, *Management in Perspective* (Boston: Houghton Mifflin, 1965), p. 137.

13. F. E. Kast and J. E. Rosenzweig, *Organization and Management* (New York: McGraw-Hill, 1970), p. 380.

14. Ya-lun Chou, *Statistical Analysis* (New York: Holt, Rinehart and Winston, 1969), p. 184.

15. *Ibid*, p. 184.

16. H. Bierman, Jr.; C. P. Bonini; and W. H. Hausman, *Quantitative Analysis for Business Decisions*, 3d ed. (Homewood, Ill.: Richard D. Irwin, 1969), p. 433.

17. *Ibid.*, p. 441.

18. T. R. Hoffman, *Production: Management and Manufacturing Systems* (Belmont, Calif.: Wadsworth, 1967), p. 316.

19. J. von Neumann and O. Morgenstern, *Theory of Games and Economic Behavior* (Princeton, N.J.: Princeton University Press, 1944).

Suggested Readings

Bierman, H. Jr., Bonini, C. P., and Hausman, W. H., *Quantitative Analysis for Business Decisions*. 4th ed. Homewood, Ill.: Richard D. Irwin, 1973.

Miller, D. W. and Starr, M. K., *The Structure of Human Decisions*. Englewood Cliffs, N. J.: Prentice-Hall, 1967.

Simon, H. A. *Administrative Behavior*. 2d ed. New York: The Free Press, 1957.

———. *The New Science of Management Decision*. New York: Harper & Row, 1960.

5

From time to time, we hear the news media complaining that the federal government manages news information. The media usually direct their complaints toward presumed attempts to present information in such a way that the news reports will reflect favorably on administration programs and actions. In discussing the management of information in organizations, we are not concerned with public relations or advertising. We are, however, very much concerned with managing information in organizations so that appropriate information is available at the right time and place for efficient decision making, for information and efficient decision making are inseparable. We must therefore study how the gathering and processing of information can be designed to aid in making better decisions.

The Black Box

Recall that we have identified the organization as a system with interrelated component parts that must be coordinated by management. To function efficiently, management must receive information from all elements of the organization. The various elements or subsystems will also be communicating (transmitting information) among themselves. Hence, we may envision the organization as a communication or information network. Information is not just transmitted internally, however. Since the organization is an open system, it interacts with the environment, and both receives and transmits information from and to outside agencies. We will assume that the organization wants communications to the external environment to be accurate and factual.

It is important for an organization to gather as accurate information as possible from its external environment. There are many ways to gather information, such as market research surveys, the Neilsen ratings for television, economic forecasts, and private newsletter services. These sources of information help an organization to predict what will happen in the future. Many of these information sources (general economic forecasts, for example) may have limited usefulness to a particular, individual organization. Therefore, it is vital that the organization develop its own historical data by making its own observations on what happens in the outside world as a result of its decisions.

Despite our best efforts, we seldom can predict with 100 percent accuracy what will happen in the future as a result of a decision we make now. This is the uncertainty we discussed in the last chapter. But we can improve our ability to predict and to make better decisions if we record what happens as a result of our decisions as we go along. The point is that the outside world, from the viewpoint of an organization, is like a black box. We cannot see inside the black box to observe exactly how things work, but we can submit inputs (decisions) and observe the responses that the mechanism inside the box makes. In this way we slowly gain ideas as to how the inside of the box, or as to how the real world, works. Then we can better control our decision-making process and more efficiently use the information we get. Figure 5–1 illustrates the concept of the black box and the organizational inputs.

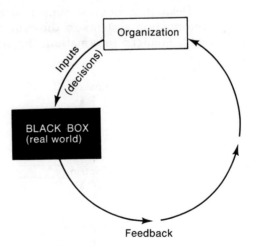

Figure 5–1 The "Black Box" concept. Feedback from reactions of real world to organizational inputs enables organization to change its inputs to real world (its decisions).

An information system (often called MIS for Management Information System) should be "designed to focus on the critical tasks and decisions made within an organization and to provide the kind of information that the manager needs to perform those tasks and make those decisions."[1] Hence the purpose of an information system is to support the manager in his decision-making efforts.

Providing this support to the manager requires that all the subsystems of the organization be recognized as interrelated, for decisions any individual manager makes will probably affect one or more of the other elements of the organization. Therefore, an information system is also an integrative device and helps management from the top down to coordinate all activities in the achievement of organizational goals (figure 5–2).

In a loose sense, one can conceive of a total information system for an organization. But in the business world, at least, most organizations are so large and complex that the term *total system* may tend to be misleading as far as thinking of a tight, highly-integrated system is concerned. John Dearden, a recognized expert on information systems, suggests that a more useful approach to the organization of an information system is "to break down the systems and data-processing activities both horizontally and vertically. Horizontally, the systems activities can be classified by the type of work performed; vertically, the systems activities can be classified by the kind of information handled."[2]

Dearden goes on to suggest that there are three major vertical information systems in the typical company. One is concerned with financial information, the second with personnel informa-

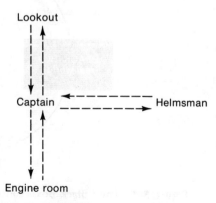

Figure 5–2 Possible information system for a ship

tion, and the third with information pertaining to the flow of physical goods. No doubt there could be other classifications of major information systems in other types of organizations. The important idea is that it may be deceptive to think of a total unified system when actually there may be two or more major systems within any given organization. And although there would be interfaces or points of contact between these major systems, it would probably be impractical at the present time to attempt to mesh them into one whole, as each will have its own unique characteristics. As information technology progresses, a highly-integrated total system will become more practical.

Designing from the Top Down

The design of an information system should be accomplished from the top down. Only top management can decide what information it needs to make decisions and how often and how soon the information is needed. This design should continue on down through the organization, with each manager specifying the nature and frequency of the information he needs for decision making. The system should not be designed from the bottom up because too much information may be accumulated. If a manager has not specified what information he wants, his subordinates will tend to give him everything they can, on the theory that somewhere in the mess the manager will find what he needs. Selection of information, then, must precede storage of information. Careful selection helps reduce the amount that must be stored.

One interesting way to minimize information storage has been developed by the Dana Corporation, a Toledo-based truck and auto parts company.[3] This company has substituted a four-channel, closed-circuit television system for the mounds of paperwork with which it formerly contended. On these television channels, the managers get current market results, leading national economic indicators, and balance sheet ratios. Thus they can compare sales and profit performance with forecasts and with the past year's results. This was a dramatic move, since records kept on paper have traditionally been the major form for information storage.

There are, of course, systems design experts. These may be members of an organization's staff or members of an outside consulting firm. The experts must work closely with the line managers to develop an efficient information system. There is little chance that the information system, as designed solely by the experts, will reflect the decisions that must be made and the information required to make those decisions. Here, as in all cases, the decision-making process must remain in contact with the concrete situation unique to the individual organization.

Another element in an information system is *feedback*. Feedback helps control decision-making processes. We discussed feedback in this regard using the concept of the black box. Management makes decisions that comprise inputs to the black box (real world). Then management observes the responses of the real world to see how closely they correspond to expectations. If everything happens as anticipated, then the decision is confirmed. In addition, the decision maker has some basis for making similar decisions in the future.

On the other hand, if the observed responses, or feedback, show a wide variance from what was expected, the decision maker will have a basis for revising his decision making in the future to accommodate what he has learned about the real world. Unfortunately, an organization could be out of business by the time adequate experience was gained. Combining theory with experience, however, can help to avoid the excessive cost connected with experience alone. Moreover, some of the techniques mentioned in the last chapter could be used to gain feedback before the final plunge is taken. Simulation might be used, for example, to gain some knowledge of how the real world will react to various inputs.

We may think of feedback as a circuit or loop; that is, information on results is "looped" back to the manager so he can improve his decision making in the future. Feedback circuits or loops are an important part of any information system. Figure 5–3 shows an example of a simple type of feedback loop.

An organization, then, generates information both from within the organization and from the external environment. The system design should provide for storing and transmitting this information in a way that recognizes the organizational decisions that must be made and the interrelationships that exist among all elements of the organization. Information constitutes the premises for decision making. And since decisions are instructions given to

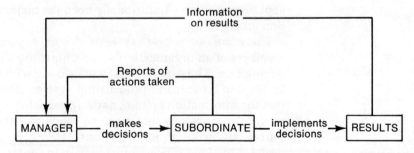

Figure 5–3 Managerial feedback loops for information flow

the various parts of the organization in order to achieve goals, the critical and vital nature of information becomes apparent.

Thus far we have omitted computers from our discussion of information systems. This omission was deliberate, since computer *hardware* (equipment) is not necessary to the design and operation of a successful information system. Human beings make computers and can handle all computational methods incorporated into such machines. It is true, though, that computers do play an important and often vital role in many information systems today.

The Computer

The computer has proved a boon to the efficient operating of many organizational information systems. Its ability to store and rapidly process vast amounts of data make it possible to greatly condense file space as well as make information quickly available.

The basic components of most computer systems include an input device, output devices, storage units, and a central processing unit (figure 5–4). Everyone is familiar with the punched computer card, having received bills in this form or registered for

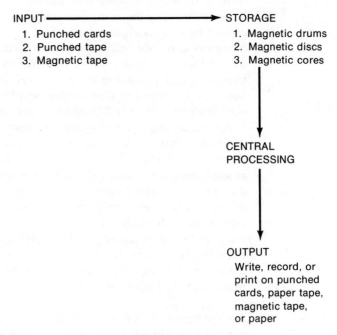

INPUT ⟶ STORAGE

1. Punched cards   1. Magnetic drums
2. Punched tape   2. Magnetic discs
3. Magnetic tape   3. Magnetic cores

CENTRAL
PROCESSING

OUTPUT
Write, record, or
print on punched
cards, paper tape,
magnetic tape,
or paper

Figure 5–4   Basic computer components

school on them. Input devices read the data punched on these cards and translate the information into a code that the computer understands. Computer systems also use paper and magnetic tape as input media.

The output devices then write or print information from the computer onto cards or tape. The information is often simultaneously issued on printout sheets. All data must be placed in storage before they can be handled by the computer. The hardware for storage often takes the form of magnetic discs and drums. A unit of information is held on a spot on the drum or disc by a charge of electricity. The increase in storage capacity in such devices has been one of the remarkable achievements of technological progress in computers over the past few years.

The computer's central processing unit does such things as adding, subtracting, multiplying, dividing, calling for data from storage, and putting data back into storage. These are the so-called hardware parts of a computer system. The *software* consists mainly of the instructions or program that a computer needs in order to operate. Since the computer is only an electronic device, without the capacity for self-starting activity, it needs detailed instructions on what to do. Information must be coded in language that the computer will understand in order for it to operate. Programming is quite rigorous, in the sense that instructions must be written in a precise way, or the computer will reject the program or make an error. The error is always the fault of the input information since a computer can only follow directions. (There are, of course, errors due to technical malfunction as well.) Several programming systems are available that make it relatively easy to write the instructions for a computer. One of the best known is FORTRAN—*the mathematical FORmula TRANslation system.*

An interesting, ongoing effort in computer science is heuristic problem solving—the attempt to program a computer so that it thinks like a human. We have discussed heuristic decision making at some length and know that most organizational problems are of the nonprogrammed variety that require a heuristic approach. For example, managers easily solve problems by some set formula or algorithm such as the computation of pay on the basis of hours worked. While heuristic problem solving on a computer has so far been limited largely to such activities as playing chess, the ultimate aim is to be able to solve those types of problems that now require the full application of human intelligence.

The Computer Generation Gap

The term *generation gap* is not confined to the human world, for the computer world has its generations as well. Since the inception of the modern computer in about 1950, there have been four distinct generations or major technological advances in computers. The first generation used vacuum tubes in its electronic circuitry. The second generation was born when the transistor replaced the vacuum tube and thereby hypercharged the speed index. A first-generation computer could take ten-digit numbers and multiply them 100,000 times in four minutes. The second generation could perform the same job in six seconds.

Then came the third generation with miniaturized circuitry on ceramic chips. It could do the same job in just six-tenths of a second. Now we have the fourth generation, which can perform many separate computations at the same time and carry out up to 200 million instructions per second. The time reduction in speed of operation between a second generation computer and a fourth generation is about 200 to one.

Today computers keep track of almost every bank check in the United States, reserve nearly all scheduled airline seats, scrutinize every federal income tax return, help to diagnose illnesses, and plan radiation therapy. One computer has synthesized the tone of a trumpet so authentically that experts cannot distinguish it from a genuine trumpet blast. One bank estimates it costs only one-three hundredth as much to post a check using a computer as to have a ledger clerk do it. And some computers are now capable of reading printed and written characters instead of having to sense data from holes in cards or from impulses on tape.

For all of its powers, however, the computer cannot guarantee results. A few years back, a simple short circuit blacked out the entire East Coast; yet the electrical generating and distribution system was and is driven by computer-generated signals and loaded by computer-calculated efficiencies. Computers have aided the telephone systems in their allocations of resources, yet many cities endure telephone service that appears to be inadequate. The F-111 supersonic aircraft was designed with the aid of computers and built with computer-run tools, yet its quality of performance has been seriously questioned, and its costs have been far beyond expectations.

Human intelligence must remain the final arbiter in most decision cases. Just one of the possible errors in model building is the use of simplifying assumptions to build a model to use on a computer and then failing to use judgment on the decision factors that were not included in the model. A computer cannot create new ideas or new solutions to new problems, nor is it capable of accepting responsibility. The last limitation probably is the most critical of all.

Real-Time and On-Line Access

Starting with third-generation computers, simultaneous processing of several jobs or programs was possible. The multiprogramming system introduced a new and increased degree of flexibility in the use of information. A computer of this type can process operational work, and can at the same time do a job for top-level planning or for the production control department. For example:

> ... suppose that the computer is processing its regular work of payroll, inventories, and so on, and a manager decides to examine the production records for the year, as of that day. If such records are available to the computer, the manager may gain access to them in an *on-line* mode; that is, he can immediately query the computer system without waiting for the present work to terminate or aborting work in process. If the receipt of information is within a very short period, say seconds, the processing can be thought of as occurring in *real-time*. Therefore, on-line implies a direct connection to the computer, and real-time implies an extremely fast response.[4]

Most airline reservation systems and many motel and hotel chains are now on a real-time, on-line basis. Oil refineries and parts of our military defense system also process information in this manner.

Time Sharing from Remote Terminals

Closely complementing the real-time, on-line feature of modern computer systems is time sharing from remote terminals. The ability of computers to do several jobs at once makes time sharing possible. Several users at the same time can plug into the computer from remote terminals, and each person can accomplish his work independently of the others. The *man-machine* interface works as follows:

> The executive leases an inexpensive remote terminal (such as a teletypewriter) and communications line (usually an ordinary telephone connection), and then "converses" with the vendor's computer much in the same way he would with another TWX station. (He types program instructions or data input onto the terminal keyboard; the computer responds with output and comments on the keyboard.) Typically, the vendor's computer is designed to allow a number of users working independently at their remote terminals to converse with the computer utility simultaneously. In other words, the utility shares the time of one high-speed computer among many users, with each user being charged at a predetermined rate only for the time he actually uses the system.[5]

Since no fixed investment in equipment is necessary for time sharing, it naturally appeals to small businesses with limited financial resources. The biggest users, however, apparently are large corporations that also are big users of other types of computer equipment. The greatest applications at the present time appear to be in the areas of financial analysis, operations research, and accounting. Users of time sharing especially like its fast response, convenience, low cost, and direct communication with the computer (rather than through an interpreter such as a programmer).

Organization Models on Real-Time

We have already suggested that it may be too early, at least from a technological viewpoint, to realistically implement a totally integrated information system and to demand efficiency from it. As yet, our capacity for design apparently is not sophisticated enough to plan an information system that will simultaneously handle the demands of all subsystems of an organization—including the demands of the various levels of management for planning, operational, and control information.

But technology does advance. We are already seeing evolutionary attempts to build computerized models of an entire corporation as an aid to management. Companies design these models to facilitate real-time, on-line information systems and to incorporate time sharing from remote terminals as a key component. An organization may have a model just for one segment of its operation, such as production. Or it may develop many models, which can then be interrelated to form a model describing the entire organization. The Potlatch Forests Company, for example, has twenty-two models to describe its various operations, groups, and subsidiaries. These can be combined to obtain a model for the whole corporation.[6]

Through remote terminals, managers can talk with these computerized models, obtain fast responses, and presumably make better decisions through more creative problem solving. The on-line model, via the computer, must maintain in its storage historical data, projected operating data, and programs for doing various mathematical and statistical analyses. This sort of system makes it easy for a manager to ask the "what if" questions: "What will happen to profits if prices are lowered?"; "What will happen to inventory if some part is manufactured internally rather than purchased?"; and so on.

James Dearden, writing in the *Harvard Business Review*, suggests that while a real-time information system, such as the one just discussed, may be satisfactory in operating situations (a production department, for example), it may not work so well for decision making at the management level.[7] In areas such as top management control, strategic planning, and overall coordination, a real-time system may be a superfluous luxury. Its high cost, inability to project future events, and inability to explain problems are just three of the factors cited to show why real-time may not be feasible for top managers. The problems encountered at top levels usually do not require instant response and hour-by-hour reporting.

Dearden and others sharing his views do not oppose real-time information systems. They merely suggest that organizations should be careful to apply these systems to those parts of the organization where a system can offer a real rather than an illusory benefit. Perhaps in a few years, a real-time, totally-integrated information system will be within reach of all types of organizations.

We have seen that information is vital to the decision-making process, that information constitutes the premises for making decisions, and that "from the standpoint of a communication network, a decision consists of instructions from one point in the network to other points."[8] The following imaginary incident may help to illustrate and emphasize the importance of these ideas.

Tom is assistant production manager in a manufacturing plant, and one of his duties is serving on a make-or-buy committee composed of himself, one of the assistant purchasing agents, and a cost accountant. Tom is currently in charge of preparing for production of a new product. He wants to find out whether a component part for the new product must be made in his own plant or must be purchased from the outside.

At a meeting of the make-or-buy committee one afternoon, Tom and the cost accountant bring along manufacturing and cost information, while the man from purchasing has information on buying the part from the outside. After going over the data, the committee decides that the part should be manufactured by their own company. Since the committee has full authority to make a decision on this type of part, an informational report only is sent to their respective bosses.

Armed with the committee decision (or instruction), Tom goes back to his own special project, where he must now make further decisions about how to make the particular part. He must also incorporate it in the production schedule for the other new parts. The committee decision supplies part of the premises for other decisions that Tom must make. Tom can be satisfied that the communication network or information system has worked well. There have been no delays, and information is being properly transmitted from one subsystem of the organization to another.

In the first part of chapter 4, we discussed some of the ways in which people and organizations actually behave in making decisions—satisficing rather than maximizing and confirming a favorite choice through the examination of one or more satisfactory alternatives. Now we are going to examine some more behavioral aspects of decision making, particularly as they relate to communication and information systems. These aspects are barriers or obstacles to effective communication.

We know that information flows in all directions in an organization—vertically, horizontally, and in all possible diagonal directions. The vertical flow causes some particularly serious problems. One of these occurs in the upward flow when a subordinate communicates with his boss. In these cases, *filtering* often occurs; that is, the subordinate will filter out information that he thinks the boss does not want to hear. Hence, the boss will receive "good news" only. The subordinate may also slant information to make himself look good or, at least, to avoid making himself look like an idiot (figure 5–5).

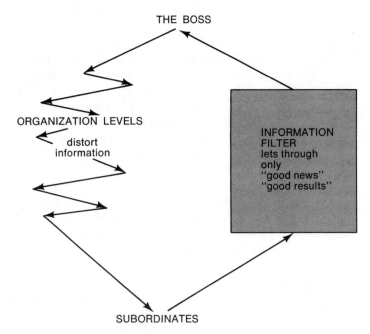

Figure 5–5 Filtering and distorting information

Unfortunately top executives tend to become isolated and really do not know what is going on in their own organizations. An executive does not have time to study all the raw data that can affect his decision making. He must depend on others to summarize and interpret data for him. The organization, therefore, must find ways to help assure that information transmitted to the top is objective and accurate. Real-time, on-line access to computerized monitoring of activities is one approach to solving this problem. In addition, executives often use staff assistance to check questionable information. Perhaps the answer lies in an organizational atmosphere that encourages employees to transmit information objectively and accurately without fear of unfair reprisal.

The downward flow of information also suffers its imperfections. Each organizational level appears to distort messages, purposefully or accidentally, so that by the time information reaches the bottom level, the top-level executive who initially transmitted the message may not even recognize his own communication. It has been said that "when the board of directors sends a message down through the levels of management, the vice presidents understand 65 percent of what is said. At the general supervisory level, 56 percent is understood; at the plant manager level, 40 percent is understood; at the foreman level, 30 percent; at the worker level, only 20 percent."[9]

Personal Attitudes and Values

Sometimes individuals in an organization hold antagonistic attitudes toward each other or hold values that are sufficiently different from those of other people that distortion of information occurs. In the imaginary incident involving Tom and the make-or-buy decision, if the assistant from purchasing and Tom had been antagonistic toward each other, Tom might have misunderstood the information from purchasing, might have distorted it somehow, or might have just plain ignored it. If Tom's value system were such that he just didn't believe in ever buying component parts from outside sources, again he may have distorted or ignored the information from purchasing. In addition, some persons digest information poorly because they have poor habits of listening and reading, and they also may be inarticulate in transmitting messages to others.

The Climate of Communicative Relationships

The climate or atmosphere in which information is transmitted has a lot to do with the effectiveness of communication attempts. Chris Argyris has noted in his research that managers display two typical behavior patterns in their decision-making meetings:

Pattern A—thoughtful, rational, and mildly competitive. This is the behavior most frequently observed during the decision-making meetings. Executives following this pattern own up to their ideas in a style that emphasizes a serious concern for ideas. As they constantly battle for scarce resources and "sell" their views, their openness to others' ideas is relatively high, not because of a sincere interest in learning about the point of view of others, but so they can engage in a form of "one-upsmanship"—that is, gain information about the others' points of view in order to politely discredit them.

Pattern B—competitive first, thoughtful and rational second. In this pattern, conformity to ideas replaces concern for ideas as the strongest norm. Also, antagonism to ideas is higher—in many cases higher than openness to ideas. The relatively high antagonism scores usually indicate, in addition to high competitiveness, a high degree of conflict and pent-up feelings.[10]

Argyris goes on to suggest that managers actually repress their feelings and their desires to take risks during decision-making sessions with other managers. The climate appears to be one of "getting the job done," not letting emotions or personalities interfere with the job, and of using direct coercion and control, backed up by rewards and penalties, to handle the involved human relationships.

A Tense Atmosphere The result of emotional repression is a rather artificial, stuffy, and tense climate that tends to stifle innovation, risk-taking, flexibility, and mutual trust. Managers will say that the stifled factors are exactly what an organization needs in order to be effective. What they say and what they do, however, are two different things. The presence of the chief executive at a decision-making meeting often results in maximizing repression, since he may have definite ideas about what he wants done. Hardly anyone tends to be very innovative and risk-taking when serious top-level displeasure will be incurred, especially when an intermediate boss may be offended too.

Argyris feels that if managers would examine their own group operations and processes and would try not to repress the interpersonal and emotional aspects of behavior, the effectiveness of the team in making decisions would be greatly improved. If the expression of feelings is valued instead of being ridiculed, group members may be less defensive and more confident about disagreeing and/or suggesting new ideas.

What Can Be Done? Overcoming the inhibitions and repressions of feelings that accompany many decision-making sessions is not easy. Many managers see themselves as nonemotional, rational, and politely open to new ideas. And yet it is certainly not rational behavior to repress new ideas and new, very possibly superior, ways of doing things.

One technique that works with some success is tape-recording an actual decision-making session. Later, the members listen to the tape and can usually see how the conduct of the meeting was stifling. Having a professional analyst present during the playback session can make it even more effective, since he can point out exactly where repression occurred and defensive reactions set in.

Another helpful technique is laboratory training or T-group training. In its most rigorous form, participants retreat to a relatively isolated location, usually in the country. They may spend up to two weeks in groups of twelve to fifteen going through their sensitivity training. Each group will have a professional advisor, but the format is very unstructured. There is no set program, and the trainees largely work out for themselves what they will do. The result is that they get to know one another quite well. After some initial jousting and fumbling around, a camaraderie usually develops that fosters great mutual trust and respect.

Sometimes feelings are hurt and egos bruised at T-group sessions, but one part of the job of the attending psychologist is to ensure that no one is seriously threatened psychologically. The other part of his job is to explain and interpret for the members what their interactions have meant for each person. The intent of sensitivity training, as of the tape-recording method, is to reduce defensiveness and to encourage more openness, honesty, and trust in each person's approach to his interpersonal relationships.

If the training results are successful and can be carried back to the job, the individual and the groups with which he associates should become more effective in accomplishment and in decision-making efforts. But the carry-back or transfer of learning is sometimes difficult. If an individual fresh out of a T-group goes back to a job where others have not had the same experience, he may rapidly pick up his former defensive habits. His interpersonal relationships will probably fall back into the same stifling patterns as before. For this reason some companies insist that all managers above a certain level go for sensitivity training if any at all are going to go. The unreliable transfer effect is one reason why the effectiveness of T-group training remains in question.

Argyris further suggests a number of problems that management information systems (MIS) themselves may create with respect to management. First he says that the designer of a MIS will try to model the system on the actual formal and informal behavior of individuals in their decision-making processes. In so doing, the designer tries to make explicit and open what previously may have been relatively hidden informal behavior and practices. The information system may appear threatening to some managers if they feel their informal methods are not really acceptable for some reason. Yet the designer must operate in this way if his information system is going to reflect the decision-making process of the organization.[11]

For example, a production control manager may find it more convenient to rely on a friend in market research than to rely on his own boss for information that helps to schedule production efficiently. The production control manager may perceive this practice as embarrassing if it becomes explicit and open in the design of a MIS. In such cases, however, the MIS designer or someone associated with him may want to find out whether the informal system is generally acceptable or whether some alternative system would be more acceptable and equally efficient. In this way, unnecessary embarrassment is avoided, and no problem develops so long as the MIS design reflects actual practice. Equally important, as Argyris suggests, is that:

... as the informal is made explicit, it comes under the control of management. The result may be that the participants will feel increasingly hemmed-in. In psychological language the participants will experience a great restriction of their space of free movement. Research suggests that a restriction of the (psychological) space of free movement tends to create feelings of lack of choice, pressure and psychological failure. These feelings, in turn, can lead to increasing feelings of helplessness and decreasing feelings of self-responsibility, resulting in the increasing tendency to withdraw or to become dependent upon those who created or approved the restriction of space of free movement.[12]

In addition, as the system and the organization become more rational and explicit, the type of executive needed may change. There may be less emphasis on power and on the individual who can take hold of an organization and make it move by personal forcefulness and compelling drive. In other words, those executives who now enjoy and pursue power, who enjoy handling some ambiguity, and who welcome personal challenges may become increasingly frustrated and confused as information systems become integral parts of organizations. Information systems may take the challenge out of managing an organization.

Argyris suggests that part of the answer to potential frustration is the development of increased interpersonal competence. We must recognize that the introduction of a sophisticated information technology is as much an emotional human problem as a technical problem. Successful implementation will probably require an atmosphere of openness and mutual trust, a willingness to cooperate with others rather than fight them, and a recognition of all the interdependent goals that must be fulfilled in an organization. Research on the effects of sophisticated information systems on organizational and individual behavior is, however, only in the initial stages.

Decision Making as an Organizational Process

The comic stereotype of the business decision maker has been that of a powerful boss making instant decisions whenever problems arise (like Dagwood Bumstead's boss, Mr. Dithers). But the stereotype rarely occurs. Major decisions made by top management in large companies are often the result of a long, drawn-out process involving lots of studies and lots of interactions among many lower-level managers. There is even evidence that the influence of top management on decisions is often merely nominal. By the time a top-level decision is made to go ahead with formal studies on a project, the remainder of the process may move automatically, carried through by lower levels to eventual confirmation and implementation.[13]

So organizational decision making is a process involving the interactions of many persons. And since many of the problems to which a manager must find solutions are general organizational problems, "he cannot rely on only one view, nor does top management want this parochialism to exist."[14] Furthermore, "... decision making is an organizational process. It is shaped as much by the pattern of interaction of managers as it is by the contemplation and cognitive processes of the individual.[15]

While decision making inevitably must be a part of the organizational process, the use of decision theory and quantitative tools is, of course, optional. To what extent is decision theory analysis used today by business organizations? According to one source, only a few United States companies appear to have used decision theory analysis for any length of time, but there is a growing recognition of its value.[16] Individual managers often continue to resist the formal implementation of decision theory methods for some of the same reasons that Argyris mentioned: it may force the release of delicate and confidential information, it may force the admission of uncertainty on the part of managers, and it may reveal, or drive underground, private and possibly embarrassing motivations.[17]

As cultural values change, however, it would become less difficult for executives to admit the presence of uncertainties in their decision processes. And as managers grow increasingly aware of what formal decision systems demand, they should more easily resist the temptation of letting personal and confidential motivations creep into the organizational decision-making process. There are, for example, quite a few stories of executives who wanted a plant moved to Colorado because they like to ski, or to Minnesota because they liked to fish, and so on.

Once established, a formal decision system can have several positive advantages. It focuses informal thinking; clarifies hidden assumptions behind a decision; and makes clear the logical implications of those assumptions. It provides an effective vehicle for communicating the reasoning that underlies a decision. It helps formulate and define problems so that information gathering and the generation of alternatives is more efficient. The clear, analytic thinking achieved by the use of quantitative tools helps to give insight into management processes in general. A formal decision system helps in getting the right information as well as the right amount of information.

Other advantages and disadvantages of decision theory could be discussed. It is enough to say here that decision theory is soundly grounded in the behavioral and quantitative sciences and that it will continue to develop and come into increasing use in modern organizations. It is not a panacea. For example, linear programming leads to an optimal solution, but the constraints and restrictions are such that real-life applications are fairly limited. Nonetheless decision theory, quantitative analysis, and information systems will continue to have an important impact on current organizational life.

Management must be interested not only in an efficient internal information system, but also in the gathering of information from the external world (the black box) in order to keep the organization running efficiently. Information helps managers adjust decisions so that the organization remains in homeostasis.

Given the present state of technology, a total and tightly integrated information system may be impossible. A total system would simultaneously link all decision centers, transmitting points, and receiving points. But linkages may be established between the major information systems of an organization so that a kind of total system is approximated.

An information system should be designed from the top down, precisely patterning both informal and formal decision-making activities. The important components of a system include the transmitting and receiving points, the decision centers, a storage facility, and feedback.

Computers, an important development in the design of information systems, have developed through four generations. There are now approximations of complete information systems, using the real-time, on-line concept with remote terminals and time sharing. There may be disadvantages involved in leaping too quickly into some type of complete system, especially for top-management decision making.

Formal decision and information systems affect managerial behavior. Efficient decision making often requires more openness and trust among managers than now exists. Individuals, because they may be antagonistic or self-protective, may distort or misinterpret information. The implementation of formal systems may be threatening to some managers because their informal practices and private motivations may be revealed. Also, there may be less operating room for the type of manager who seeks power and likes to take personal charge of operations.

Decision making is an organizational process, and while decision theory has enjoyed limited application in real life, its use is growing. Decision theory in application forces clear, logical thinking, and helps show how the total organization works and how it may be made to work better. Decision and information theory provide a basis for our continuing examination of management practice. In the next chapter, we will concentrate on the planning function of management.

Charles Babbage

We associate the computer with our present age, but the first digital computer was actually invented in 1834 by an English mathematician, Charles Babbage. Although Babbage had many interests, he was dedicated primarily to the design and development of "difference engines and analytical engines," the latter being the forerunner of the modern computer.

Babbage probably borrowed the idea of a punched card for his engine from a loom invented in 1801. A hole in punched cards instructed the loom to raise the thread in the weaving process, while the absence of a hole caused lowering of the thread. Babbage adapted the yes–no system of the punched card, which is the same as the binary system of the modern digital computer, to his engine.

The engine was mechanically operated, using an assortment of gears, ratchets, cams, pulleys, and belts. Despite its clumsiness, in comparison to electronic technology, the engine did have a punch card input system, a storage or memory device, a computational or arithmetic component, and it had the ability to follow programmed instructions. Like a modern computer, the engine could follow contingency instructions; that is, "if event A occurs, take this action; if event A does not occur, follow the normal instructions." Among many other programs, Babbage developed ones for betting on the horses (unsuccessfully), playing chess, and playing tic-tac-toe.

Upon recommendation by the Royal Society, England's scientific association, the government supported Babbage in his work until 1842. Then, despite the Society's continuing positive recommendation, the government withdrew support. But Babbage was not deterred. He continued to work on the engineering development of his machine for many years, although it was never finished to his satisfaction.

When he could spare time from his computing machines, Babbage studied and wrote on economics, manufacturing practices, the size and location of factories, unions and labor relations, and other areas. He also somehow found time to teach mathematics. His most popular book, *On the Economy of Machinery and Manufactures*, was published in 1832 and sold out 3,000 copies in two months. Within three years, four successive editions had been published.

One of his minor crusades took dead aim at the booksellers of the time, including those who were selling his own book. He felt they were acting as monopolists, keeping prices artificially high by limiting the supply of books, as was the case with his own book. In his fourth edition, he included a list of dealers, indicating those who he thought were fair in their trade practices and those who were unfair.

Babbage contributed in many ways to the initiation and development of the scientific approach to the study of management, later made famous, of course, by Frederick Taylor. Babbage advocated precise cost accounting, incentive payments to workers for increased efficiency, the division of labor for increased production, and the use of time study to determine a fair day's work. "He was conscious that principles of organization were applicable to every field where coordination of human effort was essential to the attainment of some common purpose."[18]

Babbage was accused of wild schemes at the time, but several of his ideas in retrospect are quite sound. These include profit sharing, fair trade practices (the book dealers), cash bonuses to workers for suggestions on improved methods, incentive payments, and time study.

Discussion Questions

1. The real world often is like a black box—we don't know exactly how it works, but we can at least observe the results of our actions or inputs and determine some possible cause and effect relationships. Give some specific examples of the black box concept.

2. Good design is important to the effective functioning of an information system for any organization. Try designing an information system for a short-order restaurant that employs a cook (the boss), a waitress, a busboy, and a dishwasher.

3. If you were the president of a large corporation, would you want instant access to many kinds of information via a real-time computer system? Explain why or why not.

4. In the incident "Generating Information" can you think of alternative ways in which the decision in question could have been made? Would these alternatives have changed the information system in any way? Would the changes have provided a better or a worse information system?

5. Can you remember any occasions when you filtered information while talking to a boss, parent, or friend? What were the circumstances and how did you filter the information?

6. Imagine yourself the boss in a decision-making session with several subordinates. One of your subordinates becomes honestly angry with you over an important point. What would your reaction be? How would you handle the situation?

7. In management information systems, should everything be made completely explicit and open, or should managers be allowed some leeway for satisfying private motivations through company activities?

8. Given the complexity and sophistication of the modern corporation, how much power does the chief executive really have? Does he have more power in some areas than others? In what areas might he have less power than is formally attached to his position?

References

1. W. M. Zani, "Blueprint for MIS," *Harvard Business Review*, 48 (1970): 95.

2. J. Dearden, "How to Organize Information Systems," *Harvard Business Review*, 43 (1965): 65–73.

3. "TV Replaces Stacks of Paperwork," *Business Week*, no. 2161 (1971): 48–50.

4. W. W. Haynes and J. L. Massie, *Management Analysis: Concepts and Cases*, 2d ed. (Englewood Cliffs, N.J.: Prentice-Hall, 1969), p. 684.

5. B. Allen, "Time Sharing Takes Off," *Harvard Business Review*, 47 (1969): 130.

6. J. B. Boulden and E. S. Buffa, "Corporate Models: On-line, Real-time Systems," *Harvard Business Review*, 48 (1970): 65–83.

7. J. Dearden, "Myth of Real-time Management Information," *Harvard Business Review*, 44 (1966): 123–132.

8. D. W. Miller and M. K. Starr, *The Structure of Human Decisions* (Englewood Cliffs, N.J.: Prentice-Hall, 1967), p. 17.

9. R. G. Nichols, "Listening, What Price Inefficiency?" *Office Executive*, April 1959.

10. C. Argyris, "Interpersonal Barriers to Decision Making," *Harvard Business Review*, 44 (1966): 861

11. C. Argyris, "Management Information Systems: The Challenge to Rationality and Emotionality," *Management Science*, Application Series, 17 (1971): B275–B291.

12. *Ibid.*, p. B278.

13. J. McDonald, "How Businessmen Make Decisions," *Fortune*, 52 (1955): 85.

14. L. Sayles, "Industrial Relations and Organization Behavior: Parent and Child?" in G. G. Somers, ed., *Essays in Industrial Relations Theory* (Ames, Iowa: Iowa State University Press, 1969), pp. 123–136.

15. *Ibid.*, p. 128.

16. R. V. Brown, "Do Managers Find Decision Theory Useful?" *Harvard Business Review*, 48 (1970): 78–89.

17. *Ibid.*, p. 88.

18. C. S. George, Jr., *The History of Management Thought* (Englewood Cliffs, N.J.: Prentice-Hall, 1968), p. 72.

Suggested Readings

Berlo, D. K *The Process of Communication: An Introduction to Theory and Practice.* New York: Holt, Rinehart and Winston, 1960.

Keltner, J. W. *Interpersonal Speech—Communication Elements and Structures.* Belmont, Calif.: Wadsworth, 1970.

Konvalinka, J. W., and Trentin, H. G. "Management Information Systems," in P. P. Schoderbek, *Management Systems.* New York: John Wiley, 1967, pp. 170–182.

McFarlan, W. W. "Problems in Planning the Information System," *Harvard Business Review*, 49 (1971): 75–89.

Moravec, A. F. "Basic Concepts for Designing a Fundamental Information System," in P. P. Schoderbek, *Management Systems.* New York: John Wiley, 1967, pp. 127–136.

Thayer, Lee. *Communication and Communication Systems.* Homewood, Ill.: Richard D. Irwin, 1968.

Zani, W. M. "Blueprint for MIS," *Harvard Business Review*, 48 (1970): 95–100.

Case Problem for Chapters 4 and 5

Popular Ski Company

John Edward is president of the Popular Ski Company, a small organization manufacturing and marketing a medium-priced line of skis. Edward has been concerned about getting ready to produce a new higher-priced line of skis. He very much wants to make sure all preparations go forward smoothly. He foresees nine steps in getting set up for production of the new skis. These steps listed, with the estimated amount of time necessary to complete each step, are as follows:

1. Finish addition to plant. Ten days.
2. Install new woodworking equipment. Three days.
3. Install new woodfinishing equipment. Three days.
4. Set up and test woodworking equipment. Two days.
5. Set up and test woodfinishing equipment. Two days.
6. Finish work on inspection area and install some minor equipment. Four days.
7. Install new conveyor equipment. Five days.
8. Stack raw materials and other supplies in designated areas. Two days.
9. Trial run and test of new product. Ten days.

Edward has heard of the Program Evaluation and Review Technique (PERT) and wonders if it would help in coordinating all the steps involved in producing the new skis. He calls in Lance Smith, the production superintendent to ask him about PERT and about whether he thinks PERT can help with the current problem.

Smith replies, "Yes, I do know about PERT and believe it could help considerably in scheduling activities to get ready for regular production."

Edward is interested in how PERT works and asks Mr. Smith to explain it. "Well," Smith replies, "it's really quite straightforward. A PERT network shows activities and events. An *activity* is some specific task or work that has to be done, such as finishing the addition to our plant. On a network, we also indicate the amount of time needed to complete the task. An *event* is also called a milestone and marks the beginning or end of an activity. Of course, in many cases an event will mark both the beginning and end of separate activities. Let me just show you with a sketch how two of our activities would appear along with events marking their beginnings and endings." (Smith draws the following sketch: exhibit 1.)

Smith continues: "Note that we can readily identify activities by using the events sequence as a code. For example, finishing the

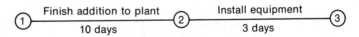

Exhibit 1 Sample PERT network

addition to the plant is activity 1–2 while installing the new woodworking equipment is activity 2–3. To get started on our project, we first have to list all the activities, their associated times for accomplishment, and the precedence restrictions. The precedence restrictions tell us which activities must be done before we can start on other activities. For example, the plant addition must be finished before any equipment can be moved in, or anything done, for that matter. Let's set up a table showing all the activities, their times, and the restrictions." (See table 1.)

"With the information in the table, we are ready to construct our initial PERT network. But before we do that, let me explain some other PERT concepts. Once we have our network, we can identify a *critical path*. This path is the minimum amount of time it will take to complete the project. We determine the critical path by finding the longest path through the network. The total project cannot be completed in less time than it takes to complete all the activities in the longest sequence or path through the network.

"Once we know the critical path, we can determine the earliest starting time, T_e, and the latest starting time, T_L, for each activity in the network. The earliest starting time would depend upon how long it takes to complete the activities preceding a given activity. The latest starting time would be the time by which any given activity must be started in order to complete the entire project on time, or to keep the critical path on time. We determine all the T_es by going through the network from front to back and all the T_Ls by going through the network from back to front.

"Once we know all the early and late starting times, we can determine the *slack* time on each activity. We do this by simply subtracting T_e from T_L on each activity. Slack time is extra time available on any activity that is not on the critical path. All ac-

Table 1 Data for PERT network

Activity	Time (in days)	Immediate Predecessor
1. Finish addition to plant	10	None
2. Install woodworking equipment	3	1
3. Install woodfinishing equipment	3	1
4. Test woodworking equipment	2	2
5. Test woodfinishing equipment	2	3
6. Complete inspection area	4	1
7. Install conveyor	5	4, 5, 6
8. Stack raw materials and supplies	2	7
9. Test new facilities and product	10	8

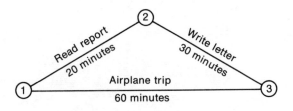

Exhibit 2 Sample PERT network

tivities do not have slack time, therefore, but we look for slack time on activities not on the critical path.

"The big advantage of knowing the existence of slack time on activities is that we can transfer productive resources, people or equipment from an activity with slack to an activity which is running behind. In this way we can try to keep the whole project on schedule.

"Let me give you a simple example of all this. Suppose you were on an airplane flight for one hour. While in transit you want to read a report that takes twenty minutes and write a letter that you estimate will take thirty minutes. A network of these activities might appear as follows (exhibit 2).

"Your earliest starting time on activity 1–2 would, of course, be time zero. The T_e on activity 2–3 would be twenty minutes or the time it should take to read the report. The T_L on 2–3 would be thirty minutes or the time it takes to finish the letter before the plane lands. The T_L on 1–2 would be ten minutes or the time it would take to complete both activities before landing. The critical path is 1–3 or the minimum time it will take to reach your destination and complete the project. Slack time on 1–2 is T_L minus T_e on that activity or ten minutes; that is, ten minus zero. Slack time on 2–3 would also be ten minutes. The only problem in this illustration, of course, is that you might find it difficult to use your slack time to get the airplane in ten minutes early."

Edward thought for a moment. "I'm impressed. Go ahead and develop a PERT network for our project. It sounds like just what we need to get done on time."

1. Draw a network illustrating this project for Edward.
2. What are the earliest and latest starting times for all activities?
3. Which activities have slack time? How much slack do these activities have?
4. What is the critical path? What is the total amount of time necessary to complete the project?

Management Decision Areas

6

Planning is decision making, and much of what we have already said about decision making in general applies equally well to planning decisions in particular. Planning decisions chart the future course of an organization, and therefore success depends profoundly upon the efficacy of plans made. *Planning is the determination of goals and the specification of means to achieve those goals,* and a *plan,* therefore, *is some predetermined course of action over a specified period of time.*

We said that planning is decision making, but this does not mean that all decision making is planning. For example, a company may plan to expand its research effort and will allocate money to hire additional scientists and technicians. Hiring a particular scientist or technician, then, is not planning but simply a hiring decision that helps to fulfill the plan. A manufacturing organization may plan to produce a certain product at the lowest cost possible, even at the sacrifice of quality. A subsequent decision to buy a machine that will produce at very low cost as opposed to one that produces at higher cost but also higher quality again is a decision that helps to achieve the goal already set—but it is not a planning decision.

Planning decisions occur before any action takes place to achieve the goal. Nonplanning, action, or operating decisions are made when action is accomplishing the goal that has already been determined.

We often think of planning as occurring predominantly at the top levels of organizations. We envision top executives as being concerned with the long-range view, with the future of the organization, and with the planning that must be done to ensure that future. But there's a twist to the story. We could call the twist Gresham's Law of Planning. You may have heard of Gresham's Law of Money—that bad money drives out the good; that is, silver coins, for example, are hoarded while paper money is spent.

Apparently, the same sort of phenomenon happens in planning. When an executive is faced with a choice between planning in an ambiguous, ill-structured problem situation and attending to routine tasks, he tends to give the latter first priority. In other words, the easy routine work drives out the hard planning work. And the busier the manager becomes, the more time he spends on routine matters and the less on planning. Eventually, he may do no planning at all.

Planning is not an easy task and it provokes a great deal of procrastination. We can see this in individuals too. Studies show that people often do not make plans for retirement until very shortly before retirement. We tend as individuals to procrastinate and to do surprisingly little planning in such important areas as financial security, careers, and even marriage. On the organizational level again: "Planning does occur in large-scale organizations, of course, but that planning is a relatively vulnerable activity compared to other activities. A person with responsibility for both routine day-to-day activities and long-term planning is likely to find the routine taking the much greater share of his time."[1]

If planning tends to get shunted aside, does this have any implications for managerial efficiency? Research studies suggest the answer is yes. One study, for example, found that efficient managers spent 61 percent more time on planning work duties than less efficient managers.[2] If the highest levels of management are lax in planning, the effect on the organization can be disastrous.

Benefits of Planning

There can be no doubt that planning is essential for organizational survival and growth. But the benefits can be specified more completely:

Effective planning prevents ad hoc decisions, random decisions, decisions that unnecessarily and expensively narrow choices for tomorrow. Effective planning gives an organization a structural framework of objectives and strategies, a basis for all decision making. Lower-level managers know what top management wants and can make decisions accordingly. But there are also ancillary benefits. An effective planning organization, for example, provides a powerful channel of communications for the people in an organization to deal with problems of importance to themselves as well as to their organization.

It is difficult to exaggerate the importance of effective comprehensive planning to an organization. It has, for many companies, provided that margin needed for outstanding growth and profitability.[3]

Through the structural framework provided by planning, management reduces uncertainty within the organization. When we define plans throughout the entire organization, people are better able to predict the behavior of others and to know how others expect them to behave. This gives all members of the organization a greater feeling of freedom to operate. Plans serve as a standard for measurement of performance and therefore are the basis for control. Finally, plans are coordinating mechanisms that help define the relationships among units and that help direct the work flow across as well as up and down the organizational hierarchy.

There are costs associated with planning, of course. Managerial manhours are expensive as well as are some of the tools used in planning—the computer, for example. An important question, therefore, has to do with how extensive planning should be in relation to various goals.

Certainly, every organization has time and money constraints that finally limit planning at some absolute barrier. But there is still plenty of room left for variation. Obviously, management should not expend great effort planning the location of a new pencil sharpener. On the other hand, management should do comprehensive planning for the introduction of an important new product. Unfortunately, since the location of a pencil sharpener tends toward the routine, we may find excessive time being spent on this while new product planning falls short of a desirable level.

At the other extreme, a command to plan carries danger. Overly expensive planning departments may be set up. Planning may be carried to the point where execution of the plan is no longer practical or possible. Management could spend so much time planning the introduction of a new product that competitors could wipe out the market in the meantime.

Effective planning requires top management to exercise good judgment in controlling the amount and type of planning done within an organization. Usually the main problem is to get people to do some planning. There also is a danger, however, of over-planning in terms of time and comprehensiveness as well as of overwhelming the planning function with expensive personnel and equipment.

Types of Plans

As you might expect, top management planning encompasses the longest period of time and has the longest *planning horizon*. As one works down through the organization hierarchy, the planning horizon becomes shorter and shorter until at the operating level, it functions entirely in the present. Figure 6–1 illustrates the concept.

Talk of *strategic planning* is more frequently heard today than in the past. This type of planning attempts to establish goals, foresee events, and plan actions over a long range (five years or more), and it provides the overall, top-level guide for planning over time periods of shorter duration. A strategic plan is not a policy. A *policy* is a general guide to action and, as such, is an extension and amplification of strategic objectives. There are overall policies as well as sales policies, personnel policies, manufacturing policies, and so on. A policy has no time limitation and will change only when plans change. For example, a company may have a strategic plan aimed at improving its community relations. A derived policy, then, could be the encouragement of organization members to participate in various community activities.

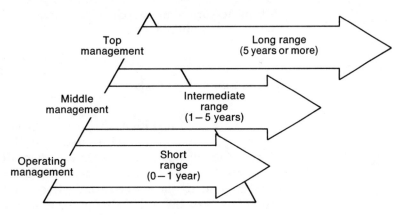

Figure 6–1 Planning horizons

Single-Use Plans   A nonrepetitive problem situation signals development of the *single-use plan*. It is set up for a particular purpose and may never be used again. A single-use plan may be used in conjunction with a major program such as the development of a new airplane or the building of a bridge. Such a plan may also be employed for lesser projects and tasks like the implementation of a new data-processing system for production management or changing the layout of an office.

Standing Plans   Repetitive situations require the use of *standing plans*. These plans are valuable in relatively stable situations where the same sorts of actions are liable to be repeated over and over again. Although policy is distinguished from strategic planning, standing plans *are* sometimes called policies and procedures. A procedure is narrower in scope than a policy and details the steps to be taken in a particular operating situation. A procedure is also a limited guide to action. Policies and procedures are usually put in written form, to help ensure their clarity and their communication to all appropriate members of the organizations.

Standing plans make possible *management by exception*. They establish a uniformity of routine throughout an organization so that even though an activity is done by different people, it will be done in about the same way. This means that top management does not have to worry about the daily routine of operations unless something goes wrong. Then the exceptional event is reported and managerial forces come into play. Management thus saves a great deal of time and can delegate many routine tasks to lower levels. A potential problem with standing plans is that activities may be routinized to the point where they become rigidly traditional. With this sort of inflexibility, new challenges are often difficult to surmount and changes in policies and procedures are met with determined resistance.

The Planning Process

The steps in planning, in making planning decisions, are the same as those needed in deciding how to decide: (1) establish goals and identify problems and criteria; (2) establish the available alternatives and the consequences of each one; (3) evaluate the alternatives in light of the criteria; and (4) select the best course of action—the one that solves the problem and attains the goal.

Top-level planning determines the organizational goals and the means of achievement. Effective comprehensive planning should also spawn operating decisions and subsidiary plans for the entire organization. Each subsystem needs to have its own plan and operating guide that is related to the total plan and the total specification of means. Ideally, comprehensive planning will integrate all the subplans, subgoals, and operating decisions with the master plan and master goals in order to coordinate organizational efforts completely. Few if any organizations realize ideal comprehensiveness of planning.

Setting Goals

The important first step in the planning process is the establishment of goals and associated criteria. We will be concerned here mainly with organizational goals as developed in strategic planning, but it should always be kept in mind that units throughout the organizational hierarchy also must develop their own subgoals. In this way there can be an orderly arrangement of resources—people, money, materials, information—to achieve the objectives. In other words, the systems approach should be used in planning just as in any other management function.

There are some general criteria for effective goal setting in any organization. These include: (1) making the goals specific and clear enough so everyone can understand them; (2) having the goals capable of measurement in some way so progress toward them can be determined; and (3) making goals realistic though sufficiently challenging to stimulate motivation.

Beyond these general criteria for setting goals, each organization will have specific criteria that reflect the organizational philosophy as well as the personal values of the executives. A company with a philosophy of minimizing risk will apply a conservative criterion to its goal setting; it will tend to reject goals that appear too venturesome. A company with a strong feeling for community service will try to incorporate this value into its goal-setting process.

Managers should become aware of their personal values, since these values have a profound effect on organization philosophy and the establishment of strategic goals.[4] The manager who tries to understand his own values as well as the values of others will have an important advantage in developing workable and well-supported plans. Since an organization usually has more than one manager, and therefore more than one set of personal values, it is likely that most organizations will have multiple criteria for goal setting.

Multiple Goals Most business organizations today do not subscribe to the idea of only one, all-important goal—making a profit for example. Instead they support multiple goals: partly out of the recognition that this is more realistic; partly out of a broader sense of responsibility to others than profit-making alone implies; and partly as a result of the claims being made on business by others.

Lists of goals vary, of course. They may include maintaining a profitable operation; providing high quality goods and services to meet consumers' demands; continuing technological advancement; maximizing the use of human resources; and taking an active and responsible role in the community. A list, however, says nothing about the priority of goals.

Everyone who has a stake in a business organization is interested in its goals, and their interests often conflict. The investors want large dividends and increases in the price of their holdings; the customers want high quality and low prices; the employees want high pay and good working conditions; and so on.

Not all goal priorities are resolved through conflict. Compromise, bargaining, and forms of coalition often work out to settle the issue. But conflict is an obvious phenomenon. The stockholders' meetings of major corporations often provide the setting for demands made by consumer groups and civil rights groups as well as by the traditional disgruntled stockholder. Conflict processes frequently lead to creative settlements, however. "Through conflict, initial, mutually exclusive alternatives (as suggested by the necessity for choice between two desirable courses of action, between two undesirable courses of action, or between a desirable and an undesirable course of action) may create a new alternative which accommodates and simplifies prior alternatives."[5]

What is the actual practice of business with respect to goal priorities? In one survey of over 1,000 managers to obtain their views on appropriate goal structures, it was found that the profit goal and the related goals of efficiency and productivity were considered most important.[6] Goals pertaining to growth and stability were ranked second, while those relating to employee welfare were ranked third. Fourth were goals dealing with social and community interests.

There is also evidence, however, that the managers of large organizations and of successful and growing firms cite public service and good products as objectives more often than do managers of small, unsuccessful, and nongrowth firms.[7] Because of public demands and other forms of persuasion, companies today are more concerned with social responsibility than at any time in the past. As profit goals are increasingly affected by public pressure and needs, and as conservative managers are replaced by managers who reflect the public interest in social responsibility, managerial attitudes toward profit as a single overriding goal appear to be changing.

The Case for Ambiguity   Earlier, in setting general criteria for goals, we said goals should be specific and clear enough so everyone can understand them. But goals can be so specific and plans for achieving them can be so exact that there is no room for adaptation. It may not always be wise to eliminate all ambiguity, especially in long-range strategic planning.

For example, top management might say that an important organizational goal is to increase gross sales of a certain product by five million dollars over a ten-year period. But economic recession or technological changes within the industry could easily make the goal unobtainable and even ridiculous in hindsight. In addition, a very specific long-range goal can lock in a company to a given plan and can remove any possibility of flexibility in planning. Changing a top-level, long-range goal too frequently makes management appear confused and not deserving of authority.

A better approach is to state long-range goals in a style that leaves room for variations in planning the means to achieve the goal. Instead of aiming to increase sales by five million dollars over a period of ten years, for example, management could say they want to show some improvement in their relative share of the market every year, on the average, over the next ten years. Then, if the total market declines, the company would still be achieving its goal. If a competitor gained a temporary technological advantage, there would be time to catch up and still show improvement over the long term. Failure, which is deadly for morale, is often a matter of oppressively high and rigid goals.

As subunits of an organization interpret the major goal and define their own subgoals, more specific statement of goals is possible. A branch sales office, for example, may set a goal of increasing its sales by 5 percent over the next year. And, of course, in those cases where managers must plan to goals that are only hours or days away, there usually is a need to be very specific.

In relating short-range goals to long-range ones, we construct a means–ends chain. Short-range goals become the means to long-range goal achievement. Increasing sales by 5 percent in a year in a given sales territory is a means to achieve an increasing market share over a ten-year period. Figure 6–2 illustrates the concept.

In general, we suggest that the longer into the future one projects a goal structure, the more advisable it is to be somewhat vague in stating the goals. This will allow flexibility in modifying the ultimate goals as well as subgoals and the means of achievement. It is simply inadvisable to get locked into a very specific goal when a more general statement will allow the exercise of numerous options in planning. Exercising these options in turn will enhance the chances for success. To modify our earlier statement,

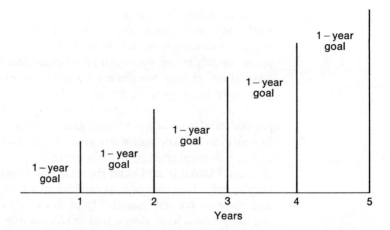

Figure 6–2 The means–ends chain. Successive one-year goals provide the means to a five-year goal achievement.

that goals should be specific, then, we may say that they should be as specific as the situation dictates and as is necessary for general understanding of the goal.

Goal Succession   What happens when an organization achieves the goal for which it was originally set up? Logically, you might say, the organization should be disbanded. But there is more to it than that. Take the case of the National Foundation for Infantile Paralysis. When polio was conquered, the Foundation did not just fold its tent and quietly steal away. Rather, it searched for other goals and finally settled on trying to eliminate childhood diseases in general. This phenomenon has been described as a case of goal succession.[8]

The process is not really illogical. The eradication of polio was not the only goal once the Foundation got under way. The Foundation was generally concerned with health, was committed to organizational growth, and the top executives had a definite interest in continuing their positions of power and prestige in the national health field. "Shifting from polio to other diseases was merely a means to these ends, as was the decision to retain the same form of organizational structure."[9] Once an organization is set up and ongoing, continued existence or survival tends to become one of a set of multiple goals. Organizations, like the individuals of which they are composed, are interested in perpetuating themselves.

Adding and Shifting Goals   Little is really known about the impact of adding or shifting goals on the organization that does so.

There is considerable controversy today about the extent to which business should take on goals of social responsibility. Some companies are trying to be more society and community oriented. Law firms, for example, allow their young lawyers time for legal work among the poor. And universities are entangled in a struggle over the proper structuring of their goals. These are highly ill-structured planning problems with few guidelines from past experience to aid in reaching solutions. Perrow describes the experience of one company in thus attempting to shift goals:

The Ford Motor Company found it quite difficult to include even the production of appliances in its output goals, let alone training hard-core dropouts or remaking the dreary city of Detroit. Ford bought Philco as a diversification measure and fully expected to rehabilitate the sickly company through the infusion of talent and capital, which Ford had in abundance. Within a short time, all but three of the top 25 men at Philco had left, voluntarily or otherwise, and Ford brought in 18 young managers in the first six months, including seven at the vice-presidential level. Within four years there were about 50 Ford men working in the Philco division. But the patient did not respond to all this new blood. Henry Ford II contended that "a good manager can run anything." But, according to *Fortune*, the man now running Philco says: "This is not true, and Ford has paid a fat price to learn it."[10]

Apparently, the skill or art required to run an auto company is different from the skill required in the appliance business. We said the science in management is transferable from one organization or country to another, but obviously one must be careful about assuming that success in one business guarantees success in another kind of business. Experience is very important to the development of expertise in a given line of endeavor. This may help explain why many companies have been cautious about adding social goals to their existing sets of goals. The following incident should help illustrate some aspects of goal setting and planning that we have been discussing.

A Planning Incident Jane and Paul were partners in a small machine shop doing jobbing or contract work predominantly for machine tool manufacturers. Due to a transportation strike, the shop was virtually shut down for a few days. The partners came in everyday, of course, and one morning Jane mentioned that it had been months since both of them had sat down to discuss their business in general terms. The daily routine had seemed to keep them so busy, there had hardly been time to say good morning.

Paul agreed and suggested they get at it right then and there. During the next two hours they discussed everything from how old their machines were to putting in new vending machines for coffee and sandwiches. What seemed to concern the partners most, however, was that the large part of their equipment was quite old, dating back to World War II days in many instances. This situation made it difficult to match their competition in quality and speed of output.

Finally Jane leaned back in her chair. "Paul, we've got to get our costs down. We can't do it overnight, but we can make that one of our major goals over the next few years. If we don't, we're just going to lose out in the bidding on new contracts."

Paul nodded assent. "You're right, and there's something else too. For a long time we've been preaching quality to our men, but it's really difficult for them with the equipment they've got to work with. We could lower costs and emphasize quality successfully if we can get some modern machinery in here. From what I've learned in the trade journals, with new machine tools, we could drop our costs 10 to 20 percent over the next five years."

The partners continued talking and planning all day long. It had taken a strike to force them to drop their routine for a while and to do some strategic planing. Their long-range goals were not overly specific—to be competitive, to keep or increase their share of the market—and they planned to achieve these goals by buying new machinery and cutting costs. They also considered some related goals that would carry down to the operating level; improved quality and increased output.

While Jane and Paul used some information inputs from throughout the organization to help in their planning efforts and were involved in setting up subgoals and subplans, they were doing it all quite informally. In the future, it probably would be better to schedule strategic planning sessions at least once a year. And they should try to systematize their approach to include all elements of problems and to gain the participation of all members of the organization who might contribute something to the decision process. Participation stimulates motivation and helps make plans more creative and innovative than if managers alone do all of the decision making. Moreover, a good planning session should involve good forecasts of the future, since forecasting can aid immeasurably in the planning process.

Forecasting

The second step in the planning process specifies the generation of alternatives as well as the consequences of each. An important associated activity is forecasting—to aid in knowing which alternatives will be feasible in terms of their predicted consequences. Forecasting also is valuable for goal modification as well as for helping to specify the means that will be used to achieve the goals. To aid in illustrating this, let us take another look at the job-shop operation of the partners, Jane and Paul.

Since the partners had been in the business of doing jobbing work for machine tool manufacturers for many years, we can assume that they had established as a long-range goal, being competitive and retaining their share of the machine tool jobbing market. Now let us also assume they are considering two alternatives—cutting costs and advertising—as means to this long-range goal.

Now suppose they obtain a forecast that strongly suggests that the machine tool industry is going to severely cut back on the amount of contract work let out to job-shops such as theirs. In view of this, the partners decide first to modify their goal—from being competitive in the machine tool market to servicing and obtaining a share of the market for jobbing work from manufacturers in general. Second, they decide to pursue both alternatives, to advertise for business as well as to cut costs, in order to remain competitive. Finally, they decide to get advertising data on various trade journals and to investigate the newer types of equipment available.

In this way, the partners use the forecast to modify one of their goals, to help select alternatives, and to help specify what should be done in order to accomplish their goal. Of course, the more reliable a forecast, the more help it will be. At the extreme, perfect information would reduce planning and decision making to the case of certainty, where there would be just one state of nature and two or more alternatives. Let us take a look at a few forecasting methods and their respective reliabilities.

Forecasting Methods *Hunches and intuition* perhaps are more commonly used than might be suspected in this age of management science and its associated techniques. All of us probably have acted on the basis of a hunch at one time or another, and if successful, we no doubt continued using intuition in our decision-making activities. In fact, evidence is accumulating which suggests that more successful managers are more intuitive than less successful managers. It is possible that the better managers have a measure of extrasensory perception which actually enables them to perceive events, both present and future, more accurately than their more fact-oriented counterparts. Certainly the case for ESP has not been disproven, so one might be advised to retain an open mind on the whole matter.

The *collective opinion* of salesmen or other presumably knowledgeable persons often provides a fairly reliable prediction—especially when the market and other aspects of the environment are relatively stable. This method has the advantages of being simple, requiring little mathematical skill, and of representing the best estimates of experts. Of course, the method may be biased by the personal attitudes of those making the predictions—some may be overly optimistic while others may be unduly pessimistic.

Historical extrapolation is a common method of forecasting. It is a bit more sophisticated than intuition or collective opinion. This method may range from simply saying that next year's sales, for example, will be about the same as this year's to *averaging, time-series analysis,* and *exponential smoothing.* A simple moving average updates the data each period by adding the most recently completed period into the average and dropping the most distant. If you were maintaining a six-month moving average on sales figures, every time a new month's data were in, you would add those to your calculations and drop out the earliest and oldest month that had been included. We can sophisticate a moving average by weighting recent periods more heavily than earlier periods or by weighting in any manner that seems appropriate. Figure 6–3 illustrates a simple three-month moving average.

Time-series analysis ranges from the simple plotting of some activity over a given time span to statistical correlations among activities over time. For example, an airline may plot the number of passenger miles flown every month. This time series may enable the airline to determine seasonal or other cyclical variations as well as to detect long-term trends. Often, two sets of data are plotted on the same chart for comparison. Along with passenger miles per month, the airline might also plot disposable personal income on a national basis. The airline may find some leading indicators that will help to predict passenger miles a month or more into the future. Under certain conditions, correlation analysis may be applied to two or more sets of data plotted on the same chart. When possible, correlation analysis will tell how reliable a functional relationship among variables is. Using correlation, for example, the airline may determine that variations in passenger miles flown do significantly depend on changes in disposable personal income, a conclusion that a visual comparison might suggest but that could not be confirmed without correlation analysis.

Exponential smoothing is a form of moving average, but with refinements. In this method, the new average is placed equal to the old average and then modified by a fraction of error between

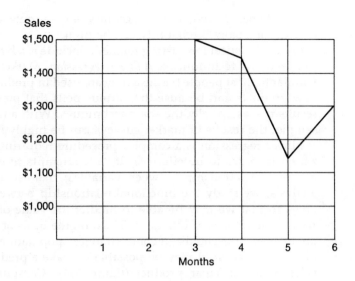

Month	$ Sales	Three-month moving average at end of			
		Month 3	Month 4	Month 5	Month 6
1	1,000	1,000			
2	2,000	2,000	2,000		
3	1,500	1,500	1,500	1,500	
4	800	4,500 ÷ 3 = 1,500	800	800	800
5	1,100		4,300 ÷ 3 = 1,433	1,100	1,100
6	2,000			3,400 ÷ 3 = 1,133	2,000
					3,900 ÷ 3 = 1,300

Figure 6-3 A three-month moving average for sales dollars

what was forecast (the old average) and what actually happened. In this way the new average, when extrapolated, will be modified by the amount of error in the old prediction. A large error in the old forecast will change the new forecast considerably. If the old forecast were perfect, the new forecast is the result of just the simple moving average. And the fraction of error that is used in the calculations will determine whether more recent periods will be emphasized (a large fraction) or more distant periods (a small fraction).

The reliability of these methods is situational; that is, it depends upon the skill of the analyst, the stability of the environment, the type of demand faced, and the accuracy of the inputs. Given favorable circumstances, reliability can be high.

Other statistical forecasting methods include *market surveys* that use sampling techniques and *linear regression*. Market surveys are familiar to most people because they are used in predicting sales of new products and because the various polls that predict election results use essentially the same techniques. With a truly random sample, the results of market surveys can be highly reliable.

Linear regression is a complex procedure requiring computerization in order to be effective. It "... attempts to establish the nature of relationship between variables; that is, in regression analysis, we study the functional relationship between the variables so that we may be able to predict the value of one on the basis of another or of others."[11] Thus, on the basis of information about new households, income changes, population growth, or new construction, it may be possible to make a prediction about sales of a particular product (figure 6–4). Computerization is necessary because the variables are so numerous and the relationships so complicated.

If we can discover the nature of the relationship between sales (the dependent variable) and other factors such as income and population (the independent variables), linear regression predictions can be quite precise and reliable. Linear regression enables the forecaster to measure explicitly any relationship or association

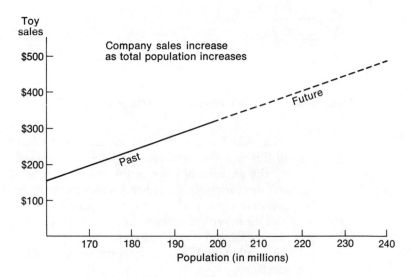

Figure 6–4 Regression analysis—the relationship between toy sales for company *A* and national population

between variables over time. And the relationship becomes the basis for the forecast itself. Highly sophisticated mathematical and statistical models are not always precise, however. In many cases, it is difficult to construct a model accurate enough to allow precise forecasts. In all cases, management judgment is needed, since uncertainty cannot be completely eliminated.

Although there are many other forecasting methods, the *Delphi Method* is the final one we will consider.

> The objective of the Delphi Method is to gain the consensus of experts on an uncertain matter by questioning them several times on an individual basis and providing them with anonymous feedback information from others in the group until there is a convergence of the estimates or opinions of the group. All questioning is handled impersonally, by a coordinator of some kind. This technique eliminates committee activity almost entirely, thus reducing the influence of certain psychological factors such as specious persuasion, unwillingness to abandon publicly expressed opinion, and the bandwagon effect of majority opinion.
>
> Both the inquiry into the reasons each expert gives for his opinions and the subsequent feedback of the reasons adduced by others stimulates the experts to take account of considerations and information that they might have inadvertently neglected. Also, feedback may cause them to give more weight to factors they were initially inclined to dismiss as unimportant.
>
> The results of a Delphi study reflect explicit, reasoned, self-aware opinions expressed by experts in light of the opinions of associate experts. Such estimates or opinions should lessen the chance of surprise and provide a sounder basis for long-range decision making than those arrived at by implicit, unarticulated, intuitive judgments. The Delphi Method has been used successfully at the RAND Corporation, TRW, and a number of other places, particularly for technological forecasting.[12]

The Delphi Method was originally designed to obtain forecasts and not to generate strategic plans.[13] It seeks a consensus on pure information rather than on an action strategy. Nonetheless, with certain modifications, such as allowing for human interaction in a planning group and the use of a coordinator as an agent for clarification and communication, a version of the Delphi Method can be used for the total planning function.

Preparing for Action

Having stated goals and made forecasts that can be applied to each of the alternatives, the organization is ready to use the general and specific criteria for evaluation and selection of a specific plan. This plan will be the specific, predetermined course of action judged best able to achieve the desired objective. Implementation of the plan naturally follows its selection. An important tool here is budgeting, which allocates organizational resources over time. Ideally, the budget plan will distribute just the right amount of men, money, and materials to the appropriate organizational subsystems so the goal can be reached. Unfortunately, the further into the future we plan, the more unreliable become our forecasts. The uncertainties of economics, politics, technology, and the social environment can overwhelm a plan. Examples of plan obsolescence abound in highly visible organizations such as the Defense Department. But since planning, and specifically forecasting, reduce uncertainty, it is generally conceded that some planning is better than none at all. It is also generally conceded that over the short range, planning tends to be much more useful than over the long range.

We might finally mention that the spirit in which a plan is implemented has a great deal to do with its confirmation, by success, as a good plan. Plans can be implemented carelessly or with great determination. Unless things go terribly wrong, even in the long run, we can usually salvage at least part of our goal. Some call this willful pursuit of an objective a self-fulfilling prophecy. You may prophesy that you are going to become a millionaire. With this as your goal, you may complete the planning process; and if you work at it, or have one of those rare strokes of luck, you just might fulfill your prophecy. Organizations can do the same thing, although obviously it is not prophecy alone that turns the trick.

Who Does the Planning?

A variety of arrangements for planning responsibility exists, depending upon the size and type of organization and the traditions it may hold. In small, privately owned companies, one man may do all the planning. With increasing size and complexity, it becomes necessary for others in the organization to help by setting their own goals and providing inputs for top-level planning. Staff assistance has long been used to aid in the search for alternatives and to furnish information for use throughout the entire planning process. More recently, explicitly structured planning departments have gained popularity. These usually report directly to the chief executive and are relatively small in size. It also appears that for companies operating in quite stable technological environments, the planning groups are formalized and occupy a distinct niche in the organizational structure. In more volatile technological environments, the groups operate more informally and often are not differentiated into formal subunits.[14] Figure 6–5 illustrates the position of a formal planning group in an organization structure.

The Contribution of Planners

The planning staff's job of contemplating long-range events—the political, economic, social, and technological scenes—and developing plans based in part on these contemplations sounds relaxed and lofty. But while the long-range aspect of formal planning is important, the job goes much farther. The planners should also be around when operating executives put approved plans into practice. In a study of 45 companies, one researcher found that planners help implement long-range plans in the following ways:

1. Operating executives, busy with pressing current problems, cannot keep properly informed about the rapidly changing external environment. Planners must, therefore, continuously study it to be certain that the company's long-range plans are attainable and desirable.
2. Planners audit the company's internal operations to help keep them consistent with the long-range plans, spot signs of trouble early, and strive for use of the firm's resources in the best overall manner.
3. Planners help operating executives in various other ways, such as assisting in drawing up near-term plans based on the approved long-range plans; helping to solve operating problems one division cannot handle alone; and preparing near-term forecasts.[15]

The value of formal planning can be seriously weakened if the chief executive does not take prime responsibility—especially for

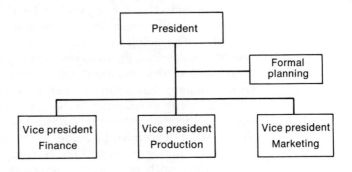

Figure 6–5 A formal planning group

long-range planning. The addition of a planning group simply recognizes that the job of planning is too big for one man; it does not mean that the chief can abdicate his role in planning. Furthermore, his interest in planning should be known to others in the organization. This will help stimulate their interest in planning and in providing the information inputs so vital to efficient planning activity at the top level.

The importance of lower-level participation in planning is suggested by a study on the accuracy of long-range planning involving sixty companies.[16] The study, now five years old and still continuing, found that the greatest accuracy results when the top executive is highly involved and when subordinates are helping to set their own goals, since subordinates tend to deliver what they promised.

However, in a preliminary report, the author of the study sounds a cautionary note: "Taking steps to improve accuracy may be effective, but only at the potential loss of some of the 'mind-stretching' benefits that could result from a less disciplined approach."[17] In other words, in striving for accuracy, the organization may stifle creativity and a willingness to take risks, and thus wind up accomplishing less than might otherwise be true. Individuals and organizations must be careful not to settle for less than the realization of our full potential, which may not be demanded by a plan.

A Tougher World

As formal planning becomes increasingly sophisticated, the business world promises to become more competitive and less rewarding. And as larger companies sharpen their planning skills and make more effective use of personnel and facilities, including the computer, small companies may find it increasingly difficult to compete. "The swing to strategic planning in large organizations constitutes a serious threat to small business management. It challenges one of the important competitive advantages which the small company has enjoyed—being faster on its feet than the larger company in adapting to changing conditions. It is perfectly clear that mere adaptation in the short run will no longer suffice. Trends must henceforth be made, not simply coped with."[18]

Another author predicts that as companies increasingly use similar data, such as economic forecasts from the same source, they also will react to the unexpected in similar ways and will influence the economy to the extent that its actual behavior will be closer and closer to behavior predicted by corporate planners.[19] This effect could introduce a heretofore unknown degree of inflexibility into long-range corporate plans as well as into the entire economy. If true, it is certainly trend-making on a large scale and substitutes constant acting toward a desired goal for reacting and short-run adapting to environmental changes.

Room for Creativity   Despite all this, there may still be room for the creative individual or organization. Filley and House suggest that successful planning is the result of successful generation of alternatives.[20] Creativity often is defined in part as the ability to link unrelated facts, ideas, or phenomena into some entity that can, for example, resolve problems in new ways. The creative individual, then, may generate alternatives not envisioned by persons in more formal planning circumstances—even though creativity and innovation receive their due emphasis in the large company.

Inflexibility may characterize the economy and the mass of large corporations in their total goal-seeking efforts, but the individual company must still remain flexible—must still develop contingency plans and possess the capability to adjust to short-run or long-run changes in the environment. Adaptation alone is not enough, but unyielding devotion to setting a trend could introduce into a company the type of inflexibility that could seriously harm it.

It would appear that when a large organization does only one or the other, adapt or set trends, the small company has a good chance of competing. When large companies decide to follow through on strategic plans, which may establish new trends as well as adapt to environmental changes, they may make it difficult for the little guy. As long as creativity cannot be quarantined, however, the small entrepreneur always has a chance. He may not be able to establish a trend; but he can do long-range planning, and he certainly should be able to adapt to changes as quickly or quicker than big corporations.

Some Planning and Decision-Making Tips

Whether associated with a large or a small organization, there are certain basic attitudes and behaviors that every decision maker should observe.

1. Be wary of always making plans to solve the most obvious and immediate problems. Often, the most important and critical problems need to be "discovered." The manager needs to analyze, dig, and think about the future to identify problems involving long-range survival and success. This is one of the most important distinctions between a poor manager and a good one. A poor manager spends much of his time "firefighting"; that is, running from one subproblem to another and rarely thinking of the long-term health of his organization. Eventually, he may find that all his minor problems are neatly solved, but that the whole organization teeters on the edge of collapse.

2. Shoot for the stars *if* the stars are reasonably attainable. There is no point in setting a goal that is virtually impossible to reach no matter how much energy, talent, and ambition you have. And a manager does a disservice to his subordinates as well if he allows them to set subgoals that are impossible to reach. To avoid frustration and disillusionment, the manager must work with his people to make sure their goals are challenging but reasonable. And he should continue to work with them, to help them achieve their goals and to set new goals.

3. Criteria for the evaluation and selection of alternatives should be as specific as possible. But the actual decision or selection of an alternative should be delayed as long as possible. New information may become available that will affect the decision. Sometimes conditions will change to the point where no decision at all need be made. But when a decision must be made a manager cannot delay too long. The decision to introduce a new product must be made at the right time, or competitors may wipe out your potential market. Each situation must be carefully examined to determine the best moment for a decision.

4. Once a decision is made, the organization should make every effort to successfully implement the decision. The organization must also be flexible, however: willing to bend, to modify, and to change in accordance with changing conditions. Blind adherence to a previously determined course of action can be as disastrous as making the wrong decision to begin with.

There are no hard and fast "how to" rules that cover every decision-making situation. The best approach is to learn the theory behind decision making; to learn how people and organizations actually make decisions and make plans; and to know some general rules covering planning and decision making. After gaining some skill in applying the theory to reality, a manager can use this general knowledge to guide his actions in any specific planning or decision-making situation.

Summary

Planning is a vital ingredient in organizational success. Planning is decision making that extends over varying ranges of time—short-run, intermediate-run, and long-run—with long-run generally held to be five years or longer. Although planning tends to get put aside in favor of more routine activities, its benefits are multiple. These benefits include allowing more predictability within the organization; providing a standard for performance measurement; and helping to structure communications and work flow.

The planning process results in strategic plans, single-use plans, standing plans, and others. Important steps in the process are setting goals and forecasting. General and specific criteria are used to evaluate goals as well as to evaluate alternative courses of action to reach the goals.

Companies have multiple long-run goals, often including those of social responsibility and employee welfare, but empirical work has indicated that profit and efficiency goals take priority. Long-run, strategic plans in particular should be kept flexible. One way of ensuring flexibility is to make the goals relatively broad, thus allowing adaptation to changes in environmental forces.

Forecasting is essential to planning since it helps reduce uncertainty about many environmental factors: technology, the economy, politics, competition, and social forces. Knowledge of future trends aids in setting goals and in selecting the specific course of action required to meet the goal. There are numerous forecasting methods, ranging from rough hunches to highly mathematical and statistical procedures.

Responsibility for planning varies in organizations, though normally the top executive should accept the prime responsibility for strategic planning. Increasingly in vogue for long-range planning are formal planning groups, who bear responsibility to the chief executive for aiding in the development of plans and for the implementation of plans. Participation of the lower levels of an organization is also necessary to the success of planning.

Some business analysts are predicting a much tougher competitive world and lower profits as formal planning becomes more widely and effectively used. While small business in particular may have trouble in such a world, as long as creativity and innovation are not the exclusive property of the large corporation, the small entrepreneur will always have a chance. And he certainly is capable of the long-range, strategic planning that he has been accused of not doing. In addition a small entrepreneur has an advantage in his ability to make short-run adaptations to environmental changes.

Management Profile

Harry Hopf

Harry Hopf was a management scholar who produced over 200 speeches, articles, and monographs during his career.[21] In 1938 he founded the Hopf Institute of Management. Yet he remains one of the least known management writers. Although he wrote a lot and delivered many speeches, Hopf never gathered his ideas into one comprehensive volume. This may account for the "who's he?" reaction when his name is mentioned.

Born in England, Hopf came to the United States at 16, without a penny to his name. He started his career in 1900 as a clerk in a life insurance company. From then until the late 1940s, his career developed until finally he was receiving fees of $500 a day as a management consultant.

Fascinated by Taylor and scientific management, Hopf applied those principles to office work. In 1915 he published his first important paper on how Taylor's concept of a planning department could be applied to an office organization. Hopf described planning as a constant process "that enters into the very heart of the activities of a business once it has been launched upon its career."[22]

He was particularly interested in the initial planning that goes into the establishment of a new business, noting that sloppy planning at this point often prevents the achievement of success. However, even if a new business were able to overcome this obstacle and stay alive, it still might not be able to realize optimal conditions.

Another of Hopf's favorite topics was optimology, or the science of the optimum. He defined the optimum as "that state of development of a business enterprise which tends to perpetuate an equilibrium among the factors of size, cost, and human capacity and thus promote in the highest degree regular realization of the business objectives."[23] Without effective planning, he said, the optimum would be impossible to attain, and the offending business would be likely to sustain losses or even fail.

Hopf did most of his work on optimology during the Great Depression of the 1930s. It is interesting that he denounced unchecked growth—apparently feeling that undisciplined growth had a direct connection with the depression disaster. Instead he advocated optimal size, which would be different for different companies and would change for a given firm over time.

Hopf perhaps deserves more fame than he has. But he needs no apologies, for the ideas in his writings are fundamental, sound, and find renewed expression today in our own search for optimality.

Discussion Questions

1. Most people find planning a relatively unattractive activity. As a top manager, what steps could you take to encourage your subordinates to want to do more planning and to do more effective planning?

2. It is best to develop a long-range strategic plan for the total organization before working out short-range plans for the organizational subsystems. What would be the consequences of first working out all the short-range plans and then developing a long-range strategic plan?

3. Why is management by exception a valuable managerial concept? Why are standing plans associated with this concept?

4. What would happen if a sales manager set his own goals without regard for any other organizational unit or the total organization?

5. In "A Planning Incident," Jane and Paul did some strategic long-range planning. Identify each of the steps they covered in the planning process. Did they do a first-rate job of planning? If not, what should they have done better?

6. How can managers such as Jane and Paul know which problems to work on first? Which problems are most critical? Which problems can be of most benefit to the organization when solved?

7. Should Jane and Paul search for problems or just solve those problems that are obvious?

8. How can managers know *when* to solve a problem or *when* to make a decision?

9. Why is forecasting so critical for the planning and decision-making process?

10. Large organizations increasingly are using planning specialists. What are the advantages and disadvantages of employing a person who does nothing but planning, as opposed to being the owner of a small business who must do many other things in addition to planning?

References

1. J. G. March, "Business Decision Making," *Industrial Research*, 1 (1959): 65–70.

2. D. E. Williams, "An Analysis of Selected Work Duties and Performance of the More Effective Versus the Less Effective Manager," *Academy of Management Journal*, 12 (1969): 516–517.

3. G. A. Steiner, "The Critical Role of Top Management in Long-Range Planning," *Arizona Review*, 14 (1966): 5–13.

4. W. D. Guth and R. Tagiuri, "Personal Values and Corporate Strategy," *Harvard Business Review*, 43 (1965): 123–132.

5. J. B. Mason, "A Reconceptualization of the Theory of the Goal Formation Process as Related to Individuals and Larger Social Units," *The Southern Journal of Business* (1971): 22–32.

6. G. W. England, "Organizational Goals and Expected Behavior of American Managers," *Academy of Management Journal*, 10 (1967): 107–117.

7. J. K. Dent, "Organizational Correlates of the Goals of Business Management," *Personnel Psychology*, 12 (1955): 365–393.

8. A. C. Filley and R. J. House, *Managerial Process and Organizational Behavior* (Glenview, Ill.: Scott, Foresman, 1969), p. 209.

9. D. Sills, *The Volunteers: Means and Ends in a National Organization* (New York: The Free Press, 1957).

10. C. Perrow, *Organizational Analysis: A Sociological View* (Belmont, Calif.: Wadsworth, 1970), p. 137.

11. Ya-lun Chou, *Statistical Analysis* (New York: Holt, Rinehart and Winston, 1969), p. 597.

12. J. C. Chambers, S. K. Mullick, and D. A. Goodman, "Catalytic Agent for Effective Planning," *Harvard Business Review*, 49 (1971): 110–119.

13. *Ibid.*

14. R. J. Litschert, "The Structure of Long-Range Planning Groups," *Academy of Management Journal*, 14 (1971): 33–43.

15. F. Greenwood, "Effective LRP Requires Action," *Academy of Management Journal*, 7 (1964): 224–228.

16. R. F. Vancil, "The Accuracy of Long-Range Planning," *Harvard Business Review*, 48 (1970): 98–101.

17. *Ibid.*, p. 101.

18. F. G. Gilmore, "Strategic Planning's Threat to Small Business," mimeographed (1966), as quoted in G. A. Steiner, pp. 5–13.

19. D. S. Ammer, "The Side Effects of Planning," *Harvard Business Review*, 48 (1970): 44.

20. A. C. Filley and R. J. House, p. 195.

21. E. R. Gray and R. J. Vahl, "Harry Hopf: Management's Unheralded Giant," *The Southern Journal of Business*, 6 (1971): 69–78.

22. H. Hopf, "Management and the Optimum," in H. F. Merrill, ed., *Classics in Management* (New York: American Management Association, 1960), pp. 355–403.

23. *Ibid.*, p. 355.

Suggested Readings

Ewing, David W. *The Human Side of Planning*. New York: Macmillan, 1969.

St. Thomas, Charles E. *Practical Business Planning*. New York: American Management Association, 1965.

Steiner, George A. *Top Management Planning*. New York: Macmillan, 1969.

Warren, E. Kirby. *Long-Range Planning: The Executive Viewpoint*. Englewood Cliffs, N.J.: Prentice-Hall, 1966.

Control

7

Establishing goals and setting specific courses of action to reach those goals are important parts of the planning process. And the goals also function as standards so we can measure organizational and individual performance. For example, you may set a goal of losing ten pounds in four weeks. It would be easy to weigh you every week and measure your progress toward your goal. Hence your goal doubles as a standard, and we could control your performance by measuring your progress periodically. This is the essence of control, and as you can see, it is tied closely to planning.

Concepts of Control

We have already said that an organization is an open system which interacts constantly with its environment to maintain an equilibrium condition called *homeostasis*. Information flow through feedback loops is an important part of this control process, since it enables an organization to be a self-regulating system. The study of self-regulating systems, with particular emphasis on information, is called *cybernetics*.

Feedback loops are integral to the study of cybernetics and of control in organizations. There are two basic kinds of loops: closed and open. The closed loop may be illustrated by the usual type of home temperature control. Basic elements of the heating system include the furnace, heating ducts, and a thermostat somewhere in the house. As the temperature in the house drops below the desired level or standard, the thermostat notes this and signals the furnace to begin operating. When the temperature reaches the standard or perhaps a degree or two above it, the thermostat signals the furnace to shut off. Note that the house temperature constantly varies around the standard and is therefore seldom precisely at the desired level. This happens because an error or a deviation from standard must occur before corrective action takes place.

The open control loop helps to avoid the problems of time lag before correction and oscillation about the standard. In the case above, we could place a thermometer outside the house and actuate the furnace on the basis of variations in outside temperature. This would require a knowledge of the exact relationship between outside and inside temperatures and the amount of heat produced by the furnace.

Thus the open control loop could anticipate temperature changes inside the house as the outside temperature rose and fell and could keep the inside temperature at or nearly at the desired standard. However, the open loop does require a precise knowledge of the relationships involved in order to function properly. Figures 7–1 and 7–2 illustrate the concepts of closed and open control loops.

Control Loops in Organizations

We have seen that feedback on some ongoing process, such as heating a house, occurs only in the closed-loop system while an open-loop system transmits information from the environment to the process and exercises control via a predetermined set of relationships. Both types are striving to meet goals, but while the closed loop measures deviations that have already occurred, the open loop attempts to prevent deviations through sound planning

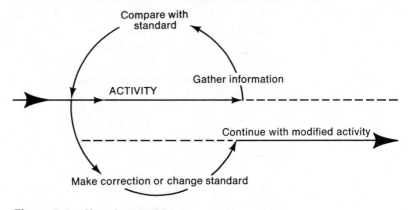

Figure 7–1 Closed control loop

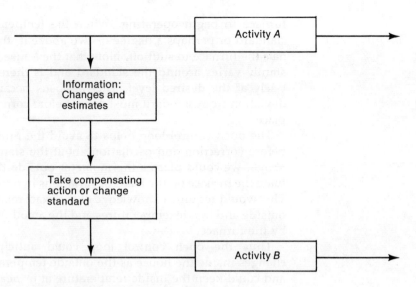

Figure 7–2 Open control loop

and coordination. In a strict sense, a self-regulating system is only possible with closed-loop control.

Some examples may help to illustrate the use of control loops in organizations. Given a prediction that the economy is going to improve, a company may anticipate hiring additional personnel. If the economic prediction is considered reliable and is precise, the company may simply prepare to activate a contingency plan that calls for a new employment level. This is open-loop control. Its nature is anticipatory and preventive.

On the other hand, the company could wait until foremen and supervisors reported they were shorthanded. Emergency action might then be quickly taken to hire people to meet the increased demands on the company. This would be closed-loop control, waiting until an error occurs and then taking action to bring about conformance to the standard.

Or the lone shoestore in a small town may learn that a competitor is moving in. Again, the store may take action in anticipation of its competition by advertising, offering specials, and providing better service. Or it may wait and see if profits are adversely affected before doing anything to correct the situation. These are further examples of open-loop and closed-loop control respectively.

However, it is not always possible to maintain an existing standard or goal. For example, the shoestore may have enjoyed an abnormally large return on investment due to its local monopolistic position. The advent of competition may make the old standard for profit unrealistic. In this case, it might be futile to try to regain the lost level. A realistic assessment of the situation probably would suggest lowering the expected return on investment. An organization must be flexible enough to modify goals and standards as well as actions to keep pace with a dynamic environment.

A Place for Closed-Loop Control   Given only the examples above, it may seem that open-loop control is always superior to closed-loop. This is not true, however, for there are many instances where we properly use closed-loop control. It is necessary and desirable in quality control, for example. To assure some minimum level of quality on outgoing production, it is necessary not only to design quality into a product but also to inspect production in process and the final product. Quality control inspectors report deviations from standard, so that the production activity may be corrected.

Companies often monitor sales performance through various reports, customer reactions, and sales volume. The feedback provides the sales manager with knowledge of deviations or variances. It also allows him to take whatever action he feels is appropriate to restore the conformity of sales performance to standard. Feedback on budgetary deviations alerts management to unusual conditions and makes possible the correction or changing of a standard to suit new situations.

So open-loop control is essential to relate two sets of circumstances or activities, such as economic activity with anticipated employment levels or style changes with inventory levels, while maintaining some single process within predetermined limits requires closed-loop control. Organizations may employ both types of loops, and develop a complex of information routes that involves loops within loops and eventually they may develop a progression of loops that encompasses the entire organizational system (see figure 7–3).

To illustrate, a company may start to produce a new product. There will be closed-loop feedback to assure a satisfactory level of outgoing quality. If all goes well, the sales department will be notified that production is definitely successful (open-loop control). Successful sales efforts may signal a need for increased production and inventories and alert management to potentially higher profits (open-loop). Throughout, the sales department and top management will maintain their own closed-loop controls. Thus the control system grows and itself requires monitoring to avoid cumbersome complexity.

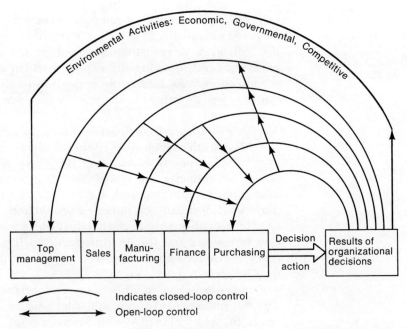

Environmental Activities: Economic, Governmental, Competitive

| Top management | Sales | Manu-facturing | Finance | Purchasing | Decision → action | Results of organizational decisions |

Indicates closed-loop control

Open-loop control

Figure 7–3   Some possible multiple control loops within an organization

Multiple Loops and Equilibrium

Although multiple loops are necessary to achieve control in organizations, problems frequently arise as each subsystem of an organization strives to maintain its equilibrium. In so doing, one or more subsystems may be temporarily unstable, out of equilibrium, and management will have to act to restore a balanced condition. This action, in turn, may upset the equilibrium of yet another subsystem, and so it goes. The conditions that produce stability for one element are often unbalancing for another. The cycle and the need for constant attention create continual work for the manager.

Another problem faces management when changes occur in the environment or within the organization. The organization must be capable of innovating or learning in order to cope with change and maintain stability. Innovation constitutes one of the toughest tests for management. It is tough enough to regulate routine events, but the decisions management makes to restore equilibrium when confronting new circumstances are much more difficult. The following incident may help to illustrate the problems involved in maintaining equilibrium.

Automating the Shipping Department

Jack was manager of the shipping department for the Radio Chassis Company. For years, Jack had operated his department very efficiently. Three men packaged the chassis in cardboard containers and stacked them on skids. Two other men picked up the skids with lift trucks and hauled them to the loading dock for truck pickup. It was all very neat, and Jack felt quite satisfied with the routine he had developed.

But as demand increased, the company decided to automate the chassis assembly line. This was done, and though things were quite chaotic in the production department for a while, stability was eventually restored. Jack now found that he had to hire additional men to handle the increased production. But with one additional man on packaging and another one to help move the boxes to the loading dock, working and storage space became inadequate.

The shipping department was upset, and Jack was worried. He appealed to the systems department, which recommended an automatic packaging machine and mechanized conveyors to carry the boxes to the dock. The equipment was installed. Now Jack only needed two men in his department. But what was to be done with the five extra men?

Jack had now restored equilibrium to his shipping department, had restructured his own closed-loop feedback system, and had no inclination toward any further disruption. Finally he turned his problem over to the personnel department to worry about.

Types of Control Systems

Determining when and how much to control and selecting appropriate control systems are among the decisions that management must make in implementing an overall control program. When to control is usually sorted into three categories: precontrol, current control, and postcontrol.

In precontrol, management attempts to institute policies, procedures, devices, and behavior patterns that will prevent deviations from standards by anticipating possible problems. The owner of a trucking company, for example, may regard any accident as a deviation from standard. To implement precontrol, he may have policies and procedures that limit hiring to those who can pass a stiff physical examination and driver's test. He may equip his trucks with all the latest safety devices, and he may run a continuing safety education program for his drivers. These guidelines and actions would all be part of a precontrol effort.

Current control, using the same illustration, would consist primarily of making sure that drivers handled their trucks on the road so as to avoid accidents. Swerving to avoid another vehicle, slowing down when the road becomes icy, and constantly checking the truck for any malfunction would be part of a current control effort.

In postcontrol, management audits some action or behavior after it has occurred to see how it measures up to the standard. For the trucking company, an examination of the accident record at the end of a year would be postcontrol. If the reasons for accidents can be determined, corrective action could then be incorporated into the precontrol or current control phases.

Most organizations will use all three of the time-oriented phases, although our trucking company could rely overwhelmingly on current control if it so desired. Its safety record would be better, however, if it used precontrol and postcontrol as well as current control (see table 7–1).

How Much to Control

Control should be exercised to the point where the organization can maintain itself in a stable condition and achieve its goals. This may pose some problems in practical application. Obtaining accurate and timely information can be one of the most difficult problems management faces in its control efforts. Particularly in open-loop control, where management requires information about the impact of one process or activity on another, severe risks can be involved if the information obtained is not reliable or if the relationships between activities are not precisely known.

For example, an organization may be tooling up to produce a new product. Unless information on the market potential is available, there will be great uncertainty as to how many units the company should be prepared to produce. There may be thousands or millions of dollars involved in equipment purchases and redesign of manufacturing facilities.

If greater reliability is simply a question of getting more information, there are methods that can help tell how much more information to get. Sampling is often used to test the market. The

Table 7–1 Safety control phases for a trucking company

Precontrol	Current control	Post control
Physical exam	Driver skill on the road	Analysis of accident record
Driver's test		
Safety devices on trucks		Corrective action
Safety education program		

more sampling that is done, the more information one has. But sampling also costs money. So we also need a way to determine the value of information from additional samples in relation to the cost incurred. When the cost of sampling exceeds the value of information obtained, we should stop sampling.

There are no hard and fast rules to tell us how much to control. The cutoff point is often complex and it may be dangerous to try to keep the control system too simple. Nor are there any specific rules on the relative weights to give to precontrol, current control, and postcontrol. Only in the case of a real-time, closed-loop, automatic system can current control be completely emphasized. Some computerized oil refineries, for example, run almost completely under current control. Unfortunately, most activites are not susceptible to automatic control, so that management must decide how to control and how much to control. Good planning will help, and it can be made even better by the consistent use of postcontrol data.

Direct Control

There are many ways to control an activity or behavior directly. A dog can be controlled by keeping him on a leash or fencing him in. A person controls some activity by doing it himself or by closely observing if some other person is doing it. An organization attempts to institutionalize its control through procedures, methods, and standardized measures. But management must decide which of many methods to implement. We will discuss a few of these methods to gain a better idea of the direct control technique.

Quantitative Methods While many direct control methods have some quantitative aspect, we are particularly interested in those quantitative methods developed specifically for control purposes. Inventory control, production control, and quality control employ broad applications of quantitative methods. Let us pick one, quality control, for a closer look.

In quality control, it is possible to inspect every item, inspect none, or inspect some portion. But inspecting every item can be prohibitively expensive in labor costs while not inspecting at all can be expensive in terms of customer dissatisfaction and lost business. In most cases, manufacturers, for example, would like to inspect a representative sample of a production lot.

But what is a representative sample? Before the application of statistical sampling theory, there was no way to tell how large a sample to take. But now, sampling theory tells us how large a sample to take and how many defective items can appear in the sample before the entire lot must be rejected. In addition, given a certain lot size, sample size, and allowable number of defects in the sample, we can also know the probability of acceptance for a production lot or run for various levels of defective parts in the lot.

For example, suppose we have production runs of 5,000 items and know that on the average, one out of every 200 pieces is defective. But in some production runs, the percentage defective could run considerably higher. If we want to assure ourselves that shipments would average no more than two per cent defective, sampling theory tells us we need to take a sample of 70 items from every run and that no more than two defective parts can be found in the sample. If three or more defects are found in the sample, the entire lot of 5,000 parts must be rejected.

We also could adjust our sample size or allowable number of defective parts in the sample if we want to improve our average outgoing quality level or if we wish to allow the average quality of our shipments to decline. Hence, statistical theory and other quantitative methods give us the means to directly control many processes and to vary the degree of control according to the situation.

Network Systems Network systems have already been discussed in chapter 4 on decision theory, and it was pointed out that systems such as PERT (Project Evaluation and Review Technique) generate good planning decisions. Network systems also facilitate direct control. For example, visualize a roadmap with several highways leading to the same destination. A different car is traveling on each of the highways, and all of the cars are supposed to arrive at the destination at the same time.

Now if you were in a control room with this large map on the wall and lights to indicate the progress of each car, this would be an analogy to a PERT system for building a bridge or whatever. In the case of a bridge, there would be various phases of construction that would have to be done separately but in time for the final completion. Watching progress on an activated roadmap or on a PERT system is an effective way to control and help assure arrival at the destination on time.

Performance Evaluation Evaluation of individual performance has been going on for years as a form of direct control. Unfortunately, it has been and is often ineffective because the available methods are not very precise and management often is careless in their application.

Performance evaluation is relatively easy on jobs where we can readily measure worker output. Work measurement techniques of motion and time study help show what average production rates should be on jobs such as assembly of component parts and repetitive machine operations. However, measuring the production of an executive is a different proposition. How do you assess the contribution of an executive to his department or to the total organization?

Companies use such factors as return on investment, cost minimization, and volume of production or sales to evaluate executives. The results vary widely. One of the problems is separating out short-term success from long-term impact. In other words, a sales manager could show remarkable success in sales volume over a two-year period, but he may do it at the expense of alienating long-term prospects. Performance evaluation is a form of direct control and must be done. But it is often done poorly, in the mistaken belief that something is better than nothing.

Evaluating the Total Organization   Evaluation at the managerial level is difficult; even more difficult are the problems in assessing the performance of the total organization. Much work has been done in this area, with few concrete results. Of course, a problem of goal incongruity is involved. A business organization may feel its sole goal is to make a profit. But people outside of the organization may assign it different goals and may declare the organization ineffective at the same time that profits are at an all-time high. And members may not feel an organization is effective unless their own personal goals are also realized. An organization must consider the needs and desires of its constituency, both internal and external, if it is to survive.

In recognition of this, most organizations plan toward multiple goals, even though some of the goals may be vaguely defined and hard to measure. A major part of the problem is simply knowing whether all the appropriate goals have been included. Given this sort of difficulty in structuring goals, then it is apparent that organizational evaluation depends in large part on the validity of the goal structure.

On the other hand, to measure its effectiveness, one could evaluate the things an organization does—such as planning, innovation, staffing, and development of personnel. If an organization does all the right things in these and other areas, one might then say the organization is effective. But this approach provides no direct measure of goal achievement and hence is not direct control. Rather, it is what we will term indirect control, since it depends on good planning, sound staffing and development, and creative innovation to develop the right goals and to achieve them.

From a narrow viewpoint, an organization can ignore its constituency, set its own goals, and content itself with evaluation on this basis. Within this context, there would be sound direct control for the total organization. From a broader viewpoint, however, this approach would be illusory and self-defeating. An organization cannot continually ignore its bases of support and expect to survive.

As we can see, direct control varies from completely automatic, closed-loop, real-time control over some production process at one extreme to uncertain evaluation of the total organization at the other extreme. Many direct control systems are current, while others, such as evaluation of results and past performance, involve postcontrol. When control is mentioned, we usually think of direct control. But there is another important variety, which can be equally effective—indirect control.

Indirect Control

While direct control usually takes current and postcontrol forms, indirect control is predominantly a form of precontrol. It tends to be long-lasting in effect and depends on an educational or conditioning process for its efficacy. Indirect control has a critical bearing on overall performance as well as on that of the system components. While the explicit measurement of deviations from standard is the strength of direct control, indirect control persuades adherence to standard in a more general way and is much more influential in setting standards than in measuring deviations from them. A few examples may help to illustrate the concept.

A management philosophy is a form of indirect control. New organizational members become conditioned to the philosophy and tend to carry out their responsibilities in conformance with organizational values. Deviations from the philosophy cannot be explicitly measured, but may be noted and one of several possible responses may be made. The company may dismiss the deviant or maverick member or transfer him to a less responsible position. On the other hand, if the deviation is innovative and offers the promise of improved organizational behavior, it may be incorporated in the existing philosophy (standard). A philosophy extends a general guide and indirectly controls behavior in all possible organizational situations.

Management Development   Closely related to the maintenance of a management philosophy, management development begins with the appointment to a managerial position and continues over a long-term period. In a broad sense, it seeks to condition the values and goals of the manager to bring about consonance with the managerial philosophy, thus sustaining the philosophy for an extended period.

Management development also seeks to change the manager, so that increased job effectiveness results. But the change that is desired is different from other kinds of changes that can be made to increase effectiveness, such as tighter controls or reorganization of the job.

The essential difference between management development and other types of change is that development requires primarily a change of *attitude and understanding;* these elements are usually not fundamental to other types of change.

Management development objectives fall into five broad categories of desired change: knowledge, attitude, abilities, job performance, and operational results. Development is thus seen as an attempt to induce a change either in managers themselves or in the operating results of managerial performance, such as scrap, turnover, profit, or cost. The change is usually intended to accomplish one of the following: (1) to improve managerial performance on the present job; (2) to prepare managers for future requirements of a present job; or (3) to prepare managers for promotion to higher level jobs.[1]

If management development is successful, it creates new attitudes, values, and understanding. And in most cases, these new values probably will agree with the philosophy of the organization. The changed managers will influence their subordinates and peers to "follow the company line," and indirect control will be in operation.

However, a manager often learns new attitudes and values that may not be in harmony with the manager's immediate environment or with the organizational philosophy. If this occurs, he may come into conflict with his superior, for example, resulting in frustration and bitterness. But if the new attitudes are better than the old, they might signal the beginning of a new standard. Even the philosophy of an organization could change as a product of the development process.

So the development process, as well as the influx of new or different values held by new members of the organization, can induce changes in standards within the organization. Management development can be a form of indirect control by helping to assure continuance of present, effective standards as well as provoking a shift to a more effective organizational posture when the old standards are no longer relevant.

Operant Conditioning Bringing about conformance to a management philosophy or to a standard of behavior or attitude usually entails a form of operant conditioning. The manager who receives a word or nod of approval for an expressed attitude in harmony with the company philosophy and who later receives a substantial pay raise is being conditionally reinforced for his public attitude. If the expressions of approval and satisfactory pay raises continue, the manager will continue to be conditioned to follow company standards.

Eventually, some gesture of approval alone will be enough to stimulate hard work and conformity, and the response—hard work and conformity—will be accomplished to enjoy again the stimulus—the approving nod of the head or the pat on the back. In terms of behavior, it is similar to the rat who learns to press a bar (respond) in order to earn food as a reward (stimulus).

The use of positive, conditioned reinforcers is not new, of course, but we are still learning many of the possibilities and pitfalls. In the area of quality control, for example, Adam and Scott point out that "One could implicitly or explicitly emphasize and condition behavior that leads to high quality output at the expense of speed, or one could condition behavior resulting in high quantity output, sometimes at the expense of quality."[2] They cite several examples of the difficulty of transferring workers from high quality work to low quality and vice versa. Once a worker becomes positively conditioned to a certain quality level, he may experience difficulty in moving to a new level.

Therefore, the establishment of a quality level is perhaps as much a behavioral problem as it is of assembling the proper equipment and tools to do the job. Extending this concept of conditioned response to the managerial level, we can see that establishment of a quality level might help maintain an outmoded philosophy to the serious detriment of the organization. This also helps to explain why it is so difficult to achieve change in the face of a set of conditioned responses of other people.

Since a perfect philosophy is so rare, it behooves management to encourage self-examination and improvement by means of changes in standards and philosophy. This, then, is why it is important for management development to generate new attitudes and understandings as well as to encourage the learning of existing values and beliefs.

We have discussed several control concepts thus far in the chapter. In particular, we have discussed closed and open control loops; direct and indirect control systems; and current control,

Table 7–2 Most likely associations among control loops and control systems

Control loops	Closed loop	Open loop
Control systems	Direct	Indirect
	Current	Precontrol Postcontrol

precontrol, and postcontrol systems. As we have suggested, management will usually apply one of the control loops in conjunction with one or more of the control systems. Because of complementary characteristics, each control loop has natural applications in association with certain control systems. For example, closed-loop control is most likely associated in application with direct and current control systems. Table 7–2 illustrates the most likely associations among all the control loops and systems that we have discussed.

Control and Organization Structure

Management employs several approaches to structure control systems in the organization. Sometimes the controller or principal financial officer will administer the whole system. In this case, controls are largely of a financial nature—budgets, financial forecasts, statistics, and audits.

In other instances, controls are scattered throughout the organization. Divisions and departments such as personnel management, finance, marketing, and industrial engineering exercise the control function for their own operations. Coordination depends on the chief executive. In recent years, there has been a trend toward charging a single agency in the organization with the overall coordination and direction of management control systems. This trend does not remove responsibility for control from operating departments but does help assure an integrated control system for the total organization.

Decentralization and Centralization

Management in every complex organization must decide whether its structure is going to be centralized or decentralized, and control is one of the most important factors that will enter into the deliberations. To centralize means to shift much of the organizational decision making to the top levels. Naturally, the necessary authority to make decisions and responsibility also shifts to the top. As a result, the middle and lower levels of the organization have relatively less authority and decision-making responsibility. Changing to a decentralized operation entails just the reverse.

Centralization and decentralization both have their advantages and disadvantages, of course. Dale lists the advantages and disadvantages of decentralization:

Advantages

1. Executives will be nearer to the point of decision making.
2. There may be a better utilization of the time and ability of executives.
3. The quality of decisions is likely to improve.
4. The amount and expense of paperwork by headquarters staff may be considerably reduced.
5. The expense of coordination may be reduced because of the greater autonomy of decision making.

Disadvantages

1. A lack of uniformity of decisions.
2. Inadequate utilization of specialists.
3. Lack of proper equipment or executives in the field.[3]

When computers arrived on the scene, there was much controversy as to whether their data-processing capabilities would encourage centralization or decentralization. Since then it has been accepted that the computer is a neutral factor, helpful no matter which direction management wishes to take. The behavioral implications of centralization and decentralization have remained more important than any technological innovations.

Lower-level managers often lament the centralization of their organization because they feel that control from the top will force conformity and reduce motivation and productivity. In addition, they feel that centralization lessens the opportunity for autonomous decision making at lower levels, thereby lowering job satisfaction and making more difficult the display of talent for the purpose of recognition and advancement. Hence the overall type of structure and control system have vast implications for the organization. These will occur not only in the control of nonhuman factors but will impinge on the behavior patterns of all managers. Whether to centralize or decentralize is an important control decision with great significance for the long-range future of the organization.

As we have just said, a centralized structure facilitates tight control from the top, whereas in decentralization management pushes much of the decision-making and control responsibility to lower levels. We also emphasized the relationship of structure and its complementary control system on behavior. In the design of control systems, however, management often ignores the nature of human response. This is unfortunate because "The decision-makers, single or aggregated—their motivations, attitudes, pressures, modes of response—must be included in management control systems design. The man (and manager) is part of the system of control, and management control system design must be viewed as a form of man-machine system design."[4]

If there are problems of human response to a control system, they will occur at the point where the system is applied. At this point the control system may also express some extraneous managerial activity—such as style of leadership. For example, workers may deeply resent a supervisor who exercises close control (and close supervision) by constantly peeping over shoulders to observe work progress.

On the other hand, some persons do not mind close supervision (control) and some may actually prefer it. The control system and style of leadership should recognize the nature of human reaction prior to implementation. The interrelatedness of management activites—control and leadership—also demonstrates the need to recognize the systems nature of organization and management. The following imaginary account illustrates the behavioral implications of control systems.

A Rebel in Research

Jasper Sandstone was a creative individual with advanced degrees in both business administration and chemistry. Out of school ten years now, Sandstone had worked two years for the Neutron Chemical Company. He was in charge of their research lab and had five people working for him. Sandstone was happy with his job because he liked the work and because he had a great deal of autonomy in running the lab. Except for general guidelines from the president's office, the lab was quite free to work out details of getting its work done.

Then a change occurred in top management. With it came a new system of tight, centralized control. In place of general guidelines, management issued detailed procedures that specified what would be worked on and when. And to add insult to injury, at least from Sandstone's viewpoint, an assistant to the president dropped in every day to check on compliance with the procedure.

Sandstone tried hard to work with the new system, but the close supervision finally got to him. He knew he had to protest. He made an appointment with the president, and mustering his best arguments, he protested the new system and asked for a return to the old. But it was to no avail. The president said the company just had to have more control over what the lab turned out.

Sandstone was dejected when he considered how many ideas had been converted to money-making products through research in his lab. He was sure the new system would not be nearly as productive, and he personally felt oppressed and frustrated by it. He felt it would take another kind of person to run the lab, and so, reluctantly, he wrote his letter of resignation to the president.

This illustration shows that control is a vital and complex managerial function. Management must not only decide on the type of control system to install but on the amount of control needed as well. Furthermore, these decisions must be made in consideration of their impacts on members of the organization. A control system must not subvert job satisfaction and motivation.

Summary

Control is vital if an organization is to maintain a condition of equilibrium and is to do those things that are necessary to adapt to a changing environment. To know what to do, the organization must receive a constant stream of information about internal and external events. This information is obtained via a closed-loop feedback system or via an open-loop system. In closed-loop control, information about a process or set of circumstances is fed back to the same process. The purpose of closed-loop control is to measure deviations from a set of standards in order to make necessary corrections. In open-loop control, information about one process is fed to another process. Closed-loop control corrects an error after a lag, while open-loop control seeks to prevent future errors by current action or by adjusting standards to accommodate changed conditions.

Control systems can be categorized in several ways. Precontrol, current control, and postcontrol comprise one way. Precontrol seeks to prevent deviations from standard through anticipation of problems, training, and other methods. Current control maintains adherence to standard while an activity is ongoing. Postcontrol checks activities after completion to find deviations from standard, to determine why the deviations occurred, and to suggest ways to prevent their recurrence in the future.

There are also several methods of direct control and indirect control. Direct control tends to be routine, to measure exactly deviations from standard, and to be specified by written procedures. Indirect control is applied where it is difficult to measure exactly deviations from standard, often depends on conditioning of individuals for its strength, and may result in the setting of new standards more often than direct control. Direct control includes several quantitative approaches such as are found in quality control, network systems, and performance evaluation. Indirect control can be exercised through management development and by means of operant conditioning.

Control systems are intimately tied to organization structure. Centralized control is designed to implement a centralized structure, while decentralized control characterizes a decentralized structure. The design of control systems should recognize and attempt to cope with behavioral patterns. People differ in their response to centralized and decentralized structures. Compatibility between a control system and personal values helps keep the organization functioning smoothly. This also suggests the importance of intelligent selection, placement, and training of personnel.

Management Profile

Henry Gantt

Although contemporary with Frederick Taylor and associated with the scientific management movement, Henry Gantt hewed a special niche for himself through his humanistic pursuits. As a young man, he joined Taylor in 1887 at the Midvale Steel Works and soon became enthusiastic over the concepts and practices that Taylor espoused.

But while Taylor produced a piece-work system that heavily penalized the worker for not reaching standard production, Gantt devised a system that simply provided a bonus for standard or better production and paid the regular day-rate for substandard work. This system, known as the Gantt task-and-bonus plan, is still used today.

In 1908, Gantt presented a paper, "Training Workmen in Habits of Industry and Cooperation," to the American Society of Mechanical Engineers. In the paper, he emphasized that workers were humans, not machines, and that a policy of driving workmen must give way to a policy of training and leading them. Today such a statement would be quite elementary, but at that time, management assumed no responsibility for training and did not begin to do so until the 1920s.

During World War I he devised the Gantt chart—a simple control device that portrayed production activity in relation to the time needed to complete it. The chart was adopted during the war by the United States Shipping Board and by the Ordnance Department of the Army. It has been widely used by industry ever since. The Gantt chart remains to this day its inventor's best-known contribution.

Gantt's humanitarian character was clearly expressed in his book *Organizing for Work* (1919). In it, he stressed the need for business to provide service first, regardless of who gets the profit, because the life of the community or of society depends on the service it gets. He urged industry to assume a full range of social responsibilities and to regard profit as a secondary, residual goal.

During World War I, Gantt was encouraged by the sacrifices that industry was willing to make, but industry's return to normalcy at the close of the war caused him severe disappointment. Gantt, though associated with management science, was no stereotyped efficiency expert. And though his scientific image may have been weakened during his career by his sympathy for the working man, in retrospect that same sympathy marks him as being far in advance of his associates.

Discussion Questions

1. What are the differences between open-loop and closed-loop control? What are some examples of both types of control in your own pattern of living?

2. a. In the case on "Automating the Shipping Department," was Jack mostly concerned with open-loop or closed-loop control? Give specific examples to justify your answer.
   b. Can you imagine other cases where a good control system could help reduce the negative impacts of the "domino" effect; that is, where what happens in one department affects another, which in turn may affect another, and so on?
   c. What should the company do about the five men who are no longer needed in the shipping department? Do you think the implementation of automation usually results in unneeded personnel? If so, should automation be restricted in application?

3. Describe how you would implement precontrol, current control, and postcontrol for police work; for waitresses working in a restaurant; and for growing a good corn crop.

4. How are both direct and indirect control applied in the navigation of a ship from New York to London? What are other examples of activities requiring the application of both direct and indirect control?

5. In "A Rebel in Research," we only gave Jasper Sandstone's view of the new system. If you were the new president, how would you justify the new system to Sandstone? Is there any absolute right or wrong in these cases? In other words, was Sandstone right? Was the new president right? Would it have been possible to keep Sandstone happy while still implementing tighter control under the new system?

6. If you were asked to appraise the performance of the manager of your local supermarket, how would you go about it? Be as specific as you can about the criteria you would use and the information you would need.

References

1. A. C. Filley and R. J. House, *Managerial Process and Organizational Behavior* (Glenview, Ill.: Scott, Foresman, 1969), p. 423.

2. E. E. Adam, Jr., and W. E. Scott, Jr., "The Application of Behavioral Conditioning Procedures to the Problems of Quality Control," *Academy of Management Journal*, 14 (1971): 175–193.

3. E. Dale, *Planning and Developing the Company Organization Structure* (New York: American Management Association, 1952).

4. E. B. Roberts, "Industrial Dynamics and the Design of Management Control Systems," in J. A. Litter, ed., *Organizations: Systems Control and Adaptation* (New York: John Wiley, 1969), pp. 287–303.

Suggested Readings

Anthony, R. N. *Planning and Control Systems: A Framework for Analysis.* Cambridge: Division of Research, Graduate School of Business Administration, Harvard University, 1965.

Emery, J. C. *Organizational Planning and Control Systems: Theory and Technology.* New York: Macmillan, 1969.

Jerome, W. T. III. *Executive Control—The Catalyst.* New York: John Wiley, 1961.

Rose, T. G., and Farr, D. E. *Higher Management Control.* New York: McGraw-Hill, 1957.

New City Parking Garage: Internal Control Procedures*

The New City Parking Garage is operated as a sole proprietorship by A. L. Lee. The operation is housed in a four-story building located in the downtown area of New City. Lee rents the garage building from an insurance company. The rental, as provided by the lease agreement, is a certain percentage of gross profit. Gross profit is defined in the agreement as "total garage income less the cost of gasoline sales." You have been asked by Lee to study the internal controls and procedures of the garage operation to determine whether or not it would be feasible for your firm of certified public accountants to render an opinion regarding the fairness of the gross profit reported to the insurance company for rental purposes under the lease agreement. You undertake the required study and obtain the following information.

The parking capacity of the garage is about 600 cars. All of the parking is on a transient basis; there is no parking on a contract or monthly-storage basis. A schedule of the parking rates is as follows:

First hour	$ .35
Next three hours, each	.25
Each additional hour	.15
Maximum: twenty-four hours	2.00

In addition to parking services, the garage sells gas and oil and other services (grease, wash and wax jobs). The garage handles the products of a major oil company and uses the credit card system of that company. All services except parking may be charged on the credit card.

The operation is staffed as follows:

1. Lee takes an active part in the management. He usually spends most of each day meeting customers and supervising the overall operation.
2. There are two front men whose principal duties consist of meeting customers, issuing parking tickets, and taking orders for service. Their working hours are from 7 A.M. to 6 P.M.
3. The dispatcher could probably be classified as Lee's right-hand man. His working hours are also from 7 A.M. to 6 P.M. His principal duties consist of supervising the work of about fifteen drivers and controlling the flow of traffic during the rush hours. Cars are moved between

*R. L. Grinaker, "New City Parking Garage," Copyright 1964 by the Board of Regents, University of Texas, reprinted in F. Greenwood, *Casebook for Management and Business Policy: A Systems Approach* (Scranton, Pa.: International Textbook, 1968), pp. 195–199.

floors by four elevators; during the rush hours, coordination of activity is extremely important in maintaining an efficient operation.

4. The day cashier also works from 7 A.M. to 6 P.M. He is relieved for lunch and coffee breaks by the dispatcher.

5. Because the garage is open on a 24-hour basis, a night crew is required. The night crew is comprised of a cashier and a driver. The duties of the night cashier are performed by two elderly men who work on alternate nights from 6 P.M. to 7 A.M.

6. The service department that houses the gasoline pumps and the wash and grease racks is staffed by three men. Only gasoline is sold at night. The night sales are handled by either the driver or the night cashier.

7. The bookkeeping and other clerical tasks are performed by a middle-aged woman who spends a normal eight-hour day at the garage. About half of her time is spent on garage business. The remainder of her time is spent in keeping accounts for other businesses on a contract basis. Because she is paid such a small salary, this arrangement has the approval of Lee.

The operation and flow of data are described as follows. When a car enters the garage it is met by one of the front men. A four-part, prenumbered, transient parking ticket is taken from the supply shelf and inserted in a time clock. The metering time is thus stamped on the customer's claim portion and on the back of the billing portion of the ticket. The supply shelf is replenished from the main supply of tickets maintained in an unlocked wooden cabinet located at the garage entrance.

The four-part parking ticket appears roughly as in exhibit 1. The customer is given his portion of the ticket (the claim check) and the remainder is placed on the windshield of the car. If the customer desires other services, they are checked off on a "service ticket," which is made out in an original and one carbon copy. The carbon copy is placed on the windshield of the car and the original is taken to the cashier.

If a car does not require service, it is driven directly to a parking stall. The driver leaves the first portion of the parking ticket on the car and removes the remaining two portions. He writes the location code on the second portion. He takes the second and third portions to the cashier's cage where they are filed in numerical order in a slot file.

If a car does require service, it is driven to the service department. Services are performed as follows:

1. If ordered, gasoline is put in first. The attendant prepares a listing showing the parking ticket number of each car and the gallonage and dollar amount of gasoline put in each car.

Exhibit 1 Four-part parking check

First portion—stays
on car for identification. . . . . . .   No. 6851

- - - - - - - - - - - - - - - - - - - -

Second portion—driver who
parks car records location
code on this part. Stays
with billing portion until
customer calls. Used to
locate car . . . .   No. 6851

- - - - - - - - - - - - - - - - - - - -

                                         No. 6851

                                         Charges:

Third portion—used to bill   Parking   _____
parking and other   Oil   _____
services. . . . .   Grease   _____
                                           Wash   _____
                                           Other   _____

                                           Total   _____

- - - - - - - - - - - - - - - - - - - -

Fourth portion—customer's
claim check . . . .   No. 6851

2. If other services are ordered, the car is driven to the grease and wash racks. The last man servicing the car removes the carbon copy of the service ticket and spindles it. These copies of the service tickets are destroyed at the end of each day.

When the servicing is completed and the cars are parked, the parking tickets are routed to the cashier. The cashier uses the gasoline reports prepared by the service department and the original copies of the service tickets to prepare charges. Amounts are entered on the billing portion of the parking tickets. For other than gasoline, he assumes that the services have been performed and takes the charges from the original copy of the service order. He knows, for example, how many quarts of oil would be required for an oil change on a '61 Ford. He prepares credit and charge tickets in advance for several of his regular customers; this procedure saves him time in the rush hours.

When a customer comes in to claim his car, he presents his claim check to the cashier and the following procedures are employed:

1. The matching ticket is withdrawn from the slot file and the location portion is torn off and given to the dispatcher. A driver is instructed to bring the car to the exit.
2. The billing portion of the ticket is inserted in a time clock and the "out time" is stamped on the back thereof.
3. The elapsed time is determined and the parking charge is computed.
4. The amount is written in the appropriate space on the front of the ticket.
5. If there are charges for other services, the billing is totalled.
6. If the customer pays in cash, the collection is made and the ticket is placed in a cigar box.
7. If the customer wishes to charge the services (other than parking) on his credit card, a credit card ticket is prepared (if not already completed) and the customer's signature is obtained. The services so charged are scratched off the billing section of the parking ticket. The credit card ticket is placed in the cash drawer and is handled like money.

The cashier works from a wooden cash drawer that has no registering device. At the end of a shift, the cashier removes all cash from the drawer except the permanent cash fund, which amounts to $150. The cashier leaving duty and the cashier coming on duty count out the $150 together to assure that the correct amount of the fund has been transferred to the next man. The amount of cash over and above the basic fund represents the day's receipts. The cashier does not count this money but simply places it (along with the credit card receipts and the billing portion of the parking ticket) in a cash bag, which he locks and places in the safe in the bookkeeper's office.

The next morning the bookkeeper takes the cash bags from the safe and prepares what she calls her "daily sales analysis." It is prepared as follows:

1. From amounts entered by the cashiers on the parking tickets and credit card tickets, sales are determined by type—parking, gasoline, and so on.
2. The cash is then counted and added to the total amount of the credit card receipts.
3. The total of the cash and credit card receipts is compared with the total sales, and the difference is charged or credited to "cash over and short." The bookkeeper stated that the "overs and shorts" varied from $2 to $5 a day. She also revealed that Lee gets a copy of the sales

analysis and really fusses with the cashiers if the shortage amounts to more than $5. The totals from the daily sales analysis are entered in the sales register by the following entries:

> Debit—Cash receivable from oil company
> Credit—Various sales accounts
> Debit or Credit—Cash over and short

4. No further use is made of the parking tickets, which are bundled together and filed by each day's business. To clear the files, the parking tickets are destroyed about every two or three weeks.
5. The daily deposit is prepared and taken to the bank.

The bookkeeper recaps the credit card tickets on a listing sheet provided by the oil company. She delivers these periodically to the oil company's truck driver to apply on account for product purchases.

As a part of her analysis work, the bookkeeper also checks the "overs and shorts" of gasoline pumped each day in terms of gallons. This is done by taking the gallonage of sales reported each day and by comparing the amount with the gallonage pumped according to meter readings taken from the gas pumps. The meters are read each morning at 7 A.M. by the day cashier. According to Lee, this procedure assures a "clean cutoff" of daily sales. At 7 A.M. on the first day of each month, the gasoline quantities are determined by "stick-gauging" the tanks. This is also done by the day cashier, just before he goes on duty.

The bookkeeper furnishes monthly financial statements to Lee. The sales figures reported on the last statement are as follows:

Parking	$15,750	Grease jobs	$600
Gasoline sales	4,650	Wash jobs	420
Oil sales	530	Wax jobs	75

Draft a memorandum to be presented to Mr. Lee. In your memo:

1. Criticize the system of internal control as related to "gross profit on sales." Point out specific weaknesses noted and give reasons why you consider the matters pointed out to be weaknesses. Support your reasoning by indicating specifically the errors that might occur and how they might occur.
2. Offer constructive remedial steps that might be taken to correct the weaknesses noted.

Variations on Organization Structure

8

Planning and control are important managerial activities carried out within the context of an organization structure. The nature of the structure determines, in part, how management plans and controls. Structure has a bearing on other components of the organizational system as well. In this chapter, we will discuss different types of structure. In the next chapter we will consider the relationship of structure and behavior, with particular emphasis on innovation, performance, and informal behavior.

The purpose of formal structure is to prescribe how the elements of the organizational system communicate with and relate to one another. Formal structure is like a web or network that usually moves up, down, and across, but that can also go in any other, diagonal direction. It spells out authority and responsibility relationships as well as specifies communication channels. Of course, formal structure as described on paper often does not exactly coincide with what happens in practice.

Structure, then, is static. It is like an empty house where various rooms such as the kitchen and laundry room specify areas of activity, and where hallways and stairways prescribe routes of travel. But without occupants, the house just sits. Not until a family moves in do the layout and structure of the house have any meaning. Family activity brings life to the house, and its layout helps in the delineation of authority relationships by prescribing certain constraints on and centers of activity for mother, father, children, and pets. So it is with an organization. Until people and management activate the structure, the organization is just a diagram on a piece of paper. Structure is highly important, however, for it guides activity toward the achievement of goals.

Selection of an appropriate organizational structure, therefore, is yet another critical decision that management must make. And there are numerous patterns from which to choose. We will examine the characteristics of basic structures, starting with traditional or classical structure.

The Traditional Form

Traditional structure, which is still predominant in most organizations, embraces a number of organizing principles from classical theory. We have already discussed some of these principles, such as division of labor and the scalar chain. And as we have said, a number of the principles are valid for organizations today.

To illustrate the classic approach, imagine that we are going to organize a company to manufacture and sell furniture. We know there are a number of jobs to be done—buying materials, manufacturing, selling, accounting, and so on. We begin to list all the jobs and find before long that our list has become rather long and unwieldy. What we have been doing is applying the principle of *division of labor*, but we find the need for some principle to organize our list.

Hence we apply the principle of *scalar* and *functional processes*. We separate our long list of jobs vertically, setting up scalar levels and establishing a chain of command from the top down to the bottom. We distribute authority along the chain and thereby establish a criterion for the assignment of responsibility. That is, the most responsible jobs should go near the top of the organization and the least responsible near the bottom. Also, we want to make sure that we follow another traditional principle—*that authority is commensurate with responsibility*. We must delegate sufficient authority to discharge the responsibility assigned. And we must not overlook the principle of *unity of command*. Each person in the organization should report to one boss and one boss only. This will avoid confusion and assure that the chain of command is unbroken.

Horizontal Separation

Having taken care of authority levels, we now want to separate our activities horizontally by functional process. In a business organization, we carry on as we started—dividing our activities into purchasing, manufacturing, selling, finance, engineering, accounting, and perhaps others. Having applied scalar and functional differentiation, we now feel our organization is ordered in a reasonable manner. We have departmentalized on a functional basis and assigned our many specialized jobs to the appropriate department (function) and scalar level.

But something is wrong. Thirty-five people report to the president, and only three or four report to some foremen. We have forgotten to apply the traditional principle of *span of control*. There are no absolutes on this, but we remember that top executives should have no more than eight subordinates reporting to them while foremen may have up to thirty. To correct our situation, we insert a layer of vice presidents between the president and the thirty-five subordinates and reduce the number of foremen.

After a few more minor adjustments, our organization structure is complete. We have established a logical relationship of functions, delegated authority down through the organization, assigned responsibility at the appropriate levels, and made each person accountable to one boss.

Coordination

Coordination will be achieved mainly through span of control and unity of command. Starting at the bottom, each foreman will coordinate the activites of his subordinates. He will report to his one boss, who coordinates the activities of several foremen, and so on up the line. Written policies, procedures, and rules will help assure there are no deviations from the way in which we intend the organization to be run.

We have just described a classical organization in the strictest sense. In practice, it would tend to be rigid and relatively incapable of coping with dynamic environmental conditions. Equilibrium would be difficult to maintain, and most organizations based on such a structure would probably fail in today's world. In the next section, we will describe some modifications of the strict classical model. These modifications do not remove the model from the traditional category but do enable it to better deal with changing circumstances. Figure 8–1 illustrates an organization chart for the strict classical structure.

Modified Traditional

While the strictly traditional structure may suffice for simple, routine activities, we need more complex organizational arrangements to deal with complex nonroutine events. As more products or services accumulate and as we serve larger geographical areas, functional departmentation, for example, is no longer adequate.

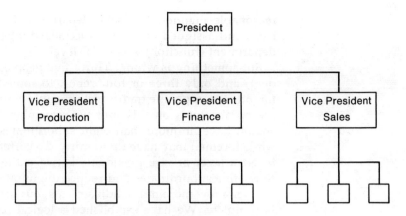

Figure 8–1 Classical structure

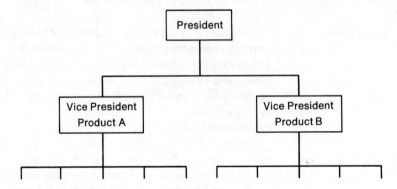

Figure 8–2a Product departmentation

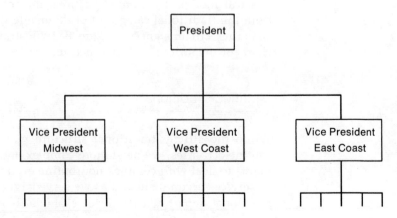

Figure 8–2b Geographic departmentation

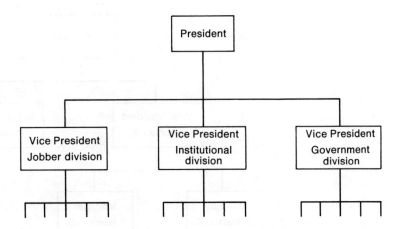

Figure 8–2c Customer departmentation

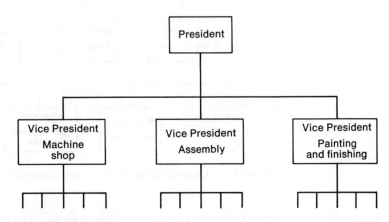

Figure 8–2d Departmentation by manufacturing process

There may be a need to departmentalize on the basis of products, geographical areas, customer, or manufacturing processes (figure 8–2a, b, c, and d).

Automobile companies typically differentiate, in part at least, by make of car, and in addition, there is often a truck division. Chain and franchise operations frequently use states or regions as a primary method of departmentalization. Some defense industries have consumer goods divisions as well as a government sales division. And manufacturing industries often find it convenient to separate their production function into departments such as raw material processing, machine operations, assembly, and painting. Today it is common to see two or more methods of differentiation in the same organization (figure 8–3).

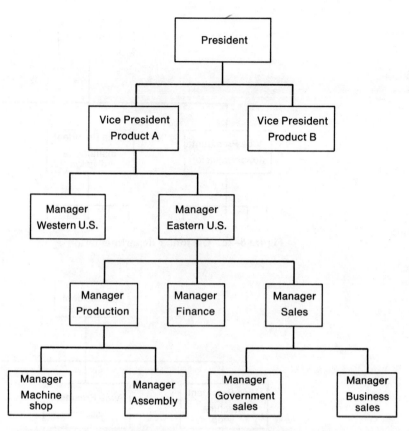

Figure 8–3 Combining methods of departmentation in the same structure

The strictly traditional form tends to be a *line* organization. Managers at all scalar levels make all decisions pertinent to their responsibilities. These decisions include decisions on hiring and firing, how to produce a product, how to sell a product, and purchases of materials and supplies. From this description it is obvious that line organization is suitable only for simple, routine activities.

As soon as events progress the least bit toward complexity, the line organization falters. This faltering occurs primarily because one man alone cannot handle all the decision problems that constantly occur. A manufacturing foreman, for example, cannot recruit, hire, train workers, and also fulfill his responsibilities on quality and quantity of production. He needs help, and he gets it—from personnel management on people problems; from purchasing on supplies and equipment; from production control on scheduling and routing the work; and from quality control on maintaining the quality of outgoing production.

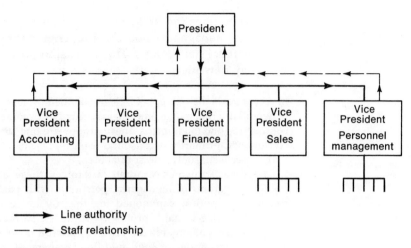

Line authority
Staff relationship

Figure 8–4 Line and staff organization

This help is called staff advice, and the organization using staff advice is called a line and staff organization (figure 8–4). Staff advice often need not be exactly followed. The personnel management staff department may recommend the hiring of a particular individual, but the final decision on hiring is usually left up to the line boss.

Distinction between Line and Staff The line, then, is that part of the organization charged with achieving the goals of the organization through their direct efforts. In a business organization, the line typically comprises the sales, finance, and production functions. Most other functions are staff, such as personnel, purchasing, engineering, and accounting. Their job is to advise the line on such matters as who to hire; what the best components to buy are; what the best sources to buy from are; what the best product design is; and what information on costs and profits pertains to current decisions.

Staff help is classified in many ways to clarify how staff works and what its place in the organization structure is. The following classification of internal staff is a reasonable one: "We can classify four basic types of internal staff aids to management: the "assistant-to"; the assistant manager; the functional staff group; and the internal trouble-shooting team. The latter has particularly been growing in popularity as company size and diversity into different product/market activities increase."[1]

The assistant-to and the assistant manager act primarily in an advisory capacity to the manager. They often may work on special assignments as a kind of internal consultant. The functional staff group is perhaps the staff group with which we are most familiar. Personnel management, purchasing, engineering, and accounting are functional staff groups. The internal trouble-shooting team is a relatively new idea:

In recent years the concept of a clearly defined professional group devoted to overall internal management consulting has become more prevalent. In contrast to functional teams, these groups are one step closer to external consultants, primarily because the team represents a mix of skills rather than expertise in only one special area.

Sometimes known as corporate task forces, these staff groups are composed of a group of managerial personnel with particular expertise in various disciplines, summoned together by top management and assigned to tackle a major problem within the corporation. They are licensed to cross all organization lines in pursuit of solutions, are typically headed by an upper or high middle management man, and report directly to top management. The group itself is temporary. . . .[2]

Blurring the Distinction   We perhaps should mention now that the distinction between line and staff is less sharply drawn in many contemporary organizations than has been true in the past. The internal trouble-shooting team, for example, may include experts from traditional line and staff classifications. And we will find later on that other variations on organization structure mix line and staff personnel to the point where these traditional terms become almost meaningless. The blurring effect may be creating a synthetically new form. Our purpose right now, however, is to point out that the line-and-staff modification of the traditional form is necessary to provide a superior way for a complex organization to deal with complex events.

Functional Authority   The chain of command or scalar process, along with unity of command, were important foundations for traditional structure. But while giving the boss total authority over his subordinates may be possible in a simple line organization, it becomes impossible given the demands of increasing size and intricacy of operation.

Concurrent with the rudimentary development of staff organization was the emergence of a type of authority that splintered unity of command, namely functional authority. Under this concept of authority, management for example, may give authority over a particular area of operations to a staff department. We indicated earlier that a manufacturing foreman may need specialized advice on his personnel, procurement, scheduling, and quality control problems. But suppose the foreman chooses to ignore advice from the quality control department and allows many products to pass inspection that otherwise would be scrapped if the standards of the quality control people were followed?

The foreman's actions would upset quality control, and eventually many others, of course. But the only immediate recourse of quality control, under the unity-of-command concept, would be an appeal to the foreman's superior. In so appealing, time might be lost and a large number of poor products shipped to customers. Therefore, management may logically conclude that in order to assure the production and shipment of a uniform-quality product, quality control should be given the authority to insist that standards be met and to take appropriate corrective action when necessary. Thus management delegates functional authority in this specific area to quality control and specifically denies to foremen the authority to tinker with quality control methods without prior approval.

Coordination

Traditional structure depended on set plans and procedures, on the chain of command, and on limited spans of control to effect coordination. This would work as long as activities were uncomplicated and as long as everyone did as they were told. But this sort of hierarchical coordination (control) system quickly breaks down under the pressure of unpredictable human behavior.

One way to combat the dysfunctional consequences of behavior on coordination is to strengthen the control system, incorporating a large number of feedback loops and building a broad system of corrective responses. But strengthening control this way just layers the organization with more networks of activity. The overload may lead to as many problems as the lack of coordination that initially sparked such a control system.

To get effective coordination, we must go beyond structural specification and advocate unifying forces such as doctrine, spirit, and morale. "This is the voluntary coordination that occurs when people know the goal of the organization, want to attain it, and know what has to be done. . . . The desirability of *esprit de corps* from which this spontaneous coordination springs has been frequently cited. The ways to attain it are . . . frequently conspicuous by their absence. . . . A key step is to inculcate the organization members with the organization purpose and values and, in this way, make the goals of all organization members the same."[3]

Through the years, management has strived hard to match the need for coordination with effective methods of achieving it. But much remains to be done. Voluntary cooperation is the most powerful method of achieving coordination, but its application is often disappointing. We will have more to say about motivating cooperation in later chapters.

Some Structural Aspects of Coordination   The method of horizontal differentiation or departmentation has an important bearing on the need for coordinative effort. If overall departmentation is by function, there will be a great need for coordination among sales, manufacturing, and purchasing. These functions are dependent upon one another. For example, purchasing has to assure a supply of raw materials and other supplies before manufacturing can begin. And manufacturing must supply products or the definite promise of products before the sales department can sell.

If an organization is departmentalized on a product basis (by automobiles and appliances, for example), these departments would be relatively independent of each other and require little coordinative effort. But within each product division, the same requirements for coordination may exist as before with respect to purchasing, manufacturing, and sales.

The amount of coordination needed varies considerably within a given organization. Overall coordination can be extremely difficult or relatively simple, depending on the overall method of departmentation. Within a given department, variations will also occur. Some manufacturing processes, for example, require a high degree of coordination among dependent processes. In others, the processes are relatively independent. It may also be possible to build up buffer inventories between processes to ease the coordination problem.

Finally, the traditional form makes coordination difficult under most circumstances. Consider our purchasing–manufacturing–sales illustration. In classical structure, coordination requires plans to be implemented through the chain of command with no provision for horizontal communication at the lower levels of the organization. Hence communication and coordination efforts constantly travel up and down the chain of command, resulting in lost time and excessive cost.

In practice, informal horizontal communication facilitates the relationship between hierarchy and process. The foreman of the assembly department talks directly to the foreman of the machining department, and they coordinate their work on a one-to-one basis. The production boss talks directly to the purchasing agent. Informal, direct communication usually saves a great amount of time and yields superior coordination. Some organizations have built horizontal communication channels into their formal structure.

In chapter 7, we discussed aspects of decentralized and centralized control, including some behavioral consequences of each control method. These variations in control application are usually associated with similar variations in structure. For example, it makes sense to administer decentralized control through a decentralized structure and centralized control through a centralized structure.

In converting a·centralized structure to a decentralized one, the usual procedure is to reduce the number of levels and extend the span of control (figures 8–5a and b). The advantages and disadvantages of the decentralized structure in conjunction with decentralized control have already been noted in chapter 7. It is worth repeating, however, that as a modification of the traditional centralized form, the decentralized structure tends to put decision making at the point of application. The combination of greater autonomy at lower levels and a more intimate knowledge of local

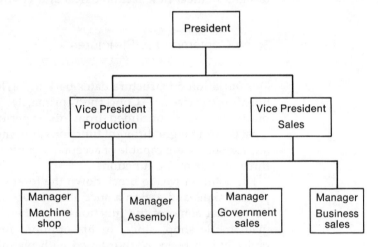

Figure 8–5a Centralized structure

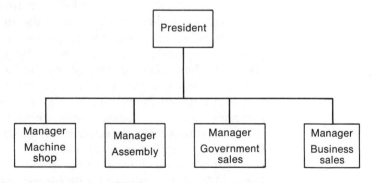

Figure 8–5b Decentralized structure

conditions is supposed to, and often does, yield better decisions. But there is a danger of too much parochialism in decentralized decisions, resulting in excessive suboptimization for the total organization. This potential problem should be prevented in the design of control and coordination systems for the decentralized structure. And the voluntary approach to cooperative effort probably has a better chance of success in the decentralized structure than the centralized simply through the recognition of its necessity for effective organizational operation.

We will consider additional behavioral consequences of the decentralized structure in the next chapter. For now, we will treat it as simply one more modification of the strictly traditional form of organization. In the next section, we will learn of some other contemporary organization structures. These other structures are more than modifications; they are advances into new organization designs to meet new technological and environmental demands.

Some Contemporary Structures

One variation on structure dates back to Taylor's time—the functional organization. Concerned primarily with machine-shop practice, Taylor concluded from his experience that a foreman must perform eight different functions and, most importantly, that few foremen were capable of acceptable performance on more than three or four of the functions.

His solution was to break down the foreman's job into its component skills and assign a specialist to each of them. He also believed that some of the functions were better done in the office than in the shop, since, in his opinion, foremen and workers typically had been overburdened with planning and scheduling. Specialists in the office were designated time-and-cost clerk, instruction card clerk, work-order and route clerk, and disciplinarian; specialists in the shop were designated gang boss, speed boss, repair boss, and inspector (figure 8–6). Under the plan, each specialist foreman was in charge of all workers with respect to the functional activity assigned to him as foreman.

A functional structure has several advantages: high specialization and detailed knowledge of a given function, separation of planning and operations, better technical supervision, and quicker training for prospective foremen. The main disadvantage is confusion—authority so diffused that workers are never quite sure whom to consult for all those in-between problems; foremen tend to blame one another for problems; and the necessary coop-

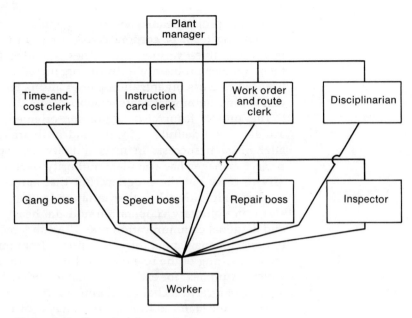

Figure 8–6 Functional organization structure

eration among foremen (or among any managers in a functional structure) may be seriously disturbed as personal differences develop.

Although in practice Taylor's new plan did not work well and was largely abandoned by 1920, his ideas on functional specialization contributed to the later development of staff specialists in line-and-staff organizations. Since Taylor's time, much planning work has been taken away from the foreman, so there has been less need for the sort of specialization he envisioned at the foreman level.

The Matrix Organization

The scalar and functional principles in classical theory established a basis for the job-task hierarchy. This means that all jobs in an organization are neatly arranged by scalar level and functional area. It is a logical arrangement, with jobs at or near the top of the hierarchy generally requiring more planning and less doing, while jobs at the bottom entail more doing and less planning. With appropriate spans of control, the typical pyramidal shape develops.

The matrix form of organization represents a major departure from traditional form and particularly from the job-task hierarchy. The antecedent of the matrix organization is the project team. Used predominantly in industry for military and aerospace projects, the project-team concept is similar to a staff-type troubleshooting team or corporate task force. In the latter, management assembles various disciplines into one team and assigns them a major problem within the organization. The staff team is licensed to cross organizational lines and is temporary in nature, disbanding upon goal achievement.

The project team also is mission-oriented, being set up to achieve some definite objective and ordinarily being disbanded after mission success. In most military and space projects, the project manager has complete authority over all activities necessary to carry out the program. But that authority usually is not applied in traditional, authoritarian style, the manager relying instead on voluntary cooperation and the heavy use of horizontal and diagonal communication lines. "A fundamental characteristic of project management differentiating it from traditional theory is the structuring of the role relationships within the project organization. A project, for example, is not generally bound by the constraints of a vertical chain of command, functional separation, distinct line and staff activities, and span of control. Instead, a project organization tends to revolve around the fluid interaction of highly skilled personnel at various organizational levels."[4]

But though the project team is a specialized, task-oriented entity, it does not exist completely apart from the traditional structure of the organization. The project must report to a designated boss in the parent organization (figure 8–7).

The Evolutionary Matrix Form The matrix organization evolved out of the project concept. Belief in the effective use of talented people supports a fluid organization "built around an array of

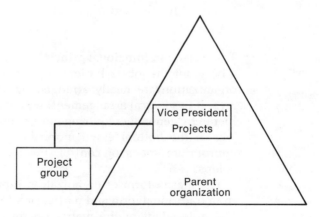

Figure 8–7 Project organization

specific projects."[5] Today it is recognized that many organizations contain a matrix or pattern of differentiated task units that can be systematically structured on a project basis.

Not all project managers in a matrix organization have complete authority over the activities necessary to mission accomplishment, however. Instead, depending on the technology and the personnel involved, some project managers have relatively little authority, while others have complete authority.[6] Likewise, some project groups are quite dependent on the parent organization and have little autonomy while other groups have almost complete autonomy.

Let us look at figure 8–8. The project group in the number one position would confront a technology requiring only fairly routine, repetitive work. Technicians would staff the group, and they would be primarily oriented to the parent organization for direction, control, and reward. In the number four position, on the other hand, the technology would be sufficiently sophisticated so that tasks would be nonrepetitive and would require creativity and independent analysis. Highly trained professionals would staff group four and would have considerable autonomy.

There is a substantial amount of empirical research that tends to support the foregoing theoretical model for matrix organizations.[7] Giving the model a counterpoint in reality, the following imaginary incident may help explain how it works.

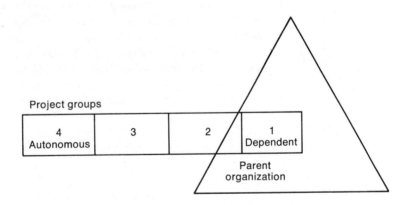

Figure 8–8 Classification of project groups in terms of autonomy from parent organization*

*Adapted from F. A. Shull, Jr., A. L. Delbecq, and L. L. Cummings, *Organizational Decision Making* (New York: McGraw-Hill, 1970), p. 191.

Barry Slade was a highly trained market researcher for a large infants' clothing manufacturer. Public and governmental pressure had forced the firm to begin developing nonflammable infants' wear. Slade was put in charge of the project and experts from throughout the company were temporarily assigned to him. These experts included chemists, fashion designers, production experts, and other market researchers.

Slade was enthusiastic. He believed wholeheartedly in the project, and, in addition, he felt this was a wonderful opportunity to display his leadership talents. Trouble developed for him quickly, however. The general sales manager, who was Slade's immediate point of contact with the parent organization, was specifying for Slade exactly how the work was to be done and was requiring that Barry report to him one or more times a day on how things were going.

The personnel in the project soon became restive. Every time one or more of them started working on a new idea, Slade would have to check it out with the sales manager. Finally, it seemed his job became one of just making sure everyone was working on his assignment. There was a general loss of interest, and the whole project seemed to bog down.

Slade was desperate. When a top-flight fashion designer said she wanted to go back to her regular job, Slade decided that action was imperative. He appealed to the general sales manager to allow the project to run its own show. Disappointed with results up to that point, the sales manager decided anything was worth a try.

With Slade coordinating, and everyone participating in the generation of ideas and decision making, the project soon got off the ground. Everyone relaxed, and Slade was immensely pleased with the enthusiastic spirit of cooperation. He felt that if he and the project had been given this degree of autonomy from the beginning, there never would have been any problems.

New Requirements

There are, of course, a number of problems that may be coincident with the development of new organizational designs:

The changing concepts in the management area of organization will require managers and operating personnel to become educated and trained for work experience in the developing organizational designs. Otherwise, they may suffer frustrations, emotional disturbances, and loss of motivation. Working in an organization characterized by change as projects are started and completed continuously is not as secure as performing a continuing function in a more stabilized work flow situation. Furthermore, can you visualize the plight of a manager if he finds himself employed in a matrix type organization and the knowledge gained from his experience only exposed him to a traditional line and staff organization? He would experience a disadvantage in competition with others comparable to being given a problem requiring calculus when his knowledge was limited to arithmetic.[8]

In addition, the project manager is in a *boundary* or *marginal* position, meaning that he is on the margin or boundary between the project group and the parent organization. Often there may be a third party involved, such as the government, which may have awarded a contract to the parent organization. As you may imagine, a boundary position can be full of frustrating and difficult situations. We will consider more of these problems in the next chapter on structure and behavior.

Free-Form Organizations

A number of utopian societies in the past have operated with a free-form type of organization design. Some communal groups today are free-form. In its purest state, a free-form organization has no leaders, no scalar chain, no span of control, and no evidence whatsoever of traditional precepts. Everyone is expected to work and to cooperate in a joint effort to determine what must be done and when. Free-form organizations hold the belief that everyone can generate and contribute ideas to the organization. Therefore, anyone who aggressively seeks to assert a leadership role defies a basic value. There must be a great deal of good faith on the part of each member, and thus it is perhaps not surprising that the failure rate is high. Although a business organization in free-form style is hard to find, there is a more practical structural approach that has great appeal in a competitive world. This structural form is the organic model.

The Organic Model If you were to take a project group as we have described it and if you were to expand the group to compose an entire organization, you would have a rough approximation of the organic form. The organic form is the opposite of the traditional or mechanistic form. Where the latter coordinates through the scalar process, the organic form integrates by continual readjustment through the interactions of members. Where the traditional organization operates under instructions and decisions from superiors, the organic depends on communicated information and advice.[9]

The organic form is fluid in its approach. Each organizational member has a commitment to the whole task, not just to a small part of it. A high value is placed on lateral and diagonal interaction. There is a general recognition that any part of the organization may temporarily control all activities, as when a mailing deadline requires everyone's attention and labor. As with the most fully autonomous project group, the successful functioning of this type of organization requires personnel who are mature professionals interested primarily in the task rather than in their own personal advancement.

Committee Structure   Most organizations have committees for various purposes. These purposes include decision making, coordinating, encouraging information flow, education, recommending action, generating ideas, and others.[10] These purposes do not distinguish one organization from another in any definitive way, however. Here we are interested in those organizations that use committees predominantly for decision making and that depend on committees for operational success.

Universities closely approach the committee form. From the department level on up to the highest administrative strata, committees make many important policy and operating decisions. The university is not representative of a pure committee form, since individual administrators also make many operating decisions. Some voluntary and/or nonprofit organizations, except for an executive secretary, may most closely approximate the pure form.

The variety of organization structures we have been discussing may serve to show that, while the modified traditional form may still be the most popular way to structure an organization, other forms may be more suitable in particular situations. It is extremely important for management to know how to structure an organization under various conditions. Accordingly, our next concern will be those factors that affect the way in which we might structure an organization.

Determinants of Design

While the form of an organization may constantly undergo minor changes in response to environmental pressures, major structural changes probably occur rather infrequently. Major decisions on structure are made at the initiation of an organization and at those times when a major change is needed to accommodate new and different circumstances.

One major determinant of structure is organizational purpose. If the initial reason for organizing is to handle a number of activities in a very routine fashion, a traditional bureaucratic form may be appropriate. If innovation and fluid development are important, a matrix or organic form may be best. As purposes are modified throughout an organization's life, structure should be modified in accordance with the new or changed goals. Relating form to purpose is an application of the contingency approach to organization design. That is, design is contingent upon a number of identifiable factors. While this approach may use a classical form, it differs from the classical approach. The classical approach would tend to structure an organization according to classical principles regardless of purpose. The contingency approach, then, advocates flexibility in form by adjusting form to changing circumstances.

We will consider only a few of the factors that can influence design. One of the most important is technology, which can have a crucial impact on organization structure.

Technology and Structure

Technology influences the structure of component parts of an organizational system as well as the structure of the total organization. At the operating level of a manufacturing plant, for example, production technology demands great coordination among two or more manufacturing sections. An automobile assembly line that produces a finished car requires intricate coordination of parts supply, flow of work, and storage or removal of the finished product. This coordination must be built into the structure of the production component of the company.

On the other hand, the production of various kinds of fasteners may require relatively little coordination among departments. One department may produce bolts and nuts, a second department may produce rivets, and a third may produce screws. Since each department produces a finished product, the need for coordination would be minimal. This, too, should be reflected in the structure of the manufacturing division of the company.

A technological advance can seriously affect structural requirements. The introduction of numerically-controlled machine tools has had a continuing impact on factory organization. Numerical control uses punched tape or a direct computer hookup to instruct a complex machine tool through many operations. The machine tool combines several operations that formerly required a separate machine for each operation.

Hence you have what is called a machining center in one machine. A numerical control system requires at least one new job—someone to program the tape. And it modifies several traditional jobs—such as setup, production control, and quality control. A numerical control installation often may suggest that structural changes should be made. A linear design, where the production process uses several machines in a row, may be changed to a modular design, where the numerical control machine is used as a focal point.[11] This change in structure should recognize the modifications of jobs as well as the changes in work flow, communication channels, and authority relationships that occur with numerical control.

Other technological advances can have similar impacts on an organization and may also require structural changes. Unfortunately, formal changes in design often do not take place when they should, because there is too much inertia, ignorance, or simply faith in the old structure. When formal structure does not adapt, informal structure springs up to handle the new requirements. We will discuss this further in the next chapter.

Technology and the Total Organization While the impact of technology may be most apparent on a particular component of the organization system, it also affects the structure as a whole. Joan Woodward has completed a study of 100 companies in England, the results from which provided persuasive evidence that technology influences structure.[12] She identified three basic types of production systems in the study: (1) unit and small-batch systems, (2) large-batch, assembly, and mass-production systems; and (3) continuous process (oil refinery systems).

The research disclosed that companies with similar production systems had similar organizational structures, despite the variety of products involved. Chain of command grew longer and span of control grew wider as one moved from the unit and small-batch type of production to the continous process type. The most successful companies in each type of process were those closest to the average span for such variables.

Other variables were included in the study, of course, but the most important point is that Woodward made a most significant contribution to the study of organizations by suggesting a way to classify organizations. Recognizing the convergence of technological and structural types allows differentiation among organizations and thereby aids in many analytical studies. The clear identification of a technical function in organizations, as distinguished from a social function, allows superior analysis. And analysis permits prescription: a mass-production technology suggests an optimal structure that has a medium-length chain of command and span of control.

Environment and Structure

Environmental forces induce certain structural patterns at the onset of an organization's life. They also force subsequent adaptive changes. An organization may be set up to produce and sell some rather mundane product—paper toweling, for example. The company schedules advertising, establishes manufacturing methods, and may eventually gain a respectable share of the market. Modified traditional structure develops, and activities fall into a relatively unruffled routine.

Suddenly, a powerful company enters the same field and initiates an attempt to dominate the market. The powerful company dramatically changes the environment. The original company must quickly change or its market could be lost. There may be new advertising campaigns, new product developments, desperate attempts to differentiate the present product, and vigorous efforts to reduce manufacturing costs.

In short, the organization must change from a mechanistic structure to an organic one—at least in part—in order to innovate more effectively and to save itself. The company may need additional coordinative devices such as liaison groups and special task forces.[13] A matrix type of design might evolve. It is not our purpose to specify the type of structure needed but rather to show the impact an environmental change can have on the organization as an open system. The environmental dynamics are not always so dramatic, but response, nonetheless, must be made. Management must be alert to structural changes required by the environment.

Rationality and Structure

The last determinant of structure we shall consider is rationality. James Thompson has developed several applications of rationality in structure.[14] We will discuss only one. Thompson, a noted management analyst, suggests that the complexity of a structure, the number and variety of its units, will reflect the complexity of the environment. The more difficult the environment, the more important it is to assign a small portion of it to one unit.

To illustrate: a general hospital confronts a heterogeneous task environment; that is, the hospital must perform a number of different jobs for its clientele. These jobs include obstetrical care, surgery, handling contagious diseases, emergency aid, and others. The rational approach for the hospital is to establish units or divisions to take care of similar cases or homogeneous segments of the task environment. The obstetrics ward accepts only obstetrics cases, surgery only surgery, and so on.

The hospital illustration, of course, is simple, and is nothing more than an application of the traditional functional principle. Nonetheless, it is a rational attempt to structure an organization into homogeneous units in order to deal effectively with a heterogeneous, complex task environment. From this viewpoint (rationality), one can go on, as Thompson does, to examine other relationships between rationality and structure—a number of which do not necessarily identify with traditional and/or bureaucratic principles.

Team at the Top

The top managerial level in most organizations typically permits leadership by only one individual, who usually carries the title of president. Most organizations expect this one man to represent them at many external affairs of a public relations and public service nature as well as to make the planning and coordinating decisions necessary to survival and growth. In one instance, a chief executive spent 40 percent of his time on speechmaking, plant visits, and public-service activities, leaving him little more than half his time to run the company.

In response to this situation, some companies now have a plural executive or executive team, and other companies are carefully considering the team concept. Among companies using the executive team are R. H. Macy, E. I. du Pont de Nemours, and Standard Oil. The growing impact of new technology, the increasingly diversified products of many companies, and the international scope of operations are reasons encouraging a trend to executive groups.[15]

Executive groups are usually small (from three to seven members). They are deeply involved in such matters as resource allocation, setting goals, establishing policy, evaluating performance, and deciding broad questions of organization structure. An executive team does not concern itself with routine operating problems.

Team Leadership Members of an executive team are all equal in their responsibility and authority within the group. It is a fact of life, however, that someone must exert enough leadership so the team functions effectively. This represents one of the problems of the team-at-the-top concept. It is a rather short step from appropriate leadership to inappropriate domination. Hence the person who is the leader must recognize the delicacy of his position and be capable of behavior that will realize the potential of the team rather than turn it into a one-man show.

Selecting team members is a major problem. Executives are aggressive and have a culturally conditioned or natural inclination to make their own decisions. These types may be hard to fit into a team. On the other hand, there are executives who do not like to make decisions, who procrastinate, and who welcome the split responsibility of a committee decision. These types may not contribute much to an executive team.

The ideal team-at-the-top member is a person willing and able to make individual decisions of organizational importance and also willing to subordinate himself to the group decision-making process. Such a person is rare, and few organizations have enough of these individuals to make a team. Therefore, the team-at-the-top is still an uncommon form of organizational government. Nonetheless, it has potential as well as a record of success with a few substantial companies.

The Board of Directors

The typical board of directors is not a team-at-the-top like the kind we have just described. Boards probably originated in Germany in the fifteenth century, when mining companies began selling shares to people in distant cities. Investors found it difficult to attend company meetings and appointed agents to look after their interests. Today, many critics feel that a board of directors is an anachronism. Corporate law today charges the board with managing a company for the stockholders. While directors rarely perform an active managerial role, they are supposed to act in a trustee relationship to stockholders. In this capacity, they presumably help to establish basic policy, engage in long-range planning, and exercise control over those charged with active management. Directors can be outsiders, or they may be appointed from the inside of the company.

But there may be quite a gulf between what a board of directors are supposed to do and what they actually do. In one study involving conversations with many executives, it was found that directors rarely establish basic objectives and policy.[16] Further, most outside directors do not have time to gather the type of information needed to ask the discerning questions a director is supposed to ask. And inside directors ask few questions because of the vulnerability of their positions.

And yet, according to rulings from state courts, a director should exercise the same degree of care that the ordinary "prudent businessman" would show in similar situations. This care includes keeping informed. The director will not be held liable for honest mistakes in judgment, but he may be held accountable for carelessness and outright negligence.

Given the record of difficulties and failures in large organizations, it seems apparent there are problems with the board-of-directors concept. Perhaps we need new laws to better define the legal responsibilities of directors. We also may need to look for other alternatives. For if business does not come up with alternatives, someone else in the community will.

Organizational Size

Is there a limit to organizational growth? Is there some point at which structure collapses under increasing complexity? Are there traditional cultural values which should be observed with respect to size? These questions are difficult to answer. On the practical side, studies indicate that as organizations grow larger and more complex, coordination becomes more difficult.[17] This in turn leads to more administrative personnel. With a high degree of complexity, management leans more heavily on impersonal coordinating mechanisms such as formal rules and procedures.

What is the end effect? On the one hand, we observe a successful giant—General Motors. On the other hand, we have observed a failure—Penn-Central Railroad. The lesson: there can be no absolute generalization about the effects of size and complexity on the ability of an organization to survive. Too many other factors are involved.

There are advantages to size. An organization builds momentum that can assure survival and even relative success for long periods of time. TWA operated successfully from about 1948 to 1962 without effective leadership, a condition that probably would have spelled disaster for most small companies. Big companies are better able to use the tools of management science since there often are built-in costs in decision-theory analysis that small companies cannot afford. Sheer size and financial resources permit a more sophisticated technology and, as a result, greater productivity and lower costs. It is not all one-sided, however. Small companies can move faster—they are more flexible. In many operations not involving massive or sophisticated technology, small companies can be more efficient. Many people prefer the more personal atmosphere of a small outfit. And on the international scene, time-lags in decision making on the part of large, multinational firms allow smaller and largely domestically oriented companies to remain competitive.[18] Furthermore, in the United States, there is a cultural bias in favor of small business. The lure of going into one's own business is as strong today as it has even been. Our national law forbids monopolies in restraint of trade, giving entrepreneurs at least the right of entry into a competitive market.

No One Best Structure

We have described an organization as an open system with various subsystems or component parts that needed to be integrated or linked together. Organization structure and the job-task hierarchy form one of the bases for the type of interaction that links the parts of an organization and tends to hold it together. The linking process yields a centripetal force, a homeostatic force that helps achieve organizational balance by keeping activities goal-oriented. "The formal structure of an organization represents as closely as possible the deliberate intention of its framers for the processes of interaction that will take place among its members. In the typical work organization this takes the form of a definition of task specialties, and their arrangement in levels of authority with clearly defined lines of communication from one level to the next."[19]

Structure and the job-task hierarchy prescribe authority lines and channels of communication. These prescriptions are not always followed; but in the traditional and modified traditional organizations, structure, hierarchy, and functional definition form an important foundation for integration. Management in a mechanistic organization depends heavily on this foundation for direction through effective operation of the exception principle.

An organization oriented toward free-form requires other means to link its component parts. A high degree of goal recognition becomes critical for all members. Informal, sometimes temporary, social groupings and patterns of influence comprise a portion of the ways by which free-form linking occurs. Between these two antithetical structures are many variations. But there probably is no one "best" organizational structure or managerial orientation. Hence there is no standard linking process based on structure and job-task hierarchy that can be copied out of a manual and applied. Each organization has a unique set of attributes that must be recognized in designing an appropriate structure. Structure must always be custom-fitted to purpose.

Summary

Structure is derived from and must change with the goals of an organization. The traditional form of structure is characterized by classical principles: division of labor, scalar and functional processes, unity of command, and span of control. Coordination is achieved largely through span of control and unity of command.

The modified traditional form uses bases for departmentation such as products, geographic areas, customers, and manufacturing processes, as well as the traditional base of function. In addition, staff advice has developed in the modified form to help the line achieve the goals of the organization. Originally formalized into functional groups such as personnel management, staff work is being increasingly accomplished through task forces that mobilize persons from throughout the organization to tackle some major problem. Functional staff groups continue to handle routine affairs, however, and often exercise some degree of functional authority in their area of expertise over line personnel.

The matrix organization recognizes differentiated task units by structuring them into distinct project groups. The group has a goal, and instead of following traditional principles, the project group tends to revolve around the fluid interaction of highly skilled personnel at various organizational levels. Project groups are not independent of the parent organization but do vary in the degree of autonomy enjoyed.

Of the contemporary organizations, the matrix organization probably is the best known. It may be considered as a representation of free-form organization. Other variations on structure include the functional organization and the committee structure. The new organizational forms frequently pose problems of adjustment for the individual accustomed to traditional methods.

There are many determinants of organization structure. Technology, rationality, and environment are three major determinants. An automobile assembly plant, for example, is organized differently from an oil refinery according to differences in technology. A hospital organizes its departments in a rational way to serve a community presenting many different health problems. And adapting to changing market conditions in the environment may force the restructuring of an organization.

A special form of managerial organization is the plural executive, often called a team-at-the-top. A principal cause for the emergence of this concept is the limited time one man can give to the varied demands made upon the chief executive of a complex organization. A board of directors is not a team-at-the-top, and is rather anachronistic today, given its limited role.

Finally, we observed that there apparently are no structural limits on organization size nor is there any one best structure. Structure helps to link the various components and activities of an organization and must be tailored to each particular situation.

Management Profile

Alfred P. Sloan

If one were to pick the outstanding businessman of the first half of this century, one might well choose Alfred P. Sloan. Sloan was the man who guided General Motors for over thirty years, starting in 1923, and who was instrumental in making GM the giant it is today. He was born and raised in Brooklyn, graduated from the Massachusetts Institute of Technology, and got his first regular job with the Hyatt Roller Bearing Company in 1895. The company at that time was shaky. It was trying to market a new kind of flexible bearing, but orders were few and far between.

Fearing the worst, Sloan left Hyatt and joined another new company trying to develop refrigeration equipment. This company was moderately successful. But then Sloan was offered an opportunity to buy into Hyatt. Borrowing from his father and friends, he bought a controlling interest and became Hyatt's general manager. He began by selling bearings to some of the many auto companies that had started up at that time.

In 1900, Hyatt got its first big order from the Olds Motor Works—120 bearings. Then Cadillac bought bearings and Ford became a customer. Hyatt was on its way. By 1915, the firm was firmly established.

In the meantime, the embryo of General Motors was developing. Will Durant had started the Buick Motor Company around 1908 and soon added Olds and scores of other companies. Durant overextended General Motors financially, however, and he was forced to quit. Then, in 1912, he started Chevrolet, and through shrewd trading of stock, he again gained control of General Motors.

In 1917, Durant called Sloan and asked if Sloan would sell the Hyatt Company. After some deliberation, Sloan agreed, and the Hyatt Company became United Motors, a subsidiary of GM, with Sloan as president. By 1920, GM was again in deep trouble. This time the financial empire of the du Pont family bailed out the company, taking in return 2,500,000 shares of GM stock.

In 1923, Sloan was named president of GM, replacing Durant. Durant had been a benevolent dictator, buying companies and spending millions on the basis of instant judgments. Sloan, on the contrary, was a careful and systematic executive. He set about restructuring GM in the decentralized style that it still maintains today. As part of the restructuring effort, he devised an organization chart that featured a group executive for coordinating purposes. Each member of this team headed up an operating team and reported directly to Sloan.

Sloan also organized a general staff to offer functional advice to himself and to the operating divisions. The operating divisions were relatively autonomous; members of the general staff had no direct authority in the activities of the operating divisions. Finally, Sloan heavily emphasized management development. He believed in raising his own executives and paying them well for success.

For decades Sloan reigned as chief executive of General Motors. He could take justifiable pride in his organization. Not a glamorous figure like Ford or Durant, Sloan, perhaps more than any other man, proved that large organizations are manageable. The example he set in restructuring General Motors has served as a model for other corporations, which have followed suit by carefully tailoring structure to their own size and purposes.

Discussion Questions

1. Design a basic, traditional organization structure for a shoe store; a hospital; an insurance company. In your design efforts, be sure to consider division of labor, scalar and functional processes, unity of command, and span of control.

2. Organizations today need much expert advice from lawyers, psychologists, engineers, and so on. What danger can you see in an organization becoming overloaded with staff personnel? What can be done to help assure a proper balance between line and staff people?

3. In what ways is the coordination required of a football team similar to that required of a business organization? In what ways is the coordination different? What could a business executive learn from the methods a football coach might use to motivate coordination?

4. In the case of "The Mismatch," why did the granting of greater autonomy to Barry Slade's project group make such a difference in its operation? What kind of person is required to handle a large amount of autonomy in the work situation?

5. Why do you suppose the sales manager in "The Mismatch" initially kept a close check on Barry Slade and his project? Could this problem involving the sales manager and the project director have been prevented? How?

6. Is the free-form organization more in harmony with current cultural values? Do you predict a bright future for free-form structure or do you foresee a return to more traditional designs? Why?

7. Which factor do you think is the most important in the determination of organization structure: technology, environment, or rationality? Explain your answer, and illustrate with examples.

8. Given a choice, would you rather be the president of a company and completely responsible for results or would you rather be a member of a three-person "team-at-the-top?" Why?

9. Do you think some organizations today are too big? If so, how would you restrict size? And how big should organizations be allowed to grow? What reasons can you give for your judgment?

References

1. J. O. Vance, "The Future Role of Staff in a Changing Corporate Environment," *Academy of Management Proceedings* (San Diego: Academy of Management, 1970), pp. 303–313.

2. *Ibid.*, p. 305.

3. J. A. Litterer, *Organizations: Structure and Behavior* (New York: John Wiley, 1969), p. 69.

4. D. L. Wilemon and J. P. Cicero, "The Project Manager—Anomalies and Ambiguities," *Academy of Management Journal*, 13 (1970): 269–282.

5. J. F. Mee, "Changing Concepts in Management," *The Student Chapter News* (Society for Advancement of Management), 2 (1966): 5.

6. *See* F. A. Shull, Jr., A. L. Delbecq, and L. L. Cummings, *Organizational Decision Making* (New York: McGraw-Hill, 1970), pp. 171–226, for an extended discussion of project managerial authority.

7. *Ibid.*

8. Mee, p. 5.

9. C. J. Haberstroh, J. A. Baring, and W. C. Mudgett, *Organizing for Innovation* (Cleveland: Case Institute of Technology, 1967), p. 3.

10. A. C. Filley and R. J. House, *Managerial Process and Organizational Behavior* (Glenview, Ill.: Scott, Foresman, 1969), pp. 321–354.

11. E. F. Lundgren, "A Modular Organization Structure for Numerical Control," *Proceedings of the Midwest Academy of Management* (Madison, Wis.: The University of Wisconsin, 1968), pp. 146–162.

12. J. Woodward, *Industrial Organization* (London: Oxford University Press, 1955), pp. 50–82.

13. J. Galbraith, "Environmental and Technological Determinants of Organizational Design," in J. W. Lorsch and P. R. Lawrence, eds., *Studies in Organization Design* (Georgetown, Ont.: Irwin-Dorsey, 1970), pp. 113–139.

14. J. D. Thompson, *Organizations in Action* (New York: McGraw-Hill, 1967), pp. 66–82.

15. D. R. Daniel, "Team at the Top," *Harvard Business Review*, 43 (1965): 74–82.

16. M. L. Mace, *Directors: Myth and Reality* (Cambridge, Mass.: Harvard Business School, 1971), pp. 185–188.

17. S. R. Klatzky, "Relationship of Organizational Size to Complexity and Coordination," *Administrative Science Quarterly*, 15 (1970): 428–438.

18. H. Schollhammer, "Organization Structures of Multinational Corporations," *Academy of Management Journal*, 14 (1971): 345–365.

19. J. Pfiffner and F. Sherwood, *Administrative Organization* (Englewood Cliffs, N.J.: Prentice-Hall, 1960), p. 18.

Suggested Readings

Lorsch, J. W., and Lawrence, P. R. *Studies in Organization Design.* Georgetown, Ont.: Irwin-Dorsey, 1970.

Thompson, J. D. *Organizations in Action.* New York: McGraw-Hill, 1967.

Woodward, J. *Industrial Organization.* London: Oxford University Press, 1965.

Structure and Behavior

9

Having learned something about the determination of organization structure and of the different types of structure, we are now going to study the interactions between structure and people. For many years, under classical theory, the idea that structure could influence behavior was largely ignored. Modern theory, however, fully recognizes this phenomenon and further asserts that people have a continuing impact on the development of organization structure. In this chapter, we will pursue these concepts, thus adding to the store of knowledge required for effective decision making. First we will delve into some of the problems arising in the bureaucratic and traditional types of structure.

Dysfunctions of Bureaucracy

We have distinguished between the mechanistic and organic forms of organization, noting that the mechanistic form is oriented to performance of routine activity, while the organic form is best suited to innovative and problem-solving effort. Both types of organizations have their place. There are, however, negative aspects to any organizational form. Let us first consider bureaucracy.

Robert Merton points out some of bureaucracy's shortcomings.[1] He observes that bureaucratic rules and procedures often result in "trained incapacity." An individual may develop skills and abilities in a specialized area over a period of time and may be consistently successful in their application. But if conditions change, an appropriate response literally may be beyond the capacity of the individual. His training and experience, repeated many times over, render him helpless.

Associated with the incapacitating effect of training is what Merton calls *displacement of goals*. People learn to attach so much importance to the means for achievement of goals that the means eventually displace the goals. The original goals are lost; instead, rigid adherence to formalized procedures is emphasized. Red tape may threaten the achievement of the organization's purposes. Merton illustrates the effects of such literal adherence to rules with the following story about Bernt Balchen, Admiral Byrd's pilot in his flight over the South Pole:

According to a ruling of the department of labor, Bernt Balchen . . . cannot receive his citizenship papers. Balchen, a native of Norway, declared his intention in 1927. It is held that he has failed to meet the condition of five years' continuous residence in the United States. The Byrd Antarctic voyage took him out of the country, although he was on a ship flying the American flag, was an invaluable member of an American expedition, and in a region to which there is an American claim because of the exploration and occupation of it by Americans, this region being Little America.

The bureau for naturalization explains that it cannot proceed on the assumption that Little America is American soil. That would be *trespass on international questions* where it has no sanction. So far as the bureau is concerned, Balchen was out of the country and *technically* has not complied with the law of naturalization.[2]

Impersonality

Probably all of us at some time have been irritated over impersonal treatment received at the hands of a large organization. We may even rage over the arrogance of one of its underlings. We all want special consideration and personal treatment. If the underling is a "servant of the people," a government employee, we are particularly incensed.

And yet, to be fair to the other person, we should recognize that bureaucracy commends its members for fulfilling impersonal roles. To act otherwise, to accord special favors and consideration to outsiders, might harvest charges of graft, favoritism, and apple-polishing. Furthermore, a member of the organization acts as a representative of the power and prestige of the entire structure. This may lead to an apparent or real domineering attitude on the part of the representative and to resentment on the part of the client. Since we must so frequently deal with bureaucratic behavior, we should try to understand it.

Staff-Line Conflict

The organizational dysfunctions of bureaucracy are readily apparent to the outsider. There are other problem areas, internal in nature, which are not so apparent. Staff-line conflict is one of these areas.

Some years ago, Melville Dalton documented several sources of difficulty between staff and line personnel.[3] His work at the time was in industrial organizations where the line had exclusive authority over production and the staff functioned in a research and advisory capacity. In three factories, Dalton found that staff officers were significantly younger than line officers. One result was that the older line men resented receiving what they perceived as instructions from younger staff men. Ideas presented by staff personnel were often ignored or regarded with amusement.

In addition, the younger staff men were more highly educated, more sophisticated socially, and more concerned about their dress. Older line managers felt the staff personnel were putting on airs and were overly concerned with status symbols—such as being invited to eat in the executive cafeteria.

The fact that top-line officers controlled movement into higher staff ranks was the real rub, however. In order to curry favor with the line, therefore, staff men often resorted to certain informal practices. They would cooperate with the line in evading rules and, by this means, obligate one or more line managers to a future favor. A staff officer might delay implementation of a new procedure in order to allow a line department time to clear up forbidden practices or inefficiencies. In other cases, funds appropriated for staff use were informally shifted over to line departments. In these ways, staff personnel sought to resolve the conflict and to assure their advancement into top spots or into the line.

Structure or Personality

Behavior may seem to be influenced not so much by staff-line structure as by the personality types that fill staff and line positions. Yet without the staff-line structure, there would be no conflict. Furthermore, while the structure gives rise to the problem, the solution may not lie in tinkering with the structure. Rather, as Dalton himself found in a later study, conflict can be reduced by reducing the visibility of status symbols (invite all line and staff officers to the executive cafeteria) and by placing individuals with similar backgrounds in both line and staff positions. Lower-line posts, for example, can be filled with young, technically-trained college graduates.[4] In those organizations where management blurs the distinction between line and staff, of course, this particular problem does not arise in such a sharp form.

Line, Staff, and Job Satisfaction

Other studies of business and industrial organizations report that engineers and scientists in staff positions are less satisfied with their jobs than their counterparts in line positions.[5] And the turnover rate has been reported as higher among staff managers than among line managers. But why should a staff person be less satisfied? Typically, he is knowledgeable, socially aware, and able to mix with many different executives through his professional affiliations and his job.

The answer apparently resides in the scarcity of decision-making opportunities afforded to a staff person. With all of his education and talent, he cannot make line decisions unless somehow he usurps some of the authority of the line. This frustration may explain not only his relative dissatisfaction but also may partially explain staff-line conflict.

Organizational Level and Job Satisfaction

Recent studies indicate that job satisfaction and morale increase *monotonically* with levels of management; that is, top management is more satisfied than middle management, and middle management is more satisfied than the lowest level of management. And the lowest level of management, the supervisory level, is more satisfied with its job than workers at the operating level.[6]

One suggested explanation is that at higher organizational levels, there is less disparity between what satisfaction is expected and what is realized. We all have certain needs that we try to satisfy. These include our needs for security, for social approval and interaction, for esteem, for autonomy, and for self-actualization or for fulfillment of what we perceive as our full potential as humans. We hope and in certain situations expect that these needs will be satisfied. In high organizational levels, it is suggested that expectations with respect to these needs are more fully realized than at lower levels. Hence those individuals at high levels are more satisfied with their jobs and have higher morale than persons at low levels. These findings apparently apply to business organizations in other countries as well as to those in the United States.[7] The manager of a Russian factory is probably more satisfied with his job than a worker in the factory. The same would tend to be true of high-ranking managers in India, China, or other countries. Regardless of varying cultures, the challenges of the job appear to be most important in determining job satisfaction.

We noted in an early chapter how organizational level affects activity. While top management tends to engage in long-range planning and decision making, for example, operating management plans on a day-to-day basis and makes decisions accordingly. Top managers interact with many persons outside the organization and strive to maintain the system in a steady state. Operating managers deal more with persons within the organiza tion, and they treat the organization external to their own depar ments as an external environment. Little research has been done to show what impacts these and other level-related activities and behavior have to do with job satisfaction, but there is little doubt that they are involved.

Organizational Size and Job Satisfaction

We have already said that no finite limit apparently exists on organizational size, at least from the standpoint that size alone need not produce dangerous levels of inefficiency and ineffectiveness. There remains, however, a question about the effects of size on attitude and performance. Let us first look at work groups on the operating level. (Little has been done with work groups at the managerial level.)

The evidence strongly suggests that workers in small subunits are more satisfied than workers in larger ones.[8] Part of the evidence consists of the fact that workers in small groups have lower absenteeism and turnover rates. We may speculate that in the smaller groups, workers get to know one another better, feel more secure in their relationships, and, in general, have a greater feeling of solidarity or cohesiveness.

The evidence on productivity is divided: some studies show small groups have higher productivity than large groups, while other studies show the opposite. The important conclusion is that *high satisfaction and productivity do not necessarily correlate.* A large group can have low job satisfaction, as expressed by individual members, and high productivity. All in all, however, the evidence suggests that smaller-sized units are best if there is a choice.

Few studies attempt to relate size of the total organization to attitudes and behavior. In two instances, studies report that job satisfaction and morale were lower in large organizations, but the evidence is far from conclusive. And we have even less idea of the effects of organization size when talking in terms of the operating level or the managerial level. Perhaps we may say that large organizational size will not reduce morale as long as work units are kept small.[9] Further research is necessary.

The Shape of the Organization

The effect of the shape of an organization structure on behavior and attitude has been a lively topic ever since 1950, when James Worthy wrote of his experiences with and observations of Sears, Roebuck and Company.[10] His observations directly contradicted classical dicta about the desirability of tall structures with relatively short spans of control, specialization, and tight coordination through close supervision. Instead, Worthy advocated a flat structure with relatively few levels and wide spans of control.

Worthy felt that a flat structure, which pushes decision making down to the lower managerial levels and shortens the vertical communication channels, would result in superior decision making, improved satisfaction and job performance, and greater individual responsibility and initiative. But studies on Worthy's prescription, done in the sixties and later, tend to refute him:

The evidence does not support Worthy's (1950) sweeping generalization that a flat organization produces greater job satisfaction and improved job performance. The evidence points to organization size as one of the factors affecting the relative advantages of tall and flat organization structures. Two of the studies reviewed found that in relatively small organizations a flat organization did appear to be advantageous in terms of producing managerial job satisfaction. However, for relatively large organizations one study found that tall organization structures produced greater job satisfaction, and one study found that tall organization structures fostered greater productivity. Thus it appears that the advantages of a flat structure not only decrease with increasing organization size, but that in relatively large organizations a flat structure may sometimes even be a liability.[11]

In a small organization, the problems of communication and coordination are not as severe as in a large organization. Therefore, the autonomy and freedom afforded in a flat structure may be fully realized in a small organization, and managerial satisfaction will be increased. The flat structure, however, may not be able to cope with the complexity of a large organization, and may result in dissatisfaction and frustration. For effective control and coordination, a tall structure may be necessary for the large organization. Managers are able to supervise more effectively, and greater satisfaction results than with a flat structure, but with less satisfaction than allowed by a flat *and* simple organization.

Centralization or Decentralization

Decentralization is usually associated with a flat organizational profile and centralization with a tall profile. Decentralization locates decision making in the lower levels of the organization to as great an extent as possible. Decentralization is supposed to improve professional development through decision making and is supposed to increase managerial motivation by allowing greater autonomy and participation in solving important organizational problems. But empirical studies "offer no clear support for the proposition that decentralization can produce either improved job attitudes or performance."[12] Current facts suggest that whether one opts for a flat or tall structure and/or a centralized or decentralized operation should depend on organization size, product line, interdependence or independence of subunits, type of personnel, ease of control, and other factors. Let us use an imaginary incident to illustrate how decentralization works.

Staff Man

Alvin Brown's first job out of college was with the quality control department of a large company. For over two months he had been working with three other men who were also new in quality control. Brown was reasonably happy, since he enjoyed working in a small group. And they were all in the same boat—learning their jobs and learning about the company. Also, a friend of Brown's from college had taken a job with the same company as a foreman in the production department. Alvin would occasionally see his friend around the plant, and they often had lunch together.

After four more months went by, however, Brown began to get a little upset. He was spending all of his time helping to set up statistical quality control plans and rarely got out into the plant unless he made it a point to go out and look around. In the meantime, his friend was always telling about all the responsibilities he had and all the decisions he had to make every day. Brown was beginning to be jealous of his friend's job.

Brown had to admit, though, that his friend was always interested in the new ideas Brown was working on. Some of the oldtimers in production simply snorted when they overheard Brown talking about these new ideas at lunch.

On the first Monday in December, Brown's boss called him into the office.

"Brown, I've been pleased with your progress, and I think you're ready to move on to a more important assignment. I'm going to put you in charge of the A section of the production line for our pump component. I've been handling that, but it needs someone's full-time attention. Now you'll be in full charge of quality control. What you say goes. You even have authority to stop production if there's a sufficiently serious quality problem. Do you think you can handle it?"

"Yes, sir," Brown replied.

The rest of the morning Brown was walking on air. He could hardly wait to tell his friend about his new assignment and his responsibilities and authority. Now he too would be making decisions.

The job worked out well for Brown. He enjoyed the combination of staff work and functional authority. He also discovered that the oldtimers in production were taking him much more seriously now than they had before.

Structure and Innovation

As we have stated, the classical, mechanistic organizational form tends to be inferior to the organic form in generating and implementing innovation. There are specific behavioral reasons for this.[13] The mechanistic form has several attributes that restrict the innovative process. Among these attributes are the inclination to isolate the unit responsible for innovation from the rest of the organization; the tendency to encourage sectional and personal resistance to innovation; and the tendency to develop many stages in the innovation process, which often necessitates transferring a project from one department or group to another via liaison agents. Furthermore, commitment to function or to means and emphasis on vertical communication rather than on horizontal communication constrain organization-wide concentration on task accomplishment.

In contrast, the organic firm tends "to invest in people, then exploit them as a resource in any way possible. ..."[14] A technical specialist in physics, for example, will be allowed to work in market development if he can make a contribution. The organic firm assigns the innovation unit a central place and role in the organization and then emphasizes lateral communication and movement of personnel. Interaction is direct; liaison specialists are eliminated or minimized. And in order to do this, the organization knocks down subunit jurisdictional barriers and deemphasizes hierarchical status.

The success of the organic organization depends in large part on the support of top management and its ability to manage:

As nearly as we can tell, "ability," in operational terms, seems to be some familiarity, either at the intuitive level or as a matter of explicit principle, with the ideas of organic organization and a willingness to use knowledge, resources, and the authority of office to facilitate the setting and accomplishment of organizational goals. We feel this definition imparts a desirable emphasis toward the conception of management as a learnable art and toward the mutual support and confidence that lie at the root of potential applications of organic ideas. It also leads away from the more traditional idea that "ability" is innate and unchangeable and avoids some of the consequences: unnecessary *ad hominem* arguments and inappropriate invidious comparisons.[15]

Problems in Matrix Organizations

We have presented the matrix organization as a contemporary type of structure that promises more effective performance than organizations structured along traditional lines. The matrix form, however, also has some behavioral disadvantages, like all other organizational structures. First, in those matrix organizations where projects are temporary, the project manager in particular may confront some disconcerting problems. These problems stem from the position in which the manager is placed. He is on the margin or boundary between the project group and the parent organization; and he may also be placed between the project group and some third party that is subcontracting the project to the parent organization.[16]

Dealing with the needs and expectations of his own people in the group can be troublesome for the project manager. Frequently, personnel in a project group are professionals, and therefore they hold certain values with respect to perfection and high-quality work. The professionals may perceive cost and scheduling constraints, perhaps imposed by the parent organization, as compromising their values. The project manager must be able to satisfy their professional goals as well as be able to meet cost and schedule demands. One helpful strategy is for the project manager to explicitly communicate the project goals to the professionals at the outset. In so doing, he defines the limits of action and helps prevent the frustration of unmet expectations.

In addition, the project manager may not be able to directly reward his people with promotions and salary increases. Managers in the parent organization—managers of departments or sections that supply the personnel to the project—often hold these prerogatives. The project manager, on the other hand, must somehow find different ways to motivate and to reward. Providing challenging work and autonomy in problem solving is one form of motivation that may be highly rewarding psychologically. If the project manager cannot or will not set up some sort of reward structure within the project, the stage is set for dissatisfaction and conflict among his project team.

Career and Job Security

Behavioral problems of the organic form exist not only for the manager but also for the project team as a whole. A study of three major aerospace companies suggests that when a project is temporary, personnel worry about loss of employment when the project ends.[17] As work approaches the phaseout period, there may be heightened worry and frustration about getting on another project or getting another job. Experience has taught some project members that returning to their old job with the parent organization is not always guaranteed.

Members of projects are also often concerned about becoming professionally obsolete. They may see that, because of their specialization and task repetition over a period of time, they may not be able to keep up with technological advances. Members also worry about career retardation. While project association frequently offers a fast route to high pay and prestigious positions, there is also the possibility that the next project, if there is one, may involve work at a lower level than the current. In contrast, the parent organization or a functional organization usually invites relatively slow but steady progression up the ladder. The member of the functional organization, therefore, may worry relatively less about career setbacks than members of project organizations.

Because project members are anxious about their own positions, they withdraw a measure of loyalty to the project. The study of the three aerospace companies suggests that after persons move around from one project to another for a while, they have less loyalty to their project organizations than members of functional organizations have to their association. The principal problem here is one of motivation. Not being inspired by organizational achievement, the pay check may well become the primary interest of the project "mercenary." And money is not an absolute incentive.

Ambiguity in the Organic Form   Although the study mentions a number of other human problems, the final one we will introduce pertains to the confusion and ambiguity often associated with organic structure. The ambiguity usually stems from loose definitions of jobs, obscure authority relationships, and helter-skelter lines of communication. For example, project managers frequently expressed feelings as follows:

"A project organization is brought into being for one purpose, namely, the accomplishment of the requirements of a specific end item. Efficiency in operation is sacrificed in order to optimize this criterion." "Sharpness in defining job responsibilities is overlooked as long as the jobs get done by someone. Duplication of effort is a universal characteristic of project organization. In a large project the same kind and quantity of work might be performed in three or four suborganizations." "There just isn't time to develop orderly lines of inter or intra communication by project organizations. This unquestionably bothers the people who are involved, but somehow the word eventually gets around."[18]

It appears that project organization generates some unique behavioral problems. As the study suggests, "The central implication of the findings is that although there may be persuasive justification for the adoption of project organization, relief from human problems is not one of them.[19] These problems were reported as primarily occurring in matrix organizations with temporary projects. The term *matrix organization* is now increasingly used in reference to organizations with a permanent array of projects—a type of free-form organization with central control over a variety of projects. A matrix organization tends to be an organic organization and therefore capable of greater innovation than the traditional, mechanistic type. It is likely that the matrix will be an important organizational form in the future as well as now. Therefore it is well to note that matrix does not mean realization of perfection. The matrix has its share of behavioral problems, with which developing managers must deal. If dealt with as the evolving, imperfect form that it is, managers may help it evolve by making its design more effective. At the same time they may benefit from its advantages.

Structure, Technology, and Informal Organization

We have been discussing some of the behavioral influences of the bureaucratic and traditional organization form as well as of the matrix design. Now we will indicate how structure aids in the development of informal organization, leaving a detailed description of its characteristics and dimensions until a later chapter. We will examine the interaction among changing technology, structure, and informal organization.

Classical theory prescribes organizing around a hierarchy of positions. Most organizations today still follow a modified form of the classical prescription—even though there is a trend toward less overt structure and toward the forming of organizations around groups of people. But position structure remains a first step in most organization and reorganization. This structure has an observable impact on informal associations.

Each position has three salient dimensions with respect to the formation of informal groups.[20] First, there is the technical dimension. This area includes all the equipment and facilities required to get the job done and the physical positioning of one job in relation to another as specified by technical requirements. In addition, there is a prescribed approach or way of thinking that must be developed in the person holding a given job.

Second, there is a sociotechnical dimension of position. The formal structuring of positions is one of the linking processes that helps integrate the organizational system. But the linking process is only activated when occupants of positions interact in the decision-making process. And third, there is a social dimension. Because of the technical and sociotechnical dimensions of positions, interactions occur. Out of these interactions, social relations grow and foster informal activity on and off the job.

In sum, then, organization structure may facilitate informal association in several ways: (1) people work physically close to one another; (2) people engage in the same kind of work; (3) people discover similar interests or attractions through formal interaction; and (4) people discover similar backgrounds and status through their on-the-job relations.[21] As people continue to interact socially and on the job, their choices of friends usually are reinforced and the initial formations of groups and subgroups are solidified.

Recognition of Informal Structure in Design

Classical theory tended to ignore the tremendous impact of human interaction in organizations. Modern management science, on the other hand, recognizes and seeks to understand organizational behavior. Let us first consider those effects of human interaction that most likely should play a role in organization design.

One such effect is that, given the informal associations of people, decision making in the organization is not always a rational choice process. Decision making is not engaged in by individuals seeking only to help in the achievement of stated organizational goals. Rather, most of the time, if not always, decision making takes place within an environment of political maneuvering and social relationships that can, in the extreme, completely remove the decision process from any connection with organizational or subunit goal achievement. In other words, severe suboptimization may occur because individual decisions may reflect special group interests. These interests, in turn, may be attuned primarily to increasing the power of the group rather than to achieving the organization goal. An imaginary incident may help illustrate the problem that informal organization presents for the organization as a whole.

The New Accountant

Bill Manx had just gone to work in the production control department of a large manufacturing company. This was his first job after graduation from college, and Manx was quite anxious about how well he would do. He was assigned a desk next to a man about five years older who was to give Bill whatever help he needed in learning the ropes.

After only a few days, Manx learned that his advisor had graduated from the same college and shared Manx's intense interest in hunting and fishing. In the course of his work activity,

Manx also became quite friendly with other members of the department. Soon Manx was on the department bowling team, and he and his wife were socializing with other members of the department and their wives. In short, Manx had been accepted as a full member of the informal group in production control, and he had become quite close friends with two of the people.

One day at lunch, a man from quality control criticized the manner in which products were routed through the production system. He pointed out how much more difficult quality control was because of the routings and suggested a way to change them. The individual in production control primarily responsible for routing, whom Manx now knew quite well, immediately jumped to defense of his methods.

Manx participated in the ensuing argument, vigorously defending his friend and his department from this unwarranted attack. Nothing much resulted. The quality control guy accused production control of blind stubbornness while Manx and his friends told the quality control man to mind his own business.

That night at home, Manx thought about the incident. In a reflective mood, he admitted to himself that the quality control man was quite right—the routing could be changed without loss of efficiency and to the greater convenience of quality control. He and his friends had been overdefensive and had reacted emotionally rather than logically, a reaction that was going to block some potential cost savings for the company. But Manx knew he would not pursue the matter, out of loyalty to his own group. Nor would anyone else in production control.

If we accept, then, that informal groups do form, we should ask what can be done in organization design to minimize the dysfunctional effects of groups and even to exploit them for the good of the organization. We may find a solution in the project-group design: "Such an organization strategy provides for overlapping group memberships of short to intermediate duration, bringing together decision-relevant groupings of specialists and administrators. Further, such groupings can be juxtaposed with departmentation for routine decision-implementation. Finally, project management satisfies the need for overlapping group membership without artificially imposing the burden of 'linking' groups solely on the departmental supervisors."[22]

Thus, in the matrix design using project groups of temporary duration, relatively permanent informal associations are more difficult to maintain than in a traditional, functional organization. Overlapping group memberships help assure representation from

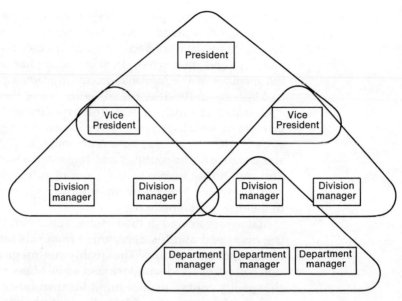

Figure 9–1 Linked groups*

*Adapted from R. Likert, *The Human Organization* (New York: McGraw-Hill, 1956), p. 50.

all elements of the organization in decision making. If management deliberately changes group memberships, the threat of powerful, parochial empires should be diminished.

Linking groups have been suggested as a way to provide overlap among groups in order to facilitate interaction among work groups from both functional areas and hierarchical levels.[23] In this design, the supervisor holds simultaneous memberships in two or more groups. He thus provides the link that enables subgroups to integrate their activities and to reduce suboptimization (figure 9–1). There is no real departure from traditional form, however, since the linking arrangement operates within existing structure. In addition, the entire burden of integration falls upon the supervisor since he is the only one with overlapping membership. In contrast to this essentially traditional pattern, the matrix form appears to offer better representation from groups to the organization and from the organization to groups.

Changing Technology and Informal Organization

In the last chapter we suggested that technology influences structure, and we cited several examples in illustration. Unfortunately, structure is not always built on the technological base, and when it is not, there are problems of communication and coordination. Lack of consonance between technology and structure may be particularly apparent in those situations where technology is rapidly changing. The point is that we are usually dealing with an existing structure and a changing technology rather than starting from scratch to build a new structure. In the first instance we have two options: to change the structure to accommodate the new technology or to make the new technology work using the old structure. If structure is not modified to fit the new technology, there will tend to be problems of communication, authority flow, coordination, and of worker morale. The need for structural adjustments is usually apparent since adjustments will be made informally if the management does not formally make adjustments.

Continuing to use one example from the last chapter, we can further explore the impact of numerical control machines in many manufacturing organizations. We pointed out how numerical control machines combine many operations into one and how a machining center is literally set up around one machine. In addition, someone is needed to program the machining operations on tape—a tape that can then be used to completely machine a part from beginning to end.

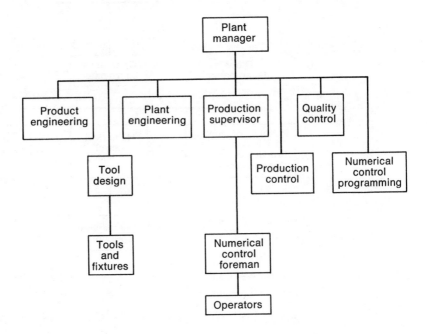

Figure 9–2 Old structure for numerical control

In the study reported, many companies using numerical control machines had made no structural changes whatever to accommodate their new technology.[24] Figure 9–2 represents their unadapted structure for dealing with numerical control. Note that programming has been placed in line with other staff functions and has formal line access to the operators only through the production supervisor and the foreman.

In practice, information and authority flows were considerably different from the structure illustrated in figure 9–2. Most work and information flow were coordinated through the programmer, and the study found that the great versatility and capability of the machine left little for a foreman to do. The study recommended, therefore, that the programmer could readily assume the vestigial duties of the foreman. Figure 9–3 illustrates the recommended organizational changes to accommodate the new technology of numerical control.

This numerical control team structure tends to follow the recommendations and research findings reported by other researchers. For example, Chapple and Sayles advocate interrelating

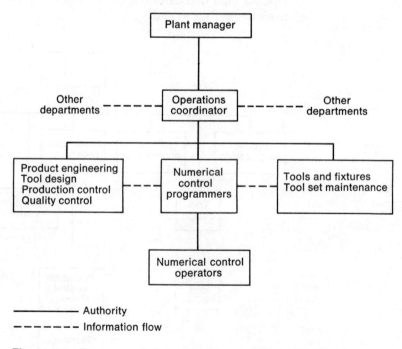

Figure 9–3 Recommended structure for numerical control

the production and organization structure with the decision-making process affecting the individual: designing the structure from the bottom up; basing the organization on the actual work flow; and superimposing structure on known technology.[25]

Rice states that any organization requires both a technological organization and a work organization to provide for interaction among those who carry out the necessary tasks.[26] He feels there has been a tendency to project the technological factor into the associated work organization and then to assume that there is only one work organization that will satisfy the conditions of task performance. This means treating groups and individuals as though they were machines and results in what has been labeled the "machine theory of organization." Then, when the work organization fails to satisfy the social and psychological needs of its members, their attitudes to task performance lower the level of productivity and prevent the full realization of technological potential. Related tasks should be so organized that those performing them have satisfactory relationships.

The numerical control team structure (figure 9–3) was predicated on the development, by the people involved, of information flows and *informal* relationships that could lead to the most efficient solution of problems. If formal organization does not change and adapt to new technology, informal organizational relationships may spring up to get the job done.

Summary

Human behavior is an important consideration in choice and design of organizational structure. Real human behavior often upsets ideal models for organization. For example, bureaucratic structure can lead people to concentrate on procedure to the point where organization goals are overlooked.

Research studies have reported behavioral conflict between staff and line personnel in the staff-line structure. The source of difficulty may be in the type of person attracted to line or staff work rather than in the structure itself. Other studies have indicated line personnel are more satisfied with their jobs than staff people, perhaps because there is more opportunity for decision making in line than in staff work.

Job satisfaction evidently increases as one moves up the organization ladder. Furthermore, workers in small groups tend to have greater job satisfaction than workers in larger groups. It remains unclear, however, what effect total organizational size has on job satisfaction either at the managerial or worker level.

Despite claims to the contrary, a flat organization structure (few levels) apparently does not necessarily result in improved satisfaction and job performance. Two studies indicated that a flat structure in a small organization did improve managerial satisfaction while another study suggested that in large organizations a tall structure enhances satisfaction. Similarly, decentralization has been advocated because it is supposed to improve job attitudes and/or performance. Again, empirical studies offer no clear evidence for this view. Whether to decentralize, therefore, can be decided on the basis of factors other than the behavioral ones.

The organic organization is more amenable to innovation than the mechanistic form. Yet the matrix organization, a favored organic form, also has its share of problems. For one, the project manager is placed in an ambiguous boundary position between the project group and the parent organization. In addition, members of a project group worry about their job security, professional obsolescence, and uncertainties in the communication and authority structures.

Finally, structure has a pronounced impact on the development of informal organizations. Every formal position has a technical, sociotechnical, and social dimension. Out of the technical and sociotechnical dimensions, social interactions occur and informal groups form. Given that informal structure does form, it should be studied and incorporated into the formal structure in order to reduce ambiguity and to allow management better control.

This chapter concludes a major part of the book pertaining to three important decision areas of management—planning, controlling, and organizing. We have discussed these areas in rather broad terms; that is, usually from the viewpoint of the total organization—the macro view. We have reviewed many of the complex and difficult decisions that management must make.

We have included the influence of individual and group behavior where necessary to illustrate their efforts. However, we have not concentrated on behavior; that is, what motivates people, why informal groups form, what their significance is for the organization, and what the components of good leadership are. Information on these topics forms a major portion of the knowledge bank that managers must possess to help in making effective decisions, and these are the subjects of the next major portion of the book.

Mary Parker Follett

Boston-born (1868) Mary Parker Follett started her career as a social worker. Educated at Radcliffe College, the Sorbonne in Paris, and Newham College in Cambridge, England, Follett became a noted social philosopher.

Observing the importance and dynamic nature of business, she began to concentrate on the organization and management of business in particular—though her ideas could as well be applied to many different organizations. She was truly a pioneering spirit, for she felt that psychological underpinnings for a philosophy of management had been completely ignored. She believed strongly in group effort as a means to superior problem solving and decision making. Her use of the term "group think" preceded by many years the popularity it began to enjoy in the 1950s. These notions, of course, were contrary to traditional thought on the chain of command, and few business leaders paid any heed to her "wild" ideas.

Her writings on authority were equally astounding at the time. Remember that in classical theory there was only one kind of authority: that which had been legitimized by the organization and gave one person power over one or more other persons. Follett, however, raised several interesting questions. Does a person have power over someone or power with someone? Is authority offensive to a person's emotions and therefore a poor basis for cooperative organization? Does authority derive from the nature of the job rather than from an official title?

On the basis of her studies over the years, Follett concluded that authority indeed does derive from the nature of the task and from the situation in which the task is to be performed. Furthermore, authority imposed on workers is a poor basis for organization; a better approach would be to secure agreement within a group about actions to be taken. Depending on the task to be performed, different members of a group could be leaders at different times as their varying knowledge and skill matched the tasks. If the group agreed on goals and tactics, their performance would be better than if there were one leader imposed on the group.

Mary Parker Follett was ahead of her time. We know now that most of what she said about authority and behavior is quite valid. Yet she was ignored by the business practitioners of her day. This is, perhaps, the fate of many creative thinkers. Much of what was advocated by turn-of-the-century management scholars has come true, and this result suggests that we should listen to contemporary scholars for clues to the future twenty and thirty years from now. Those ideas that appear wildest now may be accepted as a matter of fact in the future.

Discussion Questions

1. Can you recall any frustrating experience you have had as a client or customer of a bureaucratic organization? What do you think the organization could have done to correct the situation that caused your frustration?

2. Research studies indicate that people in the higher levels of organization are generally more satisfied with their jobs than people in lower levels. Since not everyone can be in top management, can you think of any ways in which the organization could allow persons in lower organizational levels to be more satisfied?

3. Given your choice, what type of organization structure would you prefer as a place in which to work; that is, small or large, tall or flat, decentralized or centralized?

4. In the case of the "Staff Man," should the organization have given Alvin Brown functional authority earlier than it did? What are the implications of your answer?

5. Every type of organization structure seems to involve some trade-offs. For example, the matrix structure may encourage innovation but it appears to generate problems of security and loyalty. Is it desirable to identify the trade-offs for various types of structure? Why? What are the trade-offs in a bureaucratic type of organization?

6. In the case of "The New Accountant," should the organization do anything about Manx's informal group if it becomes known that the group is at least partially responsible for not working more closely with quality control? What should be done?

7. The relationship between structure and technology is important. Why should structure be built on the technological base rather than the other way around?

References

1. R. K. Merton, "Bureaucratic Structure and Personality," *Social Forces*, 18 (1940): 560–568.

2. *Ibid.*

3. M. Dalton, "Conflicts between Staff and Line Managerial Officers," *American Sociological Review*, 15 (1950): 342–351.

4. M. Dalton, "Changing Line-Staff Relations," *Personnel Administration*, 28 (1966): 3–5.

5. L. W. Porter and L. E. Lawler, "Properties of Organization Structure in Relation to Job Attitudes and Job Behavior," *Psychological Bulletin*, 64 (1965): 23–51.

6. *Ibid.*

7. *Ibid.*

8. *Ibid.*

9. *Ibid.*

10. J. C. Worthy, "Organizational Structure and Employee Morale," *American Sociological Review*, 15 (1950): 169–179.

11. Porter and Lawler, pp. 23–51.

12. *Ibid.*

13. This discussion is based on a paper by C. J. Haberstroh, J. A. Baring, and W. C. Mudgett, *Organizing for Innovation* (Cleveland: Case Institute of Technology, 1967).

14. *Ibid.*, p. 2.

15. *Ibid.*, p. 27.

16. D. L. Wilemon and J. P. Cicero, "The Project Manager—Anomalies and Ambiguities," *The Academy of Management Journal*, 13 (1970): 269–282.

17. C. Reeser, "Some Potential Human Problems of the Project Form of Organization," *Academy of Management Journal*, 12 (1969): 459–468.

18. *Ibid.*

19. *Ibid.*

20. A. Delbecq, "How 'Informal' Organization Evolves: Interpersonal Choice and Subgroup Formation," *Business Perspective*, 4 (1968): 17–21.

21. *Ibid.*

22. *Ibid.*

23. R. Likert, *New Patterns of Management* (New York: McGraw-Hill, 1961), pp. 105–118.

24. E. F. Lundgren, "A Modular Organization Design for Numerical Control," *Proceedings of the Midwest Academy of Management* (Madison, Wis.: The University of Wisconsin, 1968), pp. 146–162.

25. E. D. Chapple and L. Sayles, *The Measure of Management* (New York: Macmillan, 1961), pp. 18–45.

26. A. K. Rice, *Productivity and Social Organization: The Ahmedabad Experiment* (London: Tavistock, 1958), p. 4.

Suggested Readings

Argyris, C. *Integrating the Individual and the Organization.* New York: John Wiley, 1964.

Whyte, W. F. *Men at Work.* Homewood, Ill.: Dorsey and Irwin, 1961.

Case Problem for Chapters 8 and 9

The Winslow Products Company*

The Winslow Products Company has a single plant employing 550 people. The main product is a metal fitting produced through a series of machine and assembly operations. The company also makes other parts similar to the one described, principally for the steel industry. The president received a degree in law, but he has had considerable experience in the sales field. He can also perform basic design work, and he holds several patents. The vice-president and general manager has engineering training, and he is well versed in manufacturing techniques and processes. He also has had long and intimate association with cost controls and cost accounting techniques and is considered to be an expert in this field.

The board of directors performs the normal duties of developing policies and passing on long-range plans. The board has some expertise in financial planning, since it is heavily loaded with individuals from investment houses and banking firms. The company treasurer works on a part-time basis and holds a partnership in a local law firm. The secretary of the company is a former salesman who is within one year of retirement. For the past two years the secretary has been afflicted with an illness that has limited his overall effectiveness.

The union in the plant is newly organized, but labor relations have been very good to date. The initial stages of unionization were accomplished with only minor problems, and the manager of industrial relations feels that the local union (United Steelworkers of America), which is now bargaining with the company, has very

*From *Management Strategy and Tactics* by John G. Hutchinson. Copyright © 1971 by Holt, Rinehart and Winston, Inc. Reprinted by permission of Holt, Rinehart and Winston, Inc.

responsible leadership. The volume of purchased parts is somewhat small, although raw materials are critical to the company in terms of total profitability. The general manager in particular likes to keep a close control over purchasing because he feels that it is a key area in cost control.

The engineering department is headed by a relatively inept manager. Most of the creative ideas and planning in engineering originate with the general manager. Without the general manager's guidance, this department would be woefully inadequate.

Winslow Products operates in a very competitive industry. Because of this, cost controls are extremely important. Moreover, the sales effort must be kept at a vigorous and continuous pace. In recent years, the company has seen its profits fall steadily. This decline has worried the president and has caused some anxiety among members of the board of directors. In general, company profits have not dipped below levels considered acceptable by the board. The president, however, feels that if present trends continue, the company will be unable to maintain its position in the industry.

1. What departments, if any, should be added, liquidated, or combined in the future to make this organization operate more efficiently? Give the reasons for your decision.
2. Draw up an organization chart showing how this company should be organized.

Case Problem for Chapters 8 and 9

The Michigan Transport Company*

In 1965 the Michigan Transport Company (MTC) bought a small chemical plant which produced heavy chemicals. Though MTC had never owned or operated any chemical installations, company officials thought that diversification was necessary if the company was to remain profitable and keep growing. The decision to enter chemicals turned out to be initially successful, as certain phases of the cold war created a demand for the product of the acquired property.

Encouraged by this early success, the company decided to enter the chemical industry in a big way. The board of directors began to investigate companies with the idea of either outright purchase

*From *Management Strategy and Tactics* by John G. Hutchinson. Copyright © 1971 by Holt, Rinehart and Winston, Inc. Reprinted by permission of Holt, Rinehart and Winston, Inc.

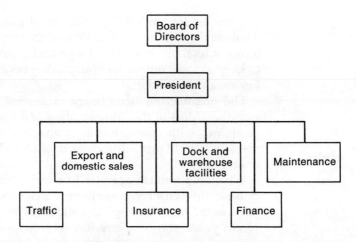

Exhibit 1 Organization chart of major operating units—Michigan Transport Company

or merger. None of the board members had much knowledge of the chemical industry, although the chairman of the board felt that their combined business wisdom would enable them to make wise purchase decisions. After surveying several dozen companies over a period of several years, the board decided, in 1967, to try to merge with a medium-sized chemical producer with a narrow but profitable line of heavy chemicals. Negotiations began in late 1967, but because of the death of the chairman of the board of MTC, no final decisions were made by the middle of 1968.

In June of 1967, the grandson of MTC's founder became president. He believed in rapid diversification and continued expansion of the company. He felt, however, that the board had not been careful in carrying out policies of diversification. For instance, all merger or purchase decisions were made by the board alone. He believed that the current organization was not well suited to investigate possibilities of expansion or diversification (see exhibit 1). The major departments of traffic, maintenance, export and domestic sales, insurance, dock and warehouse facilities, and finance were cumbersome and suited only for adequate handling of the old shipping business of the company. This organization was particularly outmoded, according to the new president, because it failed to allow for industrial development and because insurance now accounted for almost half of the company's current revenue.

The new president believed that his first job was to reorganize for growth and efficiency. He wanted to:

1. Streamline the current organization to reflect the true needs of the company
2. Provide for adequate analysis and decision making on expansion
3. Maintain a good organization operating at a profit
4. Establish central staffs in order to use the existing talent and experience of organization members in the most profitable manner

Though MTC was still profitable, revenues had been falling steadily. By the end of 1968, profits were expected to fall to 5 percent of sales. In view of this forecast, the new president planned to take strong steps to keep the company prosperous and profitable.

1. What do you think of MTC's approach to diversification?
2. Prepare a new organization chart to help the president meet his goals. Add, delete, or combine departments as necessary.

Working with People

IV

Managing and Developing People

10

This chapter will be a transition between the management decision areas of planning, controlling, and organizing and the knowledge areas of human behavior. When discussing the decision areas, we did so first from the viewpoint of top management and the total organization and then moved to the planning, controlling, and organizing decisions made by unit managers. That is, we used a macro approach.

Now we are going to change to a micro approach. We first will study individual and small group behavior and then progress to a discussion of leadership, including that which top management can apply for the entire organization. The planning, controlling, and organizing decisions of unit managers must derive from the decisions of top management in those same areas. Therefore we study such decisions with the macro approach. In leadership, however, we recognize that managerial decisions must derive from an understanding of individual and small group behavior. Therefore we study such decisions with the micro approach, attempting to understand how individuals and groups behave under varying circumstances.

Managing and developing people includes topics ordinarily considered within the province of personnel management. In our coverage, however, we will be principally concerned with those areas that are of continuing importance to most organizational managers. Therefore we will discuss such issues as transfers and promotions, but we will not consider initial selection for jobs or other activities that represent specialized functions of the personnel department.

Not many people forever stay at the same job and the same location in an organization once they become employees. Job changes are often made to satisfy the needs of the individual or of the company. Even when a company initially rejects someone who is applying for a particular job, the interviewer may discover through the testing procedure that the applicant has a high aptitude for another type of work. This is called *differential placement* and is a form of job change even before the person is hired.

A transfer is a lateral movement within the organization and usually involves no increase or decrease in pay or responsibility. As an employee, you may want to move to another location within a given plant or perhaps to another plant or even to a different kind of job, and the company will attempt to satisfy your wishes if it is possible to do so. The company may also transfer you to meet its own needs with respect to changes in work load, organizational requirements, or job requirements.

Transfers are often valuable to the employee in that they can provide a variety of experience and training. At the same time, employees often resist organizational transfers if they result in considerable personal inconvenience. For example, you may have lived all your life on the East Coast when the company informs you of a possible transfer to a small town in the Midwest. While you recognize that the transfer may provide valuable experience and perhaps mean a future promotion, you may also be reluctant to leave your old friends and familiar surroundings.

Promotions

A transfer to a higher-level job within the organization is a promotion. A promotion usually means increased pay, status, and responsibility. Companies usually make promotions on the basis of seniority, merit, or both. Seniority provides a simple, straightforward method of promotion but certainly lacks the motivational aspects of promoting on the basis of merit. However, merit has its own inherent problems, particularly the difficulty of accurately evaluating the job performance of individuals.

Companies use various methods of evaluation. A common one involves the evaluation of several attributes of job performance, such as quality of work and cooperation, on scales ranging from poor to excellent (figure 10–1). Problems arise, however, because of personal bias, overemphasis of recent behavior, a tendency to rate everyone about the same, and allowing a specific trait of an

	Poor	Fair	Good	Very Good	Excellent
Quality of work					
Dependability in carrying out assignments					
Attitude toward work					
Attitude toward company					
Ability to get along with co-workers					
Efficiency in getting work done					
Leadership—ability to influence co-workers					

Name _____

Department _____

Date hired _____

Present position _____

Date of placement in present position _____

General comments _____

_____

_____

_____

Evaluator _____

Title _____

Date of evaluation _____

Figure 10–1 Conventional graphic rating scale

individual to excessively influence the ratings on other traits. Despite these difficulties, many managers and some employees favor promotion by merit while unions tend to favor a base in seniority. The union attitude is explained by its desire to maintain solidarity of membership and to avoid any differentiation among their members such as would be imposed by merit promotions and performance evaluation.

Performance evaluations are commonly used, however, and do have value beyond their use in promotions. Evaluations provide a basis for counseling with employees on how to improve their education, training, job skills, and interactions with other employees. This sort of counseling is a delicate matter as an employee may quickly feel threatened and defensive when discussing his past performance. A recent tendency is to accentuate the positive by asking employees to set their own goals in the areas of job skill, personal relationships, and training. Then they are asked to evaluate their own performance and to set new goals in cooperation with their supervisors. This process emphasizes the future as well as the past.

In recent years, managers and subordinates have responded favorably to the method in which the employee sets his own goals.[1] The following imaginary incident may help to illustrate how this system of *management by objectives* works.

An Evaluation with a Future

John Arden had just started work with the purchasing department of a manufacturing company. He had worked for another company for five years after graduation from college but had left because he felt his talents had been largely unappreciated. John believed the evaluation system in his old company was grossly inadequate and offered little or no opportunity for recognizing ability.

A friend had told him good things about his present employer, but Arden was skeptical and was impatiently awaiting his first evaluation. After a few weeks on the job, his boss, Larry Dent, called Arden in, asked him to set down on paper some specific goals for the next six months, and to report back in a week. Arden was nonplussed. For five days he thought about it. After all, he had never done this sort of thing before.

Finally, he really put his mind to it. My job is buying fasteners (screws, bolts, and so on), he thought; what can I do in six months to improve my performance on the job? After considerable thought, he came up with just two items. His company had been buying fasteners primarily from one source, so he figured that developing some alternative, reliable sources would be one goal.

Then he added developing better relations with the production people in his own company as a second goal.

Hesitantly, Arden reported back to his boss who, to Arden's delight, seemed quite satisfied. Dent cautioned, however, that it might be difficult to measure improved relations with the production people, but he was willing to go along with it.

Six months later, Arden and Dent reviewed his progress. John had added two reliable sources for fasteners, but he was unsure about his relations with production. As it turned out, Dent had received some favorable comment from the production superintendent about Arden, so both felt some progress had been made.

Arden was very happy with the system, noting that there was no criticism of his personal characteristics and that, instead, the accent was on his continuing development. He also realized that a lot of time was involved, both for himself and his boss, in setting goals and reviewing progress every six months, but he was fully convinced that the company was getting its money's worth. The important aspects, Arden thought, were that he had to be able to set down specific goals and he had to take a problem-solving and not a critical approach in discussions of performance.

Bases for Promotion The reward of promotion may not always go to the best man. Those employees who are unable or unwilling to play the game of organizational politics sometimes may be shunted aside for the less talented. The disappointed promotion-seeker may elect one of several alternatives: to leave the company and seek a more rational system elsewhere; to lower the level of contribution; or to attempt the political game as a route to promotion. Nepotism also intrudes into the rationality of promotional systems when a favorite relative of the boss gets an unjustified boost in the organization. Perhaps the wisest course is to attempt to discover promotional practices in an organization before accepting employment. Talking to current members may be the best means of accomplishing this since formal practices may conceal actual informal practice.

Resistance to Promotion While our society emphasizes getting ahead, not all employees want promotions. People get used to familiar faces, places, and behavior patterns, and a promotion means these things will change. A comfortable feeling of security encourages everyone to resist to some degree the new, the different, and the challenging. Therefore, while it is always wise to maintain promotion opportunities and avoid blind-alley jobs as much as possible, a company should not be too disturbed if some of its employees resist promotion and feel quite satisfied with their existing levels of pay and responsibility.

Planning Ahead

In the areas of recruiting, selecting, and moving people from job to job, it is important that a company not get caught up in firefighting—dashing madly about this week to hire people who are going to be desperately needed next week. It is much better to plan ahead—to anticipate requirements a month from now and a year, five years, and even ten years ahead.

It is particularly important to anticipate managerial personnel needs. Whatever the planning horizon, a forecast of executive needs should be based on anticipated organizational growth, attrition of the present management team, and special requirements in the various managerial positions. A vital part of this planning is a current inventory of personnel showing not only the number of people but also their present talents and skills as well as potential for the development of additional skills and knowledge. In this way, the company obtains an idea of where it should concentrate efforts in terms of hiring new people and training present personnel to be ready for promotional opportunities. While it is not easy to predict future events, this is one of those fairly numerous areas in organizational affairs where forecasting is essential.

Compensation

Everyone expects to receive money for the contributions made to an organization in the course of the normal employment relationship. The pay problems include not only having the money available but in determining how much to pay each individual employee. If an employer engages in interstate commerce and comes under the provisions of the Fair Labor Standards Act of 1938, the government solves part of the problem for him since he must pay at least the minimum wage. In addition, he must pay one and one-half times the hourly base rate for all hours worked over forty hours in any given week. However, beyond this minimum, the situation is much more nebulous, a variety of factors affecting the determination of a level of wages or salary.

Among the most important of these factors is the supply and demand for labor. If the supply of labor is limited, a company is going to have to compete for labor all down the line and to pay the going wage or more in order to attract applicants. It may be that only one particular job skill is in limited supply, but if that skill is needed, the company may have to pay a premium to obtain it. If the supply of labor is large relative to the demand for labor, the company will probably have more flexibility in setting its level of wages.

However, other factors such as the cost of living limit the range of flexibility. If a company is going to maintain an efficient and satisfied work force, one of the things it must do is pay wages and salaries that enable its employees to enjoy an adequate standard of living. If the cost of living increases, most companies will want to increase pay. In fact, some union contracts provide for an automatic pay increase every time the cost of living increases by a certain amount. These contract provisions are called *escalator clauses*.

Bargaining for Wages

Companies that are unionized engage in collective bargaining to establish wage levels. At times, the bargaining reaches an impasse where neither side is willing to yield further, and a strike follows. Then the bargaining becomes a test of the economic strength of the respective parties until they finally reach some agreement— sometimes at the strong urgings of the government when the dispute involves the public interest.

In some industries where a union is particularly strong, great uniformity of wages occurs as the union imposes the same wage levels on all companies in an industry. Craft unions are usually able to effectively control the supply of labor in a local labor market. Thus this power is added to that which they might already have at the bargaining table. Craft unions are able to control the supply of a particular craft because they control entry into a craft through various admission and apprenticeship requirements. Union entry restrictions have been eased in recent years, especially with respect to minority groups, as the government has exerted pressure to reduce discrimination in the crafts.

The factors of supply and demand, cost of living, and collective bargaining compose only part of the wage payment picture, however. They have a lot to do with the overall level of wages and the minimum wages that will be paid, but the factors mentioned offer little guidance for the internal structuring of wages; that is, how much should one job be paid in relation to another. The relative worth of a job in an intraorganizational context is extremely important to a worker. Because even though he may be receiving an adequate income in terms of supply and demand and cost of living, if another worker is doing lesser work in terms of skills and responsibilities but receiving the same pay, the first worker is probably going to be quite unhappy.

For this reason a system is needed to help assure a fair and equitable distribution of wages to all employees based on the required levels of skill, mental effort, physical effort, responsibility, and working conditions in various jobs. The process of doing this is job evaluation. A number of different approaches to job evaluation have been devised; the suggested readings at the end of this chapter provide details on the various systems.

Incentive Systems

If a company has a fair internal system for distribution of wages and has set an overall level of wages based on the factors previously mentioned, it has largely accomplished the job of paying its people. This is true, assuming it is also generating sufficient money inputs to take care of all money outputs. Many companies, however, further sophisticate their wage payment systems by attempting to build into them a motivational device that financially rewards outstanding performance.

An example of such a motivational device would be a simple piecework system. Assume that the base hourly rate for assembling toy trucks is $2.50 per hour. Now let us say the company conducts a motion and time study of this job and determines that a person working at a normal pace can assemble twenty-five toy trucks in an hour. The company then says something like the following to the workers: "Look. We will pay you ten cents for every truck you assemble. If you do twenty-five in an hour, you'll get $2.50, but if you produce more than twenty-five, we'll pay you for whatever you make. And if you assemble less than twenty-five an hour, we'll still pay you the base rate of $2.50. So you've got everything to gain and nothing to lose."

There are actually many different incentive pay systems tailored for particular situations, though most are some variation of the simple system outlined above. There are group systems, too, as well as ones for individual workers. While the idea behind incentive pay systems sounds simple and almost foolproof, problems do accompany their implementation and operation. We briefly covered some of these problems when introducing the Hawthorne studies, and we will do a more complete analysis in chapter 12 when we discuss work groups.

Profit Sharing Some organizations also try to increase employee motivation through the development of financial participation plans. These include stock ownership plans, stock option plans, profit sharing, and production sharing plans (cost savings on production are shared with the workers). Stock ownership and stock option plans are most applicable to managerial levels, while production sharing plans are usually limited to production workers. Profit sharing, however, can embrace everyone in an organization and has been tried by many companies, including some very large ones.

Profit sharing involves an actual sharing of company profits, usually on an annual basis after determination of profit or loss. There are two basic types of plans, current and deferred. The current plan distributes a share of the profits to the employees in cash, while the deferred plan credits them with a share that will not be paid to the employee until a later date—usually on retirement.

The latter plan has one significant advantage: the employee does not pay taxes on his share until he actually receives the money. If this occurs during retirement, as is probable, he will most likely pay a lower tax rate than otherwise since his retirement income presumably will be lower than his income while working. Despite this advantage, many employees prefer to have cash now, which, of course, means having a current type of plan.

One problem of profit sharing is that while companies intend it to be a motivational device, the individual employee often has trouble connecting his particular work activity with the overall profit picture of the company. If the connection is tenuous, as perceived by the employee, we may question any serious motivational claims for profit sharing. Another problem involves regularity of payment. If there are a number of profitable years, and employees receive profit shares on a regular basis, they soon expect to receive this bonus every year. If, then, a year occurs in which profits are limited or negative and profit shares are limited or not forthcoming at all, the employees may be disappointed and even resentful. Thus, a prerequisite for successful profit sharing may be a rigorous educational program so that employees know there may be years when profits are low or nonexistent, and that then shares will likewise be low or nonexistent.

Executive Pay   We have said little about compensation for management personnel simply because there are few standard or even systematic plans in operation. There is wide diversity in salaries paid to executives, and generally merit counts for more in the payment of managerial personnel than it does for operative workers. Some companies have liberal bonus plans for executives who do an outstanding job during any given year while others use stock option plans to reward their best managers. The latter allows those holding stock options to exercise their options for the purchase of company stock at lower-than-market prices during a limited period of time. Deferred bonuses operate in a similar manner to deferred profit sharing and, because of the tax advantages, have become quite popular. Through salaries, current and deferred bonuses, stock options, and other means of remuneration, some executives have annual incomes totaling hundreds of thousands of dollars.

Training

A company cannot assume employees are capable of performing their jobs in an effective manner without some preparation. At a minimum, the company must provide new employees with an introduction to the organization. Have you ever gone to work for a company and remembered how strange and perhaps frightening your first day on the job was? If no one bothered to show you the ropes, you probably stood around not knowing quite what to do and feeling very much like the lost and confused person you probably appeared to be.

This is precisely the sort of situation a company should seek to avoid with respect to its new employees. It is imperative that a company have an effective orientation program for new members. In a business, the personnel department usually assumes part of this responsibility in terms of a general introduction to company policies, fringe benefits, pay, and general conditions of employment. Equally important, the supervisor of the department where the new person is to work, or someone the supervisor may appoint, should accept the responsibility for acquainting the new employee with specifics of the job routine. This will include such items as the length and time of breaks and lunch hours, introductions to fellow workers, locations of washrooms and cafeterias, and other relevant information.

On-the-Job Training Beyond initial orientation, the principal function of training is to instill job knowledge and skills. Organizations use a number of methods to accomplish this, and we can discuss them most easily by first differentiating operative training and management development. In operative training, management must first determine two things: (1) the content of training in terms of what an employee must do to perform a task or job in an effective way; and (2) the skills, knowledge, and attitudes an employee must develop if he is to perform the tasks that constitute his job in the organization. After doing such an analysis, management establishes the training methods that will help employees to be more efficient and effective.

Probably the most common method of training a new employee is on-the-job training. The supervisor or a fellow employee introduces the new person to his job and helps him along until he can begin to function by himself. This method is satisfactory for relatively simple jobs; but for complex jobs, the lack of training expertise of the supervisor or fellow employee may prove a severe handicap. In addition, pressure to get out production displaces on-the-job training and may cut into time and effort that should be devoted to training.

To overcome these handicaps, some companies segregate their training programs from the production process. One form of this is vestibule training, where trainees receive instruction on machines, for example, in an area away from the production departments. Although the duplication of equipment is expensive, there are advantages in allotting time specifically for training and in using skilled instructors. Classroom training is another way to gain these advantages. Some training methods involve a combination of on-the-job and off-the-job techniques. Apprenticeship training is an example of this combination in that a novice not only works under the supervision of a master craftsman but also spends time in a classroom situation.

Management Development

Management development is important to a business since a supply of competent, trained individuals must always be available to take over executive slots as an organization grows and maintains success. A prime requirement for a successful management development program is an inventory of current management talent and a determination of the needs of present and potential managers in terms of advancing them through the ranks of the organization. The process of determining current abilities and needs is difficult, since much of it depends on subjective appraisals. Certain types of performance, such as producing so many toy trucks per hour, are susceptible to objective measurement. Managerial jobs, however, entail a great deal of activity the results of which cannot be quantified or may not even be known for an extended period of time. Much effort has been and is being made to develop effective methods of individual appraisal.

Self-development for managerial personnel has been heavily emphasized in recent years. Self-development imposes certain conditions on an organization, however. There must be an atmosphere of encouragement for self-development; rewards must be real and not illusory; and the organization must allow the individual freedom to act and to make mistakes if there is to be a meaningful learning experience. In other words, there must be a certain level of tolerance for errors, particularly for lower-level managers. As an executive gains experience and rises to positions of increasing responsibility, the error tolerance will diminish.

Not all development depends on self-development, however. There are a number of training methods for managerial people as well as for operative personnel. Among these are job rotation, understudy assignments, committee assignments, and classroom lectures. Organizations also encourage managers to take university courses and to participate in educational and professional organizations. Many universities provide extension courses and special seminars for managerial people, and some consulting firms conduct special seminars.

A form of management development that we have mentioned earlier is sensitivity training. In its pure form, sensitivity training requires a location away from the hustle and bustle of everyday life, typically in a peaceful, isolated country setting. Trainees meet in groups of twelve to fifteen for a period of two weeks. Though a skilled trainer is present, the meeting sessions are unstructured; that is, the trainees receive no guidance from the trainer on what to do or say. The idea is that the trainees will interact in such a way that figurative mirrors develop for each person so that he can see his personality and behavior patterns as they appear to others. Feedback provides the mirror effect, with each person telling the others what he thinks of them and how he reacts to their actions.

In the process of sensitivity training, people become aware of their defensive patterns and how they really affect others. Great rapport usually develops in the groups, and, perhaps surprisingly, individual group members develop a real liking for one another. This attitude encourages change and at the end of the two-week period, the trainee may well feel more secure and less defensive in his interactions with other people. In a pragmatic sense, the goal is to enable people to work together in an atmosphere of frankness and to engage in cooperative goal-oriented activity undisturbed by personality clashes, even though they may occur, or by unproductive defensive behavior patterns.

Since sensitivity training does disturb the defense mechanisms a person may have been developing for years, trained psychologists are present to assist trainees in their acceptance of feedback that may have proven particularly upsetting. Psychological upset is a potential drawback, but a perhaps more serious problem involves transfer, the ability of a person to retain his changed personality back on the job. When returning to familiar ground—old and familiar friends and fellow workers—the same old stresses, strains, and tensions may resurrect the recently shed defense mechanisms. The effects of sensitivity training may last no more than a few days without friendly reinforcement. For this reason, some organizations insist that all managers undergo sensitivity training if any are, feeling that otherwise it is largely a waste of time and money. Sensitivity training is now often available on a more limited basis, with meetings held only a few times a week and held in a location that is convenient to a person's place of employment. Proponents of these latter arrangements claim to accomplish as much on this basis as would be true in the pure form we have described.

Evaluation of sensitivity training is another difficult process. We can give people tests before and after training, and we can observe their behavior before and after training. While these techniques are reasonably effective for certain types of training, such as learning a particular skill, they are much less reliable for other types, such as sensitivity training. Other approaches exist for the evaluation of training, but none apparently provides clear-cut standards by which to measure progress.

Measuring Employee Attitudes

The intensity of effort applied to the attempt to measure employee attitudes waxes and wanes, but most organizations maintain some minimal measure through various readily available objective indices. These indices include the turnover rate, absenteeism, grievances, and production quantity and quality. The problem with these indices is that while suggestions of relative contentment or dissatisfaction may be obtained, there is nothing in the measures that helps explain why turnover is high or low, why absenteeism is high or low, and so forth.

To correct the deficiency, organizations often conduct interviews with their employees, particularly exit interviews—that is, talks with persons leaving an organization, who might be expected to be honest in their responses because they are leaving. Serious doubt about the reliability of the exit interview still confounds many managers, however, for several reasons. Even when leaving an organization, most people may not want to burn their bridges behind them; many will persist in stating what they think the interviewer wants to hear; and it is difficult to assemble a collective opinion when interviewing departing people from many different departments and levels.

Hence, managers often turn to an anonymous questionnaire survey administered by an outside consultant. Anonymity is deemed necessary to help assure honest answers, and the use of an outside consultant presumably guarantees that no individual's answers will be revealed to the sponsoring organization. The questionnaire usually contains questions about how employees feel about organizational factors such as pay or their boss.

The answers are usually multiple-choice form and may be scaled, weighted, and combined in such a way that the organization receives just one total score. The value of this score becomes greater by comparing it to other scores based on the same questionnaire for similar companies, departments within the same organization, or particular groupings of employees. A company may also use the same questionnaire on a periodic basis to detect trends in attitudes.

A good attitude survey should be able:

. . . (1) to determine what is important within the work environment to the employee; (2) to determine the degree to which managers meet the human needs of the organization; (3) to pinpoint the specific strong and weak points of company policies and practices; (4) to evaluate the company's physical facilities and working conditions; (5) to find out what employees feel and think; and (6) to determine information and training needs. Subsidiary objectives are the release of tension through the expression of dissatisfactions and the expression by management of concern, if nothing else, about what employees feel and think.[2]

Once a survey of opinion is accomplished, management cannot sit on the results. Employees will turn off quickly if they have responded honestly and then find nothing being done to correct problems. Management should immediately communicate the results, indicate what will be done, and then do it.

Human Asset Accounting

People form organizations. Managers are people. Experts are fond of emphasizing people as an organization's most important asset. Yet we are only now trying to place a value on the human asset. This effort, human asset accounting, has developed in the last few years in recognition of the value of the individual in organizational decision making. Human asset accounting presumes that measurement of human value will help assure the effectiveness of decision making. In addition, it may be possible to aggregate measures of individuals in order to value groups such as departments, divisions, or small staff groups.

But what will this do: just place another item on the financial statement?

It is significant to note that many of the concepts and much of the terminology being used in developing human resource accounting are being adopted from conventional accounting. They are merely being applied to a problem that has been relatively ignored. Although familiar accounting concepts and terminology are being used, human resource accounting is not being designed for use in published financial statements. It is intended as a managerial tool. It is designed to satisfy information needs presently faced by operating management. It aims to provide management with relevant, timely, quantifiable, and verifiable information about human resources to encourage informed judgments and decisions. It is future oriented, and thus deals not only with transactions data as conventional accounting, but also with measurements of replacement cost and economic value. Since human resource accounting is intended as a managerial tool, it need not be constrained by accounting conventions, legal restrictions, or tax laws.[3]

Getting a handle on the value of a human asset may involve rather sophisticated mathematical models. Acquisition cost, replacement cost, and economic value are factors currently being employed in one approach and represent items that appeal to intuitive understanding.[4] Money to recruit, hire, and train comprise, in part, acquisition and replacement costs. Economic value, on the other hand, may require projection of an individual's contribution over an extended future period of time and tends to be more complex.

The value of human asset accounting could be enormous in acquiring other companies, in properly rewarding individuals, in transferring managers, or in evaluating management development methods. However, it may be some time before a body of knowledge develops about how human asset accounting should be used for planning and controlling within an organization or about the impact of such an accounting system on human behavior. The development of such a body of knowledge presumes a point in development where human asset accounting can and will be widely applied.[5]

Summary

After becoming a member of an organization, a person may experience numerous job changes. Transfers occur at the request of individuals or for the convenience of the organization. Promotions reward meritorious or long-term service. Presumably, performance evaluations form the bases for these actions, though in many cases evaluations are inexact and seniority or favored status play an overriding role.

Compensation is an important part of most organizational memberships. While supply and demand and labor negotiations often are predominant in setting the level of wages and salaries, equitable internal structuring is equally important. More difficult and more responsible jobs should command relatively more pay, and vice versa. There are many variations on method of payment, including incentive systems, profit sharing, and stock options for executives.

To make more effective use of personnel, most organizations maintain job training and management development programs. There are many different approaches to training and development. Difficulty of performance evaluation often prevents assurance that the best possible training method is in use.

Attempting to get a fix on the human asset is a continuing endeavor for most organizations. The determination of employee attitudes through interviews and questionnaires is one avenue of approach. Another and more recent one is human asset accounting. The latter strives to place measurable values on organization members in order to improve judgments and decisions about individuals.

Management Profile

Oliver Sheldon

Writer, scholar, and business practitioner, Oliver Sheldon worked during the period of development of classical theory. Although he is placed in the ranks of classical writers, Sheldon added dimensions of social responsibility and community service as he attempted a synthesis between scientific management and humanitarianism. Fresh out of the British Army in 1919, Sheldon, then 25, got a job as personal assistant to B. Seebohm Rowntree, chairman of Rowntree and Company, an English company specializing in the manufacture of chocolates and confectionaries.

Rowntree was a well-known amateur sociologist and believed that the company was a human organization more than anything else. The company employed many girls who:

> . . . sang at their work, drank cocoa at a penny a cup, enjoyed the plants that hung in the corridors, and kicked up their heels on the lawns outside. Sheldon was never to leave the place. He knew the kind of management he liked before he'd spent four years at Rowntree's. . . . As early as 1891, women welfare workers were added to the staff, and before the turn of the century a suggestion system and a pension plan were installed.
>
> Workers' councils, pensions for widows, the 44-hour, 5-day week were all adopted by 1919, and by 1933 a profit-sharing plan, a full-time psychologist, employee testing, and union agreement for the time-study of all jobs had appeared. The same year saw the factory's work rules revised and approved by Rowntree's employees. They also joined a precedent-breaking Joint Appeal Committee through which management gave up its ultimate disciplinary powers.[6]

Sheldon's major work was his book *The Philosophy of Management*, published in 1923.[7] In it he sought a synthesis between scientific management and the social ethic that permeated the Rowntree Cocoa Works. While advocating the use of science in management to develop efficiency in both the human and material elements of the factory, he also championed a policy of responsibility to the community that demanded certain practices in regard to the human element of production.

These practices included the right of workers to form associations, effective leadership, equitable discipline, worker participation in certain management decisions, the provision of an adequate standard of living and leisure time for the workers, stable employment, profit sharing according to contribution, and a spirit of equity in all relations between labor and management. Yet while Sheldon was much in favor of participatory democracy in industry, he emphasized that management still must provide leadership and guidance in order to be successful. Although no mention of Rowntree was ever made in his book, his writing nonetheless highlighted the practices of a successful company that believed in a social ethic of community responsibility and humanitarian treatment of workers.

Discussion Questions

1. Through transfers and promotions, a company may be able to recruit many if not all of the people needed to fill open positions from within

the organization. While this practice may help maintain high morale, what disadvantages might it entail?

2. Imagine yourself as a branch sales manager for a typewriter company. You've had two interviews with an applicant for a sales job, and you've been very impressed with the applicant's motivation and enthusiasm. However, results from a battery of psychological tests indicate the applicant has a low aptitude for sales work. Do you think you would hire this person? Why?

3. The incident "An Evaluation with a Future" illustrates the use of management by objectives for the job of buyer in a purchasing department. Do you think management by objectives could work for all types of jobs? Consider, for example, the following jobs: policeman, restaurant chef, bank teller, assembly line worker, construction foreman, and truck driver.

4. Inflation and a limited supply of labor in a given area can combine to produce some unhappy situations. Consider the case of an engineer, for example, who has been with the company for the three years he or she has been out of college. The engineer finds out the company is hiring new people at higher starting salaries than the engineer is making after three years. As you may expect, the engineer is very unhappy. What, if anything, can the company do to prevent these situations?

5. In guiding the development of their personnel, some organizations place the greatest emphasis on increasing knowledge about the job while others stress changes in attitude and behavior. Apparently there is disagreement about what is most important in personnel development. What is your opinion?

References

1. H. Meyer, E. Kay, and J. R. P. French, Jr., "Split Roles in Performance Appraisal," *Harvard Business Review*, 43 (1965): 123–129.

2. P. Pigors and C. A. Myers, *Personnel Administration* (New York: McGraw-Hill, 1965), p. 288.

3. R. L. Brummet, E. G. Flamholtz, and W. C. Pyle, "Human Resource Measurement—A Challenge for Accountants," *The Accounting Review*, 42 (1968): 217–224.

4. *Ibid.*

5. J. K. Link, "Human Asset Accounting," University of Missouri–Columbia, 1971.

6. "Famous Firsts: A Happy Factory that Sired a Social Ethic," *Business Week*, 1921 (1966): 126–127.

7. O. Sheldon, *The Philosophy of Management* (New York: Pitman, 1966).

Suggested Readings

Bass, B. M., and Vaughan, J. A. *Training in Industry: The Management of Learning*. Belmont, Calif.: Wadsworth, 1966.

Broadwell, M. M. *The Supervisor and On-the-Job Training*. Reading, Mass.: Addison-Wesley, 1969.

Carroll, S. J., Jr. and Tosi, H. L., Jr. *Management by Objectives: Applications and Research*. New York: Macmillan, 1973.

Fleishman, E. A. *Studies in Personnel and Industrial Psychology*. 2d ed. Homewood, Ill.: Richard D. Irwin, 1967. Section 2.

Ghiselli, E. E. *Explorations in Managerial Talent*. Pacific Palisades, Calif.: Goodyear, 1971.

Mahoney, T. A. *Building the Executive Team*. Englewood Cliffs, N.J.: Prentice-Hall, 1961.

Reeves, E. T. *Management Development for the Line Manager*. New York: American Management Association, 1969.

The Individual and the Organization

11

An organization must accomplish numerous activities to induce people to join and to stay. In the last chapter, we described some of these inducements: compensation, providing opportunities for promotion, training, and development. This is only part of the story, however. To gain the full and effective contributions of organization members, management must obtain an understanding of human behavior. Both the organization and the individual benefit from such understanding. Propositions and behavioral science research results pertaining to human behavior enable managers to make more effective decisions.

Organizations have grown complex in the last century. Individuals, however, have always been complex. The behavioral sciences (principally psychology, sociology, and anthropology) have advanced rapidly in the generation of new knowledge about human complexity. The growth of sophisticated, industrialized societies has helped expose the complex nature of man and has added new complex behavior that must be studied.

Personality

What are the unanticipated consequences of having people in the organization? Does each individual react differently to organization membership? Are there similarities in behavior? Do similarities or differences in behavior depend upon similarities or differences in personality? What is personality? And so on. We will begin our attempt to answer these and other questions by reviewing theories about personality.

Personality is the pattern of dispositions to act consistently in varying situations. Put another way, it is the stable attributes that a person carries with him and that determine his approach to the problems of living.[1] For example, one person may be disposed to anger and hostility over many events in his daily life, while another person moves along with measured calm, seldom displaying any hostile emotion beyond mild irritation.

Personality, however, is constantly affected by the environment in which behavior occurs. That is, the disposition to act in a certain way may be upset given certain circumstances. Hence, while predictions may be made about an individual's future behavior with some probability of accuracy, given knowledge of his personality structure, completely reliable forecasts can rarely be made. Under varying circumstances, the nonhostile person may react violently, or the hostile individual may pass through a stressful situation unruffled. The inability to completely explain and predict human behavior makes people interesting, of course, but also adds to the complexity involved in understanding and working with them.

Personality and the Satisfaction of Needs

Given that individuals carry with them propensities to act in certain ways, what makes them act at all? What governs much of our behavior? The answer lies in satisfaction of needs. And predominant among them are *primary needs*. We act first of all to survive—to eat, breathe, drink water, and to reproduce the species. Most people in a developed society satisfy these needs readily, but the world is full of instances where primary needs are not readily satisfied.

When primary needs are largely satisfied, other needs emerge—*secondary needs*. These are social needs, and they may be split into two categories—*affiliative* needs and *egoistic* needs.[2] "Both have to do with people, but the affiliative needs deal with belongingness, companionship, or love of being *with* people. The egoistic needs refer to a position *over* people rather than with people. Power, status, prestige, or esteem fit under this second subclassification."[3]

Behavior is motivated toward a goal structure determined by unsatisfied needs. How each person behaves as he seeks to satisfy his needs is determined largely by personality, which develops in the period up to early adulthood and remains relatively stable throughout a lifetime. Generally, then, we would not expect a person to act much differently at age 45 than at age 25 in trying to satisfy his affiliative and egoistic needs.

The differences between individuals in this respect, however, may be great. One person may aggressively seek out the friendship of many others, while another depends on the overtures of others to establish a few enduring relationships. One may blatantly strive for status and prestige, while another quietly insinuates himself into a position of power. Figure 11–1 portrays the process of need satisfaction.

Unsatisfied Needs Not everyone experiences the same level of motivation to satisfy needs; that is, the strength of various needs is not consistent from one person to another. Where one person may be highly motivated to satisfy an intense egoistic need, another may expend little effort in this direction but a lot in the satisfaction of affiliative needs. Depending on the individual's talent and ability, the satisfaction of a need for great power and prestige, for example, might be quite easily frustrated.

What happens then? First of all, an unsatisfied need generates stress or tension. When you are hungry, you endure physical stress, which is only relieved when you finally eat. Similarly, stress is encountered when secondary needs are not satisfied. People are motivated to satisfy the needs and relieve the stress associated with unfulfillment. If primary needs remain unsatisfied, people eventually die, but if secondary needs remain unsatisfied, a variety of reactions can result. Blair Kolasa describes the general patterns of response to nonsatisfaction of needs:

Nonattainment of a goal is frustrating. One way of handling this is to leave the "field" or withdraw. The withdrawal may be physical, as in flight from the scene, or it may be internalized and carried to the extreme lethargy seen in *apathy*.

A more common reaction to frustration is *aggression*, an act or force against someone or something. Aggression is most easily seen as a move outward. If there is a direct attack on the source of frustration in a way that can take care of the problem, this is often reasonable and healthy. It may not be "healthy," however, to punch the boss in the nose in order to remove this source of frustration. What happens all too often is that the

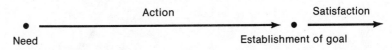

Figure 11–1 Need satisfaction

aggression is directed to third parties or objects. This circumstance is known as *displacement*. Innocent bystanders have been known to suffer from frustrations not of their doing; when a husband growls at his wife after a traumatic day at the office, the innocent spouse should be understanding but may not be. Aggression displaced toward inanimate objects may be less taxing for humans. Kicking doors and sawing wood have long been popular. A newer and perhaps more therapeutic displacement device is the dummy resembling the boss which some few companies have introduced. The worker need only retire to a special room and punch away.[4]

There are other more severe reactions to failure to satisfy needs, ranging from defense mechanisms such as compensation and sublimation to neuroses and even psychoses. In *compensation*, a person overacts in one activity to make up for deficiencies in another. For example, the boss who knows he exerts little control over his subordinates may attempt to compensate through exaggerated friendliness. In *sublimation*, a generally approved social activity substitutes for one that is disapproved or not possible. The owner–manager of a company that is unsuccessful or is successful because of questionable practices may sublimate by dedicating himself and his company to forms of community service. In each instance of defensive behavior, the individual is reacting to frustration, stress, or anxiety in the effort to protect his self-concept (figure 11–2).

With the exception of neuroses and psychoses, the defensive reactions just described are indulged by all of us to some degree.

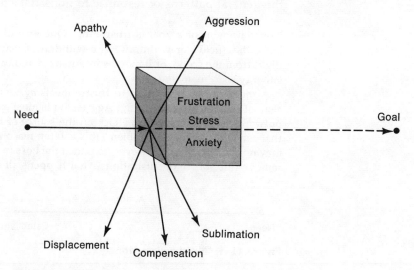

Figure 11–2 Defensive behavior

While not totally adequate in guarding a self-image, neither do they generally harm an individual as he constantly strives for need satisfaction. In those instances, of course, where defense mechanisms induce great rigidity of behavior, they can prove a definite handicap. But such behavior is then verging on the neurotic and includes such responses as phobias, compulsions, and obsessions.

Regulating Behavior It might be convenient if we could handle our needs one at a time, so that a different need would not bother us until a present need had been satisfied. Such, however, is not the case. Two or more needs often occur at the same time. We can be, for example, hungry, thirsty, desirous of companionship, and anxious to get some necessary work done all at the same time. Without some sort of system for establishing priorities, we would be dashing madly from one need to another as each established an overriding urgency.

Most people, however, are capable of satisfying one need even while others are generating increasing amounts of tension. How many times have you postponed eating until some work was finished—work that might provide added security, increase esteem, or satisfy an egoistic need? A control process is part of the motivational system and enables far more mature behavior than that based solely on impulse. These two forces, then, motivation and regulation, govern our behavior, and the particular behavior pattern that emerges manifests the individual personality.

Personality and emotion are closely related, as are motivation and emotion. We often hear remarks to the effect that someone has a happy or a dour personality, presumably meaning that the former primarily experiences happiness while the latter languishes in gloom and austerity. There may also be predispositions to act in anger, to easily experience joy, or to shed tears—all emotional forms of behavior that reveal personality. As with personality, emotional states may be thought of as distinct from motivation but closely related to it. A highly motivated person may be at the same time a highly emotional person. And the person who is frustrated in need satisfaction may react quite emotionally.

Cognition

As individuals, we are quite aware of many of our need-satisfying activities and emotional states; that is, we know what we are doing when we eat to assuage hunger pangs, and we know that we become angry, sad, or joyful. There is another activity of which we are quite aware, and that is thinking. Along with associated processes such as reasoning, problem solving, perception, judgment, and creativity, thinking defines the more generic term *cognition*.[5]

In the cognitive process, an individual abstracts from the real world through the use of images or symbols. In this way, we can reason our way through some problematic situation, make judgments based on some standard, or create something of value that is different from the ordinary.

Cognition is based on perception, which is the way an individual organizes and interprets all the data and information received from sources external to himself. "The system or organism recognizes the information, assembles it, and makes comparisons with material previously stored in the 'central information processing storage.' This involves a whole history of what has happened to the individual over his lifetime, since it is the organization of inputs through an inner process that is dynamic, that is, a constantly changing one. It is a process that shapes whatever comes in from the outside; in turn, what is there is changed by what comes in."[6]

There is, of course, a vast amount of external stimuli that can be perceived. But if you think for a moment of your own perceptive abilities and experiences, you may realize that people perceive only a small part of the total possible. Barring a photographic memory, a 30-second look at a crowded room usually results in recall of only a small percentage of its contents. We say, therefore, that perception is selective; that is, we select a limited amount of information from the outside simply because we cannot handle more.

At the same time, people often perceive more than they are aware of. After observing a crowded room, for example, an individual may be asked to write down everything he saw. After listing ten items, others may be suggested, and he may then recall having seen additional items of which he had not been aware. How often have you been unaware of some constant sound until your attention was drawn to it, or until the sound changed in some manner?

Hence, much of our perceptual awareness is determined by what commands our attention, and this in turn depends largely upon dimensions of the stimulus: intensity, size, contrast, and repetition. Advertisers exploit these dimensions to command our attention and to make us aware of their products. It is important to remember also that perceptions below the conscious level, those of which we are unaware, can influence us—the noise we do not "hear" but which is irritating, or the visual asymmetry which we do not "see" but which is, nonetheless, upsetting. Have you ever said, "I knew something about this place bothered me, but I couldn't pin it down until I saw that (or heard that or smelled that)?"

Personality Set Also influencing perception is a person's *set*, determined by a lifetime of conditioning from many sources—family, peers, education, successes, failures, and others. A set is a tendency to perceptually respond in a certain way. An individual living in a large city and walking at night may hear footsteps behind him. The way he has learned to internally process and organize information from the outside suggests danger, and he acts accordingly. A different set may apply in a very small town. In this instance, footsteps may be perceived as a likely signal for encountering a friend, and instead of running, the individual turns around prepared to issue a friendly greeting.

Hence, we have "a tendency to perceive what we expect to perceive" and "what we perceive depends a great deal on not what is out there but what we ourselves bring to the situation—our own needs, drives, and predispositions."[7] These tendencies may extend to stereotypes, a prejudiced perception of people and events. For example, a worker may perceive all managers as being harsh and exploitative, while a manager may perceive all workers as being lazy and as bilking the organization whenever possible. An infinite number of possible stereotypes exists. Most of these probably are dysfunctional to the individual in that they preclude the possibility of clear perception and therefore interfere with the cognitive process.

In discussing personality, the satisfaction of needs, and cognition, we have indicated that these phenomena are generally applicable to all humans. We noted from time to time, however, that individuals do differ. We turn our attention now to the development of individual differences.

Uniqueness of the Individual

Each of us is unique in personality, in the intensity and direction of needs, cognitive patterns, and other dimensions; particularly when these are considered in combination. What factors play a role in personality differentiation? Inherited traits are important. Size, general shape, coloring, and other physical characteristics are established before birth and initiate the differentiation process. Social interaction within the family shapes the personality during the early years. Child-rearing styles are important and include such factors as the amount of affection given to a child, the manner and severity of punishment, what sorts of values are instilled, and the activities that are encouraged.

Many studies suggest the importance of parental influence on personality formation.[8] For example, there is a close correlation in attitudes and values among family members—closer than between children and peers or between children and teachers. These latter relationships do have their impact, however. All through life, one's association with peer and other groups has a continuing effect on development, although early associations are the most influential.

Inevitable Conflicts That early experiences in the family do most to strengthen personality dimensions and to cement attitudes and values does not mean that conflicts in values or dissatisfaction with one's personality never occur. As exposure increases to outside influences—such as peer groups, schools, reading materials, and travel—the opportunity for conflict also increases even though these influences remain subordinate to the already established family influence.

Usually the family persuasion wins out, though some modification may result. In certain instances where interaction with the family has been sporadic or disturbing, teachers, counselors, and friends can help alleviate emotional problems through the development of different attitudes and behavioral predispositions. In other cases, encountered values may be so far removed from those already held that no problem occurs. Or, the individual may be unable to reconcile large differences in values and so adopts the new values as his own, though perhaps only temporarily.

The last modification most likely occurs where the first-acquired values are not deeply entrenched, and the individual gladly surrenders them for what appears to be a more attractive set. The change can go in several different directions, but we often associate it with delinquency patterns or other dysfunctional behavior, especially when we wonder something like why that nice young man from that good home turned out to be so bad.

Other potential sources of conflict, though not completely distinct from the influences we have just discussed, are the roles we seek or have thrust upon us. Imagine yourself, for example, as a policeman, a college professor, a senator, or a professional football player. Some of the demands attached to each occupation are patently different. Each demands that a certain role be "played." There are differences between directing traffic and teaching a class or between studying national defense issues and studying a game plan. And the public has some general expectations about how a person is supposed to behave in a given role. We may expect the policeman to be positive in his actions as he directs traffic; the professor to examine all sides of an issue before reaching a conclusion; the senator to combine these two characteristics as well as carry a heavy burden of responsibility; and the football player to combine dedication with high physical skill.

A person may not feel completely secure in the match between his role and his personality. In many instances, he may not want to or could not carry out certain roles. When a person can perform adequately, conflict between role and personality may tend to disappear as the role and its expectations shape personality. Years as a professor certainly will have some impact on the professor's personality as he or she seeks to meet the expectations of students, fellow professors, superiors, family, and of the community in fulfilling his or her role. And changes in attitudes and values might well be associated with the personality changes.

In sum, we know that everyone has a personality, that everyone seeks to satisfy needs, and that everyone thinks. But we also know that everyone is different. And these differences are what makes the job so tough as an organization attempts to relate to its individual members—to motivate them, to satisfy them, to induce them to be "good" organizational members. For example, let us consider an imaginary illustration of need conflict.

The Road to the Top "Hey, Charlie. C'mon, we'll be late at the first tee."

That was Henry, Charlie's good friend and coworker at the Hit-'em-a-Mile Golf Club Company. They were about to play the first round of the year in the company's golf league. Charlie hurried, but he was also thinking back to that first day on the job—now over three years ago.

The president had talked to him that day, explaining how he and his 300 employees were one big happy family. They worked together, ate together, picnicked together, and played golf together—most importantly, played golf together. And Charlie, as a member of the management team and the company family, surely would want to participate in all the togetherness, especially the golfing togetherness.

But while the president had played on one of the top college golf teams, Charlie had hated sports all his life—especially golf. The specter of chasing a little ball around acres of countryside utterly appalled him. He smiled now, thinking how his attitude had changed. "I actually like the stupid game," he thought. And his wife had told him, repeatedly, that he was more outgoing and social since coming to work for Hit-'em-a-Mile. He mused again, "It's funny how when you're sort of forced to act in a certain way, you really kind of become that way."

But one thing hadn't changed. His promotion to a vice-presidency had only confirmed what the president also told him on that first day, "The road to the top in this company is determined by what you do on the job—not on the golf course or anywhere else." And Charlie had worked hard—days, nights, and weekends. He remembered the many times he had wanted to play golf, really wanted to play, and chose instead to get some necessary work out of the way.

"But," he thought, "all those little frustrations and conflicts were nothing in the long run. My promotion is worth every kick I gave my office chair on those Saturday mornings when the weather was so perfect for a game."

Charlie grabbed his clubs. "Hey, Henry. What're you waiting for? We haven't got all day, you know."

Motivation

Our prime interest, of course, relates the individual to the organization. What we have discussed in a few pages about individual behavior does not even begin to suggest the vast literature in this area. But in spite of this accumulated knowledge, there is no widely accepted theory that explains or prescribes an effective basis of motivation within the context of a complex organization.

There are theories, to be sure, and we will examine several. And there are techniques based on theory, and we will examine some of these. But the means to effective motivation continues to plague the modern manager as it has managers over many past years. We can, for example, read in Frederick Taylor's works about soldiering on the job. Many nineteenth century writings urged sobriety, industriousness, loyalty to one's employer, and many other admonitions of similar ilk. Such writings indicate that management has always had trouble motivating workers.

On the other hand, the Protestant work ethic was influential for many years on both sides of 1900. And of even greater impact was a general work ethic nourished on the many farms where work from sunrise to sundown was common. Certainly today, however, our culture and values have changed. We no longer fervently embrace Horatio Alger; we feel free to question the loyalty and dedication demanded by many organizations; and we have the means to pursue interests away from the job—interests that may prove more fulfilling and satisfying than anything encountered in the job situation. People are basically the same today as seventy-five years ago, but the many facets of more affluent and sophisticated life styles no doubt make motivation a more complicated proposition.

Individual and Organizational Goals

Given a little knowledge about human needs and behavior, a manager might think the matter of motivating within the organizational context relatively simple. After all, it would seem that if the individual could perceive that the achievement of organizational goals would also satisfy individual goals, the whole problem would be solved right there. Management would simply have to point out the mutual interest existing between the individual and the organization, and the latter would enthusiastically work for the organization, thereby helping to assure satisfaction of his own needs and goals. It is not that easy, however.

Classical theory, for example, derived from experience with involuntary organizations such as church and army, presumed that workers would subordinate their personal objectives to those of the organization. Since monetary return represented the only reward sought by economic man, a perception of similarity of goals would be quite natural. The harder an individual worked, the more money the organization would earn; and the more money the organization made, the more money an individual would earn.

Frederick Taylor put the whole matter on a more personal basis through the use of incentive plans. The basic idea was still the same—hold out the promise of more money for harder work, and man will work harder. These simplistic notions of classical theory have been largely discounted by the recognition of other motivational factors besides material gain, although the importance of money as a motivator has not been discarded but rather cast into a broader perspective.

To date, however, research has failed to determine the proper role of financial compensation in motivation. Many questions remain unanswered. For example:

The principal research problem is to discover in what way money motivates employees, and how this, in turn, affects their behavior. For this, we must know more about the motives of employees—which motives are dominant, and how employees differ from one another in the configuration of their motives. We must also determine which of these motives can be linked to money as an incentive. Can money be linked with insatiable needs so goal attainment does not cause cessation of behavior? Can money act as an incentive for the "higher order" needs? The two main hypotheses here—that money can serve only "lower order" needs, and that it can serve essentially all needs—have very different implications for compensation practices. Investigation of this question requires not only the discovery of the motives for which money has instrumental value but also the extent to which money can serve to fulfill or satisfy these needs. Quite obviously, money serves to satisfy needs for food, clothing, and shelter, but it is much less obvious how money may be related to such other areas as need Achievement or need Power. It seems obvious that money serves these needs too, but solid evidence of a relationship is lacking. To what extent may money be a primary way of dispensing feelings of achievement, competence, power, and the like? In other words, what needs are currently served by money, and what needs, not now perceived as associated with money, may it be called upon to serve?[9]

There is much to be learned about the motivating effects of money. Obviously, it is important. But exactly how money affects behavior—in terms of amounts paid, increases in pay, and methods of payment—remains very much a mystery.

A Hierarchy of Needs

We said earlier that one possible classification of needs was on a primary–secondary basis; the latter being further subdivided into egoistic and affiliative needs. While this may explain some types of motivated behavior, it does not provide much help to the manager in attempting to motivate individuals on the job. Abraham Maslow has identified a more complete configuration of needs intended to more thoroughly explain individual motivation. He identified five human needs: (1) physiological, (2) safety, (3) social, (4) esteem, and (5) self-fulfillment. Maslow's basic idea is that people first attempt to satisfy physiological needs, then the need for safety, then social needs, and so on to the end of the list. In other words, people confront a hierarchy of needs and will strive to satisfy each one in turn.[10] Figure 11–3 illustrates this concept.

Physiological Needs These are the primary needs for food, water, and reproduction. Necessary for survival, no other need will motivate if these remain unsatisfied. Once these needs are satisfied, however, Maslow suggests we will zero in on the need for safety.

Safety Needs We need to feel protected from the many disasters that could strike: injuries, sickness, loss of job, or discrimination in promotion. Safety is not a demand for absolute security but for the knowledge that everything possible has been done by the

Figure 11–3 Maslow's hierarchy

organization to minimize the risks involved. Safety programs, job security in exchange for good work, and equitable policies on rewards and discipline are examples of things an organization can do to satisfy safety needs. When an individual feels as much has been done as can be reasonably expected, he will then manifest interest in social needs.

Social Needs   At the social level, we move out of the primary needs and into the secondary. An individual needs love, affection, companionship, and other associations that we lump into the category of social needs. Relationships on or off the job satisfy these needs, but there is no basis for a manager to expect his subordinates to make social relationships only off the job.

In some cases, however, management will discourage the formation of social groups within the organization during working hours. With his social drive frustrated, the individual may react with antagonism, noncooperation, and generally anti-organization attitudes. The lesson, of course, is to let groups form. Management is sometimes pleasantly surprised to find a socially harmonious work group performing at higher levels than expected. Once social needs are satisfied, attention focuses on the need for esteem.

Esteem Needs   The need for esteem is far more difficult for most people to satisfy on the job than the needs already mentioned. Esteem relates to the confidence and respect we want in ourselves, and want to be accorded to us from others. It may derive from knowledge, accomplishments, abilities, or other sources. Given that our physiological, safety, and social needs are met, we will strive hard for self-esteem and esteem from others. Satisfaction of the need for esteem produces a feeling of independence and confidence since the individual has successfully cleared his own judgment as well as that of others.

Many jobs in the lower ranks of organizations offer little opportunity for nurturing esteem. In particular, work which has been refined to the point of repetitive boredom simply does not allow much accomplishment nor require much ability. One or more of the manifestations of frustration over an unsatisfied need, then, may well be the result. However, if the need for esteem is largely satisfied, we reach the pinnacle of the hierarchy—self-fulfillment.

Self-Fulfillment Needs At the pinnacle, people strive for the full realization of their potential. In effect, they ask the question, "What can we really do to fully utilize all of our abilities, talents, creativity, and whatever else might be involved in us as humans?" People want to maximize every capability that is in them. Few are fortunate enough to even begin to satisfy this need. Within the organizational context, limited opportunity exists for many members to realize self-fulfillment. Their struggle may thus center on the need for esteem or even on the lower-level needs.

One of the basic ideas in the hierarchy of needs is that as one need is satisfied, the next higher need demands satisfaction and so on up the ladder. A corollary of this idea is that a satisfied need no longer motivates. Therefore, to provide an opportunity for effective motivation, opportunities for satisfying successively higher needs must be offered. Otherwise, frustration will result. Few organizations can offer these opportunities to all members.

You may wonder just what a manager can do with knowledge about the hierarchy of needs. Can it be applied to everyone in the organization regardless of their age, position, length of service, or education? How does one make the hierarchy operational; that is, put it into practice? Evidence suggests that need satisfaction may vary with degree of success, length of service, and different stages in a person's career.[11] Opportunities for need satisfaction, then, would have to be applied differentially, depending on a person's particular situation. But the question, about practice, still remains. Even though we know something about a need hierarchy and the varying requirements of people for need satisfaction, we still know little or nothing about how to put this knowledge into practice.

The Two-Factor Theory

Specifically relating needs and motivation to the job context, the two-factor theory roughly divides Maslow's hierarchy into two parts: needs that motivate effective behavior on the job and needs that merely prevent dissatisfaction. Needs that tend to motivate are at the top of the hierarchy: esteem and self-fulfillment. Satisfaction of the lower-level needs—physiological, safety, and social—prevents dissatisfaction on the job, but, according to the theory, these needs will not motivate effective task behavior.

In searching for what satisfies esteem and self-fulfillment needs, Frederick Herzberg, who developed the two-factor theory, initially questioned 200 accountants and engineers about when and why they felt good on the job and when and why they felt bad.[12] Herzberg later repeated his study with different kinds of workers in different kinds of organizations and obtained essentially the same results as the first time around.

Motivators Herzberg found several factors intrinsic to the job that produce job satisfaction, that satisfy the esteem and self-fulfillment needs, and that motivate effective task-oriented behavior on the job. These factors are (1) a perceived opportunity for achievement, (2) recognition, (3) work itself, (4) responsibility, and (5) advancement. These factors all relate to job content and have been labeled *motivators* or *satisfiers.*

There are also factors in the job environment that do not motivate or provide satisfaction but that merely prevent dissatisfaction. These include organizational policy and administration, supervision, relationship with supervisor, working conditions, salary, relationship with peers, personal life, relationship with subordinates, status, and security. These are *maintenance* or *hygiene* factors, since they are necessary as environmental elements to prevent dissatisfaction, much as we need reasonably clean air, for example, to prevent illness. The maintenance factors are also called *dissatisfiers* since their absence can cause dissatisfaction.

Herzberg makes the important point, with respect to his theory, that job satisfaction and job dissatisfaction are not opposites.[13] The opposite of job satisfaction is *no* job satisfaction while the opposite of job dissatisfaction is *no* job dissatisfaction. This distinction means that failure to provide motivators on the job largely precludes job satisfaction but does not in and of itself produce job dissatisfaction. And fully satisfying requirements of the maintenance factors does not produce job satisfaction but will help remove job dissatisfaction. Herzberg found that when most or all of the motivators are present, individuals are less affected by a poor hygiene situation than when motivators are lacking.

Placing Emphasis Where It Belongs The two-factor theory has contributed to a better understanding of motivation and why attention to certain factors such as salary or wages can remove a source of discontent but do little to motivate someone positively. Many organizations still concentrate exclusively on working conditions, money, policies, supervision, and so forth in attempting to elicit greater work interest and job satisfaction. Results have been disappointing.

The two-factor theory clearly points out that intrinsic job factors are important; that such things as the opportunity to achieve, interest in the work itself, and recognition from superiors and peers satisfy the esteem and self-fulfillment needs and contribute to job satisfaction and interest. A six-year study of an application of the two-factor theory at Texas Instruments Incorporated suggests the validity of its basic concepts.[14] In addition, the study points out that some workers simply cannot be motivated and that persons in different kinds of jobs react differently to the motivators. For example, work in itself was very important to scientists, while advancement and responsibility in work were important to manufacturing supervisors.

"Maintenance seekers," on the other hand, are motivated primarily by the nature of their environment and tend to avoid motivation opportunities. They are chronically preoccupied and dissatisfied with maintenance factors surrounding the job, such as pay, supplemental benefits, supervision, working conditions, status, job security, company policy and administration, and fellow employees. Maintenance seekers realize little satisfaction from accomplishment and express cynicism regarding the positive virtues of work and life in general. By contrast, motivation seekers realize great satisfaction from accomplishment and have positive feelings toward work and life in general.

Maintenance seekers show little interest in kind and quality of work, may succeed on the job through sheer talent, but seldom profit professionally from experience. Motivation seekers enjoy work, strive for quality, tend to overachieve, and benefit professionally from experience.[15]

The experience at Texas Instruments indicated that when maintenance seekers are in an environment of achievement, responsibility, and recognition, they tend to behave like and adopt the values of motivation seekers. Conversely, the absence of motivators apparently can cause motivation seekers to behave like maintenance seekers; that is, they get hung up over the maintenance factors in the environment. Hence, the study suggests that while some people may be difficult to motivate, placing them in an environment of motivators may stimulate them toward more positive feelings.

A Cautionary Note A number of scholars have criticized the two-factor theory mainly on the basis of the research methodology used to collect the data. Herzberg used a storytelling technique wherein respondents related situations in which they felt good or bad on the job. The criticism centers on the thought that when people feel good about something, they tend to enhance their own self-esteem by taking full credit for their achievements, assumptions of responsibility, and advancement. When people feel badly about some situation, often involving some element of failure, they tend to blame environmental or maintenance factors.[16]

Conclusions about what management should do with respect to building motivation may be unjustified, then, when based on this storytelling approach. Given an individual's propensity to take credit for success and to project blame for failure, the results of each replication using the storytelling technique would inescapably parallel the original findings that led to the two-factor theory. In addition, there is a question as to whether everyone even reacts in the same way to sources of job satisfaction and dissatisfaction.[17]

If such doubts exist, why even mention the two-factor theory? The answer applies to all theories on motivation. None of them has been proven; questions can be raised about the validity of each one. We need to work with present theories to develop better ones. The two-factor theory is undoubtedly an oversimplification, but so are all other theories of motivation. Moreover, some organizations have reported successful application of the two-factor theory.

Emphasis on satisfaction of human needs characterizes Maslow's need hierarchy and the two-factor theory. There are other theories that make certain broad assumptions about the nature of man, and that contain implications for motivation. We will examine two of these.

Theory *X* and Theory *Y*

In 1960, Douglas McGregor proposed two views of management's task, each based on certain underlying assumptions about the nature of man. He labeled the views theory *X* and theory *Y*. In the years since, these two theories about motivation perhaps have become more widely known than any other. The conventional conception of management's task is theory *X* and encompasses the following:

1. Management is responsible for organizing the elements of productive enterprise—money, materials, equipment, people—in the interest of economic ends.
2. With respect to people, this is a process of directing their efforts, motivating them, controlling their actions, modifying their behavior to fit the needs of the organization.
3. Without this active intervention by management, people would be passive—even resistant—to organizational needs. They must therefore be persuaded, rewarded, punished, controlled—their activities must be directed. This is management's task in managing subordinate managers or workers. We often sum it up by saying that management consists of getting things done through other people.

Behind this conventional theory there are several additional beliefs—less explicit, but widespread:

4. The average man is by nature indolent—he works as little as possible.
5. He lacks ambition, dislikes responsibility, prefers to be led.
6. He is inherently self-centered, indifferent to organizational needs.
7. He is by nature resistant to change.
8. He is gullible, not very bright, the ready dupe of the charlatan and the demagogue.[18]

The assumptions of the conventional view comprise a serious indictment of human nature—if true. The manager subscribing to the theory X view may seek to direct and control his subordinates by constantly observing them, holding over them the threat of disciplinary action, and demanding exact adherence to company rules and policies. Or he may go to the other extreme, doing almost anything to satisfy subordinate demands and keep them happy—hoping thereby that they will accept his direction and control.

McGregor points out that the conventional view is inadequate because it is based on the satisfaction of only the physiological and safety needs of individuals and ignores higher-level needs. People may behave as described in points 4 through 8 above, but they do so not because this is their basic nature but because the organization forces them into this mold. However, if an organization can make it possible for workers to satisfy social, esteem, and self-fulfillment needs, a completely different behavior pattern may be established. And a different view of management's task also emerges—McGregor's theory Y.

1. Management is responsible for organizing the elements of productive enterprise—money, materials, equipment, people—in the interest of economic ends.
2. People are *not* by nature passive or resistant to organizational needs. They have become so as a result of experience in organizations.

3. The motivation, the potential for development, the capacity for assuming responsibility, the readiness to direct behavior toward organizational goals are all present in people. Management does not put them there. It is a responsibility of management to make it possible for people to recognize and develop these human characteristics for themselves.
4. The essential task of management is to arrange organizational conditions and methods of operation so that people can achieve their own goals *best* by directing *their own* efforts toward organizational objectives.[19]

How can management switch from a theory X view to a theory Y view? Or to put it another way, how can management make it possible for organization members to realize their social, esteem, and self-fulfillment needs? We will confront these questions in chapter 13 on leadership and on the approaches management can take to influence behavior.

A Supporting View Argyris is one of those analysts who states that the typical manager looks at his employees as being lazy, uninterested and apathetic, money-crazy, sloppy, and wasteful. But if the employee fits this mold, it is because the formal organization makes him so. Argyris suggests that the individual is predisposed toward maturity—that he does not want to behave in childlike ways but would much prefer to be relatively independent, to accept challenge, and to exercise awareness and control over self.[20]

However, specialization of task, tight control, and highly directive leadership do not allow adult behavior. Hence, both individual and organizational goals are frustrated and neither party achieves self-actualization. Through a *fusion* process, implemented in part through more free-form structures and improved leadership, the goals of the individual and the organization can converge until both parties realize success.

Positive Reinforcement

Rather than searching for internal sources of motivation and attitude, which critics claim cannot be measured anyway, advocates of *positive reinforcement* suggest simply the consistent rewarding of good performance. Based largely on the work of B. F. Skinner, positive reinforcement is an application of operant conditioning, which we discussed in chapter 7 on control.[21]

A fundamental Skinner principle is that behavior can be engineered, shaped, or changed by a carefully controlled system of rewards—a process that he calls "positive reinforcement." In an industrial setting, this means devising ways of letting an individual employee regularly learn how well he is meeting specific company goals, and rewarding performance improvement—chiefly through frequent praise and recognition. But such reinforcement, Skinner contends, should always be positive. In contrast with "carrot and stick" management approaches, Skinner believes that punishment for such things as poor performance can only produce negative results. It is much more efficient, he argues, to shape behavior by rewarding positive results.[22]

Manipulating behavior sounds sinister to some people, who argue that the end result could be a totalitarian control of mind and body. Nevertheless, there are companies applying positive reinforcement and discovering success. For example, the Emery Air Freight Corporation uses the approach in their sales, customer service, containerized shipping, and other departments.[23] Praise and recognition, plus daily feedback on performance have raised efficiency from 30 percent of standard to 90 percent in some departments. And the results persist after several years.

What You See Is What You Get As we have learned, individuals have various needs they are seeking to satisfy—perhaps sequentially as in Maslow's hierarchy and perhaps concentrated at the esteem and self-fulfillment levels, as suggested in positive reinforcement. Not all persons have the same need intensity, however, and their levels of aspiration will vary according to their past histories of success or failure.

Thus people strive to satisfy varying needs and goals and are willing to work, with varying dedication, to achieve their goals. Some individuals want more money for what it can bring them—a new car, a new house, greater security, a vacation trip. These purchases in turn may satisfy social, esteem, or self-fulfillment needs. Others may seek an increase in status on the job or seek the kind of work that holds intrinsic reward simply through its performance. Most of us obtain a sense of pleasure, satisfaction, or fulfillment through successful performance of some kinds of work, though we tend to label such work a hobby or avocation.

The path-goal theory postulate is that if an individual perceives that hard work will result in achievement of his goal(s), he will be motivated to work hard. But if the desired reward is not perceived, he will not act. Hence, if "what he sees is what he gets" is true, he will work hard to get it.

The Path-Goal Approach   This approach to motivation has been called a path-goal approach,[24] a preference-expectation theory,[25] and an effort-reward expectations theory.[26] The path-goal label is easiest to use in describing the concept that if an individual perceives high performance as a path to a desired goal, he will be motivated to perform. If he does not make the connection between performance and goal achievement, if he does not perceive performance as a path to his goal, he will lack motivation. Hence, a person's effort will be proportionate to his perception that it will lead to the reward he wants.

If the path-goal system is to work, the administrator of the reward must properly evaluate the importance of the reward to the individual. In other words, for the process to work, the reward has to be relevant. So the administrator has to properly perceive the reward needed to motivate the employee. This requires the administrator to know something about the perceptual process and to seek reliable evidence before making arbitrary decisions in the rewarding process[27] (figure 11–4).

Generating Job Satisfaction   Early human relations theory held that a satisfied, contented, and happy worker would also be a productive worker. Yet need theory suggests that unsatisfied needs motivate an individual to act to satisfy his needs and that a satisfied need is not a motivator. Is there any correlation between satisfaction and productivity? Apparently so, if we look at the relationship from a different viewpoint. Instead of saying that satisfaction motivates high performance, we might say that high performance yields satisfaction.

That productivity breeds satisfaction is consonant with the path-goal approach. An individual who is working hard apparently has perceived that hard work will achieve some desired goal. This knowledge followed by goal achievement produces satisfaction. Thus the source of satisfaction is different from the sources of satisfaction generally advocated by some human relations experts: good working conditions, a friendly boss, and/or a variety of fringe benefits.

Therefore, management should strive first to relate rewards to individual goals, thereby motivating high performance, and expect satisfaction to follow. Good working conditions and fringe benefits should be provided, of course, but not with the expecta-

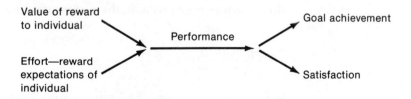

Figure 11–4   Path-goal approach to motivation

tion that these alone will assure productivity. Edward Lawler and Lyman Porter have studied the production–reward–satisfaction relationships and suggest that:

1. If there is a strong positive relationship between production and satisfaction, the organization is effectively distributing rewards based on performance.
2. If there is no relationship between satisfaction and production, then rewards are not being effectively related to performance.[28]

Thus the productivity–satisfaction relationship points out the shortcomings of an organization's rewarding practices. If the company is not linking rewards to performance, the employee does not see satisfaction related to performance. The employee does not believe that an increase in effort will lead to greater reward, and he is not motivated to higher productivity.

What should a company do when it finds that it has no positive relationship between productivity and satisfaction? Porter and Lawler make the following suggestions:

1. The organization must offer rewards which are relevant to the worker.
2. The organization must differentially reward the superior performer over the inferior performer.
3. The organization must maintain credibility about its reward practices. The worker must believe that if he gives a better performance, he will be properly rewarded.[29]

Some Constraints The crux of the path-goal approach is the determination of the most highly valued goals of employees and then the assurance that good performance will spell goal achievement. However, it may be quite difficult in complex organizations for managers to determine the goal preferences for each individual member. In addition, many reward systems simply do not have the flexibility required to tailor rewards to individuals or groups. Under union contracts, for example, across-the-board adjustments in pay and fringe benefits are common, and unions tend to frown on differentially rewarding workers in the same job category. So even if a determination of desired goals could be made, institutional factors may preclude their inclusion in a reward system.

Theory and Practice

Well-developed theory is a basis for sound practice. Hence, if the theories of motivation are well developed, we should expect to find effective application in practice. While we cited some instances of success in providing opportunities for motivation, we can at the same time see many organizations, perhaps the vast majority, floundering in their attempts to motivate members. Either they are not applying known theory, then, or current theory is not adequate to guide motivational efforts. The latter conclusion is probably more correct.

Personality theory and the theories of motivation that we have discussed tell a lot about human behavior and the reasons for behavior. They do so, however, in a general way that is difficult to apply in particular situations. There is considerable evidence in support of each theory, but there are some exceptions as well as a lack of comprehensive replication. The method of positive reinforcement appears to work well in some situations, but it is doubtful whether effective feedback on performance can be supplied in all cases and whether it lasts over a long-term duration.

There is need for much more knowledge about financial incentives, about the application of need theory, about the determination of goals that people really seek—about the basic nature of humans. We need more information about people at different levels in organizations, in different jobs, and in the various stages of a career. With respect to the hourly worker, for example, Bernard Karsh states: "As I see the industrial world today, efforts to make the hourly worker a participator are fading fast, although many managers may refuse to believe it. We are rapidly returning to the old scientific management view that we will buy the worker's muscles for eight hours a day and give up trying to get an ownership attitude out of him. If he is to fulfill himself as an individual, he will have to do it on his own time."[30]

While an ownership attitude may not be possible, many still believe much can be done to relieve the monotony and boredom associated with types of hourly work. At the Saab-Scania plant in Sweden, for example, teams of four workers each are assembling entire automobile engines, whereas in the past each worker on an assembly line did only a small specialized part of the assembly job.[31] The hope is that such job enrichment efforts will "humanize" the assembly job and provide some intrinsic satisfaction to the worker.

An assessment of future trends suggests that different approaches may have to be used for the component elements of an organization and even for different work groups and individuals. Organization level, type of job, career stage, and the individual himself all appear to demand tailored conditions. New values, new technology, and new organization structures constantly challenge our knowledge but at the same time hold forth new opportunities for learning and problem solution.

Furthermore, man does not function alone, even on the job. An individual associates with others and forms groups, and management must not only work with the individual but must also recognize the group. Failure to do so exposes management to unexpected behavior and could precipitate serious conflict situations. We will explore the nature of groups and their implications for managerial decision making in the next chapter.

Summary

Personality is the pattern of dispositions to act consistently in varying situations. The motive power behind action usually is the drive to satisfy some need. Human needs embrace primary and secondary needs; that is, the need to survive in the first instance and the need for social satisfaction in the second. When needs are not satisfied, tension builds, frustration occurs, and one or more of several reactive patterns may follow.

People regulate their behavior, not always acting on impulse but deliberately choosing many times to give one need priority over another in their need satisfaction schedule. People think or engage in cognition, and part of this action is selective perception of external stimuli. Much of this selection process is subconscious, as is the manner in which people internally organize information for their own use. Their cognitive perception also depends on their set or tendency to perceive what they expect to perceive, which in turn is conditioned by years of exposure to reference groups and experience.

Finally, there may be conflict between the roles people play and their personalities. Years of development into a particular personality pattern are not easily shaken if people are asked suddenly to adjust to a new and strange role. In some cases, people cannot adjust: in other cases, the new role also adds personality dimensions, perhaps to the point where the role is no longer disturbing.

Several theories of motivation discussed were the classical theory, Maslow's hierarchy of needs, the two-factor theory, theories X and Y, positive reinforcement, and the path-goal approach. In conclusion, motivational theories tend to be too general for effective application in many specific cases and more information is needed about people at different levels in the organization, in different jobs, and in various stages of a career.

Management Profile

Hugo Munsterberg

Enticed to the United States from Germany by Harvard University, Hugo Munsterberg achieved tremendous success here but was never able to forget his homeland. This attachment to a country that had denied him academic employment cost him dearly. For Munsterberg attempted to influence President Wilson not to intervene in World War I against Germany, thus incurring loss of good friends, attempts to oust him from Harvard, and even threats on his life.

What sort of man was this—rejected by his own country yet demonstrating unfailing devotion to it? Complex, possessing genius, diversified, and prodigiously productive (he once wrote a book in three weeks), Munsterberg is the creator of industrial psychology. Trained at Leipzig under Wilhelm Wundt, the father of modern experimental psychology, Munsterberg arrived at Harvard in 1892 at the age of 29. He built the first laboratory for experimental psychology in this country and launched a career that was amazing for its breadth as well as its depth.

Included among his publications are *Psychology and Life* (1899), *American Traits* (1902), *Eternal Life* (1905), and *Principles of Art Education* (1905). In addition, he wrote many articles for popular magazines such as the *Ladies' Home Journal* and for supplements in the Sunday papers.

Our interest, however, centers on his work in industrial psychology. A great admirer of Frederick R. Taylor, Munsterberg expanded the approach of scientific management to include the measurement of differences between workers, the use of psychological tests to fit the worker to a job, and methods of motivation. But while Taylor had struggled for proper recognition, Munsterberg was lionized.

Businessmen flocked to Harvard for his advice. Munsterberg was invited to visit many of the largest companies in the nation at that time. He devised many tests for individual organizations, counseled on training and motivation, and argued vigorously for the marriage of industrial psychology and industrial engineering.

Munsterberg's introduction of applied and experimental psychology to the world of business and industry marks a milestone in the advancement of knowledge about people and organizations. He died in 1916 at the age of 54, but though his career was cut short, his students and disciples carried on his work. His assistant at Harvard, for example, developed the first standardized mental tests for the Army in 1917.

Discussion Questions

1. What do you think of the idea of having a dummy which resembles the boss so that employees can ease their frustrations by punching the dummy? Is this a mature way to relieve frustration? Are there other ways that could be superior to having a dummy available?

2. A lifetime of conditioning affects the way we perceive events and things. Does this mean, then, that we are prisoners of our own experiences and the influence of family and friends with respect to perception? Is it possible to learn to perceive events and things in different ways? Explain your answer.

3. In the incident "The Road to the Top," Charlie apparently adapted very well to the role expectations of his new job. Can we always expect people to be able to adapt to new roles? Would you anticipate that some individuals might have difficulty in fulfilling a supervisory role for the first time in their careers? Why?

4. Think back to some job you have held—even a very minor part-time or short-term job. Was there any opportunity to satisfy the needs for esteem or self-fulfillment on your job? In other words, were any of Herzberg's five motivators present on your job? If not, what could have been done with the job to enable it to satisfy higher-level needs?

5. Do you believe the path-goal approach to motivation would work better with the theory X approach to management or the theory Y approach? Or doesn't it make any difference? Why?

6. How can a supervisor in a complex business organization determine the goals of his subordinates?

7. What is your view on motivating the unskilled and semiskilled worker? Have we run out of ideas to apply? Have we tried hard enough to apply known theory? Is there a need for new ideas and new theory? What motivation methods would you suggest, and what difficulties in application do you foresee?

References

1. R. S. Lazarus, *Adjustment and Personality* (New York: McGraw-Hill, 1961), p. 24.

2. B. J. Kolasa, *Introduction to Behavioral Science for Business* (New York: John Wiley, 1969), p. 250.

3. *Ibid.*

4. *Ibid.*, pp. 256–257.

5. *Ibid.*, p. 211.

6. *Ibid.*, p. 212.

7. *Ibid.*, p. 217.

8. *Ibid.*, p. 388.

9. R. L. Opsahl and M. D. Dunnette, "The Role of Financial Compensation in Industrial Motivation," *Psychological Bulletin*, 66 (1966): 94–118.

10. A. Maslow, *Motivation and Personality* (New York: Harper & Row, 1954), pp. 35–58.

11. A. C. Filley and R. J. House, *Managerial Process and Organizational Behavior* (Glenview, Ill.: Scott, Foresman, 1969), pp. 374–378.

12. F. Herzberg, B. Mausner, and B. Snyderman, *The Motivation to Work*, 2d ed. (New York: John Wiley, 1959), pp. 30–37.

13. F. Herzberg, "One More Time: How Do You Motivate Employees?" *Harvard Business Review*, 46 (1968): 53–62.

14. M. Scott Myers, "Who Are Your Motivated Workers?" *Harvard Business Review*, 451 (1963): 73–88.

15. *Ibid.*, p. 76.

16. V. H. Vroom, *Work and Motivation* (New York: John Wiley, 1964), pp. 128–129.

17. R. J. House and L. A. Wigdor, "Herzberg's Dual-Factor Theory of Job Satisfaction and Motivation: A Review of the Evidence and a Criticism," *Personnel Psychology*, 20 (1967): 369–389.

18. D. McGregor, "The Human Side of Enterprise," in D. E. Porter, P. B. Applewhite, eds. *Organizational Behavior and Management* (Scranton, Pa.: International, 1964), pp. 452–463.

19. *Ibid.*

20. C. Argyris, *Personality and Organization* (New York: Harper & Row, 1957), p. 123.

21. "New Tool: Reinforcement for Good Work," *Business Week*, no. 2207 (1971): 76.

22. *Ibid.*

23. *Ibid.*

24. B. S. Georgopoulos, et al., "A Path-Goal Approach to Productivity," *Journal of Applied Psychology* (1957): 345–347.

25. Vroom, pp. 15–28.

26. L. W. Porter and E. E. Lawler, "What Job Attitudes Tell About Motivation," *Harvard Business Review*, 46 (1968): 118–125.

27. S. S. Zalkind and T. W. Costello, "Perception: Some Recent Research and Implications for Administration," *Administrative Science Quarterly*, 7 (1962): 218–235.

28. E. E. Lawler and L. W. Porter, "The Effect of Performance on Job Satisfaction," *Industrial Relations*, 7 (1967): 20–28.

29. Porter and Lawler, pp. 118–125.

30. B. Karsh, "Human Relations versus Management," *University of Illinois Bulletin*, 66 (1969): 35–48.

31. "Sweden Tests a New Assembly-line Concept," *Business Week*, no. 2218 (1972): 70.

Suggested Readings

Costello, T. W., and Zalkind, S. S. *Psychology in Administration: A Research Orientation*. Englewood Cliffs, N.J.: Prentice-Hall, 1963.

Kolasa, B. J. *Introduction to Behavioral Science for Business*. New York: John Wiley, 1969.

Maslow, A. H. *Eupsychian Management*. Homewood, Ill.: Richard D. Irwin and The Dorsey Press, 1965.

McGregor, D. *The Professional Manager*. New York: McGraw-Hill, 1967.

Tosi, H. L.; House, R. J.; and Dunnette, M. D. *Managerial Motivation and Compensation*. East Lansing, Mich.: Division of Research, Graduate School of Business, Michigan State University, 1972.

Vroom, V. H. *Work and Motivation*. New York: John Wiley, 1964.

Case Problem for Chapters 10 and 11

The Marginal Purchasing Agent*

Dale Sumner was rarely asked for his professional advice at a Sunday afternoon backyard barbecue, but this was the exception. Having recently moved to San Diego, Sumner and his wife were pleased to have a get-acquainted neighborhood party held in their honor at a nearby home.

---

*R. D. Joyce, *Encounters in Organizational Behavior: Problem Situations* (New York: Pergamon Press, 1972), pp. 118–121.

About midafternoon Sumner found himself engaged in an interesting conversation with Lloyd and Natalie James, host and hostess of the party. James was the Director of Material Procurement for the privately financed Phipps Institute for Ocean Research, and Sumner asked numerous questions about the Institute and its work.

"I don't think I caught your specialty," asked James.

"Human behavior in organizations," replied Sumner. "I recently accepted a position in the Business Department at California State University, San Diego, which is what brought me to this part of the country. I also had a small management consulting practice in Indianapolis, which I hope to reestablish here."

"That sounds very interesting," said Natalie. "What might you consult with a company about?"

Sumner smiled. "I work primarily in the areas of personnel morale and motivation."

"You're the expert who knows how to 'turn people on' to their work?" asked James.

"I wish motivation were as simple as a mechanical turning on or off. Unfortunately, it is a very complex set of overlapping variables. Behavioral scientists have found some of the answers but in many areas we still know very little."

"You know," offered James, "I've been thinking as you were talking. I have a man working for me who is absolutely impossible to motivate. Maybe you can give me some ideas on what I can do..."

Natalie broke in and attempted to change the subject. "Lloyd, darling, this is a party. Don't bother Mr. Sumner with your office problems now."

"That's quite all right, Mrs. James," replied Sumner. "I don't know if I can be of any help, but I'd be very interested in hearing more about your problem employee."

Lloyd James needed no further prompting to tell Sumner about Allen Whitney, the marginal purchasing agent.

"It's not that he doesn't know his job," said James. "Allen Whitney has been in the procurement business for years and knows someone in every sales and order department between Santa Barbara and Tijuana, Mexico. But, somehow, he can't seem to concentrate on his work and even the routine procurements usually take him longer than any of my other purchasing agents."

"If it's not lack of training, perhaps it's a low energy or ability level?" asked Sumner. "We must admit to quantitative differences between individuals relative to innate abilities and energy."

"That's not it either," replied James. "Whitney is a friendly, enthusiastic, high-energy guy. Everyone likes him, including the people he works with by phone as well as others in the office. The problem is that his enthusiasm and energy seem to be all directed outward toward other activities and he has little left for the job."

"Could you give me an example?" asked Sumner.

"Actually several," replied James. "For one thing, Allen is president of the San Diego County Association of Purchasing Agents, an organization he has been active in for years. Phipps Institute supports and encourages employees to be active in outside professional societies and associations. We even cover his small out-of-pocket expenses associated with the nonsalaried association presidency.

"I see," said Sumner. "While the Phipps Institute unofficially supports Whitney in this professional society, his efforts in carrying out the duties it entails takes away from his productive time as a purchasing agent."

"Exactly!" said James. "Whitney spends excessive amounts of time on the telephone organizing association meetings and conducting its other business, and he constantly falls behind in his schedule of procurements."

"You mentioned numerous examples. Can you cite others?" asked Sumner.

"Professional activities mostly," replied James. "But Allen Whitney is also very active in the Boy Scouts of America and a local Republican organization."

The two men were interrupted by Jill Sumner who steered them to the potluck table for a second helping of food. Still eating, Sumner then followed his wife around the large yard and garden area as she introduced him to other neighbors she had met that afternoon.

Later, when most of the guests had left and their two wives had gone into the house, Dale Sumner joined Lloyd James poolside with a can of beer and suggested they continue their earlier conversation.

"Have you spoken to Whitney about the interference of outside activities with his work at the Institute?" asked Sumner.

"On numerous occasions but, regrettably, I don't get very far. Whitney's attendance record is very good and he does get his job done and so I can't get him to see the problem."

"Please continue," said Sumner.

"Last week, for instance, I spoke with him about some procurement which had been delayed. I hoped to show him he was just doing marginal work. But, in each instance, he had a plausible excuse as to the reason for the delay . . . some logjam beyond his control."

Sumner broke in. "And you feel that if Whitney expended even part of the energy he does on his outside activities toward his regular job he could break those logjams he spoke of?"

"Yes, that's it." said James. "It's a matter of priorities. If he were constantly calling his stockbroker or handling other personal business on the job I could have him stop it or face termination. As it is, however, these outside activities are tacitly approved by the Institute and Whitney has a perfect alibi."

"So you want to get Whitney to see the need to reverse his personal set of job priorities and increase his motivation toward his procurement work?" asked Sumner.

"Right! But how do I do it?" asked James in return.

"It may not be possible," replied Sumner after some thought. "Without knowing the man personally and hearing his side of the story it is not possible to be sure. Offhand, it appears that Allen Whitney no longer finds challenge and growth in his daily work as a purchasing agent. He does what is absolutely necessary and then turns his efforts outward to those activities in which he can further grow, achieve, and be recognized for his personal contributions. Like the majority of employees, Allen Whitney self-actualizes in outside activities and hobbies."

1. What did Sumner mean by his last statement? Discuss.
2. What steps might James take to alter Whitney's set of priorities?
3. Can a restructuring of priorities take place without the full consent and support of Whitney? Why?
4. James said that Whitney does marginally acceptable work. Should James have a technique or method to determine what exactly determines or establishes marginally acceptable from unacceptable performance? How is this done on jobs which cannot be easily measured?

The Group and the Organization

12

Individuals have social needs; they seek the company and camaraderie of others. To the consternation of some managers, this phenomenon occurs on the job as well as off. Socializing and the emergence of groups is a matter of concern to all managers—not in any foreboding sense, but simply as a human activity that must be considered in many areas of managerial decision making.

Reasons for Group Membership

In chapter 9 we discussed how certain aspects of organization structure facilitate the formation of informal groups. But a discussion of these aspects does not get at the underlying reasons for the emergence of groups. What attracts individuals to groups and causes them to seek acceptance as a member?

We may assume that groups have one or more goals, though a goal may be simply to satisfy the social or affiliative needs of individuals. Friendly banter, jokes, and talk on topics of mutual interest can do much to enliven the work scene, relieve tedium, and ease the embarrassment and discomfort of being alone. Even more important, perhaps, is the security anticipated and usually found within a group.

Support

An employee may perceive threats to his psychological and physical well-being from several sources: the organization, his immediate superior, and his fellow workers. The employee may perceive the organization as exploiting him through penurious wage policies, his boss as endangering his health by making him work too hard, and his fellow workers as ridiculing him or as offering too much competition for a limited supply of jobs.

Standing alone, the individual may feel insecure and unable to cope with the forces threatening and frustrating him. But in alliance with others who face similar fears, the employee discovers strength and support. Collectively, his group may find the courage to demand higher wages, they may tell the supervisor that his behavior is decidedly unpopular, and they may attempt to remove competition for jobs by spreading the work around and making sure everyone has enough to do—even to the point of deliberately slowing down production.

For example, one study found that groups of workers, as opposed to individuals standing alone, were more aggressive toward their supervisor, disagreed more often with the supervisor, expressed greater dissatisfaction with the supervisor's failure to give reasons for his behavior, and argued more vehemently for their own positions as opposed to that of the supervisor.[1] The comfort enjoyed through the supportive relationships of a group is very important to the individual.

Belonging to the Elite

The first-string team, the elite military unit, the back-room boys in politics—all of these groups hold forth the promise of prestige and status to the individual member. If the individual so perceives the group, membership may satisfy much of his need for esteem, both from himself and from others. Perhaps the most obvious examples of these groups occur at the high school level, where certain cliques are highly regarded by many students and desperate attempts to join signal the great importance of membership.

The power to influence behavior of others is often associated with a high-status group. The game team generates loyalty among its fans, the military unit sets standards, the political group decides who shall run for office. The individual can savor this power as an ego-fulfilling experience. Such prestige occurs not only as a facet of simply belonging but is also the end-product of contribution—the feeling that one has helped the group in its chosen role.

Within organizations, high-prestige work groups form, who claim a reputation by virtue of their high standards of output or by the nature of work they perform. In some organizations, staff groups are the most prestigious, particularly the personal staff of the chief executive. In other organizations, the line units rate high status. Sometimes the most dangerous work marks an elite. During World War II, airborne units enjoyed an extremely high status, with squads of group size vying for top positions. Whatever the situation, prestige plays an important role in the struggle for satisfaction of egoistic needs.

A final reason we shall mention for desiring group membership (although our list is not, or is it intended to be, all-inclusive) also relates to a need for support. People are often not completely sure about their perceptions or interpretations of many things. This uncertainty is as true of organizational procedures, practices, and supervision as of anything else.

A new employee is particularly affected by uncertainty about various organizational requirements. He wonders how to take his new supervisor; what certain rules mean; what exceptions from standard practice the company allows; and perhaps a host of other things. To get answers, he asks questions; and as he is more and more accepted as a member of his work group, the answers he gets are more to the point and representative of the consensual view of the group. Thus the individual gains confidence in a perception or an interpretation because it is shared with others, and he has been able to check the reality of his own views. A person whose perceptions are supported by other people feels supported and usually extends the same support to others. The bond of mutual support in the face of uncertainty is a strong cohesive force in groups.

Some Attributes of Groups

Just as individuals can be described in part by various attributes, such as personality dimensions, so groups can be described in part by attributes such as cohesiveness and the ability to set and enforce standards governing behavior of members. Cohesiveness can be thought of as the "attraction of members to the group in terms of the strength of forces on the individual member to remain in the group and to resist leaving the group."[2] The forces working on the individual to remain in a group include those we have already mentioned—desire for social interaction and support, the appeal of high status, and a need for confirmation of perceptions.

Stanley Seashore has suggested that the organization can facilitate group cohesiveness if it will take certain actions designed "(1) to lend prestige to the group members, (2) to structure the organization so that there is provision for groups of relatively small size, and (3) to help maintain a continuity in group membership over a period of time.''[3] Figure 12–1 indicates the forces that help to build group cohesiveness.

Group Norms

A norm is a standard of conduct that influences many facets of an individual's behavior. Norms established by neighborhood gangs often prescribe a style of dress and a set of attitudes toward parents. In work groups, norms frequently set a certain production range to be maintained by all group members. Particularly in companies using incentive plans, a group norm often dictates that no member will exceed the company standard for output by more than 30 percent.

Cohesiveness and the ability of a group to enforce its norms relate closely; that is, the more cohesive a group, the more likely its norms will be observed. Cast in more specific terms, the more a person desires to be a member of a group because of his needs for support, status, and confirmation of perceptions, the more likely he is to follow the group norms.

We are all subject to some tendency to conform to a group judgment. It is difficult to stand alone with one's opinion when several others in your immediate presence hold to a different view. A

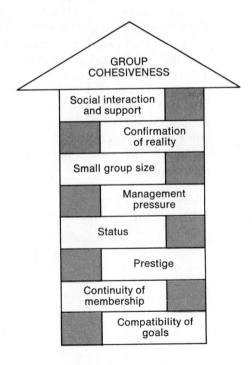

Figure 12–1 Forces creating group cohesiveness

number of experiments strongly confirm this tendency toward conformity. A study done by Solomon Asch is one of the best known.[4]

The subjects in the Asch study were asked to view some lines drawn on two cards (figure 12–2). When members of the group were then asked to match the line on card 2, which was the same length as the line on card 1, virtually no mistakes were made. However, Asch then rigged an experimental group so that all the members except one were instructed to give incorrect responses. When faced with a unanimous opinion on the part of the other members that one of the shorter lines on card 2 was the same length as the line on card 1, the unknowing person showed a distinct tendency to go along with the group's faulty judgment. Some individuals, however, stood their ground and refused to go along with the group. Asch also found that if only one other person supported the subject's opinion, the subject usually gave the correct answer even though the rest of the group responded with an incorrect answer. The Asch study and other studies help to show how powerful a group can be in controlling the behavior of its members through conformity to group norms.

There are, of course, instances in which group members do not always conform to group norms. For the most secure members of the group—the leaders or those who have been members for a long time—some deviation is tolerated. When the group considers a deviation to be serious, however, the group will act to force the deviant member back to conformity. Sarcasm, hitting, or ignoring the offending members are methods the group might use. Where deviation persists or is particularly flagrant, the group may exclude the deviant individual from further participation. The group considers such actions necessary to maintain their solidarity and effectiveness.

Research Findings on Cohesiveness

Studies by Seashore reveal a number of interesting effects of group cohesiveness.[5] He reported, for example, that members of highly

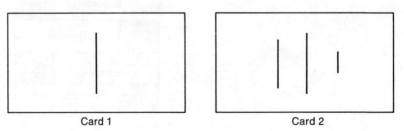

Card 1   Card 2

Figure 12–2   Lined cards similar to those used in the Asch study

cohesive groups showed less anxiety than members of less cohesive groups. They felt less nervous, felt under less pressure to produce at a high level, and were not particularly bothered by lack of support from the company. The highly cohesive group also controlled the production output of its members more effectively than less cohesive groups and, in addition, dared to set their own production standards at a greater distance from company standards than the less cohesive groups.

What are the implications of cohesiveness for management?

The administrator of an organization may draw from these findings some hints regarding policy and action. It is clear that the association of employees in cohesive groups may generate influences that are or may be of considerable consequence to the success of an organization. With respect to employee morale—in the context of anxieties at work—the cohesive work group appears to have a favorable influence. But with respect to productivity the positive value of cohesiveness in the work group appears to be contingent upon the administrator's success in developing among the employees a feeling of confidence and security in the management of the organization. The popular admonition to supervisors that they should develop a cohesive team, if carried out indiscriminately, may merely lend force to the divisive influences within the larger organization. To assure a positive benefit to the organization from group cohesiveness the adminis-

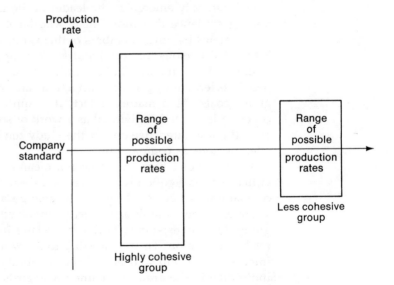

Figure 12–3 Relative abilities of highly and less cohesive groups to set their own production rates

trator might well take steps first to provide the basic conditions of equity and supportiveness which warrant employee confidence in management. A policy of "divide and conquer," as expressed in an emphasis on man-to-man relationships and suppression of group processes, may be partially effective; but the greater gains appear to lie in a policy to "unite in common cause," as expressed in the positive emphasis upon the formation of cohesive work teams.[6]

It is apparent from Seashore's comments that cohesiveness can be a powerful force within an organization. If the cohesiveness of work groups is generally high, employees feel relatively secure psychologically. Moreover, the impact of group cohesiveness on productivity can be dramatic. Strong group norms may influence production to high or low levels, depending on the organization's leadership ability to motivate groups and, in particular, on leaders of groups (figure 12–3). The leadership problem will be considered in the next chapter, but there is a specific related question that we will consider now: how does leadership emerge in a group?

Leadership of a Group

It is often assumed that the most popular member of a group would naturally emerge as the leader of the group. There is supporting evidence that individuals who have been rated high on certain items by other members of their group tend to select other high-rated persons for social and work companions.[7] Items used in the study included influence, attitudes, task orientation, ideas, people orientation, physical attraction, and contribution toward group goals. As a matter of fact, it is quite rare for anyone to choose a low-rated individual as a work or social companion, for even the low-rated persons in the study tended to choose high-rated persons as companions.

But this choice hierarchy does not mean that a high-rated individual who is frequently selected as a desirable work and social companion is necessarily going to emerge as the group leader. There are other complicating factors involved. For one thing, the group does not exist in isolation, but relates in various ways to the total organization. The relationship to the whole has an important impact on a group's goals and on the ability of the group or an individual in the group to define those goals.

Furthermore, a group leader is not perceived so much as directing the members of a group but rather as bringing a particular type of resource to the group, which they have perceived is needed and which can be used at the discretion of the group.[8] While the leader is likely to be a popular participant, it appears that the reason he is the leader has mostly to do with his ability to respond to the perceived requirements of the group for the leader's role.[9] Group leadership, therefore, is a pragmatic phenomenon. Work groups select leaders at specific times on the basis of situational factors, which may at one time or other have to do with the relationship of the group to the total organization; with the current goals of the group; with the ability of one individual to facilitate communication within the group and between the group and outside agencies; or simply with the composition of the group in terms of age, education, seniority, and work history. The following imaginary incident may help to show how a group leader arises and is accepted.

Lead the Way

Dark was fast closing in as the five hunters moved cautiously through the brush. Jed Smith was leading the way. The quietest member of this group of friends, he was usually quite willing to go wherever and do whatever his buddies wanted. Now they were on their annual deer hunt. Today, however, they had gotten lost, wandering through country that was new and strange. All day they had walked, getting a couple of chances at deer but not cashing in. Around four in the afternoon, they had realized they were deep in the woods and with no sure knowledge of how to get out.

"Well, Jed," someone said, "it's up to you."

"You lead the way, Jed, and we'll follow."

With these few words, the group formed around Jed. After a few moments, he moved off. The other four followed. Since he had vast experience in the woods and a sure instinct for finding his way, Jed accepted this challenge of leadership, not confidently, but knowing that he was the logical one at this point to lead the group.

Two hours later, the friends stumbled onto a gravel road. Within an hour, they had found their car and were back at the motel.

"Hey, let's drive up to Lem's Restaurant, have a steak, and celebrate our escape from the woods," Joe Cook yelled.

There was general acclaim for the suggestion, and everyone hurried to finish cleaning up. Jed quietly went along with the idea. Someone else had assumed leadership, now that the needs of the group had changed. Jed Smith would lead them in and out of the woods—Joe Cook would lead them to good food and good times.

Some Types of Groups

Many types of groups have been identified and any one particular group may be classified under more than one type. A first-order differentiation is between *primary* and *secondary* groups. In chapter 1 we differentiated between a group and an organization in saying that a group had to be small enough to allow close face-to-face interaction while an organization is too big to allow this type of interaction to be possible. A group as defined in chapter 1 is a primary group. That is, it requires close face-to-face interaction over a relatively long period of time. Warmth and emotional support characterize primary groups.

A secondary group is more remote and impersonal, not requiring close face-to-face interaction. Rational association to achieve some goal is typical of a secondary group. Hence, a total organization may be considered a secondary group. Our concern here is with the smaller and more intimate primary group.

For a quick preview, there are *ingroups* and *outgroups*; *membership* and *reference* groups; *formal* and *informal* groups; *interest* and *friendship* groups. There are others, too, but the list would become too cumbersome for reasonable presentation. The names of the groups we have mentioned reveal quite a bit about what they are.

The ingroup, for example, holds a position regarded by its members and others as desirable or dominant because the group represents current values held in high esteem or occupies a power position due to member prestige and influence. The outgroup, on the other hand, may share in appreciation of the values, but for one reason or another cannot experience whatever the values represent nor can the outgroup enjoy the power brought about by prestige or influence. The outgroup may be a majority or a minority in a particular collection of individuals, but is always looked upon as subordinate or marginal in their culture. Of course, it is important to remember that events and values change, and what is "in" at one time may be "out" at another.[10]

People *belong* to membership groups; belonging may be attested to informally by the other members or formally by membership card, certificate, or by a place on a membership roster. A person *identifies* with a reference group, however, because he finds the group attractive. Hence, there is a potential for conflict between the values and norms of a membership group and those of a reference group.

For example, an individual may be a member of the shipping department in a company and may also look upon the top executives in the organization as his reference group. If he aspires to an executive position, he may work long and hard, whereas his fellow members in the shipping department may be quite content with doing enough to get by. The conflict engendered inside such an individual could be quite uncomfortable unless he chooses to completely ignore the values held by his cohorts in shipping.

Formal and Informal Groups In an organization, groups that have been clearly defined and structured in the organization charter or by managerial action are considered formal groups. These range from the board of directors to a group of workers mailing packages in the shipping room. A class in school is a formal group, too.

There is considerable overlapping among all the groups we have mentioned. Informal groups may also be friendship and interest groups. A formal group also may be an ingroup or outgroup, membership or reference group—as may an informal group. Usually, however, an interest or friendship group will not also be a formal group.

People with particular interests—such as in music, sports, art, or whatever—would seldom find all other members of a formal group sharing the same interests. We seek out others with interests similar to ours. On the job, this may mean looking for friends in other departments and among superiors and subordinates. Or a club may form that is devoted to a special interest and that may include among its members executives as well as operative workers. In pure friendship groups, on the other hand, there may well be a general sharing of interest in many areas, but members are much more likely to be attracted to others at their own level in the organization. Other factors such as closeness in age and background also play an important role in friendship formation.

As we observed earlier, the technical and sociotechnical aspects of work have much to do with the formation of informal friendship groups. The physical layout of the work and the need to communicate in order to get work done cause interaction among people on the job. And, of course, they talk not only about work but about other matters as well. Friendships form that may include several individuals and that may extend beyond the job into recreational activities, hobbies, and family get-togethers. Cohesiveness develops, norms governing behavior unfold, and before long the group is capable of exerting a considerable influence on the organization, if the group so chooses.

The informal friendship group that forms within an organization is the main focus of our interest. Whether it is also an ingroup, outgroup, or some other type of group may be important, but we are still primarily interested in the effect of the group on each member's willingness to contribute to the organization and the achievement of its goals.

Some Special Types of Informal Groups   Not all informal groups that develop in organizations are the same. They differ in terms of purpose, tactics, characteristics of membership, and cohesiveness. Leonard Sayles identified four general work-group types in a study of 300 groups in 30 different industrial plants.[11] The *apathetic* groups were composed largely of low-skilled workers, had weak leadership, low cohesiveness, and posed little problem to management. The *erratic* groups, formed as a result of frequent member interaction on the job, performed inconsistently. At times, these groups enjoyed highly effective leadership and could mount strong challenges to the organization. At other times, they were weak though easily excited, and they were frequently quite ineffective during these periods. The erratic groups could also shift from being anti-management to being pro-management.

The more highly skilled workers who performed their jobs with less interaction than the previous two groups composed *strategic* groups. These groups appeared to be more cohesive and more unified in their pursuit of goals than apathetic or erratic groups. Their leadership demonstrated a capacity for the planning and execution of goal-directed tactics. Due to their influence with other employees, perhaps because they represented ingroups as well, the strategic groups were an important consideration in management planning. As you might expect, they also formed the core of union activity and pressure.

The fourth type Sayles identified as *conservative* groups. Not so much task groups as the previous three, their membership came from employees who held high-status positions in the organization, though still short of managerial ranks. Members of a particular conservative group could be from widely differing and spatially separated jobs in an organization, yet a group could be highly cohesive when pursuing a specific objective. Generally, they held somewhat aloof from the other groups.

There are other ways of classifying informal organizational groups. Most of them, however, can be considered task groups; that is, they form through interaction in the performance of some job. A task group might also be a command group, whose members report to one boss or supervisor. Figure 12–4 diagrams various types of groups and indicates where possible overlap may occur.

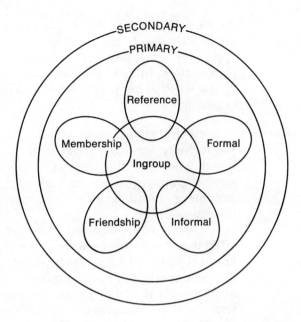

Figure 12-4 Some types of groups and examples of possible overlap

Effects of Group Size

Group size can have an important impact on such factors as cohesiveness and member productivity. To a limited degree, size can be controlled by management through the way a job is designed. Hence, it is valuable for management to know something of the effects of group size, and therefore we will investigate this structural variable.

First of all, what is the effect of size on member satisfaction? Using some criteria, it is difficult to say what the effect of size is on satisfaction. However, in terms of group discussion and the amount of participation that one individual has in the discussion, research findings suggest that the smaller the groups, the more satisfying it is to members.[12]

One study specifically indicated that a group with five members was most satisfying when a particular research task was involved.[13] The same study indicated there was more tension in small groups than large groups but that large groups did not provide enough time for participation. It appears that in small groups, two to five members, there is considerable tension, but people seem to try hard to be supportive of one another in order to reduce the tension. There is also ample opportunity for participation in group activities. In larger groups, ten to twenty members, there is apparently much less tension but also much less opportunity for participation. In sum, an individual's personality would seem to dictate whether he would find a small group or a large group most satisfying.

Size and Productivity
A number of studies show that quality of performance and group productivity are higher with large groups (under certain conditions), whereas on the basis of sheer speed in getting a job done, smaller groups appear to have an edge.[14] However, other studies indicate no relationship between size and productivity for blue-collar workers.[15]

The nature of a task is one of the important conditions that can affect the relationship between size and productivity. If you have a group of people picking peas in a field, the more workers you have the more productive the group will be. Of course, if you add so many people that they get in one another's way, you do reach some limit on productivity. In another situation, simply adding people may not help much. If you have four carpenters installing cabinets in a kitchen, each one may have his own particular job to do, and it probably complements the work of the other three. Because of the complementarity and limited physical space, adding a fifth carpenter could disrupt the system and possibly even lower productivity.

There may be a preferred group size for various jobs that will tend to maximize productivity. In this instance, the managerial job is to determine as accurately as possible what that preferred size is. The practice of determining best group size in relation to the task is widespread. It helps explain why three astronauts fly to the moon; why baseball teams have nine players on the field; why military units have specified numbers of personnel; and so on.

Size and Cohesiveness
As group size increases, cohesiveness appears to decrease. Therefore it is less attractive to join and stay in a large group than in a small group. One reason for this is that as groups grow larger, they inevitably develop more organization and structure. Members are assigned specific jobs to do, leadership becomes more formalized, and eventually, when face-to-face interaction is no longer possible among all members, the group is no longer a group but an organization.

Can anything final, then, be said about the desirability of group size? Remembering that the task involved may be the real arbiter of size, we may say that a relatively small group—from five to twelve members, for example—provides the best opportunity for management to understand and work with it. Cohesiveness can be high in such a group. And with proper motivational opportunities, productivity may reach and stay at high levels. While the smaller group engenders greater tension, it also offers more participation and the potential for greater satisfaction from that participation. There is greater risk in encouraging the formation of small groups, but there also appears to be potentially higher rewards from superior productivity and from overall satisfaction with the group.

Critical to the problem of motivation and high productivity is the reward system that must be structured. Companies can seriously err in setting up a competitive, individual piece-rate system, for instance, where worker cooperation is necessary to get a job done. In the pea-picking case, for example, an individual incentive system might be appropriate because each worker is on his own and need not depend on other workers to help pick his peas. However, for the carpenters installing cabinets, an individual incentive system could be disastrous. At least two alternative group reactions to such a system are possible, provided it were practical for one carpenter to work somewhat faster than another. In the first instance, the other carpenters might resent the one or ones capable of working faster and earning more money. The former might deliberately slow down, and if some job interdependency does exist, the whole group would be forced to work at a slower pace. The second option for the group would be simply to ignore the potential reward for any one individual in the plan and to set a pace for each member. Then everyone would receive the same incentive payment. A highly cohesive group could easily control their production in this manner. Under the first alternative, serious bickering and dissension could result. Under the second, there could be effective group solidarity and cooperation. In both instances, the company might well suffer from excessively low productivity. If an incentive plan were desired in the case of the carpenters, it would probably be better to adopt a group incentive plan under which each worker would share equally or in proportion to his normal rate of pay.

Groups and Problem Solving

There is no question that groups are essential for the performance of some tasks—sailing a large boat, for example—but the real question of interest to us is whether groups are more effective than individuals in the performance of some task where a group is not absolutely required. In other words, if you, as a manager, had a choice between using a group or an individual to solve some problem or generate ideas, what would be the best choice for you to make?

It is safe to say that most of the studies in this area report a superiority of group over individual approaches although at least one ... does not. It may be that the source of disagreement lies mainly in the conditions surrounding the task and in the individuals who are subjects. The preponderance of expert opinion, however, is in favor of superiority of the group in problem-solving performance.

There has been further interest in a specific variant of group problem solving known popularly as "brainstorming" where the focus is on unrestricted and uninhibited associative responses by members of an assembled group. The group is under instructions to be unconcerned about the logic or validity of an idea and to respond with as many as possible.[16]

Hence there appears to be substantial evidence to support the superiority of the group over the individual in a process of logical problem solving. Evidence pertaining to the concept of brainstorming is less clear. There are indications that group effort generates a greater variety of creative ideas, but there are also studies that show this is not true. However, as a manager facing some specific problem situation, you would be taking preferred action by forming a group to solve the problem. The choice assumes that the members of the group are competent with respect to the problem and that the problem is amenable to group action (that it is not an emergency situation, for example, which might demand an immediate decision).

We can now see the value of group action. We also know that groups are ubiquitous and that management should make the effort to understand group dynamics, since groups can play a powerful role in affecting productivity and morale. Now another question arises with respect to group effectiveness: does the manner in which a group is structured have any impact on output and efficiency?

Group Structure

We are going to talk about the effect of structure on the efficiency of communication and then relate this to performance. Several interesting studies have been done on *communication networks*, the communication structures that direct the flow of communication from one individual to another. These studies attempted to discover which kinds of networks were the most efficient and the most satisfying to group members.

Alex Bavelas conducted the earliest and perhaps the best known of these studies.[17] His basic interest lay in discovering which of two or more possible communication patterns would give the best

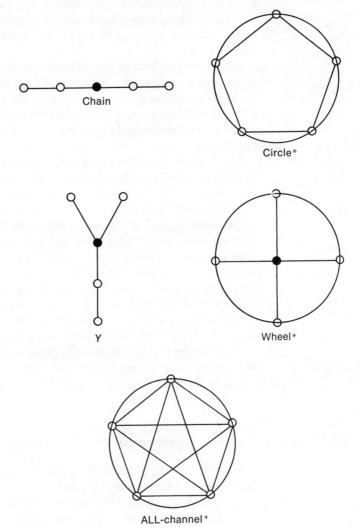

Figure 12–5 Communication network

*The outer circles in these figures are not intended to represent communication channels that may not exist. They are simply intended to illustrate the pattern.

performance. In addition, he was interested in the effect a communication pattern might have on leadership, on organizational development, and on the ability of the organization to adapt to environmental changes.

Through task structure and the control system, the organization may fix a certain communication pattern on a group. This particular pattern may be one that encourages inefficiency and develops poor leadership. Bavelas thought that if there is a choice among several communication networks, management could structure the most effective one—if it could be determined—and reap the benefits.

Let us look at two of the networks that concerned Bavelas, the circle and the chain (figure 12–5). In the experiment, he found a greater number of errors occurring in the circle than in the chain network. However, he observed better overall morale in the circle network and particularly poor morale at the two end positions on the chain.

Subsequent experiments by other individuals added other types of communication networks to the comparisons—the Y network, the wheel, and the all-channel.[18] In some cases, it was found that the circle still committed the most errors. However, when the circle, wheel, and all-channel networks had achieved efficient arrangements over time, they all had approximately the same speed of task performance. Furthermore, when the problem to solve was complex, the circle proved faster than the wheel, although for simple problems the wheel was superior.

In terms of overall morale and satisfaction with the job done, the circle proved superior to all other networks (not counting the all-channel). In the other networks—the chain, Y, and wheel—those occupying central positions (identified in the diagrams by the black dots) had by far the highest morale and satisfaction compared to those in the outlying positions.

General Conclusions

Two general areas of findings appear to stand out from the several experiments with communication networks. First of all, in terms of group effectiveness, the wheel was more efficient and faster than the circle, at least during the initial startup phase. But once underway, the circle network (and the all-channel) was just as fast and was superior in solving complex problems. The Y and the chain occupied middle positions.

Second, in the wheel, chain, and Y networks, leaders developed at the focal points for communication. A leader would emerge in the circle too, of course, but it took more time for this to happen. The circle leaders enjoyed the highest morale and the greatest job satisfaction of all participants; and the circle provided the highest morale and satisfaction for all members of any network.

The nature of the task, the speed and efficiency involved, and the personalities of the group members are important considerations in the structuring of any group. But from the standpoint of morale, satisfaction, and general problem-solving capability, the circle and all-channel networks appear to hold an edge. They encourage complete communication among all members and encourage participation in the decision-making process, thereby enhancing motivation and improving performance. In addition, they are better able to adapt to changing conditions, perhaps because they involve all members in the decision process.

We find, then, that a group can have many positive aspects. What conditions seem to be necessary for positive and effective group action? In general, effective groups are those:

whose practices and procedures enable them to carry out systematically the steps in problem solving and whose members have skills appropriate to the nature of the problems faced;

that have received training in problem-solving strategies and whose efforts are appropriately motivated;

that have a stable status system, familiar to all its members;

whose size is large enough to accomplish the task but not so large as to introduce distracting organizational problems;

that are cohesive, interacting cooperatively with members possessing compatible personality characteristics; and

that are operating under mild to moderate but not extreme stress.[19]

Criticisms and Shortcomings of the Group Process

Some criticisms have been leveled at the group, and a number of shortcomings attend the group process in its problem-solving and other goal-oriented activities. No doubt the pervasiveness of groups, both formal and informal, in organizational life is a major contributing factor to the alarm expressed by some about the impact of groups, particularly with respect to *loss of individuality*. The United States has a tradition of rugged individualism. The pioneer and the lone cowboy or trapper have been romanticized in books and movies as tough, self-reliant individuals, able to fend for themselves and to handle any threatening emergency. Many of us retain a Walter Mitty-like self-image as persons fully capable of solitary battling against nature and man, eventually emerging in absolute victory, and all the while receiving the acclaim and admiration of our fellows.

The reality, of course, is that we live in a complex system both nationally and in the lesser organizations with which we associate ourselves. And formal groups and committees, as well as informal groups, accomplish much of our work. In 1956, William H. Whyte attracted national attention with his book *The Organization Man*.[20] In this book, he expressed great concern about our loss of individuality to the group, not only in business and government organizations but also in our general lifestyle. He cited the clustering of homogeneous people in look-alike suburban houses and the development of identical patterns of life activity for thousands and millions of people—all results of conforming to group norms. He said that we were threatened by an invidious uniformity in our national life and by a loss of individual creativity and effort. Dullness and boredom would predominate in such an atmosphere, and a national resource of the first magnitude, our rugged individualism, would be lost.

Some of the fears Whyte expressed probably have materialized in our culture. As our society continues to grow even more complex and sophisticated, we may see yet more group action and uniformity. Obviously we cannot return to the lifestyle of pioneer days. With respect to loss of individuality in a group itself, Walter Nord offers the following commentary:

Much modern writing on groups has seen them as functional, necessary, inevitable, and costly to individual growth. While it is recognized that social approval and peer relations are important for the stability and identity of individuals, both advocates and critics of groups emphasize that approval of one's peers, often being contingent on conformity to group norms, requires one to sacrifice the expression of individuality. Benne (1961), however, explored the possibility that groups could be developed to reward nonconformity and innovation.

He argued that the pressures for conformity need not suppress individuality. Citing his own experiences in sensitivity training groups, he proposed that under some circumstances interpersonal relationships enhance individuality and freedom. For example, an environment can be created to help members move beyond the traditional mode of stereotyping each other and work toward developing a perception of each other guided by the assumption of a multiplicity of personalities. Under such conditions, people can explore and examine the social and psychological forces which often seem so powerful that they can control our behavior, although we remain unaware of them. Benne leaves us with the provocative challenge to provide ways of using authority and peer-group relations to promote individual freedom and growth as well as group and organizational goals. The establishment of groups and organizations which support individual growth requires an understanding of group processes. Additional insights can be acquired through an exploration of the topic of leadership.... [21]

<table>
<tr><td>**Limitations of
Groups**</td><td>There are limitations in the group process. Earlier we indicated that groups often are superior to individuals in solving problems. It has also been suggested, however, that groups are best in handling problems of moderate difficulty—that individuals are best at very easy and very difficult problems.[22] In addition, groups tend to be slower than individuals in problem solving; for one thing, the group requires time to get organized before it becomes relatively effective. And even in the instance where the group is faster than the individual, the output per man-hour is likely to be less for the group than for the individual. Therefore, the cost of group problem solving and decision making is likely to be higher.</td></tr>
</table>

Even when the group is organized and operating relatively effectively, coordination of individual effort remains a problem. Ordinarily, such coordination would be accomplished through the group leader. Leadership thus introduces another criterion for success, of course; not all groups are going to have good leaders. In some cases, participation in the group process is curtailed because the formal leader is psychologically unable to accept decisions made by the members of the group.

The Positive Outweighs the Negative

Early management literature devoted considerable space to advising managers how to combat or at least neutralize groups. We now realize that groups are an integral part of organizational life, and that our concern should lie mainly in how best to use the group. Furthermore, we realize that a group is naturally more effective than an individual in a number of ways. The conclusion that the positive effects of groups outweigh the negative simplifies the managerial task of using groups to best advantage.

Informal groups are always with us; the managerial job is to know enough about these groups so they may contribute to the organization. With respect to formal groups, it is not enough to say that their positive values outweigh their dysfunctional qualities, and that therefore the thing to do is to always use them.

Rather, management must decide which tasks are most suited to groups and which to individuals; what environmental conditions favor the group; what kinds of group members are available; and what sort of organizational characteristics pertain to formal group formation.

For example, the job of working out a new-product program in a company requires inputs from various departments—marketing, production, finance, engineering. Assuming each department has people who are capable of and want to participate in group effort, this kind of job may be well suited to a group. Related benefits of group action here include communication by representation among all concerned departments and easing of the coordination problem that always attends the introduction of a new product. On the other hand, a highly sophisticated and complex mathematics problem might best be handled by one qualified individual.

Summary

Groups offer support and security to the individual, affording him comfort and strength that he could not find alone. Groups also hold forth prestige and status and provide perceptual reinforcement; that is, the individual can check his views, feelings, and interpretations with other members of the group.

Groups influence individual behavior through the establishment of conduct and attitude norms. The greater the attraction of an individual to a group, the more cohesiveness the group tends to have and the more influence it has on behavior. Only in the case of the most secure members of the group, perhaps the leaders, is any significant deviation allowed from the group standards. If flagrant and persistent deviations from the group norms occur, the offending member eventually may be forced out of the group.

Leadership arises in a group to meet the needs of the moment and therefore may change from time to time. The most popular member is not necessarily the leader.

There are many different types of groups: primary and secondary groups; ingroups and outgroups; membership and reference groups; formal and informal groups; and interest and friendship groups. A person may belong to more than one group at a time, and a given group may be classified in several ways at any one point in time. A formal group, for example, also may be an ingroup, a primary group, and an interest group.

Group size is an important variable affecting group effectiveness. Small groups tend to provide greater satisfaction for their members than large groups. Large groups are most productive in some cases and small groups in others. Small groups appear to be more cohesive than large groups.

Groups are often more effective than individuals in solving problems of moderate difficulty, though the cost per man-hour is higher than for an individual. In terms of group structure, the wheel model is initially more efficient, but once organized, the circle is often more effective and affords higher morale and satisfaction to its members. Circumstances will usually dictate which structure is most effective for a specific job.

Critics charge that the group causes a loss of individuality, but others contend that groups can be structured in such a way that individuality need not be suppressed. Some suggest ways in which groups actually enhance individuality. The good points of groups appear to outweigh the bad, and therefore managers have a responsibility to learn about groups in order to use them effectively.

Management Profile

George Elton Mayo

George Mayo is already known to us through his role in the Hawthorne studies. Mayo, who was born in Australia in 1880, received his M.A. in Logic and Philosophy from the University of Adelaide. Moving to Scotland, he then taught at Queensland University until 1923. Then he emigrated to the United States, holding a faculty post at the University of Pennsylvania from 1923 to 1926. In 1926, he went to Harvard, remaining there until his retirement in 1947 and until his death as professor emeritus in 1949.

In 1928 Mayo began his participation in the Hawthorne studies. The Hawthorne studies placed great emphasis on the group and on the organization as a social system. Mayo's own subsequent writings, though based on the Hawthorne studies, ranged far beyond the specific Hawthorne research results. Indeed, much of his work can be classed as social philosophy.

For example, Mayo was greatly concerned about the effect of the factory system on the traditional social organization of individual lives. For centuries, people had found identity in their work and extended family—a niche in the larger system. It was often a cramped niche, but at least it provided psychological security.

Technological progress, with the correlated emphasis on efficiency and division of labor, destroyed this social niche, leaving in its stead rootlessness and loss of purpose. Mayo felt that there was too much managerial emphasis on technical efficiency and that far greater concern for the social needs of employees must be built into the supervisory job. This social end could be accomplished by training supervisors in human relations and particularly by encouraging supervisors to listen to and counsel with their subordinates. In this way, the worker could realize satisfaction of his social needs and could again feel a part of the social system.

Mayo also challenged the "rabble hypothesis," which conceives of society as a mass of people, each one avidly pursuing his own selfish interests with no regard for others. He countered this concept by suggesting that cooperation is more important than competition; that persons act as much or more to protect their group status as they do to protect their self-interest; and that thinking is guided more by sentiment than by logic. Society, he felt, should be built on cooperation, using the small group as a base and building up to larger groups. Given a group orientation, which Mayo claimed was more natural to man than competition, there would be no place in society for the animalistic behavior described in "the rabble hypothesis."

Both Mayo's views and the Hawthorne studies have been severely criticized. Critics have said that Mayo's views of society were unrealistic; that cooperation in a complex society is not necessarily natural; that contentment and happiness do not necessarily lead to organizational success; and that total concentration on the group ignores other important factors such as economic incentives.

Hindsight is invaluable in making criticisms, of course. No doubt Mayo made his share of mistakes in philosophy as well as in research methodology, but he will always be regarded as a management pioneer who made a great contribution. At the very least, he stimulated a tremendous amount of further research in the areas of individual and group behavior.[23]

Discussion Questions

1. Are the reasons for joining a group at work the same as for joining some group completely removed from the job situation? In other words, would an individual join an informal task group at work for the same reasons he would join a small stamp-collecting club at his local YMCA? Explain your answer.

2. As a combat military commander, would you prefer that your troops form informal groups with a high degree of cohesiveness, with a very low level of cohesiveness, or that they form no groups at all? What are the reasons for your answer?

3. In the imaginary incident "Lead the Way" do you believe Jed Smith would have continued being the group leader if he had not been able to get out of the woods within a reasonable time? What might have happened to his role?

4. List all the formal and informal groups you belong to. How many overlap? Are there any conflicts among the goals of the various groups? Are there conflicting norms among the groups? What conflicts have you personally experienced?

5. With respect to the groups you belong to, classify them as small (less than ten members) and large (ten or more members). Which groups, by size, afford you the most satisfaction? Which are most productive (if relevant) and which most cohesive? Are your findings in accord with research results? If not, what are the reasons?

6. Would you prefer to work with a group or work alone in solving some problem or doing some work? Does your answer depend on the type of problem or work, or is it purely a personal preference? Do you think that in certain kinds of work, such as police work, the individual should be given a choice with respect to working alone or working with one or more other persons? Explain your answer.

7. In all of the studies on communication networks, the leaders of the groups enjoyed the highest morale and greatest job satisfaction of all members. Why should this occur? Would this also be true of groups and their leaders in real work situations? Why or why not?

8. As a manager, would you do everything you could to facilitate the group process within your part of the organization or would you heavily emphasize individual initiative and activity? Could you do both at the same time? How?

References

1. E. Stotland, "Peer Groups and Reactions to Power Figures," in D. Cartwright, ed., *Studies in Social Power* (Ann Arbor, Mich.: Institute for Social Research, University of Michigan, 1959), pp. 53–68.

2. S. E. Seashore, *Group Cohesiveness in the Industrial Work Group* (Ann Arbor, Mich.: The University of Michigan Press, 1954), p. 97.

3. *Ibid.*, p. 101.

4. S. E. Asch, "Opinions and Social Pressures," *Scientific American*, 193 (1955): 31–35.

5. Seashore, pp. 97–102.

6. *Ibid.*, pp. 101–102.

7. G. H. Graham, "Interpersonal Attraction as a Basis of Informal Organization," *Academy of Management Journal*, 14 (1971): 483–495.

8. *Ibid.*, p. 494.

9. W. J. Duncan and C. D. Roberts, "An Analysis of Choice Consistency and Perceptual Uniformity in a Paramilitary Organization," *Academy of Management Journal*, 15 (1972): 33–47.

10. B. J. Kolasa, *Introduction to Behavioral Science for Business* (New York: John Wiley, 1969), pp. 451–452.

11. L. R. Sayles, *Behavior of Industrial Work Groups: Prediction and Control* (New York: John Wiley, 1958), pp. 7–40.

12. E. J. Thomas and C. F. Fink, "Effects of Group Size," *Psychological Bulletin*, 60 (1963): 371–383.

13. P. E. Slater, "Contrasting Correlates of Group Size," *Sociometry*, 21 (1958): 129–139.

14. Thomas and Fink, pp. 371–383.

15. L. W. Porter and E. E. Lawler, "Properties of Organization Structure in Relation to Job Attitudes and Job Behavior," *Psychological Bulletin*, 64 (1965): 40.

16. Kolasa, p. 466.

17. A. Bavelas, "Communication Patterns in Task Oriented Groups," *Journal of the Acoustical Society of America*, 22 (1951): 725–730.

18. *See*, for example, H. Leavitt, "Some Effects of Certain Communication Patterns on Group Performance," *The Journal of Abnormal and Social Psychology*, 46 (1951): 38–50.

19. T. W. Costello and S. S. Zalkind, *Psychology in Administration* (Englewood Cliffs, N.J.: Prentice-Hall, 1963), p. 444.

20. W. H. Whyte, Jr., *The Organization Man* (Garden City, N.Y.: Doubleday, 1956).

21. W. Nord, *Concepts and Controversy in Organizational Behavior* (Pacific Palisades, Calif.: Goodyear, 1972), pp. 503–504.

22. H. H. Kelley and J. W. Thibaut, "Group Problem Solving," in G. Lindzey and E. Aronson, eds., *The Handbook of Social Psychology*, 2d ed., vol. 4 (Reading, Mass.: Addision-Wesley, 1969), pp. 1–101.

23. D. A. Wren, *The Evolution of Management Thought* (New York: Ronald, 1972), pp. 290–295.

Suggested Readings

Cartwright, D., and Zander, A., eds. *Group Dynamics*. New York: Harper & Row, 1968.

Collins, B., and Guetzkow, H. *A Social Psychology of Group Processes for Decision Making*. New York: John Wiley, 1964.

Hare, A. P. *Handbook of Small Group Research*. New York: The Free Press, 1962.

Homans, G. C. *The Human Group*. New York: Harcourt Brace Jovanovich, 1950.

Luthans, F. *Organizational Behavior*. New York: McGraw-Hill, 1973. Chapters 19 and 20.

Tannenbaum, A. S. *Social Psychology and the Work Organization*. Belmont, Calif.: Wadsworth, 1966.

Thibaut, J. W., and Kelley, H. H. *The Social Psychology of Groups*. New York: John Wiley, 1959.

Leadership

13

A knowledge of leadership is one of the requirements for managerial success. Does this mean that not all managers are leaders? Precisely, for we can easily distinguish between a manager, in a formal sense, and a leader. A manager can also be an outstanding leader if he or she develops the requisite knowledge and skills.

An organization appoints managers to formal positions within the hierarchy and places certain resources at their disposal. An organization also grants powers to managers to act in its behalf. Managers are able to bind the organization to legal contracts, to order subordinates to perform certain actions, and perhaps to hire and fire employees. In broader terms, managers plan, control, and organize. But designated managerial powers do not automatically make a manager into a leader.

What Is a Leader?

A leader is able *to influence others to behave according to the leader's goal-oriented expectations;* that is, he is able to influence others *to strive toward a goal with enthusiasm and diligence.* The latter is particularly important; any manager can force his subordinates to work by virtue of the manager's official authority, at least for a while. The manager can even threaten to fire any employee who does not work hard enough. Of course, in a labor market where the employee could easily get another job, this is not much of a threat. But only a leader can inspire genuine cooperation.

Hence, in making a distinction between a leader and the formal position of a manager, we are also distinguishing between power and authority. Power is the ability to command, while authority is the right to command. What are a leader's sources of power? Some derive from the legitimate base of the organization, while others derive from the individual. The first sources relate to authority while the second sources have to do with power as we have defined it.

All of the words necessary to our discussion—leadership, management, power, and authority—offer great possibilities for confusion. Ordinarily, for example, if we say a boss has the authority to fire someone, we also mean he has power. The equation may be true in certain situations, but in other instances it may not be true at all. In a totalitarian regime, authority can mean great power, since the individual may have no alternative but to obey. Disobedience could mean imprisonment or worse, all backed up by the legitimate authority of the state (organization).

But institutional and cultural factors can change the definitions of power and authority considerably. Where there is a strong union, for example, an individual manager may encounter great difficulty in firing a person without specific, serious charges, that may have to be allowed by the union contract as well. In the United States, there also is a cultural tendency not to give up on an employee who is performing poorly until every possible approach has been used. Many managers regard poor subordinate performance as a personal affront and take pride in fully developing all their subordinates. We can observe this phenomenon in baseball, for example, where a player who is judged to have great potential, but who has never realized it, is picked up by team after team. Each manager thinks he can develop the potential in the player, though each club may finally give up and trade the player.

In the cultural and institutional setting of the United States, we assume that authority is not necessarily consonant with power, that the individual generally has enough protection and/or alternatives so that he need have little fear of organizational discipline. And our cultural disposition is to persuade and not order, to influence and not force. Within this framework, therefore, a manager may have authority, the right to command, but little power, the capacity to command. He may be able to manage in a process sense—planning, controlling, and organizing—but he may not be able to lead. Authority and management are linked to the formal, legitimate aspects of the organization, but power and leadership frequently relate closely to and spring from the individual. The opportunity to exercise power and leadership usually resides in a formal managerial position in an organization, but it is up to the individual to know how to use his position as a base for leadership and power.

Sources of Power

John French and Bertram Raven have analyzed power and influence in organizations. While other analyses of power and influence have been done, the French and Raven model appears to be the most widely accepted. They postulated power as emanating in five ways:

1. *Reward power.* This includes the absolute rewards which a manager can garner for subordinates. Pay raises and promotions are examples. In addition, however, reward power depends upon how subordinates perceive the ability of the manager to reward them. Subordinates may perceive that a manager can get the same pay raise for them that everyone else is getting. Perhaps more important is the question: can he get something special or something extra?

   A manager who suggests to his subordinates that he has influence with higher executives, but really does not, is asking for trouble. He is building expectations in his subordinates that he cannot meet, and the results probably will be low morale and productivity. On the other hand, if the manager is perceived as having power (influence with higher executives) and really does have but does not use it, subordinates again may be disappointed and lower their productivity levels.

   The ability to reward is important, but it must be handled properly. A manager should not boast of power he does not possess. But if he does possess power, and others know it, he should be willing to use it for the benefit of his work group.

2. *Coercive power.* This is the "stick" of the "carrot and stick." Coercive power is the actual and perceived power to punish; hence, the associated motivational drive is fear. In most cases, the most severe punishment is that of being fired. But as we explained earlier, there are institutional constraints on many disciplinary measures, and there is a tendency generally to minimize the use of coercive power.

3. *Legitimate power.* The ownership of private property is a broad economic base underlying the concept of legitimate power. Supplementing this base are traditional and cultural values, sometimes incorporated in a charter or constitution and sometimes simply accepted by a majority of individuals as normal procedure. Most of us recognize that persons in formal positions of authority have the culturally defined right to issue orders to us if we find ourselves in a subordinate position.

   We also recognize that as individuals we can reject the authority of a formal position and then suffer the consequences. Consequences include loss of a job if a private company is involved, or jail, if we are rejecting the authority of the government—refusing to pay income tax, for example. Authority can be reduced by effective rejection, too.

A mass, collective refusal of authority can seriously damage an organization.

4. *Referent power.* The more subordinates identify with their superior, the more power the superior has. Subordinates may simply like the superior personally. He may be a "regular guy," or he may have *charisma*—that magic quality so cherished by politicians. A charismatic leader is able to attract and influence by force of personality alone, perhaps enhanced by his association with some great and popular cause.

5. *Expert power.* Possessing expert knowledge in a given area affords great power in certain circumstances. If only one individual knows how to open a bank vault so the bank can do business on a daily basis, he has considerable power, at least temporarily, if he cares to use it. Expert power is largely set through the perception of others, based on their own knowledge in a given area, about how much knowledge the one individual really has in that area. If the bank employees did not perceive that one of them actually had the knowledge to open the vault, that one would have had no more expert power than anyone else in the group.[1]

Some power sources are derived predominantly from the organization, while others are derived most closely from the individual. A manager receives his authority to reward, punish, and issue orders from an organization, while his referent and expert power is generated largely by himself. Sources of power in the organization—that is, the authority granted by the organization—may not amount to much. French and Raven speculate that referent power may be the broadest. Referent power appears to enhance organizational authority as well as expert power. Referent and expert power tie in most closely with our concept of leadership, while reward, coercive, and legitimate power relate most closely to our concepts of authority and the manager in an authoritative position.

Authority by Consent

In 1938 the management scholar Chester Barnard postulated a theory of authority that differed diametrically from the classical, top-down theory.[2] In the classical concept of the scalar chain, authority flows from the top of the organization to the bottom. At each level, managers delegate a portion of their authority to the next lower level. It is assumed that orders will be obeyed on an impersonal basis.

The differing approach to authority, an *acceptance theory* of authority, has been described as follows:

The essence of the Barnard thesis was that people differ in the degree of effort they will contribute to achieve the objectives of an organization. Hence at any given time the individual members will be putting forth varying percentages of effort, with a consequent effect on their production. The organization must in some way secure their willingness to cooperate, and financial incentive is not the important way to do this. The degree of effective authority possessed by a leader is measured by the willingness of subordinates to accept it; and the acceptability of orders to the individual member can be graded on a time-point scale. There are those which are clearly unacceptable, those on which there is a neutral attitude, and those which are unquestionably acceptable.

Authority, then, is in a sense delegated upward. The web of authority is maintained by a system of communications which is in turn supported by the willingness of individuals to cooperate. Even in the military—Barnard argues by quoting a famous general of World War I—authority is based upon the willingness of members to accept it. Indeed, there are many inducements and compulsions to cooperate in an organization, not the least of which is our long training in the significance of hierarchical status. . . . [3]

When people function as subordinates, most are neutral or indifferent over the question of whether they will obey a given order. Sometimes, however, if an order violates a closely held moral precept, a person may reject the order and refuse to obey it. On the other hand, if someone received an order to take a day off when the weather outside was beautiful and he wanted to play golf, he would enthusiastically accept the order. As long as the willingness to accept orders persists, authority is effective. In contradistinction, the refusal to accept orders by a substantial number of subordinates weakens authority and can seriously damage the organization. Mass refusal to accept orders rarely occurs, but it may be observed from time to time in such dramatic events as mutinies and revolutions. Figure 13–1 shows areas of acceptance, rejection, and the zone of indifference with respect to authority.

We have distinguished between authority and power on the one hand and a leader and a manager on the other. These terms, however, are not mutually exclusive. A manager may also be a good leader; and authority granted to an individual by the organization does generate at least a minimal amount of power. But for the holder of authority to have *effective* power, his authority must be accepted by his subordinates. Acceptance may come about through the referent power of the manager—that is, his subordinates like and respect him; through the manager's expert power; through the manager's use of an effective leadership style; or through a combination of these factors. An imaginary incident may help to illustrate how some of these factors combine in a real managerial situation.

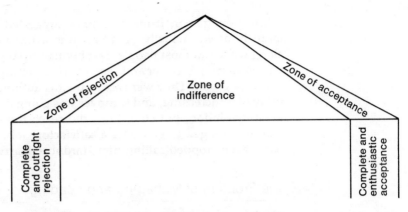

Figure 13–1 Reaction of subordinates to authority

Hardnose Harry

When the production superintendent appointed Harry Sherman to the job of foreman of the assembly section, Sherman was worried. In ten years with the company, Sherman had never risen higher than "wrap-up" man on the assembly crew. This meant that Sherman had been responsible for finishing the assembly of various parts and for making sure that the entire assembly was correctly done. In any event, Sherman had never imagined, even in his wildest dreams, that he was foreman material. Perhaps the new superintendent saw qualities in Sherman that the old one missed.

Anyway, Sherman was willing to give it a try. One good thing—he didn't have any good friends on the assembly crew. There was too much turnover, and Sherman never knew anyone long enough to form a friendship. The old foreman, who had retired, had really been Sherman's only friend in assembly. The old foreman had been a rough old guy and Sherman seemed to be the only one who could get along with him.

Sherman tried to follow the old foreman's pattern, though Sherman didn't have the old guy's ability to intimidate subordinates. Sherman just turned out mean—so mean that employees began calling him Hardnose Harry. Turnover continued at a high rate, production fell off, and Harry often found himself arguing loudly with a recalcitrant subordinate.

The superintendent noticed what was happening, of course, and sent a young man from personnel around to talk to Sherman. After a while he suggested to Sherman that perhaps Sherman was trying too hard to imitate the old foreman. Part of the problem apparently was that Sherman really wasn't the type, and so his subordinates were rejecting his authority and getting him into great difficulty.

The young man from personnel suggested that Sherman be more himself. Actually Sherman was a likable person and got along well with most people. So Sherman tried just being himself. He found his job easier and seemed to be getting along better with his work group. They were accepting his authority better, productivity was increasing, and turnover was going down. There was no great revolution, but conditions did reach the point where Sherman was judged to be doing a satisfactory job. And his subordinates even stopped calling him Hardnose Harry.

The Problem of Managing and Leading

Envision yourself moving into a managerial position. Like Sherman, you would be expected to get out the required production, but you could not do it without the cooperation of your subordinates. They would have to accept your authority, your leadership. Now, rejection of authority need not be obvious. It may be a subtle slowdown of production that is barely noticeable, at least at first, or deliberate mistakes that can be extremely difficult to pin down.

Hence your leadership would be vital to the effective performance of your job. You would have to understand the dynamics of your work group and how to motivate the group—as a group and as individuals. You would have to know how to satisfy the needs of your workers. You would have to find out what they want and clearly show how performance would get them an appropriate reward. Futhermore, if you had a firm belief about the nature of man, it would affect your leadership style—perhaps a style suggested by theory Y or one by theory X.

We have already learned something about motivation and group dynamics. There is also much research on leadership available too. We will review some of these theories and make some recommendations about how effective leadership should be developed and maintained.

Theories of Leadership

Any book on management and administration published prior to World War II, and containing a section on leadership, probably has a list of traits that any person should possess or acquire if he aspires to a leadership position. Lists of traits included factors such as physical appearance (strong, tall, and athletic), courage, decisiveness, honesty, fairness, and intelligence. Hardly anyone would argue with the desirability of most of the traits, but they do not describe leaders in all situations. Differing situations will require differing leadership approaches.

Subsequent studies deny much of trait theory as an overly simplistic approach to the leadership problem. These studies show that other factors have a lot to do with how effective anyone can be in a managerial slot. These factors include the types and varieties of technologies at the work place, physical facilities and equipment, and the personalities and skills of the workers.

But trait theory is far from being completely dead. Edwin Ghiselli, for example, conducted extensive studies on the characteristics of successful managers. For a trait to be considered a managerial trait, it had to satisfy three conditions. First, managers had to rank highest on the trait, workers lowest, and line supervisors in between. Second, there had to be a strong relationship between the trait and managerial success. And third, the relationship between the trait and success had to be highest for managers, lowest for workers, and in between for supervisors. Ghiselli showed that *supervisory ability* stood alone as the most important trait contributing to managerial success. It is the ability to plan and coordinate, to guide and direct the work of others. Supervisory ability is closely related to the managerial process—that is, to planning, controlling, and organizing. It is perhaps more commonly termed *administrative ability*. Its importance reflects the traditional importance of these managerial functions.

Following supervisory ability in importance was a cluster of five traits: the *need for occupational achievement, intelligence,* the *need for self-actualization, self-assurance,* and *decisiveness.* Ghiselli indicates that these traits are about equal in importance, and together constitute a major part of managerial success. The relative importance of the traits will vary from one situation to another, of course. One final note: a need for high financial reward ranked far down the list as a component of managerial talent. This need may well be present in most if not all managers, but it is not a factor in making someone a good manager.

Some traits Ghiselli mentioned can be learned, while others appear to be internalized through inheritance. Everyone can learn supervisory ability, for example, if he has the intelligence to be an effective manager. Given some minimal level of intelligence and a strong need structure for achievement and fulfillment, many people are capable of becoming relatively successful managers.[4]

The trait theory, however, does not offer much guidance in how to behave or structure a work group. And since many studies suggest that good traits alone cannot assure effective leadership, we must therefore consider factors that a manager can manipulate in order to achieve success.

Laissez-faire Leadership

A hands-off approach characterizes the laissez-faire style of leadership. The leader allows his subordinates complete freedom in planning their activities and offers guidance only in response to direct questions. While there may be certain situations where the laissez-faire style is appropriate, indications are that groups operating under the laissez-faire system are low in productivity, low in quality of work, and low in satisfaction.[5] And within the context of formal organization, it is not likely that many supervisors and managers would care to risk the loss of control inherent in the laissez-faire style. An exception may be found in university structure, where faculty members often have great freedom to plan their own work. But even in a university, teaching schedules are set, committee assignments are made, and there is usually considerable pressure for research output of acceptable quality.

Autocratic Leadership

One way to fill the vacuum created through laissez-faire leadership is to lead autocratically. The autocratic leader does not try to get particularly close to his group, remaining aloof while he issues orders. Like the laissez-faire leader, he does not consult with his subordinates, does not ask for suggestions, and rarely offers any explanations or reasons for his actions. The autocrat depends on his ability to reward and punish to get work out; the motivational technique is largely the production of fear.

Autocratic leadership appears to generate less satisfaction and productivity than other styles of leadership. However, there are certain situations in which autocratic leadership may be best. For example, where actions must be taken very quickly or where work is very routine, the autocratic approach may be appropriate. The military style, particularly in combat, is autocratic. Some subordinates may even prefer the autocratic approach. If subordinates tend to be dependent and do not feel capable of working without explicit direction, the use of anything but autocratic leadership could be a mistake. In those instances where autocratic leadership is correct, motivating by threat of punishment should be deemphasized, to diminish the usual backlash of resentment.

Supportive Leadership

Some overlap occurs among supportive leadership and the two remaining leadership theories that we will discuss. The supportive approach contrasts most sharply with the autocratic since there is in the former a concern for the individual and frequent attempts to involve subordinates in the leader's decision-making role. In dealing with supportive leadership, we will discuss several pertinent areas: group participation in decision making; consideration and initiation of structure; employee-centered versus production-centered leadership; and close versus general supervision. These are all important aspects of the supportive approach and deserve individual consideration before we pull them all together in summing up the supportive type.

Participation The intent of participation, as with any of the leadership approaches, is to inspire high productivity and maintain a satisfied work force. Participation seeks to achieve these goals through involvement of subordinates in the decision-making process, presuming that participation will increase satisfaction, stimulate interest, and thus provoke high productivity. Studies made generally support participation though there are studies which strike a cautionary note.

The degree of participation allowed can vary, of course. A manager may simply invite questions with respect to a decision he has already made; he may ask for suggestions; or he may allow subordinates full freedom to make decisions within prescribed limits. The last approach may sound like the laissez-faire approach; but under participation, the manager will continue to make some decisions himself and will maintain a concern and interest in the decisions made by subordinates. Table 13–1 illustrates some of the possibilities for the participative approach.

The theory postulates that participation results in decisions that are perceived as fair. Everyone gets a chance to express his views and to appraise the views of others. From the decision alternatives available, the group chooses the one most acceptable. A group that feels involved is more satisfied and more productive than one that does not feel involved.

Table 13–1 The scope of participative decision making

Autocratic— no group participation	Manager asks for questions	Democratic— group initiates and makes decisions in many areas
	Manager asks for suggestions	
	Group makes minor decisions in limited areas	

Midsection of figure indicates that these three levels of participation may exist simultaneously.

Choosing the alternative most acceptable to the group may not yield the best decision in all situations, however. Therefore, the manager must reserve some decisions to himself. Generally, management should make those decisions requiring expert knowledge of objective facts—those rational, logical decisions that might particularly affect cost and profit. The design and method of manufacture of a product, systems of maintenance for equipment, and purchases of materials are examples of such decision areas. Decisions affecting feelings and attitudes profit most from participation. Scheduling vacations, allocating equipment, and scheduling work within the group are examples of decision areas that may be open to participation.

Successful participation requires that management believe people have a sincere desire to contribute and requires management to create an encouraging environment for participation—to allow subordinates to make as important decisions as possible. Success also requires subordinates not only to be capable of contributing to the decision-making process, but to be confident of their ability to work without highly directive supervision.

As we mentioned earlier, there are studies the results of which suggest caution against the unrestricted use of participation. A study of a government organization, for example, found that increased involvement in the decision-making process resulted in higher worker morale; but that productivity did not rise.[6] The researchers suggested that the principal reason for the lack of increase in productivity was that many of the workers were not prepared to participate—that they preferred the dependent relationship found in a more authoritarian leadership style. The researchers also pointed out that it takes time for people to become involved and that when they do, the very nature of the involvement—the increasing number of relationships and interests, the development of multiple objectives, and the possible loss of informal leadership—all tend to hamper improvement in productivity. The key to effective use of participation, the researchers suggested, is " . . . the manager's being able to find that trade-off point between participation and morale on the one hand and high productivity on the other which gives him the best overall results."[7]

Bernard Karsh comments on participation as follows:

Decision-making authority is an absolute requisite within organizations. Though small groups may ultimately achieve some consensus about what needs to be done and how to do it, the modern large-scale organization can hardly afford the luxury of relegating decision authority, except perhaps on relatively trivial matters, to those who are neither legally nor functionally responsible for taking into account and accommodating conflicting points of view and interests. Participative management would indeed suggest that organizations can be handled through consensus as in democratic politics or, even more ideally, in the tradition of the Greek city-state or the New England town meeting, in which all citizens were presumably equal participants. As I have noted, such has seldom been tried in industry under any modern political system. It seems to me that it can be tried only when there is a greater concern for morale than for productivity, where there is greater concern for achieving consensus than for making a profit.[8]

Finally, Joan Woodward notes that in her studies participation in decision making did not overcome resistance to change, as long as the change appeared threatening to the economic and socio-psychological values of the participants.[9] Therefore, we cannot look upon participation as any panacea for organizational problems. If used as we have suggested—with regard for the situational variables (mainly the ability and confidence of subordinates in participation) and with regard to the manager's ability to correctly allocate those decisions he should make and those subordinates should make—participation can be an important contributor to success.

Consideration and Structure Initiation   Two basic dimensions of leadership behavior, consideration and initiating structure, were identified through a large-scale project carried on at Ohio State University during the 1950s. These dimensions describe leader behavior as perceived by subordinates and as the leader himself perceived his own attitudes toward his role.

Consideration includes behavior indicating mutual trust, respect, and a certain warmth and rapport between the supervisor and his group. This does not mean that this dimension reflects a superficial "pat-on-the-back," first name calling kind of human relations behavior. This dimension appears to emphasize a deeper concern for group members' needs and includes such behavior as allowing subordinates more participation in decision making and encouraging more two-way communication.

Structure includes behavior in which the supervisor organizes and defines group activities and his own relation to the group. Thus, he defines the role he expects each member to assume, assigns tasks, plans ahead, establishes ways of getting things done, and pushes for production. This dimension seems to emphasize overt attempts to achieve organizational goals.[10]

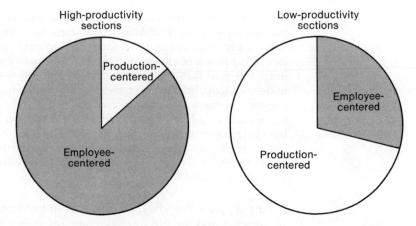

High-productivity sections

Production-centered

Employee-centered

Low-productivity sections

Employee-centered

Production-centered

Figure 13–2 Differences in emphasis on production and employees between high- and low-productivity sections*

*Based on research by R. Likert, "Patterns in Management," in P. Weissenberg, ed., *Introduction to Organizational Behavior* (Scranton, Pa.: Intext, 1971), pp. 453–469.

Initiating structure is similar to the trait of "supervisory ability," which we discussed earlier. It is certainly vital to a manager's effectiveness, but most research suggests that the manager rating high on consideration achieves better results than the manager rating high on initiating structure.

Employee-Centered and Production-Centered Leadership The terms *employee-centered* and *production-centered* are closely akin to consideration and initiating structure respectively. The employee-centered boss seeks to instill cooperation in his work group, wants to help his subordinates with their problems on and off the job, and is friendly and supportive. The production-centered boss sees to it that work is getting out, that subordinates are always working, and that proper methods are being used.

The Survey Research Center of the University of Michigan conducted a series of experiments designed to explore these two dimensions of leadership. Rensis Likert is the chief expositor of the results. They showed that when a supervisor also pays attention to the technical aspects of a job, the employee-centered approach is superior to the production-centered in raising both morale and productivity. Hence the employees can satisfy their needs at the same time the organization realizes goal achievement.[11] Figure 13–2 illustrates the difference in productivity between groups with employee-centered bosses as opposed to those with production-centered bosses.

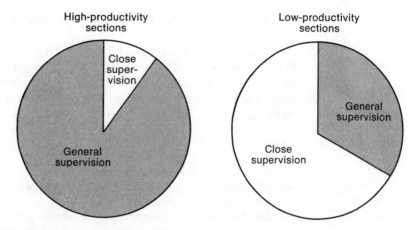

High-productivity sections

Close supervision

General supervision

Low-productivity sections

General supervision

Close supervision

Figure 13–3 Differences in emphasis on supervision between high- and low-productivity sections*

*Based on research by R. Likert, "Patterns in Management," in P. Weissenberg, ed., *Introduction to Organizational Behavior* (Scranton, Pa.: Intext, 1971), pp. 453–460.

Close Supervision and General Supervision In close supervision, the boss directs his subordinates in every detail, hovering over them constantly to make sure work is properly done. In general supervision, just the opposite is true. The boss gives his subordinates leeway in doing their jobs. He may issue guidelines and work with them, of course, but he does not hover over them, making sure that every operation is subject to his observation. We usually associate close supervision with production-centered leadership and general supervision with employee-centered. Research findings show that close supervision tends to be associated with lower productivity, while general supervision tends to be equated with higher productivity. Likert also indicates that "Closeness of supervision is also related to the attitudes of workers toward their supervisors. Workers under foremen who supervise closely have a less favorable attitude toward their boss than do workers who are under foremen who supervise more generally."[12] Figure 13–3 shows some results of research on close and general supervision.

Conclusions on Supportive Leadership Likert states, "These data add confirmation to early findings that the more supportively a manager behaves and the more often he uses group methods of decision making, the greater is the capacity of his organization to achieve highly coordinated efforts directed toward accomplishing its objectives and the greater is its success in attaining these objectives."[13]

On the other hand, although many studies confirm the claims of the supportive style, we are still not able to predict the effects of the style on work-group behavior. We have not as yet pinned down the variables to the extent that prediction is possible. We do have guidelines, however, as to the conditions under which the supportive approach may prove effective. Conditions are good when:

1. decisions are not routine in nature,
2. the information required for effective decision making cannot be standardized or centralized,
3. decisions need not be made rapidly, allowing time to involve subordinates in a participative decision-making process;

and when subordinates:

4. feel a strong need for independence,
5. regard their participation in decision making as legitimate,
6. see themselves as able to contribute to the decision-making process,

and

7. are confident of their ability to work without the reassurance of close supervision.[14]

Used in the appropriate situation and under the guidance of a skilled leader, supportive leadership should measure up to the claims suggested by all the study results.

The "Great Man" Theory of Leadership

We have given rather short shrift to the structure-initiating, task-oriented, and production-centered style of leadership. This style of leadership is included, however, in what is perhaps the most effective style we have yet considered—that of the "great man."[15] A leader who fulfills the requirements of the "great man" theory combines a task orientation that concentrates on meeting production requirements with a considerate and supportive approach toward his subordinates. Managers tend to regard their managerial subordinates highly if the subordinates are task-oriented, if they push hard to get production, and if they generally show the type of supervisory ability discussed under trait theory.

Subordinates, on the other hand, most keenly appreciate the supervisor who is supportive; that is, who is considerate, allows participation, and supervises in a general way. Obviously this situation creates a problem for the supervisor. If he pleases his superiors by being task-oriented and by tending toward autocracy, he will receive high marks from his superior but tend to alienate his subordinates. They, in turn, are likely to have high turnover and grievance rates. If the manager pleases his subordinates through a supportive relationship, he runs the risk of low marks from his superior and decreasing chances for promotion. Figure 13–4 shows the supervisor's dilemma.

However, if a supervisor can combine his abilities in planning, organizing, and controlling with a supportive style, the "great man" theory suggests he can be an effective leader in any situation. More specifically, if supervisors initially rated high on support increase their structure and task-orientation, there will be very little negative reaction from subordinates. Production and satisfaction will not decrease significantly, grievances and turnover will increase only slightly.[16] Combining these two styles of leadership apparently reduces tension and hostility within the group while at the same time providing a sense of security to the group against outside influences. The only problem seems

His superiors promote and reward
for a task-oriented, production-centered
approach

Subordinates respond to supportive,
considerate leadership

Figure 13–4 The supervisor's dilemma

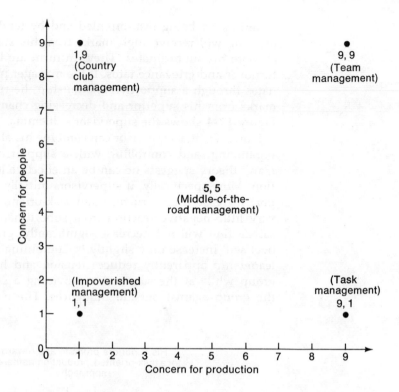

Figure 13–5 The managerial grid*

*From *The Managerial Grid* by Dr. Robert R. Blake and Dr. Jane S. Mouton. Copyright 1964 by Gulf Publishing Company, Houston, Texas. Used with permission.

to be that individuals possessing these differing sets of abilities are rare, although training certainly could overcome some of the deficiencies.

Management Development and the "Great Man"

Separately developed but related to the "great man" theory is the managerial grid, developed by Robert Blake and Jane Mouton.[17] Their theory underlies the managerial grid, which is a diagrammatic presentation of various leadership styles (figure 13–5). The grid also serves as a map to show the objectives of a comprehensive management development program.

The grid is numbered from one to nine on two axes. The horizontal axis is concern for production—the task-oriented, structure-initiating type of leadership. The vertical axis represents concern for people, the supportive approach. As indicated in figure 13–5, Blake and Mouton identify several leadership styles that result from various combinations of the concerns for production and people. They describe these styles as follows:

Impoverished management—(1,1). Effective production is unobtainable because people are lazy, apathetic, and indifferent. Sound and mature relationships are difficult to achieve because human nature being what it is, conflict is inevitable.

Country club management—(1,9). Production is incidental to lack of conflict and good fellowship.

Middle of the road management—(5,5). Push for production but don't go all out. Give some, but not all. Be fair, but firm.

Task management—(9,1) Men are a commodity just like machines. A manager's responsibility is to plan, direct, and control the work of those subordinate to him.

Team management—(9,9). Production is from integration of task and human requirements into a unified system of interplay toward organizational goals.[18]

Their training program moves managers toward a (9,9) classification, Team Management, and we can now see the similarity between team management and the "great man" theory. Blake and Mouton go beyond the "great man" concept, however, through the explicit introduction of teamwork in their training program. Interaction among the various groups in an organization and training of the entire management structure (as opposed to an isolated segment) helps develop the team approach.

In considering various theories and styles of leadership up to this point, we have implicitly suggested that a manager should be consistent in the application of a given style. A supportive manager should always be supportive, a "great man" should always be a "great man," and so on. Even in trait theory, the presumption is that the same set of traits that make a man a leader in the first place will always continue to do so. But this probably is a naive assumption. Many factors differ from one leadership situation to another, and these differences should be considered. Our final leadership theory adapts dynamically to dynamic situations.

The Contingency Model

Many factors can affect the leader–follower relationship: the personality of the leader, the personalities of the subordinates, the nature of the job to be done, the organizational environment, and so on. Finding out which situational factors are the most important and which of these relate to a particular leadership style is a difficult task. A contingency model developed by Fred Fiedler provides answers that have been supported by many research studies. The model defines a situation as being favorable or unfavorable to the leader based on three variables:

1. *Leader–member relations.* The degree to which subordinates trust and like their leader and are willing to follow him.
2. *Task structure.* The degree to which the job is routine and capable of being specified in detail as opposed to being vague and undefined.
3. *Position power.* The degree of formal power held by the leader to reward and punish and otherwise carry out the organizational mission.[19]

Situations in which leader–member relations are good, the task is well defined, and the leader has adequate formal power are favorable to the leader. In this situation, subordinates are willing to follow the leader; the leader can easily plan, organize, and control the task; and the organization backs up the leader in the exercise of his power.

The three variables are not always favorable. However, Fiedler's model is valuable because it specifies the leadership style that is appropriate for various combinations of the variables.

This theoretical formulation, which has been called the "Contingency Model" of leadership effectiveness, by and large fits our everyday experience. In the very favorable conditions in which the leader has power, informal backing, and a relatively well-structured task, the group is ready to be directed, and the group members expect to be told what to do. Consider the captain of an airliner in its final landing approach. We would hardly want him to turn to his crew for a discussion on how to land.

In the relatively unfavorable situation, we would again expect that the task-oriented leader will be more effective than will the considerate leader who is concerned with interpersonal relations. Consider here the disliked chairman of a volunteer committee which is asked to plan the office picnic on a beautiful Sunday. If the leader asks too many questions about what the group ought to do or how he should proceed, he is likely to be told that "we ought to go home." This also reflects the old army adage that it is better in an emergency that the leader make a wrong decision than no decision at all.

In situations which are only moderately favorable or which are moderately unfavorable for the leader, a considerate, relationship-oriented attitude seems to be most effective. Under these conditions, in which the accepted leader faces an ambiguous, nebulous task, or one in which the task is structured but the leader is not well-accepted, the considerate, relationship-oriented style is more likely to result in effective team performance.[20]

Fiedler goes on to point out that in committees, chances are the leader will be well accepted but will have low position power and a relatively unstructured task to accomplish. In order to gain the value of suggestions and contributions from committee members, the leader should be permissive and nonthreatening. The committee chairman usually cannot force his decisions on the group. Under conditions of severe stress or danger, Fiedler suggests the leader should be permissive and considerate to lessen tension and anxiety and to thus improve performance. In his work, Fiedler spelled out the complete set of possible variable combinations and their appropriate leadership styles. He also developed testing techniques to determine whether an individual tends toward task orientation or toward consideration.

The contingency model stresses that effective leadership relates to situational variables as much as to qualities in the leader. But as Fiedler points out:

A person's leadership style, as we have used the term, reflects the individual's basic motivational and need structure. At best it takes one, two, or three years of intensive psychotherapy to effect lasting changes in personality structure. It is difficult to see how we can change in more than a few cases an equally important set of core values in a few hours of lectures and role playing or even in the course of a more intensive training program of one or two weeks.

On the other hand, executive jobs and supervisory responsibilities almost always can be modified to a greater or lesser extent both by the incumbent of the position and, even more readily, by his organization. In fact, organizations frequently change the specifications of a management job to make it more appealing to the executive whom the organization wishes to attract or whom it wishes to retain. If anything, many organizations change executive jobs and responsibilities more often than might be necessary.[21]

The contingency model recommends *organizational engineering* as the most feasible approach to effective leadership. The organization changes the situation to fit the ingrained or natural style of the individual. The organization does not rely on the traditional steps of recruitment, selection, and training to develop leaders. The rationale is that it is easier to modify a situation than to attempt changing the personal core values related to leadership.

An organization can increase formal position power, for example, simply by granting the leader additional authority to reward and punish. Management can make a task more structured by developing explicit procedures for accomplishment. Leader–member relations can be improved by changing the composition of the group. Finally, management can learn what a leader's style is and then assign him to appropriate situations. The organizational engineering approach is a major departure from traditional practice and has the potential for overall leadership improvement at lower personal cost to the individual and lower dollar cost to the organization. Most people are relieved when they learn that they do not have to change facets of their basic natures to be effective leaders. The following imaginary incident describes some aspects of leadership that must be considered in effective organizational engineering.

The Complaining Complaint Department

Fred Baker had recently been moved into the home office of Midway Electronics as Customer Service supervisor. For the previous three years Baker had been assistant sales manager for the Cleveland territory. Baker was easygoing and had allowed the sales representatives directly under him considerable freedom in working their territories. Management felt that Baker's experience and ability to get along with people would make him an excellent supervisor for customer service. And Baker himself was eager to get the new assignment.

Baker continued his easygoing style and, in addition, took an interest in his ten subordinates. He tried to develop a warm relationship with each of them. All but three of the subordinates initially responded very well to Baker. For various reasons, the three did not get along with Baker and missed no opportunities to annoy him and to complain about him to others.

There were detailed procedures in customer service for handling work. As a result the employees had little opportunity to plan their work or make judgmental decisions. In addition, Baker had to approve almost all work output. For example, he had to approve every letter to a dissatisfied customer before it could be sent.

After a few weeks, there were more complaints about Baker. Even those subordinates who seemed to like him at the beginning were complaining. And Baker found his personal relationships with all of the subordinates were deteriorating. The situation soon came to the attention of Baker's boss, Roy James, who stopped by Baker's office one day to chat with him.

"Hi, Baker. How's it going?"

"Pretty good, Mr. James, We're right up to date on our work."

"Well, that's fine, Baker. Any problems with any of your people?"

"No," said Baker. "Everything seems to be going just fine."

But then Baker thought, "No, that's not true. Everything is not fine and James knows it. I might as well level with him." So Baker told him the whole story about how things had started out so well but had steadily gotten worse ever since.

After Baker's story, James thought for a minute.

Then he said, "Baker, you never had any real problems with your people when you were in sales. You had good production and always got along well with your subordinates. But now we've changed your situation, and things aren't working out as well. I'm convinced it's not your fault, Baker, so don't worry about that. I believe the reason for our problem is in the different situation. You were successful before, so let's see if we can change this situation to more closely match your last one. I think the main difference lies in the degree of job structure. Your last subordinates had relatively unstructured jobs to perform. Let's cut out some of the detailed procedures for your present subordinates and give them more freedom to plan their work, make some decisions, and use their own judgment. We'll enrich their jobs. I'm convinced your style of supportive leadership is more adapted to a relatively unstructured subordinate task. In addition, you tell me two or three of your people apparently don't like you. Well, I can't understand that, but again I think your supportive style is appropriate. So rather than fire or transfer them at this time, let's wait and see how things work out."

Immediate action was taken to loosen the procedures and controls on the work in customer service. Among other things, Baker no longer had to read every letter before it went out. After a few weeks, Baker felt almost as comfortable and happy as he had in his old job. Productivity was good, and he was again getting along quite well with most members of the department. The three persons who hadn't liked him originally still didn't like him very much. But at least they had stopped complaining so much.

A Leadership Montage

There is no one leadership style that will work best in every possible situation. Conversely, and more positively, the best approach overall appears to be flexibility backed up by knowledge and skill. Let us go back to the beginning and see if we can build a montage of leadership, arranging and superimposing one theory or style in relation to the others.

Going back to trait theory, we find that supervisory ability—the ability to plan and coordinate and to guide and direct the work of others—is important to leadership. Supervisory ability may be compared to task orientation in some respects, but it need not imply an autocratic approach. Other important traits included the leader's need for occupational achievement, intelligence, his need for self-actualization, self-assurance, and decisiveness. Let us accept these traits as a starting point and add one more, self-awareness. A leader should be aware of his own personality, the personalities of others, and of the effect he has upon other people. Sensitivity training can help to develop self-awareness.

We found that supportive and task-oriented leadership each has its advantages and disadvantages. Supportive leadership generally develops better morale while task-oriented leadership often results in greater productivity. The supportive approach can result in higher productivity when intragroup cooperation is required. Our conclusion was, however, that a combination of these approaches—the "great man" approach—might be best.

Let us now revise this conclusion in light of the contingency model, and say that the truly effective leader can be supportive at one time, task-oriented and directive at another, or both simultaneously. The result is a leader who possesses the six traits we mentioned; who possesses the ability to be supportive, task-oriented, or both; and who has the flexibility based on knowledge and skill to vary his style according to the situation.

Management can hardly go out in the street and find such a man on every corner. So management must be practical and do one of two things: engineer the job to fit the man or match the person and his particular style with the situation. For an organization to have truly effective leaders in all the managerial slots is an impossible dream, given our current knowledge and training capabilities. But an organization can develop an organizational engineering program by matching people and situations.

Organizational engineering does not mean that all leadership training should be thrown out. On the contrary. Training should remain as important as ever, for while it may not be able to change basic personality factors, it can develop greater flexibility and understanding. Training and organizational engineering go hand in hand: the more flexible a person is, the easier it is to match him to a situation or to engineer the job to fit the person.

There remain some leadership factors not included in the montage above, which should be mentioned. For example, leaders find *open communication* with their subordinates increases subordinate satisfaction with the job, with the company, and with the supervisor.[22] The importance of accurate and honest two-way communication between the superior and subordinate has been stressed for a long time. The direction of influence seems to be that if the superior is open and honest, the subordinate also will be, although the reverse apparently is not true.

High standards and expectations held by the leader are important. Whether the subordinate involved is a school-age child or an adult, he seems able to perceive the standards and expectations held by a teacher or supervisor, even though the latter may think these standards are held in secret. It is wise, therefore, to explicitly set high standards and expectations, since the perception of low expectations will usually be followed by low performance. Human beings tend to respond as others expect. A supervisor who has high standards, has power to reward, and who is willing to use that power leads groups that tend to have high production standards.[23]

Organizational level appears to affect leadership style. One study showed that at the lowest level of supervision, both high consideration and high initiating structure were essential to effective leadership in most cases.[24] However, at higher levels of supervision, the most successful managers scored high on consideration but low on initiating structure. Since technical skills also appear to be more important at lower levels, it seems that most operating supervisors such as foremen confront complex and challenging leadership assignments. The job of a foreman may often be more difficult than that of a vice president.

The *chain of effect* influences leadership style from the top of the organization to the bottom. According to one study, managers who work for considerate bosses tend to be more considerate themselves than managers who work for less considerate bosses.[25] The same phenomenon was true for initiating structure. The leadership style set at the top of an organization, therefore, can permeate the entire organization. Leadership at the top of the organization is critical to leadership throughout the organization and can have a marked impact on the total organizational climate.

The montage, a useful device for meshing the best aspects of many approaches, is now complete.

Leadership, Motivation, and Future Trends

Leadership and motivation are closely related. We can discuss motivation as an intervening variable between leadership and results—that is, productivity and satisfaction. With this concept, we see that a good leader provides motivational opportunities that produce the desired results. Good leadership results in high productivity and satisfied workers:

Effective leadership → provides motivational opportunities → which result in high productivity and employee satisfaction.

The leader must provide opportunity for satisfaction of needs. As we noted in the chapter on motivation, the needs for esteem and self-fulfillment are particularly important. The two-factor theory suggests that these two needs may be met through motivators or satisfiers. These motivators are: (1) a perceived opportunity for achievement, (2) recognition, (3) work itself, (4) responsibility, and (5) advancement.

Some of the motivators are easier to structure in a job situation than others. For example, there are many ways to give recognition to someone—a pat on the back, a raise in pay, a three-day pass, a new title. Skinner's positive reinforcement theory details a complete system of recognition. Advancement, one form of recognition, is sometimes difficult if not impossible to offer to everyone who does a good job. Still, it should be used whenever possible.

Various methods have been used to build into a job a perceived opportunity for achievement, interest in the work itself, and responsibility. Many jobs, such as routine assembly work are boring and inconsequential, at least from the worker's viewpoint. How can we change these kinds of jobs so workers can perceive a possibility of achievement, can be interested in the work, and can feel they carry some responsibility?

Job enrichment is one suggested answer. For example, consider a routine assembly where one worker does only a very small part of the total assembly. Perhaps a group of workers could do the whole job, making some of their own decisions about the best way to go about it, and being allowed to experiment a bit. If they were rewarded for improvement as well as production, they might well be more interested and feel they had some responsibility as well as an opportunity to achieve something. Job enrichment may not be the best answer, but structuring motivators into some work situations is a tough job. Nonetheless, it is part of leadership because of its impact on motivation.

Recall the path-goal approach to motivation. It stated that if an individual perceives high performance as a path to a desired goal, he will be motivated to perform. The supervisor then must be supportive enough to offer a range of rewards and distribute these in accordance with individual desires. The supervisor also must initiate structure so that the subordinate can see exactly the nature of the path to be followed to reach the goal. And finally, there should be more than one path to success, for otherwise the full potential of all subordinates will not be realized. "The implications of the motivation theory and the theory of articulation between leader behavior and subordinate motivation are clear. Supervisory behavior will only have an impact upon worker behavior and satisfaction if the following conditions are met: (1)

Supervisory behavior is related to the path instrumentalities perceived by the worker. (2) Path instrumentalities are related to satisfaction and performance."[26]

All of us have a need for esteem and self-fulfillment. It is quite possible that interest in our work, recognition, and the other motivators will satisfy these needs. If we can clearly see in our work situations that certain kinds of behavior will lead to desired goals that will be likely to satisfy our higher-order needs, we will be motivated. It is primarily up to the leader to provide the required opportunities. Hence, it is not enough for a leader to simply say: "I am going to be supportive and task-oriented." He must know how to be supportive and how to initiate structure in order to be effective. This knowledge and skill are required of leadership no matter what the situation. We may even speculate about a total leadership system and say the contingency model should operate only on the assumption that all leaders are trained to the minimal qualifications level suggested above.

But speculating about the future direction of leadership training and style is difficult. There is much yet to be learned about both leadership and motivation. Doubtless there will be continued and perhaps increased emphasis on supportive leadership: our society is very much attuned to satisfaction and fulfillment on and off the job. Nonetheless, we cannot overlook the task and job structure. Research must continue on at least three fronts: the supportive or considerate approach, the effects of task orientation and initiation of structure, and advancements in the situational or contingency models.

Summary

Leadership is one individual's ability to influence others to behave with enthusiasm and diligence according to that individual's goal-oriented expectations. A manager holds the formal authority granted him by the organization, but he is not necessarily a leader. He has the right to command but not necessarily the ability to command. Command ability develops through the accumulation of power.

Power, in turn, derives from five sources within the organization: (1) the means to reward, (2) the means to coerce, (3) legitimacy of formal position within the organization, (4) the identification of subordinates with their manager, and (5) expert knowledge. Referent power (the identification of subordinates with the manager) and expert power appear to be the most effective sources a manager can tap.

In recent years, an acceptance theory of authority has developed. It states that there is no authority and certainly no power unless subordinates accept the authority of their boss. Referent and expert power seem to invoke greater acceptance of authority than any other source of power.

There are numerous theories of leadership. We discussed trait theory, laissez-faire leadership, autocratic leadership, the supportive approach, the "great man" theory, and the contingency model. From these, we concluded that the individual who can be supportive at one time, task-oriented at another; or who can be both supportive and task-oriented at the same time has an excellent base for leadership effectiveness. In addition, if such an individual can adjust his style contingent on the situation, he can upgrade his effectiveness considerably.

It is often most practical to adjust the situation to the individual leader or at least attempt a match between a certain leadership style and a given situation. The former approach is called *organizational engineering*. Organizational engineering is practical because it is so difficult to change through training a person's natural style of leadership. However, the difficulties encountered in training for leadership does not mean training should not be used. Rather than depend solely on training, however, it is suggested that training be used to bring a person to a point where he can more easily use the contingency model.

That point of training involves knowing how to be supportive and how to initiate structure and be task-oriented in order to relate leadership to motivation. When an individual is trained to this point of knowledge and has also developed some skill he will find it much easier to implement the contingency model, either by adjusting his style or by engineering the situation to match his style.

Management Profile

Niccolò Machiavelli

Born at about the end of the Dark Ages in Florence, Italy, in 1469, Niccolò Machiavelli lived and worked during the Renaissance. Machiavelli began his observation and analysis of national political forces when sent to the court of Emperor Maximilian in Germany and to the camp of Cesare Borgia, Duke Valentino, who at the time was attempting to consolidate the Papal States for his father, Pope Alexander VI. Machiavelli thus witnessed the intrigues that culminated in Borgia's murder of his disloyal captains.

Machiavelli recorded these events in his *Method Adopted by Duke Valentino to Murder Vitellozzo Vitelli*.

Scheming or Practical Politics?

The adjective Machiavellian often carries derogatory connotations, as though such a person were unscrupulous, cunning, and even vicious. Many readers of Machiavelli interpret him in this manner. His most famous book, *The Prince*, was narrow in intent, however, for it was addressed only to a prince or a king and was not intended as a universal prescription for behavior. Machiavelli expressed the view that men are bad and will resort to evil means to achieve their goals if not controlled by law and, if necessary, force. In *The Prince*, for example, he says:

> There are two ways of contesting, the one by the law, the other by force, the first method is proper to men, the second to beasts; but because the first is frequently not sufficient, it is necessary to have recourse to the second. . . . A prince, therefore, being compelled knowingly to adopt the beast, ought to choose the fox and the lion; because the lion cannot defend himself against snares and the fox cannot defend himself against wolves. Therefore, it is necessary to be a fox to discover the snares and a lion to terrify the wolves.[27]

Are Machiavellian precepts immoral? As far as the methods are concerned that he advocates, these are not out of harmony with thoughts expressed by Aristotle and Plato. But whereas Plato was seeking a perfectly just state and Aristotle considered the state as necessary for human happiness, Machiavelli offers no grand purpose to justify the means he advocates. He was offering advice to rulers on how to remain rulers, immensely practical and down-to-earth advice. He had little to say to the common man nor did he intend to develop a universal philosophy of life.

Machiavelli and Management

At least one modern writer has suggested that management could benefit from an examination of Machiavelli's ideas. In 1967 a book entitled *Management and Machiavelli*, by Antony Jay, was published as "an inquiry into the politics of corporate life." Jay claims that the increasing size and complexity of modern-day corporations makes it necessary to study them as political institutions since, as they grow, they begin to take on the apparatus of states.[28]

For example, Jay feels that Machiavelli suggests a solution to the problem of how best to incorporate a company that has been bought into a larger operation. He quotes from *The Prince*, chapter III, as follows:

The other and better course is to send colonies to one or two places, which may be as keys to that state, for it is necessary either to do this or else to keep there a great number of cavalry and infantry. A prince does not spend much on colonies, for with little or no expense he can send them out and keep them there, and he offends a minority only of the citizens from whom he takes lands and houses to give them to the new inhabitants; and those whom he offends, remaining poor and scattered, are never able to injure him; whilst the rest being uninjured are easily kept quiet, and at the same time are anxious not to err for fear it should happen to them as it has to those who have been despoiled. In conclusion, I say that these colonies are not costly, they are more faithful, they injure less, and the injured, as has been said, being poor and scattered, cannot hurt. Upon this, one has to remark that men ought either to be well treated or crushed, because they can avenge themselves of lighter injuries, of more serious ones they cannot; therefore the injury that is to be done to a man ought to be of a kind that one does not stand in fear of revenge.[29]

In other words, senior men in firms that are taken over by another company should either be welcomed into the fold and encouraged or they should be fired. If they are fired, there is little harm they can do; but if they are simply demoted and moved to some supposedly harmless lateral position, they retain some capacity to strike back and injure the conquering organization. Jay indicates that this is the principle by which the Romans enjoyed so much success—generosity through full Roman citizenship for a conquered people or brutality by way of execution or enslavement.

Jay talks about politics in organizational life on a grand scale—a macro scale. But politics function on a micro level, too. Every manager faces organizational politics to some extent at one or another time during his career. However, his subordinates rightfully expect to be sheltered from organizational politics, and it is part of a leader's job to structure his group and the job to be done so his subordinates do not feel threatened. An ambiguous, ill-defined situation does not afford a sense of security. Machiavelli did not make any direct contribution to modern leadership concepts, but a knowledge of his work, perhaps as interpreted and applied by Jay, may offer insights into the political situations managers may sometimes face.

Discussion Questions

1. Do most managers use all five of the power sources that we have discussed? Would some managers use certain sources of power more regularly than others? If so, indicate which ones and why you think this would be true.

2. Cite some organizational examples in recent years where it has been possible to observe the acceptance theory of authority in operation. Look for cases where the top level of authority in an organization has made changes in response to perceived demands for change.

3. What type of leadership style would make you feel most comfortable in the role of a manager? Do you feel you could change to another style if you had to? How do you think most other people would feel regarding both of these questions?

4. In terms of the contingency model of leadership, what kind of situation would be most appropriate to your favored leadership style? Do you personally believe that engineering this situation would be the most effective way to motivate your subordinates and achieve results?

5. Consider trying to pattern your leadership style after someone you might know who is a highly successful leader. Do you perceive any problems with the imitative style? What are they?

6. In the imaginary incident "The Complaining Complaint Department," would Baker be even more successful if he included a substantial amount of subordinate participation in his leadership style? Also, should James have recommended that the three subordinates who didn't like Baker at least be transferred out of Baker's department?

7. The chain of effect theory states that the style of leadership of top management affects leadership throughout an entire organization. How far can we carry this idea? For example, does the President of the United States affect leadership styles throughout the entire federal government?

8. What is the relationship between leadership and motivation?

References

1. J. R. P. French and B. Raven, "The Bases of Social Power," in D. Cartwright and A. F. Zander, eds., *Group Dynamics*, 2d ed. (Evanston, Ill.: Row, Peterson, 1960), pp. 607–623.

2. C. I. Barnard, *The Functions of the Executive* (Cambridge, Mass.: Harvard University Press, 1938), pp. 166–185.

3. J. M. Pfiffner and F. P. Sherwood, *Administrative Organization* (Englewood Cliffs, N. J.: Prentice-Hall, 1960), p. 78.

4. E. E. Ghiselli, *Explorations in Managerial Talent* (Pacific Palisades, Calif.: Goodyear, 1971), pp. 97–99.

5. R. White and R. Lippitt, "Leadership Behavior and Member Reaction in Three Social Climates," in D. Cartwright and A. Zander, eds., *Group Dynamics: Research and Theory*, 3d ed. (New York: Harper & Row, 1968), pp. 318–335.

6. R. M. Powell and J. L. Schlacter, "Participative Management; A Panacea?" *Academy of Management Journal*, 14 (1971): 165–173.

7. *Ibid.*, p. 172.

8. B. Karsh, "Human Relations *versus* Management," *University of Illinois Bulletin*, 66 (1969): 35–48.

9. J. Woodward, *Organization Theory and Practice* (New York: Oxford University Press, 1966), p. 194.

10. E. A. Fleishman and E. F. Harris, "Leadership Behavior Related to Employee Grievances and Turnover," in P. Weissenberg, ed., *Introduction to Organizational Behavior* (Scranton, Pa.: Intext, 1971), pp. 483–484.

11. *See* R. Likert, *New Patterns of Management* (New York: McGraw-Hill, 1961), pp. 6–25.

12. R. Likert, "Patterns in Management," in P. Weissenberg, ed., *Introduction to Organizational Behavior* (Scranton, Pa.: Intext, 1971), p. 458.

13. R. Likert, *The Human Organization* (New York: McGraw-Hill, 1967), p. 69.

14. A. C. Filley and R. J. House, *Managerial Process and Organizational Behavior* (Glenview, Ill.: Scott, Foresman, 1969), pp. 404–405.

15. R. F. Bales, E. F. Borgatta, and A. S. Couch, "Some Findings Relevant to the Great-Man Theory of Leadership," *American Sociology Review*, 19 (1954): 755–759.

16. *See* Fleishman and Harris, pp. 483–493, for a detailed discussion of the effects of consideration and structure.

17. R. R. Blake and J. S. Mouton, *The Managerial Grid* (Houston: Gulf Publishing, 1964), p. 10.

18. R. R. Blake and J. S. Mouton, in E. H. Schein and W. G. Bennis, *Personal and Organizational Change Through Group Methods: The Laboratory Approach* (New York: John Wiley, 1965), pp. 169–183.

19. F. E. Fiedler, *A Theory of Leadership Effectiveness* (New York: McGraw-Hill, 1967), pp. 22–35.

20. *Ibid.*, p. 147.

21. *Ibid.*, p. 248.

22. R. J. Burke and D. S. Wilcox, "Effects of Different Patterns and Degrees of Openness in Superior-Subordinate Communication on Subordinate Job Satisfaction," *Academy of Management Journal*, 12 (1969): 319–326.

23. M. Patchen, "Supervisory Methods and Group Performance Norms," *Administrative Science Quarterly*, 7 (1962): 275–292.

24. S. M. Nealey and F. E. Fiedler, "Leadership Functions of Middle Managers," *Psychological Bulletin*, 70 (1968): 313–329.

25. E. A. Fleishman, "Leadership Climate, Human Relations Training, and Supervisory Behavior," *Personnel Psychology*, 6 (1953): 205–222.

26. M. G. Evans, "Leadership and Motivation: A Core Concept," *Academy of Management Journal*, 13 (1970): 97.

27. N. Machiavelli, *The Prince*, in R. M. Hutchins, ed., *Great Books of the Western World*, Vol. 23 (Chicago: Encyclopedia Britannica, 1952), p. 25.

28. A. Jay, *Management and Machiavelli* (New York: Holt, Rinehart and Winston, 1967), pp. 22–28.

29. *Ibid.*, pp. 5–6.

Suggested Readings

Bassett, G. A. *Management Styles in Transition*. New York: American Management Association, 1966.

Blake, R. R., and Mouton, J. S. *Corporate Excellence Through Grid Organization Development*. Houston: Gulf Publishing, 1968.

Drucker, P. F. *The Effective Executive*. New York: Harper & Row, 1966.

Fiedler, F. E. *A Theory of Leadership Effectiveness*. New York: McGraw-Hill, 1967.

Knowles, H. P., and Saxberg, B. O. *Personality and Leadership*. Reading, Mass.: Addison-Wesley, 1971.

Likert, R. *The Human Organization: Its Management and Value*. New York: McGraw-Hill, 1967.

Tannenbaum, R., Massarik, F., and Weschler, I. R. *Leadership and Organization: A Behavioral Science Approach*. New York: McGraw-Hill, 1961.

Case Problem for Chapters 12 and 13

What's Wrong with Wong?*

It was brown-bag time for the night shift maintenance mechanics. Pike and Monico were already eating at a small workbench next to the parts storage bins when Hazard arrived.

"Where have you been?" asked Pike.

"Servicing the conveyor belts in department B–9," replied Hazard as he snapped open his lunch bucket and took out a sandwich.

"You did that last week," said Pike. "Isn't that a monthly preventative maintenance job?"

"I guess so," said Hazard, "but Jimmy Joe wanted me to recheck the bearing and look for belt wear."

"Please," said Monico, "let us speak more respectfully of our great leader. You know we should refer to him as Mr. James Joseph Wong."

"Oh, no," countered Pike, "I believe the master of night shift plant maintenance would prefer to be called General Wong."

"Most certainly, General Wong . . . the . . . autocrat," said Monico, playing along.

Monico and Pike bowed their heads ceremoniously.

"I think you guys are being too hard on Jimmy Joe," said Hazard, between bites.

"Come on, Hazard," said Monico. "Face it. Ever since they promoted Wong to supervisor three months ago he's been different . . . a regular dictator."

"That's right," added Pike. "Wong was completely different when he was just one of us guys in maintenance. But he really began to give the orders the moment he took over."

Pike continued, "None of the old procedures were good enough for him. He had to reschedule everything. Then he promised management even more output on our shift. He really changed when he was given more power."

"I've seen this before," said Monico. "Promote a good guy from the ranks and he turns on you. When a man gets a blue stripe on his badge he's not the guy you used to know."

"Hey, that's clever. That's exactly how to describe Wong," said Pike, smiling broadly. "Try this fellas . . . where's the Joe I used to know?"

---

*R. D. Joyce, *Encounters in Organizational Behavior: Problem Situations* (New York: Pergamon Press, 1972), pp. 40–42.

Monico and Pike roared with laughter, and even Hazard smiled.

"I've got another," said Monico. "How about ... what's wrong with Wong?"

"Crazy!" said Pike applauding.

"Well, I don't know," said Hazard, pouring coffee from his thermos. "I don't see Jimmy Joe that way. He's certainly nice to me and I don't feel I've been working any harder since he took over. In fact, I think Jimmy Joe has improved our operations. You have to admit it was a little sloppy when Haney ran it."

"You rate-busting kids never seem to learn," said Pike shaking his head. "We have pre-set standards for charging our time that allow for emergencies you can't predict. So, even though battery replacement in a lift truck takes only twenty minutes, we charge thirty minutes. The extra time is for emergency repairs as they come up ... that's what you and General Wong don't seem to understand about the maintenance business."

"Right," said Monico. "Wong is squeezing out all our emergency time to make himself look good at our expense. Boy, will it hit the fan around here the first time we have a major breakdown."

"I don't happen to feel that way," said Hazard finishing his coffee. "I think the new standards are fair ... they correct some excesses created by equipment changes over the years." Hazard stood up and closed his lunchbox. "Look you guys," he said, "I've got to get back to check that conveyor again. But if you're that upset about the rates, why don't you talk to Jimmy Joe?"

"That won't do any good," said Pike, "He's locked in like granite."

"Can't talk to him about anything anymore now that he's such a big, important man," added Monico as Hazard left.

"Got time for a cigarette?" asked Pike.

Monico glanced at his watch. "Yes, I guess we have five minutes yet." The two mechanics lit up and exchanged predictions about the coming Sunday's pro football schedule.

"Mind if I join you guys?" It was Wong holding a vending machine sandwich and a cup of coffee.

"No, not at all, Jimmy Joe," said Pike as he put out his cigarette. "But, I've got to get back and finish that assembly department repair job."

"Me too," said Monico. "I'm behind schedule now."

James Joseph Wong ate alone.

1. What is the basic leadership problem(s) suggested by these discussions?

2. Is Wong overreacting to his new leadership responsibilities or has the group perception of him changed? Or both? Discuss.
3. What is the perception of Wong, the leader, as seen by:
    (a) Pike and Monico?
    (b) Hazard?
    (c) Wong himself?
4. What is the proper leadership role for a supervisor who works with his former peer group?
5. What should the leader do when he finds himself alienated from part (or all) of his work group?
6. Discuss this case in terms of:
    (a) organizational communication.
    (b) leadership styles and techniques.
    (c) team building.

The Job and the Challenge

V

14

We have been studying most of the activities that require managerial decisions and most of the knowledge areas that management must learn about to make effective decisions. The activity areas center around planning, controlling, and organizing. There are also many subsidiary areas in the total organizational system that require decisions. These subsidiary areas include personnel decisions on hiring, training, and promoting; legal decisions on new laws and regulations; decisions on the extent of organizational commitment to community service; and many others. Knowledge areas include decision theory or learning to decide how to decide, the elements of management information and communication systems, the theoretical classical and behavioral underpinnings of organizational structure and process (managerial activities), and the quantitative methods that can be applied in both the activity and knowledge areas.

Now in this last major section, it is time to draw together some components of our learning in order to discuss the predominant ongoing, operational activity of any organization—operations management. In addition, in the last two chapters we will discuss important organizational phenomena such as growth and change, and we will examine some current and future issues facing management.

A Definition

Operations management, or the management of operations, pulls together all the activity and knowledge areas. It also draws on such functional areas (at least in business organizations) as finance, marketing, purchasing, engineering, and accounting, which require extensive specialized study. *Operations management plans, controls, organizes, and directs the principal line function of any organization; that is, the conversion of organizational inputs to outputs.* Furthermore, operations management must accept the principal responsibility for the continued survival of an organization and, in certain instances, for organizational growth. Quite obviously, operations management cannot do this alone. It requires inputs and cooperation from all other functional areas. If even one area (engineering, for example) remains ineffective for a long enough period of time, the organization will be seriously hurt or even fail.

Examples of Operations Management

Perhaps some examples of operations management within varying contexts will help to clarify its nature. Suppose you inherited a defunct gold mine but wanted to put it into operation. Your immediate goal would be the output of gold in salable form—perhaps in gold bars. To accomplish this, you would need a number of inputs. One of the inputs would be the mine itself, supplying the gold ore as raw material. Other inputs would include your labor and the labor of others, as well as whatever equipment would be needed to carry on mining operations.

You would have to hire people, purchase equipment, and find the money to do all of this. It is obvious that you will require expertise from three specialized areas—personnel management, purchasing, and finance. You could use consultants, hire specialists, or develop your own expertise as you go along. The important point is that operations management quickly identifies the major area of activity and suggests where and when the organization needs specialized help.

Consider a manufacturing firm, one making radios, as an illustration. The outputs are radios in the appropriate quantities and styles to meet market demand. The marketing department plays an important role here, for it must determine the nature of the market and provide forecasts to the organization. With such market information, top management can marshal inputs in the proper quantities to convert them to the desired output. Inputs will be raw materials, purchased parts from other manufacturers, labor, money, and physical facilities. The nature of the inputs and the required marketing information again suggest the types of specialized knowledge and skill needed by the organization. How about a bank, or a corner grocery store, or a governmental agency?

All of them have inputs that the organization must convert into some sort of output. A bank has the usual inputs of labor and physical facilities, but its main input is money that people deposit in the bank for savings. These savings are then converted into a number of outputs: personal loans, business loans, mortgages. In addition, a bank converts some of its inputs into other services such as safety deposit boxes and checking accounts.

Convenient service to the consumer is the principal output of a corner grocery store. Primary inputs are wholesale quantities of meats, vegetables, canned goods, and other items. The grocer converts these inputs as well as his labor and physical facilities into convenient service by stocking small quantities of each item on his shelves; by offering his personal assistance to the customer; and by arranging the physical facilities in a manner that is convenient to the consumer.

Ordinarily, the principal output of a governmental agency is service to the citizen, although the output hierarchy may vary considerably. The Federal Aviation Administration, for example, seeks to assure safe flying, regulates rates of commercial airlines, assigns routes, and generally oversees airport operations. All of these outputs provide service to the citizen. Inputs to the FAA include persons skilled in aviation operations, physical facilities, and money appropriated by Congress to pay employees and purchase facilities and equipment.

These examples should help illustrate that all organizations confront the challenge of converting their inputs to valuable outputs and, further, that all organizations must manage these operations as their principal line activity. Hence, operations management consumes a major portion of the time and effort of managers throughout an organization and requires the types of activities and knowledge that we have discussed so far in the book. Now it is time to get into some of the specific problems involved in operations management. We will consider these problems under two broad managerial functions—planning and controlling. Figure 14–1 illustrates the concept of operations management.

Planning for Operations Management

One of the first items confronting an organization as it plans how to best fulfill its mission is that of location. Where should an organization locate to best acquire and use inputs? Where should it locate to assure maximum use of its output? You may have noticed advertisements in national magazines extolling the advantages of

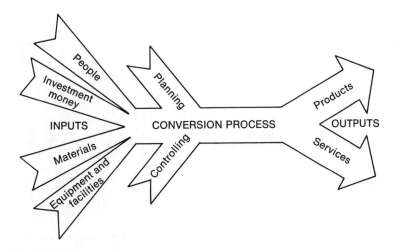

Figure 14–1 Operations management

certain states in order to entice industries to locate there. But the location can be narrowed down far more than to areas enclosed by state boundaries. The question may be whether to locate in or out of a city, or in what part of a city, or in what shopping center, or even in what specific location in a shopping center or on a city block.

Factors to consider in location analysis include taxes, labor supply, initial land and facilities cost, power sources, and ecological impact. With respect to an organization's employees, the availability of good churches, schools, hospitals, stores, and housing is always important. In particular situations, other factors such as parking may be critical. Location analysis is a complex problem to which certain quantitative techniques offer help.

One quantitative method simply weights the various factors by location. Suppose we were considering three possible locations for our organization: A, B, and C. We could use a scale from one to five and assign a weight to each location for each factor. If a rating of "five" indicated the most favorable rating while "one" was the lowest, all we would have to do is total our ratings to obtain the best location (table 14–1).

In other situations, a special application of linear programming provides the best solution (see chapter 4 for an explanation of linear programming). If we were trying to locate a new warehouse to function as a distribution center and to receive factory shipments, the transportation costs from various factories to the possible warehouse locations would be an important factor. The particular linear programming approach for determining the low-cost

Table 14-1 Location analysis

Factors*	Location		
	A	B	C
Taxes	4	1	5
Labor supply	5	2	3
Land cost	1	3	2
Power	4	1	3
Ecological impact	4	3	1
	18	10	14

↑
Best
location

*Assume that all factors listed are of equal importance.

system of shipping routes from factories to warehouse is called the *transportation model*. It is a deterministic model and leads to the best possible solution for minimizing transportation costs. For example, we have factories in Los Angeles, Chicago, and New York and warehouses in Atlanta, St. Louis, Phoenix, and Seattle. We want to add another warehouse but are not certain whether it should be located in Minneapolis or Detroit. Assuming we know all the transportation costs from factory to warehouse, we can set this up as a transportation model and quickly solve it.

Table 14-2 shows the initial set-up which will eventually lead to solution. Note that unit transportation costs are in the cells which connect horizontally by rows with the factories and vertically by columns with the warehouses. For example, it costs $12 to ship one unit of product from Los Angeles to Atlanta. Note also that supply and demand figures are shown along the righthand and lower margins of the matrix. For example, Los Angeles has a capacity to supply 6,000 units per year while the Atlanta warehouse has a demand for 4,800 units per year.

Table 14-2 Initial set-up for transportation model

Factories	Existing warehouses				Proposed warehouses		
	Atlanta	St. Louis	Phoenix	Seattle	Minneapolis	Detroit	Supply
Los Angeles	12	8	5	6	7	9	6,000
Chicago	5	2	7	10	2	2	18,000
New York	6	8	11	14	9	6	10,000
Demand	4,800	10,000	5,200	8,000	6,000	6,000	34,000

The transportation model will not only show us the best place to locate a new warehouse, Minneapolis or Detroit, but will show us the best overall system of shipping. That is, we will know how much to ship from Los Angeles to each warehouse, from Chicago to each warehouse, and so on. The answer will be the absolute lowest-cost system of shipping, given the route costs, supply capacities, and demands. The problem can be worked by hand through a rather slow repetitive method, but linear programming problems such as this are quite adaptable to computer solution.

Process Design

Once we have decided on a location for our operation, the next problem might be how to set up a system or process that will efficiently convert inputs to required outputs. Location involves the "where" of operations management. Process design involves the "how." That is, how or by what system, process, or method are we going to convert inputs into desired outputs. Most of the time, inputs will include people and physical facilities. The big variable input usually is materials. These materials may vary from iron ore for a steel mill to money deposited in saving accounts in banks.

Process planning involves two elements: process analysis and operations analysis. Process analysis determines the best flow of work and materials within the organizational system while operations analysis determines exactly what work must be done and how it must be done. In a savings bank, money flows in for deposit. Someone must keep records on how much each depositor has in his account, and how much interest is earned as well as handle the daily deposits and withdrawals. Information must flow from the savings department to the various loan departments on how much money is available for loan purposes.

If record-keeping machines are to be used, management must determine the proper types to purchase and the proper methods for their maximum use. Finally each employee should receive instruction on the exact nature of his job, including what he is to do and how he is to do it. Figure 14–2 illustrates the process flow for this simple type of banking operation.

The corner grocer must answer the same types of questions. How will shipments from wholesalers be received? Where will shipments be stored? How will goods be moved from storage to the shelves? How will the shelves be organized? What will the traffic pattern be for customers? Where will the cash register be?

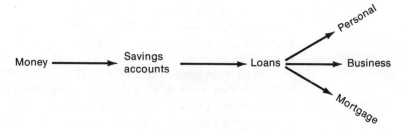

Figure 14–2 Process flow for a simple banking operation

What will the employees do and how will they do it? Answers to these and other questions will determine the process design for the corner grocery. Management uses process design to systematize the operation so the most efficient and effective methods can be used. Physical layout is important in assuring an efficient flow of materials and work. Use of physical equipment is important, as is the study of individual jobs and the training of personnel to do their jobs.

Changing Output

Having learned something of the where and how of operations management, let us now consider the "when" portion—when to change outputs. We are all aware of changing styles and tastes in music, clothes, and appearance. Length of hair varies drastically, to give only one small sample of the vast changes occurring every day among the products and services in the world's economy. These necessary changes in output pose perhaps the greatest challenge for today's organization. And these changes affect not only businesses but the whole array of organizational entities— churches, governments on every level, foundations, and social clubs.

Most products and services have a life cycle; that is, some identifiable period of time before major or minor modifications must be made. In certain instances, the life cycle is short and ends in absolute demise. Fashions in clothing are often of this nature. A particular style in shoes, for example, may be born, prosper, and die all within the period of a year or two. In other cases, a product or service may exist for years without change and then be subject to only minor modification. Barbers offered essentially the same service for many years before the popularity of hair styling forced a change.

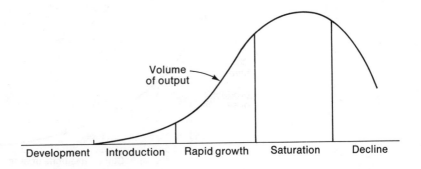

| Development | Introduction | Rapid growth | Saturation | Decline |

Figure 14-3 Demand cycle for a product or service

We can graphically portray an example of an output life cycle (figure 14–3), recognizing, of course, that the portrayal is not characteristic of all products and services. If we assume that this product or service is new in some respect, then we must recognize that there is a developmental period during which no actual output occurs. An introductory period follows. Then, if the product or service is successful, rapid growth occurs, leading eventually into saturation of the market and thus to ultimate decline.

The Learning Curve Much happens during an output life cycle, both within the organization and external to it. Environmental factors always have an impact, of course, but a phenomenon often occurs within the organization that is of great interest and value. The phenomenon is the application of the learning curve. A change in output usually is accompanied by a change in process, and this means that workers must learn new jobs when a change in output occurs.

At the beginning, they are apt to be clumsy and unproductive. With experience and with modifications and improvements in the equipment and facilities, the workers' productivity increases until finally it reaches a point where further improvement is very limited. Figure 14–4 illustrates a possible learning curve.

Awareness of the learning curve leads an organization to expect that during the introductory phase of a new output, and perhaps into the rapid growth phase, costs will decrease as a result of the learning curve as well as decreasing from the increased volume of business. On the other hand, if an organization is unaware of the learning curve, it may overestimate its costs and decide not to introduce some new product or service. For a business organization, knowledge of the learning curve is very helpful in predicting profit margins over a product or service life cycle. The learning curve, of course, is only part of the story. Adequate volume of

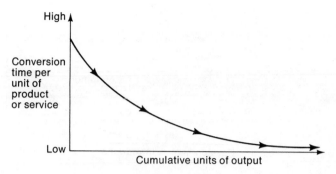

Figure 14–4 A learning curve

output is a necessary condition to a change in output. Before an organization finally decides to change its output, therefore, it would like a forecast of what volume might be expected.

Forecasting Throughout the Life Cycle

Knowledge about when a product or service will begin to decline can immensely help an organization's timing in changing output. Forecasting can yield this knowledge. In chapter 6, on planning, we discussed several forecasting techniques. These included hunches and intuition, collective opinion, historical extrapolations, market surveys, linear regression, and the Delphi technique. Hunches, intuition, collective opinion, and the Delphi technique are qualitative methods. Historical extrapolation involves statistical techniques but is, of course, based entirely on historical data. Linear regression is the most sophisticated method and may incorporate market survey information as well as results from historical extrapolation. The regression model relates the product or service to be forecast to other factors such as economic phenomena, similar products or services, and socioeconomic forces.

Of course, we would like to know much more about a life cycle than simply that moment when decline sets in. At the beginning, a forecast of volume is helpful, including the approximate time when rapid growth will begin (and how long it will last), and the expected volume during the saturation phase (and how long it will last). This is a tall order and probably cannot be filled at the very beginning of an output life cycle. However, different methods of forecasting can be used throughout a life cycle to fill in the gaps.

At the very beginning or during the developmental stage, we would have to rely on some type of qualitative forecast. Historical data would not be available nor would there be sufficient information for the type of analysis needed for a regression model. As quickly as possible, perhaps during the introductory phase or early in the rapid growth phase, additional forecasts should be made using historical extrapolation. We would like to make these forecasts as long-range as possible, but we also recognize that the further into the future we predict, the more uncertain are the expected results.

Well into the life cycle, perhaps during the saturation phase, we could very likely make the sort of analysis required for a sophisticated regression model. By relating our product or service sales to economic and social forces and competitive actions, we should gain an idea of the expected duration of the life cycle and when we should begin serious planning for a change in output.

Hence forecasting is critical to success in changing output and to operations management. Different forecasting methods need to be used at different phases in the life cycle, though we must remember that the cost of forecasting plays a role. Generally the more sophisticated the technique, the more it costs. A regression model costs much more than somebody's hunch. On the other hand, more sophisticated methods tend to be more accurate, so there is a cost here too—the cost of making a mistake. The organization must weigh these costs and decide whether trying to avoid errors is worth an expensive forecasting method or whether the cost of an error is not important enough to warrant use of something like a regression model. Forecasting volume is important, but it is really only half the solution. We will have to determine if we can make a profit and, if so, how much volume will be necessary. The breakeven model can help in this determination.

The Breakeven Point   Any organization interested in making a profit should be interested in breakeven analysis, for the breakeven point is where a firm will begin to make money if volume continues to increase. A breakeven chart plots the intersection of total cost and total revenue (figure 14–5). Two components make up total cost—variable cost and fixed cost. Fixed costs are those that continue regardless of level of output. Insurance premiums, payments for guards around physical facilities, property taxes, and maintenance are examples of fixed costs.

Variable costs are those associated with varying levels of output and are the inputs required to generate output. Materials, purchased parts, and labor are examples of variable costs. As output increases, more material and more labor are required, forcing variable costs higher. The chart shows variable costs as a straight line, steadily increasing to the right as volume increases. This linear relationship with volume very likely oversimplifies reality since a

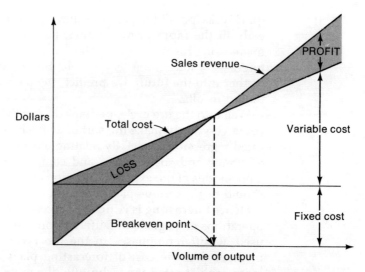

Figure 14-5 A breakeven chart

true-to-life representation may well have the variable cost line curving downward or even upward as volume increases to high levels. Using a straight line is a convenient abstraction, however, and usually is sufficiently accurate to be useful.

Total revenue derives from the arithmetic product of price per unit and quantity. The two equations below describe the total cost and revenue functions:

$$TC = FC + VC(Q)$$

where TC = total cost, FC = fixed cost, VC = variable cost per unit, and Q = quantity or the number of units. For the revenue function:

$$R = P(Q)$$

where R = total revenue, P = price per unit, and Q = quantity.

Now, in order to obtain the breakeven point, we set total cost equal to total revenue, or:

$$TC = R$$

In terms of our previous equations, we have:

$$FC + VC(Q) = P(Q)$$

Moving variable cost to the right-hand side of the equation:

$$FC = P(Q) - VC(Q)$$

$$FC = Q(P - VC)$$

Then, we isolate Q by dividing both sides of the equation by $(P - VC)$, and the result is:

$$Q = \frac{FC}{P - VC}$$

where Q mathematically identifies the breakeven point. The mathematical model is superior to graphic analysis in that a more precise determination of the breakeven point can be made. In addition, the mathematical model yields additional valuable information when properly manipulated, such as finding new breakeven points when cost figures change or determining varying amounts of profit for different volume levels.

Now when we are considering changing output, we have forecasts as to expected volume throughout a product or service life cycle and information on the breakeven point, indicating the volume required to make a profit. There is at least one other aspect of the total picture that we should consider, however, before finally making a decision on changing output—research and development costs.

Research and Development

Although the breakeven point shows where we begin to make a profit, it does not tell whether a new product or service will be profitable over its entire life cycle. There usually are research and development costs that must be recovered before total profitability is assured.

Basically, there are two kinds of research—pure and applied. Pure research generates knowledge that may or may not have practical application. Not many business organizations engage in pure research since the payoff is quite uncertain. Universities and special research organizations are more likely candidates for pure research. Applied research strives for solutions to particular problems; perhaps *development* is the more appropriate term.

Organizations undertaking output changes usually must sink some money into developmental work, and this investment must be recovered before final profitability occurs. This complete recovery point will occur sometime *after* the breakeven point is reached, because prior to breakeven the organization is losing money and going further into debt. Not until the firm begins to make a profit can developmental cost begin to be recovered. Figure 14–6 graphically illustrates this. Note how cumulative earnings may initially dip quite low and then continue to increase even though annual earnings are falling off. Cumulative earnings would continue to increase, of course, even though annual earnings reached and held to a very low level.

Now given that we have favorable forecasts on costs, price, and volume; given that our breakeven point is satisfactory; and given that we will recover all costs before the end of the product or service life cycle, we may decide to go ahead with a change in output. There still may be constraining factors involving the total pattern of organizational outputs or perhaps an inability to raise investment money. Decisions must be made on such factors as well before a final go-ahead occurs. One of these factors might be the organizational capacity to handle the increased volume of a new product or service. Physical facilities, for example, may not be up to capacity.

Capacity Analysis

Analysis for the purpose of making rapid capacity adjustments is a complex matter. We will only consider it briefly, but urge further outside study of the financial side of operations management.

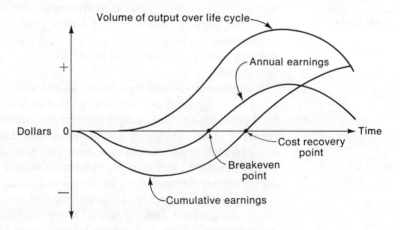

Figure 14–6 Recovery of development costs over the life cycle of a product or service.

Capacity adjustments involving capital investments are made for several reasons. The potential of a new product or service may advocate new equipment and facilities. A company may want to replace old or obsolete equipment in order to increase output and sales revenue, or perhaps new equipment will yield superior quality and, as a result, increased sales. Whatever the reasons, it is apparent there may be strong competition for available funds and that some criterion must be established to determine which projects receive a go-ahead and which do not. We will confine our present discussion to our previous line of thought about changing output through the addition of a new product or service. Moreover, we will consider only two of the several possible methods for determining the advisability of capital investment with respect to some new output.

The simple rate of return and its reciprocal, the payback period, is one approach to the problem. Assume we have the following figures on the capacity adjustment (purchase of new equipment and/or facilities) required to introduce our new product or service:

Required investment	$100,000
Estimated salvage value	20,000
Estimated first-year earnings	75,000
Estimated first-year costs	30,000

The equation for the simple rate of return (SRR) is:

$$SRR = \frac{\text{First-year earnings minus first-year costs}}{\text{Required investment minus salvage value}}$$

and so we have:

$$SRR = \frac{75,000 - 30,000}{100,000 - 20,000} = \frac{45,000}{80,000} = 56.2\%$$

The payback period is the reciprocal of the simple rate of return, or:

$$\frac{1}{0.562} = \text{approximately 1 year and 10 months}$$

If the organization had a criterion of a maximum of two years to pay back an investment, our project would qualify since it pays back in less than two years; that is, approximately one year and ten months. Simple rate of return and payback are quite commonly used, however: "Payback and simple rate of return are perhaps good, rough yardsticks for ranking alternatives, but they suffer from a common weakness; they do not reflect enough of the future. Money is not invested just in order to recover it; hopefully the investment will be recovered and additional money will be earned on the investment. In fact, income received after the payback period may be the most important."[1]

A more sophisticated method is the *present value model*. This model emphasizes the time value of money, which basically means that a dollar today is worth more than a dollar, say, five years from now. Let's put it this way. Would you rather have a dollar in your pocket or an IOU for a dollar to be paid in five years? Most of us would prefer the dollar today. Or would you trade one dollar today for $1.05, $1.10, $1.25, or $1.50 five years hence? We probably would not trade for $1.05 because we know we could put one dollar in the bank today and have more than $1.05 in five years. But at some point we would trade—perhaps for $1.50 in five years.

Our trade-off point relates to two factors, the degree of risk we perceive in the investment opportunity and the going rate of interest. Obviously, we are not going to give up a dollar today unless we can make more on it than we can by simply sticking the dollar in the bank. And if we do perceive some risk, we are going to want to make proportionately more than a savings account offers.

Let's go back to our example and identify some terms. Assume we would trade one dollar today for $1.50 five years from now. The addition of fifty cents represents *future earnings*, spread over a five-year period. Considering the total amounts involved, one dollar is the *present value* of $1.50 five years hence.

Organizations can use roughly the same approach in deciding whether to make an investment. They too want an estimate of future earnings, although their main interest is the determination of the present value of future earnings to see if the present value is greater than the required investment. If it is, this is one more indication that the investment might be a good one. The equation for present value is as follows:

$$PV = \frac{FE_1}{(1 + i)} + \frac{FE_2}{(1 + i)^2} + \cdots + \frac{FE_n}{(1 + i)}$$

where FE = future earnings for years 1, 2, and on through n years; PV = present value; and i = the going interest rate. We will plug some figures into the equation and see what results we get, starting with the data from our previous example on payback period.

Assume our new product or service has a life cycle of only three years and that the following data apply:

Required investment	$100,000
Estimated first-year earnings	75,000
Estimated second-year earnings	100,000
Estimated third-year earnings	10,000
Going rate of interest	10%

Plugging these data into our present-value equation, we have:

$$PV = \frac{75,000}{1.10} + \frac{100,000}{(1.10)^2} + \frac{10,000}{(1.10)^3}$$

Carrying out the squaring and cubing operations yields:

$$PV = \frac{75,000}{1.10} + \frac{100,000}{1.21} + \frac{10,000}{1.33}$$

Then we divide the interest rates into the future earnings, sum the results, and we have the present value:

$$PV = 68,090 + 82,645 + 7,519 = \$158,254$$

The present value of future earnings is $158,254, and this is considerably more than the required investment of $100,000. Therefore, we have a strong indication that the investment might be a good one. The big advantage of the present value approach over the simple rate of return or payback method is that the former does take into consideration the time value of money. It is often difficult, however, to determine the going rate of interest.[2]

In changing output, in considering a new product or service, it is important to estimate the life cycle; to be aware of the effects of the learning curve; to know where breakeven occurs; to know at what point complete recovery of costs occurs; to know if new or changed capacity is required; and to know whether returns from the project on a present-value basis will cover the required investment.

Even after all of this analysis, there are still other factors to consider. Are there alternative investment opportunities that might prove superior? Will the new project require new employees with different or higher skill levels and, if so, how much will this cost? And it may be apparent by now that the key to success in all of this analysis is the reliability of our forecasts. We need long-range forecasts but recognize that short- and medium-range are more accurate. The tough problem faced by those doing forecasting is threefold: (1) deciding which forecasting methods to use; (2) deciding at what points in the life cycle to forecast and with which method; (3) and coming up with the proper mix of short-, medium-, and long-range forecasts to most effectively do the job.

Operations Management and Control

Control has already been discussed in chapter 7. Now we will consider some applications of control theories in the context of operations management. For example, it is important for any organization to control the quality of its output, whether output is a product or a service. Consumers expect a minimal level of quality in the products they buy, such as automobiles, and in the services they buy, such as from a restaurant.

An organization must decide what quality level it desires in its output. The decision depends for the most part on how the organization wants to compete. A restaurant may charge very high prices and expect to compete on the high quality of its food and service. Rolls-Royce emphasizes quality in the automobile market. On the other hand, some cafeterias compete on the basis of price, and do not provide either high-quality food or service.

A first step, then, is to decide on an appropriate quality level. If the quality level is above an absolute minimum, real problems arise in trying to maintain quality during operations. Hiring and training conscientious employees help. Operant conditioning also helps.[3] If workers become accustomed to high quality, they tend to maintain their standards. Thus it might be a mistake for a high-class restaurant to hire a waiter from a greasy spoon.

Most of the burden for assuring that output conforms to standards falls upon some type of inspection process. Numerous methods may be used. In a restaurant, the boss simply may observe the employees. If the establishment is large or has several dining rooms, he may delegate the inspection responsibility to another person or may install closed-circuit television. In addition, he may periodically sample the food and ask his customers to make comments about the quality of service. In a factory, inspectors may check every part produced, or they may use a sampling technique to cut down on the work and cost.[4] Factory inspectors also can use modern inspection devices such as X-ray machines, ultrasonic listening machines, and television cameras.

There are certain ground rules about inspection, all of which apply to factories and some of which apply to restaurants and other types of organizations:

First, incoming materials should be inspected as they are received and before they are put into storage. This prevents substandard parts and materials from entering the production process and causing difficulties along the way. Next, inspection should occur before certain operations: (1) costly operations, (2) operations that hide defects from subsequent detection prior to failure, (3) operations in which faulty inputs may cause damage to the equipment, and (4) assembly operations that cannot be undone—for example, welding. In addition, inspection should occur after operations that are likely to produce defective items. Last, finished parts or products should not be put into inventory before they are inspected.[5]

The cost of inspection is an important factor in determining how much to inspect. If there is 100 percent inspection of every item, we would expect the quality level to be near perfect except for items that slip through due to human error. However, 100 percent inspection is very costly. As the percentage inspected decreases, perhaps through the use of sampling, the number of defective items increases. This too is costly—particularly with respect to customer dissatisfaction. In terms of total cost, it is possible to find a minimum cost point (figure 14–7).

Note that as the amount of inspection increases, the cost and quality level also increase. As the amount of inspection decreases, inspection cost declines, but the cost of undetected defects goes way up. These two cost curves combine to form a total cost curve, with the bottom point of the total cost curve representing the optimal amount of inspection that balances the cost of inspection

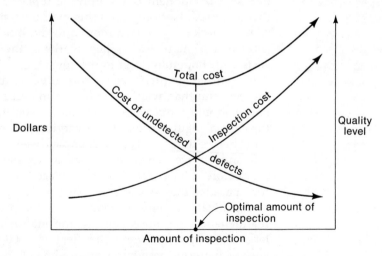

Figure 14–7 Minimum total cost point for inspection

as opposed to the cost of undetected defects. However, if a company wants to compete on a quality basis, it will inspect more and build the inspection costs into the price of its product or service. Similarly, a company competing on a price basis may do less inspection and incur a greater number of defects. In most cases, quality is controllable. It is up to the organization to set its level of quality, based in large part on the market segment the organization perceives it is serving, and then to choose the equipment and methods that will do the job.

Maintenance of Equipment and Facilities

Any organization that uses physical equipment and facilities in its operation (and it is hard to imagine one which does not) must keep its equipment in reasonable working condition. This includes such mundane jobs as sharpening pencils and changing ribbons on typewriters. If an organization does not maintain its equipment, breakdowns eventually occur and downtime results—time during which equipment and perhaps operators are idle but during which certain costs continue. These costs include salaries and wages for idle workers as well as lost output.

Though expensive, one way to approach the problem is as indicated above: simply wait for failures and then repair. This is the policy most of us follow with respect to appliances, for example, in our own homes. We wait for failure and then call the repairman. In partial recognition of the downtime that often occurs under this system, many manufacturers now replace component parts rather than repair them. Most television sets now use modular construction so a component can simply be replaced upon failure rather than repaired. Not only does this method generally get the television set back in operation more quickly, but it enables the repair shop to use more less-skilled workers, thereby lowering labor costs and, hopefully, cost to the consumer.

Preventive maintenance is more effective and less expensive in the long run than waiting for failure to occur. Preventive maintenance should reduce downtime and associated breakdown costs through a regular program of service and even replacement of parts before they fail. For an example closer to home, people lubricate and service their automobiles and sometimes even replace a part before it fails. People often replace the battery in a car or the tires because they suspect the parts are very close to failure.

Organizations tend to follow the same pattern with respect to maintenance. Suppose you are the maintenance manager for a large taxi company, one with a fleet of 1,000 cabs. On some parts such as batteries, you know approximately how long the part will last. A battery is a *wearout* item and usually will not fail prior to some minimum period. Let us say all the batteries you buy have a

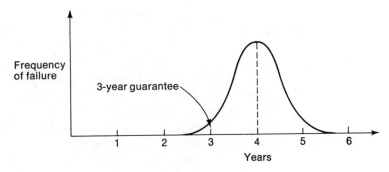

Figure 14-8 Pattern of battery failure

three-year guarantee and that the vast majority of them fail some-time between three to five years. Figure 14-8 illustrates this pattern and shows a peak failure rate at four years.

Knowing the wearout pattern is extremely advantageous. For example, you could buy all your batteries at the same time and also replace them at the same time—probably after the end of the third year of life but before the peak failure time at the fourth year. This policy is called *group replacement* and often is less expensive than individual replacement of failed parts. And the most likely time for group replacement can be computed mathematically using probabilities associated with the wearout pattern.

On the other hand, some items are not so predictable. Tires, for example, do wear out in a predictable fashion, but nails and glass in the streets cause unpredictable punctures. You could put four brand new tires on a cab in the morning and by the end of the day, you might have had to fix one or more punctures on those new tires. To put it another way, if you bought 4,000 new tires for the 1,000 cabs and drove on them long enough over city streets and alleys, eventually every one of those tires would get a puncture. Figure 14-9 illustrates random failure of this nature.

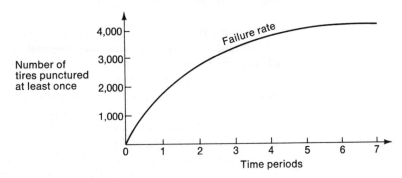

Figure 14-9 Random failure: tire punctures

Note that starting at point 0 the failure frequency is high but then declines as more and more parts fail, eventually reaching zero as the last part fails—or the last tire is punctured. Preventive maintenance is most applicable to the wearout pattern. Keeping water in the batteries helps assure they will last three years, for example. And group replacement of batteries at an appropriate time increases reliability and decreases the possibility of battery failure. However, there is not really much one can do about preventive maintenance with respect to random failure. Tire punctures are both unavoidable and unpredictable. The best course of action is simply to be ready to repair punctures as expeditiously as possible.

This, then, is roughly the situation you would face as maintenance manager for a 1,000-unit cab company. You could predict the failure of some parts and replace them before they fail as much as possible. In other cases, you would simply have to repair as failure occurred. One of the most critical problems you would have is figuring out how much equipment and how many people you would need to most economically and efficiently handle the maintenance problem.

Fortunately there is help to be found for this problem in the waiting-line or queuing model. If you got four calls on tire failure within a ten-minute time span and only had one service person, three of those failures would have to wait a given time for repair; then two would have to wait additional time; and finally one would have to wait even more time. What you have, then, is a waiting line or queue, impatiently waiting for service.

The waiting-line problem has its analogy in many other situations: the number of checkout counters required in a supermarket to handle customers, for example; or the number of agents to have at an airlines ticket counter; or the size of a maintenance crew. And the problem becomes more complicated if there are times when facilities are extremely busy and times when they are quite slack.

There are two approaches to solving the queue problem. One is a mathematical approach that requires certain homogeneous conditions with respect to people and equipment. If these rather rigorous conditions cannot be met, we can resort to simulation (see chapter 4 for a discussion on simulation). By assigning probabilities, where possible, to the arrival of customers or to the failure of parts at various times, we can construct a model that simulates the actual situation. In a few minutes of computer time, we can simulate many days or even months of operation and come up with a reasonable solution to the question of the amount of labor and equipment required.

But even arriving at such a solution does not mean there will never be waiting lines or, conversely, idle service people. We all know there are times when we zip through a supermarket checkout counter and other times when we tediously wait in line. What the waiting-line model tries to do is strike a balance between minimizing the amount of waiting that can occur and minimizing the cost of people and equipment.

Maintenance is a tough job. The maintenance manager hopes his equipment is reliable and designed for easy maintenance. Beyond that, he must see that the equipment operates within performance limits, and he must set up a system similar to the one we have been talking about.

Control of Inventories

All organizations have inventories of some kind. Even people are sometimes considered an inventory problem. For example, the size of a maintenance crew, which we just talked about, may be resolved through waiting-line analysis, but it also is an inventory problem. So is the number of typists in a typing pool. And in managerial development, one of the important steps is to develop an inventory of managerial abilities, noting for each manager his strengths and weaknesses.

In other instances, inventories range from huge ocean-going tankers to minute grains of valuable metals. Money is required to maintain inventories, but the advantages are worthwhile. Inputs to the conversion process can be stored until needed, thus reducing the dependency of the conversion process on suppliers. Without inventories, input acquisition would have to be finely coordinated with conversion. If you were running a retail ice cream store, you would not want to run to the wholesaler for supplies everytime someone ordered an ice cream cone. Similarly, inventories of finished goods simplify the linkage between output and distribution. In an ice cream store it is easier and more convenient to package ice cream in pints, quarts, and so forth, and to store it that way until sale rather than to package it at time of sale. Finally, inventories can help to smooth out the entire operations system by storing output when demand is low and then using the stored output to help meet demand when it is high. In this way, the number of employees and the amount of equipment and facilities can remain relatively constant, along with output, as demand rises and falls.

The basic question is whether it costs less to maintain inventories or to synchronize all the stages of the conversion process in the absence of inventories. On the basis both of hunch and of cost analysis, most organizations opt for the former; that is, to use inventories. This decision being made, another important question immediately arises: how much inventory should be maintained so that one does not run out of anything but at the same time that costs of inventory do not rise too high?

An Inventory Model Fortunately and as with the maintenance problem, there is a mathematical model to which we can turn for help in deciding inventory size. The model can help us answer two questions: (1) how much to order at any one time; and (2) when to order. Suppose that in an ice cream store we have been selling 100 pints of ice cream per day on an average. We forecast a continuation of this demand for the short-range future. Forecasts of demand requirements are just as important to inventory control as they are to other decision areas. If there is a five-day delivery or *lead* time on orders to the wholesaler, we might decide we should order 500 pints every five days to maintain our inventory. Thus we might think that we had logically established an appropriate time to order and an appropriate quantity to order.

But from a management science point of view, it is very possible we have overlooked some important cost factors. Application of the inventory model will reveal these. As with the maintenance situation as well as others, there are opposing costs that must be balanced. One of these is the cost of ordering, the labor and equipment costs required to place an order. If you have ever sent an order to a catalog company, you know how costly the process may be.

Second, there is a *carrying cost* on the inventory. This is mainly the interest charge on the money tied up in inventory. We charge an interest rate since that money could be used for some other income producing purpose if it were not tied up in inventory. Such costs are also called *opportunity costs* since we pass up other opportunities for investment in order to hold inventories. Other carrying costs include costs of storage space, insurance, and spoilage. We usually compute the carrying cost as a percentage of average inventory on an annual basis.

Now, the more we order at any one time and the larger the inventory is, the higher the carrying costs are. On the other hand, if we order frequently and in small quantities, ordering costs are high but carrying costs are low. Figure 14–10 shows the effects of size of order on these costs. Note that as carrying cost increases, ordering cost decreases, and vice versa. Note also that the intersection of these two cost curves identifies the low point on the total cost curve, which in turn is composed of carrying cost and ordering cost. Dropping a line straight down from the low point of the total cost curve shows the optimal quantity to order.

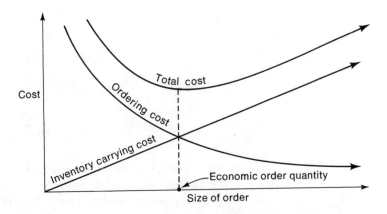

Cost

Total cost

Ordering cost

Inventory carrying cost

Economic order quantity

Size of order

Figure 14–10   Graphic determination of economic order quantity

The Mathematical Solution   The mathematical solution to the inventory size problem is precise and easy to obtain. Let us set up the following symbols:

Q = the quantity that we should order (This is what we want to determine, and it is called the *economic order quantity* or *EOQ.)*
I = carrying cost or interest charge
D = total demand over a year's time
O = ordering cost
C = cost per unit

Hence the carrying cost is:

$$\frac{CIQ}{2}$$

where we multiply the cost per unit (C) times the annual carrying cost (I) times the average inventory in units ($Q/2$).
   The order cost is:

$$\frac{OD}{Q}$$

where we multiply the ordering cost per order (O) times the number of orders placed in a year (D/Q). Since we know that low total cost is at the intersection of the cost curves for ordering cost and carrying cost, we can equate the formulas for these two costs and solve for Q in four consecutive steps:

$$(1) \quad \frac{CIQ}{2} = \frac{OD}{Q}$$

$$(2) \quad CIQ^2 = 2OD$$

$$(3) \quad Q^2 = \frac{2OD}{CI}$$

$$(4) \quad Q = \sqrt{\frac{2OD}{CI}}$$

Thus we obtain Q or the economic order quantity. Now let us plug in the figures from our ice cream store, remembering that we were selling 100 pints per day and had a lead time of five days from the wholesaler. We had figured we should order 500 pints every five days. We will assume the following data:

$$I = 0.20$$
$$D = 30,000 \text{ pints (100 per day over 300 days}$$
$$\text{during the year when we are open)}$$
$$O = \$1.00$$
$$C = \$0.30$$

Using our EOQ equation:

$$Q = \sqrt{\frac{2OD}{CI}}$$

or
$$Q = \sqrt{\frac{2 \times 1 \times 30,000}{.3 \times .2}}$$

and
$$Q = \sqrt{\frac{60,000}{.06}}$$

and
$$Q = \sqrt{1,000,000}$$

and finally $Q = 1,000$ units

So our EOQ is 1,000, twice as much as we had earlier figured it would be. This means we should start with an inventory of 1,000 pints, giving us a ten-day supply, and then reorder five days before we are due to run out. Figure 14–11 illustrates our inventory situation: the diagonal lines indicating the steady depletion of our inventory and the reorder point shown as five days before complete stockout.

This inventory model has been but one of several. The others tend to be more complex, incorporating such factors as safety stock, variable demand, and variable lead time. The more sophis-

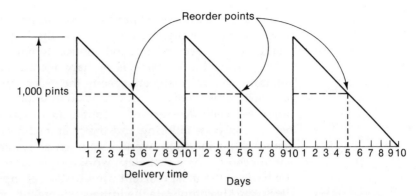

Figure 14-11   Inventory pattern for ice cream store example

ticated models tend to be more realistic and overcome some of the simplistic assumptions we made; to wit, that lead time would never vary from five days and that demand would average 100 pints per day.

Sometimes the value of items in inventory modifies the control method applied. We would be much more careful with diamonds than toothpicks, for example. We might count our diamonds every day but keep our toothpicks in a jar with a red line marked on the jar about halfway down. When the toothpicks got down to the red line, we would reorder, but we would not keep an individual count. Thus we must adapt the control system to conditions, and it is as much a mistake to overpower the item, such as making a daily count of toothpicks, as it is to use a weak system, such as keeping diamonds in an open tray on a countertop.

Conversion Control   While control of quality, maintenance, and inventories is vital to effective operations management, these areas do not zero in on the core activity—the conversion process itself. These controls contribute to the conversion process through their assurance of continuous, smooth operations at the proper quality level, but they offer little or no help on such problems as when to use a specific input, such as labor or equipment, or when to schedule one of several possible outputs for in-process work or completion.

Scheduling the conversion process is an important aspect of control. Howard Timms and Michael Pohlen have this to say about scheduling: " . . . the planning of output is really concerned with scheduling conversion operations and scheduling the acquisition of skills and materials. Controlling these functions is essentially a task in following up on conversion and acquisition operations so as to ensure that schedules are met or appropriate corrective action is taken. Practitioners of production planning, scheduling, and control often identify the total task by the last element—control—and use the term 'production control' to embrace the whole."[6]

The scheduling problem is perhaps most acute in a job shop situation, where customers specify the exact nature of output, as opposed to the relatively continuous output of some standardized product or service. Specified output is the difference, for example, between custom tailoring and the manufacture of ready-to-wear clothing. In a job shop, work must often be assigned daily to men and machines. As a first step, work assignments can be made on the basis of the most efficient combination of inputs, but delivery dates quickly complicate the initial assignment; or bosses find this man or that piece of equipment urgently needed on another job.

To deal with complex scheduling problems, organizations use a variety of methods in conversion control. Network techniques such as the Program Evaluation and Review Technique (PERT) facilitate planning as well as control. (See chapters 4 and 7 for a discussion of PERT.) Time schedules are an integral part of a PERT network, and where PERT is applicable, the boss can tell when a project or part of a project is falling behind. He then can shift resources from one part of the network to another to implement a "crash" effort, or he may revise the network. Managers also use many other kinds of master schedules, charts, and display boards for control purposes (figure 14–12).

Smoothing the Conversion Process   An important duty of operations management is to smooth out the potential ups and downs in the conversion process; that is, times when people and facilities might be extremely busy, even overtaxed, and other times when everyone is standing around wondering what to do next. The effective use of inventories will help in smoothing—depleting inventories during periods of high demand and building up inventories during slack periods. Other smoothing aids include

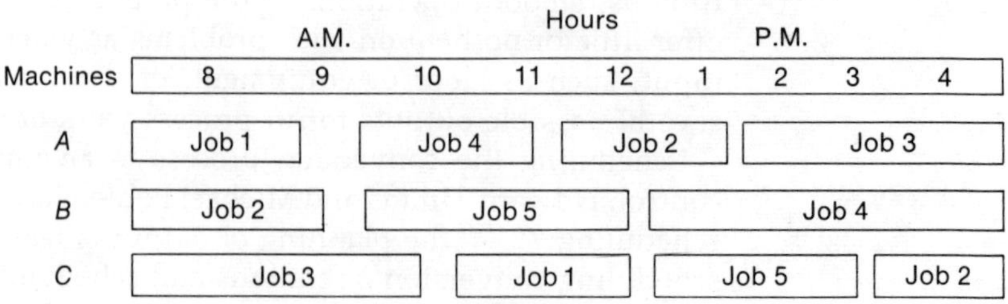

Figure 14–12   An example of a control chart in conversion scheduling running five jobs on three machines in one day

scheduling, working overtime or undertime, and hiring or laying off workers as needed. Management must determine which of the alternatives (or which combination) is the most economical and most efficient. There are a number of quantitative models that can help in the resolution of this problem.

Product Mix   The difficulty of scheduling in job shop situations suggests that it also is more difficult to smooth operations in a job shop than in an organization with a standard output. Standard output, however, has its own distinct problem—determination of the appropriate product mix, or what kinds of products to produce together. It is usually essential to work closely with the marketing function in determining product mix. Marketing supplies information on the demand and potential price structure on various products, which in turn suggest the expected profit margins. But while profit to a business organization is obviously important, the sole consideration of profit in product mix may not yield an optimal solution.

To accomplish the latter, the costs and capacities of the conversion process must have a place in the product-mix decision. Linear programming is the recommended method for achieving an optimal solution. We illustrated the solution of a product-mix problem in chapter 4, on decision making.

Perhaps an imaginary incident in the life of a college student will help illustrate the planning and controlling that must be applied to the conversion process.

A Student's Dilemma

Bill Hanes, a home economics major at Outstate University, arrived home one night, beat and frustrated from a hot day in his classroom kitchen. He had three things he absolutely had to do that night: study for an exam in meal planning; bake a cake for his girlfriend's birthday the next day; and do his laundry. He was on the edge of panic by the time he finished his TV dinner.

Then an idea occurred to him: why not lay out a schedule for the night, including times for his several activities. Then he could control his progress. Inputs would include himself, of course, his books, all the cooking utensils and cake ingredients, the oven, his dirty clothes, and the laundry machines. Outputs would be acquired knowledge, a delicious cake, and clean laundry.

Hanes did exactly that (see figure 14–13). Then he got to work. By midnight Hanes was finished. He felt confident about his exam, all the laundry was done, and the cake, other than having a slight list to the side, was beautiful. Hanes felt that he had managed all his jobs smoothly and effectively.

TIME*

7:00–7:15	7:15–7:45	7:45–8:30	8:30–8:45	8:45–9:30	9:30–9:35	9:35–9:40	9:40–10:30	10:30–11:00	11:00–12:00
Put laundry in washer			Put laundry in washer and dryer			Put laundry in dryer		Fold laundry	
	Mix cake and put in oven				Take cake out of oven				
		Study		Study			Study		Study

*Space per time period has been telescoped to allow for description of breakdowns. Note the time allotted for STUDY is greater than visually apparent from this figure.

Figure 14–13 Hanes' schedule

Value Analysis

Once the conversion process is underway, changes in product or service are usually quite difficult and therefore costly to make. For this reason, it is wise to make a value analysis—to ask a number of questions prior to starting conversion. These questions include:

1. What does the output (product or service) do?
2. What does the output cost?
3. What else does the same thing?
4. What does the alternative to the output cost?
5. Which output is least costly to the organization?

Answering these five questions before conversion can save much grief later on, though it is advisable to continue value analysis even during conversion for purposes of improvement and cost reduction. Philosophically, value analysis concentrates on what a product or service does rather than what it is.

For example, the lecture method is widely used in colleges and universities. When we ask what it does, we may be tempted to say it lulls students to sleep, though it is intended, of course, to impart knowledge. Tutoring does the same thing—that is, impart knowledge—but it is far more costly than the lecture and is not often used. Therefore the lecture method probably will continue in wide use.

Consider the use of coal as a fuel to heat buildings. Low-grade coal is inexpensive. Gas and electricity do the same thing, namely heat, but their cost per Btu (British thermal unit) is generally higher than coal. But when one considers total cost, electricity could turn out to be the least expensive method, given the cost to society of pollution from low-grade coal.

The subjects of value analysis vary from the broad-range type just mentioned to the most minute components of a product or service. Value analysis is a never-ending process that helps assure low cost and efficiency in the marketplace.

Summary

Operations management is the predominant operating activity in any organization. It oversees the conversion of organizational inputs to outputs. In a business organization, the price of the output not only must cover the cost of conversion but must yield a profit as well. In other types of organizations, some sort of measurable benefits must exceed the costs.

Planning for operations management includes making decisions on where to locate; how to convert inputs to outputs; and when to convert inputs to particular outputs. Location analysis is complex, but there are some quantitative models, such as the transportation model, that aid in reaching a decision. How to convert inputs to outputs involves process planning and its two basic components: process analysis and operations analysis. The former determines the best flow of work and materials, while the latter determines what work must be done and how it must be done.

The time factor in the conversion process covers the timing of changes in output. Changes in output are tied closely to a product or service life cycle, and management must predict as best as possible the length of the cycle and the quantities of output required during various stages of the cycle. All of this information is vital to operations management as it plans and controls the conversion process. In addition, management uses the breakeven model to determine the volume of output required to make a profit and another quantitative model to estimate the complete recovery of developmental costs on new products or services.

Management must also plan adequate capacity to produce its output. On occasion this may require financial analysis to see if investments required for new equipment and facilities can be justified by the return on a proposed new product or service. There are several approaches to resolving an investment decision. One of the most commonly used is the simple rate of return or payback method. A more sophisticated though less commonly used method is the present value model.

Another important component of operations management is control. Important control areas include quality, maintenance, inventory, and the conversion process itself. In quality control, the cost of inspection must be balanced against the cost of undetected defects. In maintenance, the cost of maintaining equipment counteracts the costs of breakdown and lost production; while in inventory control, we seek the intersection of the cost curves for carrying costs and ordering costs to determine an economic order quantity and thereby minimize total costs.

Conversion control reaches to the heart of operations management, for it must specify when to use a specific input and when to schedule any one of several outputs. These specifications are vital since a mistake could seriously waste resources as well as damage market potential through either a failure to meet demand or the creation of more output than demand warrants. Additional responsibilities of conversion control include smoothing the conversion process and, in cooperation with marketing, determining the correct product mix. Finally it is important to maintain value analysis on a continuing basis, to keep the conversion process operating correctly.

Management Profile

Adam Smith

Scottish philosopher and political economist, Adam Smith (1723–1790) was the author of perhaps the most famous book in economic annals, *Wealth of Nations*. He was the father of the classical school of economics. His interest in manufacturing, particularly in process design, is an important part of his total economic philosophy.

Adam Smith's analysis of market forces led him to the conclusion that economic activity should be completely free from government regulation. He felt that an "invisible hand" would guide market activities in a way that would effectively deploy resources. With each individual, organization, and nation working to enhance its own economic self-interest, prosperity would result.

To Smith, manufacturing, especially the developing factory system, was a necessary ingredient in his economic broth. As markets expanded and trade flourished, factories would be needed to supply products. At the time Smith wrote, the new atmosphere of competition and entrepreneurship was encouraging the formation of factories and the entry of the industrial revolution.

Of particular interest to Smith was a manufacturing method that represented a radical departure from traditional systems. This method used division of labor. The now famous example he used to illustrate the economies of division of labor involved the production of ordinary pins. He pointed out that an unskilled man would be lucky to make one pin per day, but that when the manufacture of pins was divided into eighteen distinct operations, eighteen unskilled workers, each performing one of the operations, could turn out twelve pounds or many thousands of pins every day. We know about the progress of division of labor since Adam Smith's day. Specialization has become so prevalent and so refined that we now worry about its psychological effects and strive to find ways to relieve its monotony and tedium. However, division of labor has greatly contributed to high productivity and has greatly facilitated the production of complex, sophisticated products.

In addition, Smith recognized the need for capacity analysis and adjustments. He wrote about buying new machinery and even advocated the payback method of justification for equipment investments.[7] Thus we see that Smith demonstrated a great interest in manufacturing, especially in the process aspects, and that he fully appreciated the potential in technological progress. If alive today, he probably would show great interest in the field of operations management.

Discussion Questions

1. What are the inputs and outputs of a hospital? A church? An Air Force bomber wing?

2. What might be some of the relative advantages and disadvantages of locating a farm equipment manufacturer in St. Louis, as opposed to San Francisco?

3. Do you think process design would be easier in an insurance company employing 2,000 people than in a manufacturer of furniture also employing 2,000 people? What are the reasons for your answer?

4. Consider a manufacturer of small electronic calculators and a manufacturer of steel fence posts. How would their approaches differ with respect to the use of:

a. product life cycles?

b. forecasting?

c. the breakeven model?

d. research and development?

5. In determining the advisability of making an investment in new equipment, would it make sense for a very small company with limited resources to use the simple payback method and for very large companies with ample cash reserves to use the present value method?

6. There are various cost trade-offs in the control phases of operations management. These involve inspection costs and quality levels, ordering costs and carrying costs in inventory control, and the direct costs of maintenance versus the costs of breakdowns. What are some situations in which we would *not* attempt to balance these costs: for example, to inspect less or more than at that point where cost of inspection equals the cost of undetected defects (see figure 14–9)?

7. In the incident "A Student's Dilemma," could Hanes have used a PERT network to solve his problems just as well as the method he did use? Try drawing a network for his situation. Would there be any advantages to his use of a network?

8. Apply value analysis to your ownership of an automobile for personal use in your usual daily activities. Does it appear advantageous for you to own a car in comparison to other alternatives?

References

1. T. R. Hoffmann, *Production Management and Manufacturing Systems,* (Belmont, Calif.: Wadsworth, 1967), p. 146.

2. *See* R. W. Johnson, *Financial Management,* 2d ed. (Boston: Allyn & Bacon, 1962), chapter 8, for a discussion of this problem.

3. *See* E. E. Adam, Jr., and W. E. Scott, Jr., "The Application of Behavioral Conditioning Procedures to the Problem of Quality Control," *Academy of Management Journal,* 14 (1971): 175–193, for a discussion of operant conditioning and quality control.

4. *See* H. L. Timms and M. F. Pohlen, *The Production Function in Business* (Homewood, Ill.: Richard D. Irwin, 1970), chapter 12, for a discussion of sampling in quality control.

5. Hoffmann, p. 208.

6. Timms and Pohlen, p. 469.

7. C. S. George, Jr., *The History of Management Thought* (Englewood Cliffs, N.J.: Prentice-Hall, 1972), p. 54.

Suggested Readings

Buffa, E. S. *Modern Production Management.* 4th ed. New York: John Wiley, 1973.

Chase, R. B., and Aquilano, N. J. *Production and Operations Management.* Homewood, Ill.: Richard D. Irwin, 1973.

Garrett, L., and Silver, M. *Production Management Analysis.* New York: Harcourt Brace Jovanovich, 1966.

Levin, R. I., McLaughlin, C. P., Lamone, R. P., and Kottas, J. F. *Production/Operations Management.* New York: McGraw-Hill, 1972.

Starr, M. *Production Management Systems and Synthesis.* Englewood Cliffs, N.J.: Prentice-Hall, 1964.

Timms, H. L., and Pohlen, M. F. *The Production Function in Business.* Homewood, Ill.: Richard D. Irwin, 1970.

Case Problem for Chapter 14

Standard Truck Parts Company*

The Standard Truck Parts Company was a distributor of truck, tractor, and construction equipment parts and supplies for the southeastern United States. Generally Standard carried an entire line for each manufacturer whose products it handled and provided local stocks for rapid delivery to customers. The items that Standard stocked were mainly used in the maintenance, modification, and manufacture of trucks, off-highway construction equipment, and heavy-duty tractors. In some cases, these standard lines were also of high enough quality for use in the production of certain kinds of military vehicles.

Standard had grown from a small two-man operation to a $15 million per year business in a span of twenty-five years. The growth of its dollar volume was based on an excellent reputation for good service, coupled with the general expansion of industry in the Southeast. From its inception Standard had been a profitable business in sound financial condition.

Despite the continued growth of profits in absolute terms, however, Standard found that profits as a percentage of sales declined to well below the level that the company had enjoyed in the past. When management became aware of the seriousness of the problem, it decided to undertake a thorough review of policies and procedures in the areas that could have a significant influence on costs and profits—product line, sales methods, stock handling and storage methods, billing and record keeping, and inventory replenishment. The last area was included as a major area for study because the company had been experiencing increasing difficulty with stockout situations and unbalanced inventories.

Up until the time that the review of the inventory replenishment policies and procedures was begun, there had been no formal study of this phase of the company's operations. Since maintaining inventories was one of the company's major functions, Standard had always used experienced personnel to control the placing of orders and had relied on their judgment to make correct decisions. One thing that became immediately apparent as this phase of Standard's operations came under scrutiny was that the inventory replenishment problem had become vastly more complicated in recent years, since the variety of items carried had tripled from what it was five years previously to more than 15,000 separate

*Adapted from A. N. Schreiber; R. A. Johnson; R. C. Meier; W. T. Newell; and H. C. Fischer, *Cases in Manufacturing Management* (New York: McGraw-Hill, 1965), pp. 315–320.

stock items. No formal study had been made previously of the inventory replenishment operations. Management decided, as a first step, to get some general information about order placement costs and inventory carrying costs and also to analyze in detail several typical items of inventory.

Several years earlier Standard had installed an IBM punched-card system for maintaining inventory records and for writing purchase orders. The data-processing equipment also was used for other record-keeping functions, and to efficiently schedule the equipment the inventory records were updated only once weekly. Purchase orders were also prepared on a schedule of once each week.

Purchase requisitions were turned in daily by the supervisors responsible for various types of stock, and these were accumulated until Friday when they were used to initiate purchase orders. In effect, updating of inventory levels occurred once every five days, and, in fact, almost all the supervisors turned in their purchase requisitions only once each week immediately before the scheduled machine run. This caused no particular scheduling or processing problem because the purchase requisitions were themselves punched cards on which the stock man wrote the quantity desired, which was then keypunched into the card. In total, the out-of-pocket cost of preparing and processing a requisition, preparing a purchase order, and making other necessary record changes was estimated to be $2.50 per order.

Analysis of the company records indicated that the following were reasonable estimates of the variable cost per year of carrying inventories (as a percentage of dollar value of average inventory):

Item	Percent
Capital cost	6
Obsolescence	5
Insurance	1
Taxes	1
Storage and handling	8
Total	21

One of the typical items of inventory that was analyzed in detail was a heavy-duty battery cable. The cable was purchased for $4 and sold for $5. The manufacturer from whom Standard procured the cable did not offer any quantity discount on the cable, but it would not fill orders for less than fifty cables without adding a flat charge of $25 to the order. There were other distributors in

Standard's immediate vicinity that could supply a comparable cable made by another manufacturer. Because of this, orders that Standard could not fill immediately were lost, and Standard's sales manager felt that the company lost at least another dollar per cable in other lost business and lost goodwill in addition to the dollar of lost margin on the cable.

The cable was ordered from the manufacturer located about 1,500 miles away and was shipped to Standard by truck. An analysis of the time taken to receive the cables from the day the purchase order was prepared until the cables were received indicated that this varied between five and fourteen working days. A record of the time between the preparation of the purchase order and receipt of the cables is shown in exhibit 1. It was estimated that inspection of the shipments, preparation of receiving reports, and related activities cost Standard $2.25 per order.

Exhibit 1 Procurement Lead Time

Days	Number
5	2
6	4
7	8
8	8
9	6
10	4
11	2
12	2
13	2
14	1

Exhibit 2 Customer Daily Orders

Sales	Number
0	75
1–5	9
6–10	28
11–15	39
16–20	46
21–25	24
26–30	17
31–35	11
36–40	7
41–45	4
	260

The customer daily orders for one full year (260 working days) were tabulated for this cable and are shown in exhibit 2. Further analysis of the records pertaining to this cable revealed the fact that the replenishment orders for the cable were always for lots of 500 and that the amount of stock on hand averaged about 115 units on the days that purchase orders were issued for replenishment stock.

1. Make specific recommendations as to the proper lot size for ordering heavy-duty battery cables.
2. Discuss or make recommendations for the stock level at which cable orders should take place. In your analysis consider minimum, maximum, and average lead-time demand. Point out advantages and disadvantages of using minimum or maximum lead-time demands.
3. Discuss whether the costs of stockouts justify carrying more than the average lead-time demand.
4. Based on the information available, what possibilities appear to be present for improving inventory management procedures in the Standard Truck Parts Company?

Organizational Growth, Change, and Development

15

Growth, change, and development—these topics cover a lot of territory. We want to pull together our previous discussions of organizational management in order to study these important aspects of organizational life. In the last chapter, we studied operations management or the conversion of organizational inputs to outputs. Now we want to see not only how organizations grow but how they can change and develop to become more effective, from the viewpoint of the individual as well as the organization.

How Organizations Grow

The Horatio Alger of yesterday has his modern counterparts. One example is a young man who started the Leasco Company when he was just two years out of college. With a loan of $25,000, he built Leasco into a billion-dollar corporation within ten years.[1]

We mention this success as one bit of evidence in support of the relevance of growth theory to our present-day world. Not all organizations are big and long-established. Small ones start all the time, and while many will stay small or fail, some will grow into large, successful operations. At any given moment, many organizations in various stages of growth coexist in our economy.

An organization need not start small, however. In fact, in certain industries it is mandatory that one start with a relatively large organization to have a chance for success at all. It would be most difficult, certainly, to go into business in basic steel or automobile manufacturing without substantial size. Our interest, however, is in the *process* of growth as opposed to the *state* of having grown large.

The Growth Model   The growth model we will discuss in summary form is one developed by Alan Filley and Robert House.[2] The model builds on a particular definition of growth and on certain assumptions: "... growth is the achievement of a sudden and accelerated increase in absolute increments of change in growth indexes, principally sales, assets, and employment—generated from internal sources."[3]

The definition rules out growth resulting from merger, acquisition, or any external phenomenon. It includes only growth that results from the exploitation of the existing resource and technological base within an organization. This restriction does not preclude multiple products, however, since many products could develop from the technology and resources associated with a single product base. What the model does preclude is its application to the growth situation involving the exploitation of multiple product bases and their dependencies on distinctly different technologies and resources. Hence, the model is oriented to internal growth based on the development and use of existing resources within the organization.

Other assumptions of the model include:

1. Demand conditions do not limit growth; that even in a stable industry, there could be growth through a shift in demand or the creation of demand by means of innovation;
2. Environmental conditions must be such that a rational bureaucracy could develop. These conditions most likely are to be found in relatively advanced countries; [and]
3. There is a similarity of structure, function, and pattern for varying kinds of organizations throughout the growth cycle.

In other words, the structure of a business organization at varying points in the growth cycle will correspond to the structure of other kinds of organizations—a nonprofit organization, for example—at similar stages of the growth cycle.

The model suggests that organizational growth occurring within these assumptions goes through three stages: (1) traditional craft, (2) dynamic growth, and (3) rational administration (figure 15–1). A skilled craftsman often starts a small company that may exist for years in the traditional craft stage. He runs the company and hopes to makes a living for himself as well, perhaps, as for his friends and relatives. He keeps very few records, considering

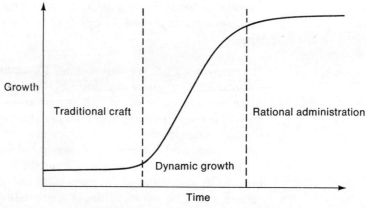

Figure 15–1 Stages of growth*

---

*From *Managerial Process and Organizational Behavior* by Alan C. Filley and Robert J. House. Copyright © 1969 by Scott, Foresman and Company. Reprinted by permission of the publisher.

them a nuisance, and relies on advice from attorneys and accountants rather than have his own staff specialists. He very likely knows all of his employees quite well, and his managerial philosophy may be summed up as: "Whatever policies and practices brought success in the past should be continued because they will no doubt also bring success in the future."

Dynamic Growth Many if not most of the small businesses in the United States are in the craft stage. Most of those in the craft stage will stay there, but a few will take the exciting leap into dynamic growth. Once embarked, there is no turning back without running the risk of severe loss and even failure. What brings a firm to fast growth? Some kind of innovation—a new product or service, a new conversion process, a new market—sets the stage. But there are other requirements. There must be a new kind of leader: an entrepreneur, a promoter, a person who is daring, loves to compete, and has enough charisma to inspire others.

In addition, the firm will need investment money for expansion. Usually it will raise money through the sale of stock, though after initial success, considerable borrowing may be possible. There must be the potential of great reward for participants in the enterprise, and there must be a great desire to bring about the changes demanded by growth. The leader generates the desire for change in his followers mainly through his referent power; that is, his enthusiasm and optimism cause his followers to identify with him and share his desire for change (growth).

A mixture of many different kinds of people following their "hero" leader characterizes dynamic growth. The leader or boss runs the show, avoiding such formalities as written policies, records, and procedures. When the firm needs a change in policy, he makes it. With a few exceptions, he does not appoint specialized staff members, preferring to rely on handpicked personal assistants for advice. The exceptions occur where expert advice is absolutely needed. If the innovation is of a highly technical nature, he may not only need the advice of scientists and engineers but may have to delegate considerable decision-making authority to them to get the job done.

The mood of the organization, certainly during the first half of the growth stage, is one of optimism and solidarity growing out of confidence in future success. During the second half of the growth stage, certain signs appear to indicate that the organization is beginning a shift into rational administration. A management structure begins to form as functions such as finance become essential. Certain staff units—purchasing, personnel, quality control—may be added. These additions and changes mark a much more gradual transition to the rational administration stage than was true in going from traditional craft to dynamic growth.

Rational Administration The changes accompanying the period of transition to rational administration are substantial.

[Transition presumes] the development of a rational, decentralized organizational structure, full functional development, market-oriented organizational objectives, written records and policy, professional management, a full staff complement, and homogeneity of values and philosophy among organization members....

By the time a firm reaches the third stage of growth, it has become much larger and more complex than it was in the first stage. The dynamic period of growth is replaced by a period of institutionalization. The entrepreneur who exercised face-to-face leadership, or at least direct influence, has evolved into or been replaced by executives who perform more rational processes of planning, organizing, directing, and controlling. Attitudes are more conservative. Action is undertaken only after careful consideration of consequences.[4]

The organization no longer dances to the tune of one fiddler. Activities are now fully orchestrated, with specialized staff, separation of top administration from operational management, and a more impersonal atmosphere. Increased profits result more from internal control of costs than from exploitation of external markets. Employees must find job satisfaction in the work itself and in group relations rather than through identification with a glamorous leader.

What happens to an organization after it reaches the third stage of rational administration? If the organization becomes too rational and too conservative, it risks slipping back into a traditional mode. It may grow larger through merger or acquisition of other organizations. If it retains sufficient innovative spirit and risk-taking proclivity, it may experience further growth through one or more additional dynamic growth cycles. Such added growth cycles are often implemented through project-type organizational structures. Under this arrangement, the parent organization continues in the third stage, but various project groups may be experiencing second-stage growth and operating under second-stage conditions. A final though perhaps rare alternative for an organization in the third stage is for nothing to happen; that is, the organization just continues along a very stable path, neither growing nor contracting, and it maintains this posture for an indefinite period of time.

Problems of Growth

We may guess that growth does not occur without problems involving organizational structure and process. Larry Greiner identifies many of these problems, particularly for organizations moving into and perhaps out of the third stage of rational administration.[5] A change in the type of leadership required may be a problem in going from the traditional stage to dynamic growth and from dynamic growth to rational administration. On entering rational administration, many firms continue a form of the centralized managerial planning and control so typical of the dynamic growth phase. However, to be more sensitive to client or customer needs, to generate more ideas for new products or services, and to encourage development of local markets, a more decentralized structure might be desirable.

But decentralizing under rational administration may be difficult at first, not only because top managers are reluctant to give up portions of their power and responsibility, but also because lower-level managers are not prepared by training or experience for decision making. Given a perceived need for decentralization, however, and a willingness to try, we may assume that most firms implementing decentralization ultimately reach some satisfactory level of success.

Unfortunately, solutions to one set of problems often seem to generate new problems, and in this case decentralization as a solution appears to be no exception. Under decentralization, top managers begin to feel they are losing control over an independent and often parochially-oriented field organization.

Hence top managers seek new solutions. One alternative returns all control to a centralized managerial headquarters. This usually fails because by this time the organization has grown too complex and large for simple centralized control. A better alternative institutes coordination through formal systems. For example:

Decentralized units are merged into product groups.

Formal planning procedures are established and intensively reviewed.

Numerous staff personnel are hired and located at headquarters to initiate companywide programs of control and review for line managers.

Capital expenditures are carefully weighed and parceled out across the organization.

Each product group is treated as an investment center where return on invested capital is an important criterion used in allocating funds.

Certain technical functions, such as data processing, are centralized at headquarters, while daily operating decisions remain decentralized.

Stock options and companywide profit sharing are used to encourage identity with the firm as a whole.[6]

These systems encourage managers to think of the welfare of the entire organization as they make decisions within their own bailiwicks. However, some of the worst aspects of bureaucratic organization begin to slowly choke life out of the organization. The formal programs and systems proliferate, and the result is exponentially increasing red tape. Procedures supersede goals as priorities turn upside down. What to do?

No Final Answer Greiner suggests collaboration as a solution to red tape. He emphasizes: ". . . greater spontaneity in management action through teams and the skillful confrontation of interpersonal differences. Social control and self-discipline take over from formal control. This transition is especially difficult for those experts who created the old systems as well as for those line managers who relied on formal methods for answers."[7]

The collaborative stage closely resembles the organic, matrix type of organization we discussed in chapter 8. The team approach and team action occupy a prominent place, with team membership drawn from the various functional areas within the organization. The old formal systems and procedures are simplified, and the headquarters unit consults much more than it directs. The organization encourages innovation, deemphasizes hierarchical levels and the scalar chain, and promotes open and honest communication and interaction throughout the organization.

What problems arise from the collaborative solution? Greiner is not sure, though he suggests that many United States organizations are in the collaborative stage. He speculates that the problems ". . . will center around the 'psychological saturation' of employees who grow emotionally and physically exhausted by the intensity of teamwork and the heavy pressure for innovative solutions."[8]

Of what value is knowledge of the growth cycle and the problems that may accompany development from infancy to maturity and beyond? The value lies in the ability to predict impending changes, to prepare for them, and to enhance the learning experience involved in progressing through a growth phase. Although managers may be aware of an organization's position in the developmental sequence, Greiner cautions against the temptation to skip a phase. Just as humans need a wide range of challenges and problem-solving efforts to reach full maturity, so an organization may need the full range of developmental crises to gain the confidence and capacity required to function as a big, sophisticated component of society.

Finally, management should recognize that there are a limited number of correct solutions to the problems that arise in growth. There is always danger that management will pick the wrong structure to solve current problems as well as fit the next phase. Hence managers need not only knowledge of growth but awareness of their managerial styles and the ability to persuade others to change in order to make change effective. Figure 15–2 adds solutions to growth problems to the basic three-stage growth model that we discussed earlier.

The President's Lawn

The following is a true incident, with names changed, and may help to show the difficulty an executive may encounter when he remains in charge while the organization moves from one growth stage to another. Frank Bell was president and founder of an organization that was gradually shifting into the rational administration stage of growth—although Bell was only vaguely aware of this shift. He had nurtured the company through its early struggling

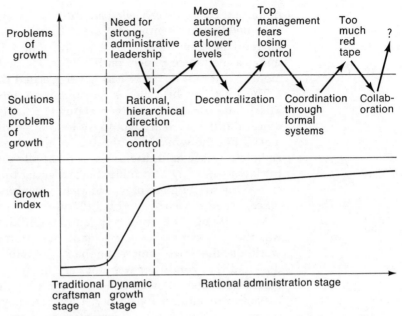

Figure 15–2 Solutions to problems of growth in the rational administrative stage.*

---

*From *Managerial Process and Organizational Behavior* by Alan C. Filley and Robert J. House. Copyright © 1969 by Scott, Foresman and Company. Reprinted by permission of the publisher. Also from L. E. Greiner, "Evolution and Revolution as Organizations Grow," *Harvard Business Review*, 50 (1972): 41.

traditional phase and had conceived the innovations that had launched the company into fast growth.

Moreover, Bell had proven remarkably adept at leadership during the great expansion period. He inspired those around him and fastened their gaze as well as his own on distant goals. He always maintained tight control and prided himself on his knowledge of everything that went on in the organization. He hired people; kept a constant, close check on shop activities; and took particular pride and enjoyment in overseeing the landscaping around the plant. He personally supervised the lawn care, often going out in the middle of the morning or afternoon to place a sprinkler in the right position.

But Bell had a gut feeling that all was not well. Things seemed to be getting out of hand. He never had time for anything away from the shop, since he was putting in sixteen to eighteen hours a day. Yet the work piled up. Events came to a head one day when an important customer cancelled an order that was two months overdue. Bell lost his temper that day, striking out at anyone within range. Late that night, however, he found the order—buried under a mound of papers on his desk. He had misplaced it two months before. The order had never reached the shop floor.

The next day he called a consultant. A few days later, Dirk Melch, the consultant, arrived about 11 A.M. Bell was not in his office, but the secretary would try to locate him. Just then, Melch looked out the window to the side of the plant. To his utter and complete amazement, there was Bell happily puttering around on the lawn—moving a sprinkler here, digging up a weed there. Bell spilled out his long tale of woe to Melch over lunch, and later in his office, asked if Melch could help him.

Melch thought he could help, and he said the first place to start was the president's lawn. He made Bell promise to never again work on the lawn unless he had absolutely nothing else to do—and that condition was not very likely to occur. Bell promised. Melch then showed Bell how to effectively delegate some of his authority and responsibility. Together, they set up specialized functional activities and some staff assistance. They generated some written policy and procedures statements and set up a formal planning system: in other words, all the formalities of rational administration.

Bell took a long time to become accustomed to the new way of doing things, but he was able to make the switch. Today the company thrives, and Bell is deeply engrossed in adjusting his organization to the demands and problems of organizational life span and growth.

Organizational Change

Change is a necessary concomitant to continued organizational life. In addition to the specific problems of growth that we mentioned, change occurs for a variety of other reasons. The external environment poses constant challenge to an organization because the environment is dynamic and demands constant adjustment for the survival of the organizational entity. Most environmental changes occur independently of any actions the organization might take. But in certain instances large corporations in particular can affect their environment.

They do this through political lobbying, through market domination, through technological leadership, and in other ways. Nonetheless, markets, technology, laws and regulations, and social ambience change regardless of the best efforts of organizations to influence these factors one way or another. The organization must face up to these external changes and must recognize that internal modifications often will be necessary to effect the adjustment process. Solutions may involve the development of new products, the adoption of new technologies, the creation of new jobs and new relationships among jobs, and the learning of new attitudes and values on the part of employees. Adjusting to environmental change will likely cause serious internal repercussions. (

Change emanates from within the organization as well. Communications get out of whack; structure begins to hinder more than to help; group processes bog down; morale drops; production falls off; and many other changes can sour a situation in a short time. Part of management's job is to recognize symptoms, to know when a system, a department, a group, an individual, or the whole organization is getting into trouble and needs a change effort.

To the onlooker, it may seem a simple matter to spot impending difficulty. But the record suggests that a situation often worsens and worsens until some debacle occurs. There may be an unexpected strike, a lost market, or hopeless technological obsolescence. Detecting potential trouble is as much a matter of experience as of learning. Good indicators of trouble include production records, profit trends, attitude surveys, budget variance, and level of quality. The organizational control system should be designed to pick up signals that will alert management. The control system should include the types of feedback processes already discussed in chapter 7 so that change and adaptation are built into the ongoing organizational life.

Resistance to Change Change is usually not easy. As individuals we tend to resist change in our lives. We find it particularly difficult to change long-ingrained habits and values. This is why leadership training can only do so much—why it is extremely hard to change a person's natural task-oriented style, for example, to a supportive one. Organizations are made up of individuals, of course, and so it is not surprising that organizations also find it difficult to change.

Perhaps the principal reason people in organizations resist change relates to disturbed social relationships. We know how important group membership can be to an individual. Organizational change often threatens membership ties, raising the specter of starting all over again to establish new social relationships. Change often requires new and different job duties, and the individual may not trust his ability to cope with new methods or tools. He may fear financial loss, decreased status, and lowered job satisfaction. Finally, everyone has some reluctance to leave the old and familiar for the new and strange. Most of our ensuing discussion will center on ways to reduce or overcome resistance to change, beginning with consideration of two basic approaches to change.

Structural and Behavioral Approaches to Change

The structural approach to change emphasizes changes in the formal relationships and task flows that characterize an organization. William Glueck describes the structural approach:

> The first structural mechanism (widely used by organization planning departments and management consultants) is to try to solve organizational problems by clarifying and defining jobs, changing job content, relationships, coordinating mechanisms, division of functions logically with minimal overlap, and small spans of control. The second structural mechanism (called the social engineering approach) tries to improve task performance by modifying the flow of tasks to fit the flow of the work. This may involve transfer of people to fit the new structure. The social engineers . . . argue that you will modify the organization structure when you modify the behavior of people leading to improved task performance.
>
> The third mechanism is to modify the structure to fit the communication needs of the organization of jobs (for example, centralized communication structures for repetitive tasks, open systems for unstructured tasks). The fourth structural mechanism is decentralization to reduce the cost of coordination and increase the controllability of subunits, to increase the motivation of goal oriented behavior through the use of smaller centers of decision, power, and information, giving greater flexibility and speed of response through local autonomy.[9]

The basic idea of the structural approach, then, is that improved performance follows some type of facilitating structural change. The behavioral approach, on the other hand, first seeks to modify the values, attitudes, and beliefs of organization members. Once modification is accomplished, the people themselves will make whatever structural and process changes are necessary to improve performance.

Specific methods of implementing the behavioral approach include participative decision making, sensitivity training, and such structured training programs as the managerial grid (chapter 8). If successful, the behavioral approach modifies not only an individual's attitudes but also improves interpersonal relationships, particularly with respect to group processes, and intergroup relationships.

There is nothing to prevent an organization from combining the two approaches into one overall program. Management can make the structural changes that appear necessary and at the same time work with individuals and groups to modify attitudes and bring about improved interpersonal and intergroup relationships. A combination approach would seem to be the most practical, since certain structural modifications often are desirable and since certain special situations, such as that described below, require careful application of behavioral knowledge.

The Group and Change

In overcoming resistance to change, special attention frequently should be paid to group pressure on individuals.[10] If, for example, we single out one individual from a group for special training intended to improve his job performance, we must recognize that no change, no improvement, is likely to result if: (1) group members perceive the training results as violating group norms; and (2) the group strongly influences the individual who received the training. Under these conditions, the individual probably will ignore his training in order to remain in good standing with the group. If he does follow up on his training, tension and hostility with other group members may degenerate into a serious morale problem.

If a group has high cohesion, any effort at change ordinarily must involve the whole group. Management may see a need for change, but this usually is not enough. Affected groups also must perceive a need for change. A good way to induce this group perception is for group members to participate in the decision-making process leading to the change. Participation of this nature is one of the components of the supportive leadership style. Furthermore, successful participation requires open and honest communication within the group as well as that directed to the group from outside sources (mainly management). But as Cartwright points out, removal of restraints on communication often results in the communication of pent-up hostility, to the point where the group threatens to fall apart.[11] Under such conditions, in the fear that things are getting out of hand, management may stop the change process. In most instances, however, management's wisest course would be to move ahead with change on the generally realistic assumption that the group will settle down and become more effective.

For a group, the participative process of reaching a decision and the degree to which group consensus is obtained and perceived are vital in overcoming resistance to change.[12] One of the problems in the behavioral approach to change is fade-out, the inability to sustain attitude change under job conditions over a relatively long period of time.

It is a common practice to undertake improvements in group functioning by providing training programs for certain classes of people in the organization. A training program for foremen, for nurses, for teachers, or for group workers is established. If the content of the training is relevant for organizational change, it must of necessity deal with the relationships these people have with other subgroups. If nurses in a hospital change their behavior significantly, it will affect their relations both with the patients and with the doctors. It is unrealistic to assume that both these groups will remain indifferent to any significant changes in this respect. In hierarchical structures this process is most clear.[13]

Hence the recommendation is that organizational change should involve at least three levels in the hierarchy: the level representing the prime target and the levels immediately above and below the prime target area. In this way, new attitudes and behavior patterns of the prime group receive reinforcement from the new expectations of both the superior and subordinate groups. Otherwise, the prime group must try to change alone and will probably fade under constant negative pressure (figure 15–3).

Organization Development

Representing the first concerted, research-based effort by many management scholars and practitioners to develop and implement effective change programs, organization development (*OD*) today attracts wide interest and application. Wendell French and Cecil Bell define *OD* as:

. . . a long-range effort to improve an organization's problem-solving and renewal processes, particularly through a more effective and collaborative management of organization culture—with special emphasis on the culture of formal work teams—with the assistance of a change agent or catalyst and the use of the theory and technology of applied behavioral science, including action research.

By the term *culture* in our definition we mean prevailing patterns of activities, interactions, norms, sentiments (including feelings), attitudes, values and products. By including products we include technology in our definition, although changes in technology tend to be secondary in organization development efforts. However, technology—if one includes procedures and methods along with equipment—is almost always influenced, and is an influence, in organization development activities.[14]

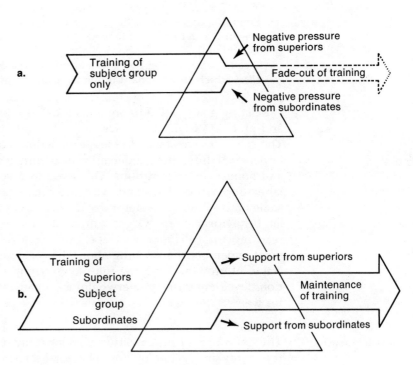

Figure 15-3 Maintenance of training improvement

The term *culture* incorporates informal organization and its associated phenomena of norms, pressures to conform, interactions, and communicative processes. *OD* focuses on both formal and informal aspects of organization, although attitudes and feelings manifested informally generally attract the initial focus of interest. Hence, it is perhaps not surprising that ". . . the key unit in organization development activities is the on-going work team, including both superior and subordinates."[15]

What is the value of organization development? Several benefits may be listed:

1. Providing opportunities for people to function as human beings rather than as resources in the productive process;
2. Providing opportunities for each organization member, as well as for the organization itself, to develop to his full potential;
3. Seeking to increase the effectiveness of the organization in terms of *all* of its goals;
4. Attempting to create an environment in which it is possible to find exciting and challenging work;

5. Providing opportunities for people in organizations to influence the way in which they relate to work, the organization, and the environment; [and]
6. Treating each human being as a person with a complex set of needs, *all* of which are important in his work and in his life.[16]

Relating goals of *OD* to organizational growth, we find that the end-product of *OD* resembles the collaborative stage of growth. The collaborative stage stresses team action, confrontation of interpersonal differences, a deemphasis of formal systems, and open and honest communications. *OD* seeks to involve people in collaboration with others and with the organization, while at the same time allowing greater individual freedom to adopt a particular behavior pattern. Organization development is a means of reaching the collaborative stage. An organization applying *OD* must remember the warning about the consequences of skipping stages of growth. Applying full-blown, comprehensive organization development may overwhelm an organization not yet ready for it.

Action Research

The definition of organization development recommends use of the theory and technology of behavioral science, including action research. Action research is a diagnostic process whereby an organization determines its actual and potential problems, its ability to change, and where and how to begin the change effort if change is indicated. Data are gathered, usually by means of interviews and questionnaires, though hunches and observation also may provide valuable input.

Once data are gathered, the organization does not simply receive a report. Instead, the organization, through its members, participates in the analysis and interpretation of data. Members may decide that additional data are necessary for further analysis. Thus the diagnostic process goes on, pinpointing areas of greatest stress and identifying beginning points for change—which, by the way, may not coincide with a high-stress problem area. Kenneth Benne says, "Points of stress between opposing forces are thus potential starting points in change. But which of the points of strain are at present so 'full of dynamite' that the client cannot talk or think about them rationally? And which, while presenting difficulties, can be openly faced, probed, and dealt with by the client system? The most stressful points in the client system are thus not necessarily the best starting points for change. Which points of stress, if handled adequately, would open up others to examination and resolution? Which are dead ends?"[17]

Action research involves the client system (the organization) in the whole question of change. But another important element, also mentioned in the definition, must be considered.

The Change Agent   Our concern is *planned* change, a deliberate effort at improvement from the standpoint of individual members as well as the organizational entity. So far we have discussed the client system, the organization or some part of it, and the knowledge generated from action research and required for diagnosis. But there is a third element necessary for planned change—the change agent. The change agent intervenes in the change process to guide, stimulate, help plan and diagnose, and develop mutual trust and confidence in order to regulate the quality, thrust, and pace of the desired change. He is a catalyst.

Initially, at least, the change agent should probably be someone or some group from outside the organization. Where only some portion of an organization is involved, a department or other subsystem, the change agent could be a member of the organization but not of the subsystem. The change agent does not operate in the traditional mode of the consultant; that is, he does not simply make recommendations. Instead, he actively works to implement change. To be effective, the change agent must develop trust for himself in others and must stimulate trust among members of the client system. Warren Bennis suggests that the ability of the change agent to influence largely depends on his representation and transmittal of values admired and desired by the client system.[18] These values include concern for our fellow man, openness, honesty, flexibility, cooperation, and democracy.

Once *OD* is underway, a group or individual within the client system may function as the change agent. In so doing, the group or individual will continue to intervene in the change process just as the outside party did. And similar to the outside party, the inside group or individual must be sufficiently attractive and prestigious to influence others involved in the change.

All well and good, you may say. We have an organization (client system) whose troubles have been diagnosed, and we have a change agent to help. But what kind of intervention should we specify?

Intervention   Most organization development specialists have their favorite means of intervention. We have discussed most of them at one time or another in the book within varying contexts. Intervention is the action phase of *OD*. It is not a final step, but rather a mode for facilitating continuous action. The most common intervention probably is an evolution of the T-group in sensitivity training. As originally practiced, sensitivity training involved getting diverse strangers together for short periods of time—usually two weeks. Through their own interactions, participants developed considerable trust and confidence in one another. Confrontations occurred in an open and honest atmosphere. Under the prevailing spirit of cooperation and collaboration, each individual learned a great deal about himself and others. This type of sensitivity training still goes on, but it labors under the serious handicap of fade-out where organizational commitments are concerned. Persons returning to organizations from a T-group experience rarely retain their new attitudes and feelings unless their peer group, superiors, and subordinates have undergone the same experience.

Hence the evolutionary form of the T-group places more emphasis on total organizational involvement, on intergroup as well as intragroup relationships, and on being directed toward the problems of organizations as well as individuals. Blake and Mouton use an evolved form of sensitivity training in their managerial grid approach to organization development.[19] For example, many conflict situations between groups occur because there is no basis for understanding—no communication between the groups and no appreciation of problems besetting the various parties.

By bringing members of the groups together in an intergroup laboratory, each group has an opportunity to view conflict from the position of the other group. Increased understanding of the attitudes and motivations of other groups develops, and new bases for solutions to conflict situations emerge.

Sometimes structural adjustments form part of the intervention. In these cases the change agent usually tries to establish a more open type of organization as opposed to a bureaucratic type emphasizing conformity to written policies and procedures. Structural adjustments may involve building teams into a collaborative type of organization and emphasize cross-functional cooperation within an overall matrix pattern. There are many specific interventions that can be used, depending on the situation. More kinds are developing all the time; to attempt a complete catalog at a given point in time is futile.[20] "In brief, if an intervening activity in an organization (a) responds to a felt need for change on the part of the 'client', (b) involves the client in the activity of planning and implementing a change event and (c) leads to a normative change in the organization's culture, then it is an organization development intervention."[21]

We have presented a rather positive view of organization development as an effective approach to change. But *OD* is not without limitations and criticism. For example:

> Organization development does not deal with power dynamics very effectively. In fact, it seldom deals with them at all. Since *OD* practitioners seek outcomes such as collaboration, high interpersonal trust, openness, honesty, decentralization of decision making, and a sharing of authority, the technology for coping with the realities of power is rather limited. Nevertheless, *OD* technology to deal with power is needed. For example, it is very difficult to conduct a team building session if the team leader refuses to attend the meetings or if he is reluctant to share power in the decision making process. Or, for another example, interdepartmental conflict can rarely be dealt with effectively if upper management reserves the right to overrule whatever problem solution the two groups might develop.[22]

W. Warner Burke mentions other limitations. Members of minority groups, women, and older persons entering into rewarding relationships with organizations receive little support from *OD*. Most *OD* interventions are long-range projects; but managers tend to concentrate on short-term problems. A method is needed that will produce faster results. *OD* has been widely practiced, but its theory development is limited. Hence there is a need for more conceptualization about *OD*, its practice and potential.

The role of the change agent remains unsettled. We have presented the change agent as one who intervenes in order to facilitate the development of conditions conducive to organizational change and renewal. Some critics take the view that the change agent should do more—that he should insist on modifications in the structure and goals when necessary. They also believe the change agent should be a team, composed of people from both inside and outside the organization and representing a variety of disciplines. There should be more emphasis on systems analysis, engineering approaches, and solutions to conflict that are not necessarily based on development of a love-trust model. Argyris may be correct in suggesting that the role of the interventionist is: "... about where the role of the medical doctor was in the early 1700s."[23]

Problems in Implementation Organization development is long-range in outlook, so an initial problem is maintaining long-range intervention. A compounding factor is the difficulty of measuring results. Many variables, both within and outside the organization, can affect *OD*, and it is often impossible to show any direct connection between successful change and *OD* efforts.

Managers want immediate results. If they cannot see results, many managers will be tempted to discontinue organization development. And there is little the change agent can do by way of measurement to convince management otherwise. Implementation of an *OD* program is often shortcircuited, therefore, by an inability to demonstrate effectiveness.

Furthermore, organization development requests people to act in ways to which they are not accustomed. It is not customary for persons to confront each other candidly over areas of disagreement, and with even more daring, to trust the other person to react honestly and without malice. Yet this is what *OD* demands. It is not customary for people to continuously monitor their methods for getting a job done, for goal achievement. Yet this is what *OD* demands. Such deep modifications in behavior require a long-term investment—a continuing process, one which management is frequently loathe to embrace.

To turn our discussion around, to overcome these problems and have a successful implementation requires:

1. The complete support and involvement of top management;
2. The application of intervention techniques on the job;
3. Understanding of and participation in the change by affected members of the organization;
4. As much trust as can be generated between the change agent and the client system;
5. Perception by the client system that the new values proffered by the change agent are desirable; and
6. A willingness to make organization development an ongoing, long-term process.

Conclusions The *OD* process and its intended end result are shown in figure 15–4. The process includes action research (data gathering and diagnosis) and intervention by a change agent. The end result of successful *OD* is a self-renewing organization characterized by (1) collaboration rather than competition; (2) open and honest confrontation among individuals and groups as a means to conflict and problem resolution; (3) an atmosphere of trust; (4) flexibility and innovation; (5) team leadership through consensus rather than through individual rule; (6) open communication in all directions; and (7) a reward system related to individual as well as organizational goals.

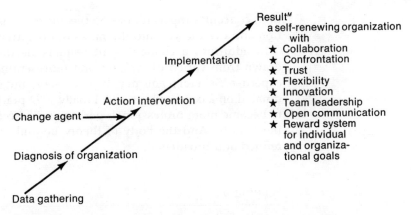

Result[M]
a self-renewing organization
with
★ Collaboration
★ Confrontation
★ Trust
★ Flexibility
★ Innovation
★ Team leadership
★ Open communication
★ Reward system
for individual
and organiza-
tional goals

Implementation

Action intervention

Change agent

Diagnosis of organization

Data gathering

Figure 15–4   Organization development—process and result

Exactly how does organization development differ from other, more traditional approaches to change? French and Bell offer several differentiating characteristics of *OD*:

1. An emphasis, although not exclusive, on group and organizational processes in contrast to substantive content;
2. An emphasis on the work team as the key unit for learning more effective modes of organizational behavior;
3. An emphasis on the collaborative management of work team culture;
4. An emphasis on the management of the culture of the total system and total system ramifications;
5. The use of the "action research" model;
6. The use of a behavioral scientist "change agent" or catalyst; and
7. Viewing the change effort as an ongoing process. Another characteristic, (8), a primary emphasis on human and social relationships, does not necessarily differentiate *OD* from other change efforts, but is nevertheless an important feature.[24]

OD and the Future   What will happen to organization development? Will it flourish as a seminal approach to change or will it fade away as just another fad out of the management grab-bag of tricks? If progress can be achieved in the right directions, chances are good that *OD* will flourish. A more integrated systems approach to *OD* is needed, for example. Fade-out is still a problem in behavioral changes because not enough consideration has been accorded the interactions among all components of an organizational system. Blake and Mouton's management grid approach perhaps is the most systems-oriented of any extant *OD* intervention, concentrating as it does on the entire management organization and even lower into the ranks of operative workers.

In addition, a change agent team is needed, with members drawn from varied disciplines and representing several kinds of expertise. Several teams may be necessary, and they must be coordinated on a continuing basis. Finally, *OD* practitioners will have to become more professional, perhaps with accrediting or certifying boards. And the body of theory behind *OD* will have to be refined and broadened.

Summary

All organizations are in or going through some stage of growth. Progressing from one stage to another means change—change in structure, in process, in technology, and in people. Even for those rare organizations that remain a long time in one growth stage, changes are essential if for no other reason than to adjust to a changing environment.

We have examined three major stages of growth: traditional craftsman, dynamic growth, and rational administration. A traditional organization often is a one-man show. Dynamic growth is characterized by a charismatic leader surrounded by personal assistants and with all members looking toward a bright, exciting, and prosperous future. Rational administration emphasizes rule of law, impersonal administration, separation of administration from operations, and developing structure.

Growth entails problems. Even after reaching the rational administration stage, management must nurse the organization through succeeding evolutions in managerial style and organization structure and process. These evolutionary phases may include, in order: tight centralized control from the top down; decentralization; coordination through formal systems; and collaboration within a matrix structure. It may not be possible to skip a phase without losing the experience necessary for maturity.

Hence change is an integral part of organizational life. Two basic approaches to change are the structural and the behavioral. The former stresses structural change, while the latter seeks first to modify the values, attitudes, and beliefs of organization members.

Organization development is a new approach to change that emphasizes client participation in diagnostic research and continuing intervention by a change agent to help the client system achieve permanent change. Intervention devices include sensitivity training, intergroup labs, team-building labs, various forms of consultation, and others. Organization development currently requires long-term intervention for success, but the technology could be developed for the short-range programs demanded by practicing managers. The future of *OD* looks good if theory development continues, if it moves toward a more integrated systems approach, and if the practice of *OD* becomes more professional.

Management Profile

Robert Owen

Robert Owen (1771–1858) was a man who sought to change the world. Reformer and successful manufacturer, Owen spent his lifetime trying to convince others of the values of humanitarianism and to put his own ideas into practice. He left home at the age of ten to seek his fortune. After working in London for a few years, Owen, at the advanced age of eighteen, started his own textile mill in Manchester, England. The mill was immediately successful. Around 1800, when he was 29 years old, Owen bought into and managed several mills at New Lanark, Scotland.

For the next quarter-century, New Lanark was Owen's base of operations for humanistic reform efforts in business, education, and labor law. He treated his own employees with paternalistic kindness and advised other manufacturers that if they treated their employees as well as their machines, profits would increase up to 100 percent.

After much vigorous effort, in 1819 Owen was able to help push through a factory bill that prohibited the employment of children under the age of nine, allowed children to work only during daylight hours, and limited total hours per day to ten and one half. Previously pauper children of all ages had been working thirteen hours per day with an hour and one quarter off for meals. Unfortunately, the 1819 law was never enforced.

Owen appreciated the importance of education. He was one of the first to establish an infant school; he inaugurated programs of adult education; and his Institution for the Formation of Character was widely hailed as embodying a forward-looking educational approach.

During the years at New Lanark, Owen was formulating his conception of a new society. Feeling that individuals had little opportunity for character development when subject to the harsh treatment and exploitation of industrial society at that time, he advocated small communities of from 800 to 2,500 members where agriculture and industry would be combined and production and consumption would be organized on a cooperative basis. Each member would perform many different jobs. He felt that the associated moral and material environment would develop good character.

In 1817 he elaborated his plans and inaugurated a great propagandist effort, which produced widespread discussion but not the practical test he desired. Discouraged with his progress in England, he came to the United States in 1824 and established the New Harmony cooperative community in Southern Indiana. The United States greeted him with great enthusiasm, and in the spring of 1825 he spoke to an audience in Washington, D.C., that included President Monroe and incoming President Adams.

By 1827, however, the New Harmony experiment ended in failure, wiping out most of Owen's fortune in the process. His popularity remained high in the United States until 1829, when he tried to show in a public debate that the principles of all religions are erroneous. Contrary to some church doctrine that all persons are responsible for their own character and must eventually answer for it, Owen believed that the individual was a prisoner of his environment and that he exercised little control over his own character development.

Shortly after the debate, Owen returned to England. He tried again with another experimental community, but it too ended in failure. Discouraged but not defeated, Owen vigorously continued his propagandizing efforts until his death at age 87. Like many visionaries, Owen saw reality far before its acceptance and even recognition by others. He called for a systems approach to the management of labor. He spoke against the division of labor as degrading. He advocated education for all and worked hard for the passage of child labor laws. Owen urged humanitarian concern for workers one hundred years before the Hawthorne experiments.

Owen and men like him tried to be change agents. Unfortunately, his contemporaries resisted his innovations, just as men like him have always been resisted. The advocacy of change and the recognition of its inevitability have always been easier on paper than in real life.

Discussion Questions

1. Could a firm in the dynamic growth stage avoid entering the stage of rational administration—that is, continue indefinitely in dynamic growth? How?

2. Despite warnings to the contrary, might it not be possible for a company just entering rational administration to immediately use a collaborative form of management? Explain your answer.

3. One author speculates that in the collaborative stage organizational members might become emotionally exhausted because of constant, intense teamwork and the demand for creative problem solving. Do you believe this to be a realistic possibility? Why or why not?

4. In the incident "The President's Lawn," the founder of the company had great difficulty in learning how to delegate. People from outside an organization often can quickly pinpoint what appear to be quite simple organizational problems. Why can't managers like Bell analyze their own problems and figure out their own solutions?

5. Since change is so much a part of organizational life, why don't people rationally recognize the need for change and accept it without resistance? Or is it possible to have an organization with an atmosphere of change so that resistance is minimized? How would you go about encouraging an atmosphere of change?

6. While combining the structural and behavioral approaches to implement change may be the best overall approach, which of the two basic approaches do you believe to be intrinsically superior? Give your reasons.

7. Do you believe all members of an organization would automatically embrace the values and goals of organization development? Why might some organizational members criticize or fear *OD*?

8. One problem with organization development is that it is a long-range program, while managers look for immediate results and therefore become impatient with *OD*. But it is part of the managerial job to do long-range planning and to work at long-range programs. Is the conflict lodged in the rational theory, or is it between the theory and the practice? How would you resolve the conflict?

References

1. " 'Don't take no for an answer,' " says builder of billion dollar corporation," *The MBA Executive*, 1 (1972): 1.

2. A. C. Filley and R. J. House, *Managerial Process and Organizational Behavior* (Glenview, Ill.: Scott, Foresman, 1969), pp. 436–481.

3. *Ibid.*, p. 439.

4. *Ibid.*, pp. 448–449.

5. L. E. Greiner, "Evolution and Revolution as Organizations Grow," *Harvard Business Review*, 50 (1972): 37–46.

6. *Ibid.*, p. 43.

7. *Ibid.*

8. *Ibid.*, p. 44.

9. W. F. Glueck, "Organization Change in Business and Government," *Academy of Management Journal*, 12 (1969): 440–441.

10. Adapted from D. Cartwright, "Achieving Change in People: Some Applications of Group Dynamics Theory," in L. L. Cummings and W. E. Scott, eds., *Readings in Organizational Behavior and Human Performance* (Homewood, Ill.: Richard D. Irwin, 1969), pp. 722–731.

11. *Ibid.*, p. 730.

12. *See* chapter 13 on leadership for a discussion of participation in decision making and limits on such participation.

13. Cartwright, p. 730.

14. W. E. French and C. H. Bell, "A Definition and History of Organization Development," *Proceedings of the Thirty-first Annual Meeting of the Academy of Management* (Atlanta: Academy of Management, 1972), p. 146.

15. *Ibid.*

16. N. Margulies and A. P. Raia, *Organization Development: Values, Process, and Technology* (New York: McGraw-Hill, 1972), p. 4.

17. K. Benne, "Changes in Institutions and the Role of the Change Agent," in P. R. Lawrence and J. A. Seiler, *Organization Behavior and Administration* (Homewood, Ill.: Irwin-Dorsey, 1965), p. 958.

18. W. Bennis, *Changing Organizations* (New York: McGraw-Hill, 1966), p. 169.

19. R. R. Blake and J. S. Mouton, *The Managerial Grid* (Houston: Gulf Publishing, 1964).

20. *See*, for example, R. L. Burke and H. A. Hornstein, "Introduction to the Social Technology of Organizational Development," *OD Practitioner* (April, 1970).

21. W. Warner Burke, "Organization Development: Here to Stay?" *Proceedings of the Thirty-first Annual Meeting of the Academy of Management* (Atlanta: Academy of Management, 1972), p. 172.

22. *Ibid.*

23. C. Argyris, *Management and Organization Development* (New York: McGraw-Hill, 1972).

24. French and Bell, p. 148.

Suggested Readings

Bennis, W. F. *Organization Development: Its Nature, Origins, and Prospects.* Reading, Mass.: Addison-Wesley, 1969.

Dalton, G. W.; Lawrence, P. R.; and Greiner, L. E. *Organizational Change and Development.* Homewood, Ill.: Irwin-Dorsey, 1970.

Filley, A.C., and House, R. J. *Managerial Process and Organizational Behavior.* Glenview, Ill.: Scott, Foresman, 1969. Chapter 18.

Greiner, L. E. "Evolution and Revolution as Organizations Grow," *Harvard Business Review,* 50 (1972): 37–46.

Lawrence, P. R., and Lorsch, J. W. *Developing Organizations: Diagnosis and Action.* Reading, Mass.: Addison-Wesley, 1969.

Margulies, N., and Raia, A. P. *Organizational Development: Values, Process, and Technology.* New York: McGraw-Hill, 1972.

Current and Future Issues

16

A stranger to this world might assume that possession of the knowledge found in a basic text on management and in more advanced texts, applied with skill gained through experience, would be sufficient for success in organizational management. There is more to success, however: burning issues in the United States and throughout the world command the attention of all types of organizations. These issues constitute our main interest in this final chapter, although we will make some limited predictions about the nature of management and organization in the future. We will direct our attention primarily to the business organization since this has been our central focus throughout the book and since much of the current discussion on the issues centers around what business can and should do. The focus on business is not meant to suggest that other types of organizations should not share the responsibility for confronting the many problems of our society.

Issues Facing Business Management

There are business leaders who still disclaim responsibility for social problems. The great majority of business leaders, however, increasingly accept responsibility for problems beyond the traditional boundaries of their organizations' interests. There has been a growing concern over quality of life in the United States and in other countries in recent years. Pollution, decay of cities, poverty, and discrimination against minority groups all contribute to this concern. The mood has become increasingly antibusiness, perhaps because business is not seen as having done enough to alleviate living conditions.

A survey by the Opinion Research Corporation of Princeton, New Jersey, showed that pollution, cost of living, using up natural resources, deceptive packaging or labeling, employment opportunities for Negroes, and slums or urban ghettos are among the most important problems that people think corporations should worry about. The survey also indicated a strong antibusiness mood. Over one-half of those surveyed expressed a low approval of business. Over one-half felt business was doing very little about pollution compared with ten percent who thought it was doing a great deal. One-fifth felt they had been cheated or deceived recently on the purchase of a service or product.[1]

Serious misconceptions also were revealed. Those surveyed believed the after-tax profits of corporations average 28 percent of sales when they actually average 4 percent. Business has a problem, brought on by its failure to act in certain cases and by its failure to communicate the real nature of business activities in those instances where business has acted in areas outside their immediate interest. Kenneth Schwartz advised business, "Through direct action and communication, corporations must overcome misconceptions about their activities while correcting abuses for which they are accountable."[2]

Student attitudes have sometimes been upsetting to business as well. Students have indicated they want business to be more socially conscious and to lobby for legislation in social areas. They also want more challenging jobs rather than jobs that require them to spend months or years in tedious training programs. Business people often respond by saying they are already doing these things, but students do not perceive it and mutual understanding does not follow.[3] Students suggest they do not want to make the company their entire life. They do not want to have to do things they do not believe in, and they would like as much autonomy in their work as possible.

So business is playing to an unappreciative audience. With this brief survey of popular mood as a background, let us go on to examine the issues involved.

Pollution

Concern over air and water pollution built rapidly in the 1960s, stimulated by fear of smog that periodically settled over cities and large areas of the country. Industry did virtually nothing to control the emission of pollutants until forced to do so by pressure groups and, finally, by the federal Environmental Protection Agency and various state agencies. Under the new regulations, there has been much activity. In one case, a single factory was turning out more soot than the entire city of New York. At times, the smoke completely blotted out the sun. The Environmental Protection Agency gave the company three years to clean up.[4]

Pressure for change comes from many sources. A local of the United Steelworkers Union has battled hard for a cleanup of coke ovens, which were emitting hazardous tar pitch particles and gases. The Sierra Club, a daring conservation group, has more than once forced utility companies to modify plans for construction of nuclear power plants on rivers and lakes, charging thermal pollution of the water and subsequent destruction of fish and marine life. The State of Delaware has even prohibited certain oil companies from locating refinery and drilling operations within the state boundaries. Pollution will remain an important issue for many years. In addition to complying with government regulations, many companies are initiating and will initiate programs of their own, not only to reduce pollution but to beautify their physical environments.

Minority Groups and Discrimination

The business world today is making an intensive effort to hire and train members of minority groups. This effort is relatively new, though many businesses and individual business people have worked hard for a long time to open up opportunities for everyone. The passage of the Civil Rights Act of 1964 marked a real turning point, however. The act requires most organizations to consider all persons without regard to race, color, religion, sex, or national origin. The Equal Employment Opportunity Commission enforces the act by making sure the proportion of minority-group members on a given work force approximates the proportion of each minority group in the local population. Where the government funds operations, such as with grants to universities, enforcement power resides in the threat to withhold funding.

Then there are groups such as the Colorado Economic Development Association in Denver, which "has helped to get financial aid totaling more than $15 million for more than 500 minority businessmen, a record unapproached by any similar group in the country." The association not only loans money but also offers a short course in management as well as professional management assistance while a new business gets underway.[5] Business has done a great deal in this area, but much remains to be done. The greatest emphasis has been and will be on the availability of jobs.

Urban Redevelopment

The relationship between urban redevelopment and business is more tenuous than that between business and pollution or minority group hiring. The latter areas appear more easily subject to direct action by business. Government at various levels has been involved in programs to salvage cities, but some business people feel that governmental efforts bog down in endless discussion and political maneuvering. Critics contend that business should be involved in urban redevelopment. But what is the business viewpoint? John S. Pillsbury, Jr., chairman of the Northwestern National Life Insurance Company, makes the following point about urban redevelopment:

So a situation that endangered the physical and financial welfare of our policyholders and endangered the value of our assets obviously endangered our business. If the prospects for our cities and our society were bleak, what would be the prospects for life insurance companies or, for that matter, for any business? Short range, both figuratively and literally, we could hold our noses and shut our eyes to what was immediately about us as we made our way to our air-conditioned offices; we could bar our windows against vandalism and we could perform our services or manufacture our products at a price and in quantity to produce a good profit at year end.

Long range, however, it was clear that we must have social, political and economic stability and a greater affluence in which a much broader cross-section of our population participates and shares in a meaningful way if our businesses are going to grow and prosper.[6]

Pillsbury goes on to suggest that business invest a portion of its profits to improve the urban environment and its economic well-being so there will be broader and better markets for products and services in future years. We have quoted Pillsbury because his opinion is that of many forward-looking business leaders.

Growth Versus Stability

For years our national economic policies emphasized the importance of continuous economic growth to national prosperity. Businesses, too, regarded growth as essential to success. However, as environmental pressures increasingly command our attention, the values of growth have been called into question. Business growth takes many forms: through the development of a single product base, through purchase of other companies, and through merger. But growth also creates problems.

The government controls growth that reaches monopoly proportions through its antitrust regulations. And we are not prepared to say that large companies have any greater potential for despoiling the environment than small companies. But, even aside from monopoly considerations or impacts on the environment, certain aspects of growth draw criticism.

For example, a study of acquisitions of Wisconsin companies by out-of-state organizations drew several conclusions. Operating under the control of out-of-state headquarters, the companies used fewer local professional services—such as accounting and legal services—than formerly. Company employment grew less rapidly after the acquisition than before, although the post-acquisition period was one of rapidly growing employment in the state.[7] Added to these immediate economic effects is the multiplier effect obtained when professionals with reduced incomes in combination with lower employment rates spend less money in the community, thus reducing the incomes and expenditures of many others. Willard F. Mueller writes: "Clearly, the conglomerate merger movement of the 1960s has caused a drastic transformation in the geographic pattern of corporate control in America. These developments may have a far-reaching and enduring impact on numerous communities across the land. But even more important, these changes reflect an erosion in the fundamental premise that a wide diffusion of economic decision making fosters social and political, as well as economic, institutions that Americans have traditionally valued highly."[8]

We cannot predict the future trend of mergers and acquisitions, though we can say with certainty that not all observers will agree with the view expressed above. Arguments over growth versus stability will probably occupy management's attention for some time to come.

Consumerism

Consumerism is another problem that business cannot ignore. Spurred on by their own experiences with shoddy and defective merchandise and by the hard-hitting attacks of consumer advocates such as Ralph Nader, consumers individually and collectively are pressing demands for higher quality and lower prices. In recent years courts have increasingly sided with the consumer in his attempts to gain legal redress for faulty products. "The law of a manufacturer's liability for harmful products has come full cycle: from non-liability, even when negligent, to strict liability— responsibility imposed simply on the basis that the defendant is the father of an unreasonably dangerous or defective product, regardless of all other considerations. This is a spectacular development, born of the recognition that the risk of loss is more easily shouldered by profit-making enterprise than by the consumer, his family, or governmental welfare programs."[9]

Thus business finds itself under considerable pressure. Business probably must incur greater cost in product design and manufacturing to build higher quality and safer products at the same time that consumers are rebelling against high prices. Industry is pressing for higher worker productivity which represents a partial answer. A full solution may depend on technological advances in years to come.

The issues mentioned above are not the only ones facing business, of course, but they represent a fair sampling of the important ones. Some of them are interrelated. Urban decay and discrimination, for example, compound the whole problem of poverty. Solving one problem could help ease another problem, or could conceivably aggravate another problem. Therefore, many experts advocate a total systems approach to problems of society. What is the direct impact of these problems on business management?

The development of organizational strategy requires the development of short-, intermediate-, and long-range plans to achieve agreed-on-goals. Matters of public concern such as we have been discussing exercise perhaps their greatest influence on business in the area of goal formation. How is this influence exercised? Groups and individuals representing various interests boycott company products, picket in front of corporate headquarters, and circulate petitions for submission to top management. Interested persons also write reports for general circulation in the media; attend annual meetings of corporations; seek membership on corporate boards of directors; and lobby at local, state, and federal levels. They often appraise past business performance and report these results in the attempt to influence business goal formation for the future.

Appraising performance or evaluating results is a sticky issue in itself, however. How does one evaluate performance on urban redevelopment, for example, or on the hiring of minority-group members? Fred Luthans and Richard Hodgetts suggest the following:

For poverty and civil rights, several representative criteria come quickly to mind: "What has been done to improve housing in the slum areas?" "How many minority or hard-core unemployed were hired throughout the year?" "How many hard-core–unemployed training programs were conducted?" "Has the equal employment opportunity of women in the firm improved?" "What has been done in the area of promoting black entrepreneurship?" Some firms will put these criteria in quantitative terms; others will employ only qualitative measures.... Both objective and subjective, quantitative and qualitative measures can be used. Simply counting the number of minority-group members hired is not sufficient. It overlooks the type of work they were given and the opportunities that exist for growth and development. . . . The same reasoning applies to the ecological concerns of the firm. It can use objective criteria for evaluation, such as the specific changes instituted in the manufacturing process or antipollution equipment introduced throughout the plant. Subjectively, it can evaluate the relationships with the local community, the time and energy expended in studying new and potential ecological legislation, and the research and development effort to come up with new products and productive processes that will not damage the environment. For the issue of consumerism the company can establish objective criteria, such as the number of complaints or number of lawsuits over the previous year. The subjective side could include such criteria as new consumer-oriented policies that were instituted and the status of relationships with local and national consumer groups.

In the final analysis all performance criteria are dependent upon the individual firm. Its operations, size, and location will dictate the specific social-responsibility objectives and methods of measurement. However, it should be pointed out that an evaluation of these objectives is possible and can be conducted on an objective and subjective basis. Each firm will have to determine its own approach, but the important point is that some form of evaluation is used.[10]

Some critics feel business should be held accountable to the public by means of a social audit. These audits would be made available to the public just as financial audits by certified public accountants often are. Now, given that there is and has been so much pressure to include social objectives among organizational goals, we should look at the record of business in this respect. In this way we will be making an informal audit of the kind suggested.

What Is Business Doing about Social Problems?

We have already touched on some business activities directed toward social problems. There is a lot more that business has been and is doing. Hallmark Cards invested $200 million in an 85-acre urban renewal project in Kansas City. Dow Chemical Company has spent millions to develop "zero discharge" plants that completely recycle waste. The Reverend Leon H. Sullivan, first black member of General Motors Board of Directors, has persuaded and helped GM to increase its number of black dealerships, to increase the number of blacks attending the GM institute, to upgrade hundreds of blacks into salaried jobs, and to pour millions into black banks and insurance companies as well as to assist in the development of black business. International Business Machines Corporation (IBM) successfully established a plant employing hundreds in the nation's largest ghetto, the Bedford-Stuyvesant area of Brooklyn. In addition, IBM and other companies grant leaves for public service, for up to a year, so employees can take time off, usually with pay, to work in areas of social need.[11]

Technological substitutes for social action are also developed by business. While we recognize the power for change inherent in the ability to change values and attitudes, we also know that value change usually is a long-range proposition. Therefore we quite frequently turn to technological approaches for partial, if not full, solutions to vexing problems. For example, safety experts have found it more effective to design safety into equipment rather than change attitudes toward safety. Social engineers try to do both, of course; but you can imagine what highway accident rates would be if they concentrated solely on changing driver attitudes.

Many other examples could be cited, but the fact is that business involvement in social problem areas is widespread. In addition to those activities already mentioned, business sometimes runs day-care centers for children of its employees, conducts educational programs on drug abuse, landscapes and beautifies the environment, and finances housing for core-city areas. In 1972, *Business Week* stated, ". . . corporate social responsibility is no longer unique, startling, or, in most cases, controversial. Social responsibility has become part of the business of business.[12]

There is another side to the question of the social responsibility of business, of course. The *Wall Street Journal* says, "Economist Milton Friedman, for one, still argues that the corporation's responsibility is to produce profits and that the cost of corporate social goals amounts to a hidden tax on workers, customer, and shareholders."[13] It is also true that many companies have not accepted the notion of corporate responsibility for social ills. And of those who profess to have done so, a certain percentage no doubt have an interest only in the public relations value.

Some attempts in the late 1960s at rectifying social problems were sincerely motivated but ill-conceived and poorly implemented. During that period, Jules Cohn surveyed 201 companies and found ". . . tokenism, recession-caused layoffs, poorly conceived job-training programs, and corporate frustration born of the realization that executives underestimated the difficulty and cost of solving urban problems."[14] Cohn said, "Businessmen can serve the public by continuing to play a limited role in urban affairs, cleaning their own houses through expanded employment and training programs, and providing revenues for the cities through taxes and donations."[15]

For some the controversy continues. For many, perhaps most, businesses, recognition of business responsibility for social action is an accepted fact. Their acceptance primarily stems from three sources: (1) voluntary recognition by business of the need for social action and of its responsibility to share in programs to meet that need; (2) governmental requirements that force business action; and (3) public pressure on companies to redefine their goals toward more active involvement in the social arena.

When companies take on social goals, they must, of course, develop plans for the achievement of these goals. Stating an official goal, such as aiding minority business in a given area, is easy. Making the goal operational—developing plans for action, implementing them, and measuring the results—is the tough part. We have cited some guidelines for appraising social efforts. Developing and implementing plans requires knowledge and experience of the specific problem being tackled.

Some time ago, *Business Week* suggested nine commandments as composing a manual for social action:

1. *Don't argue over goals.* Profits will always remain a central concern of a business organization, but unless social ills are addressed, there may be no society stable enough to permit business operation.
2. *Be sure the top man is committed.* Without a complete commitment, no program will ever get off the ground.
3. *Don't expect clear cost figures.* Don't expect to find a profit on your balance sheet as a result of social action, but don't be surprised at some unexpected benefit.
4. *Forget about structure.* Be informal. Don't get wrapped up in red tape.
5. *Be concerned about credibility.* Be honest with the public about what you have done, including both successes and failures.
6. *Get all employees involved.* Unless employees do more than authorize a deduction for a charitable contribution, your program is doomed.
7. *Get the directors involved.* Support from the top is always important.
8. *Give seed money along with advice.* When aiding minority-owned business, both professional help and money usually are absolutely essential to success.
9. *Don't make the program a maverick.* Keep your programs in the mainstream of company activity or they will wind up as stagnant backwaters.[16]

A business person committing his organization to social action could find at least two good reasons for doing so. First, there is a moral imperative for doing the right thing. Many businesses have treated employees humanely, fought discrimination, and in general have strived to be a "good citizen" because they feel a moral obligation to contribute to the well-being of society.

Second, there is the doctrine of enlightened self-interest:

There is broad recognition today that corporate self-interest is inexorably involved in the well-being of the society of which business is an integral part, and from which it draws the basic requirements needed for it to function at all—capital, labor, customers. There is increasing understanding that the corporation is dependent on the goodwill of society, which can sustain or impair its existence through public pressures on government. And it has become clear that the essential resources and goodwill of society are not naturally forthcoming to corporations whenever needed, but must be worked for and developed.

This body of understanding is the basis for the doctrine that it is in the "enlightened self-interest" of corporations to promote the public welfare in a positive way. The doctrine has gradually been developing in business and public policy over the past several decades to the point where it supports widespread corporate practices of a social nature, ranging from philanthropy to investments in attractive plants and other programs designed to improve the company's social environment.[17]

To put it more bluntly, business can help assure a long-term profit by contributing to the making of a healthy society, but if business does not voluntarily contribute, it may be forced to anyway by public pressure for governmental regulation. If society and the physical environment as we have known them are largely destroyed, what possible place could business find for its operation? Much has been done in the area of social responsibility: much remains to be done. Figure 16–1 illustrates expanding areas of business responsibility.

What Is in the Future?

We will largely confine our discussion of future trends to business, although much of what we say may apply to other organizations as

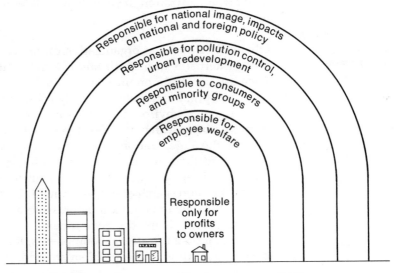

Figure 16–1 Expanding areas of business responsibility

well. A dream persists that one day we will have a theory—easily understood and communicated, precise, and comprehensive —that will explain everything about organizational management. A corollary dream persists that some day we will have one type of organization that will serve perfectly in all possible situations. At the moment, both dreams appear unrealistic. Therefore, we must separate our discussion of business from other kinds of organizations.

A variety of organization structures will continue to be required over the next twenty years at least. There will continue to be a need for the traditional hierarchy with tight, directive control. There will continue to be a need for the completely free-form organization with a total absence of structure and central direction. For the immediate future, we expect a continuation of the trend toward a more organic, collaborative organization—characterized by a team approach, deemphasis of formal structure, open communication, innovation, flexibility, trust, autonomy for the individual, and recognition of individual goals as well as organizational goals.

Change and development will be the rule rather than the exception. There will be many temporary task forces organized around problems, with members representing diverse professional skills. Each member of the organization will have greater influence on ends and means. One of the most important functions of this type of organization will be maintenance and development of the conditions that facilitate operation of the collaborative organization. In short, organization development will be a continuing requirement.

Research and Development

Obviously a business organization cannot concentrate exclusively on its internal relationships and the well-being of its employees. Business' most important goal is still survival through profit return, and profit is not always easily achieved in today's competitive, dynamic environment. Hence there will be an increasing emphasis on research and development (R and D) as an integral part of the organization. New products, value analysis, more efficient methods of manufacture and service, higher product quality and safety, and technological substitutes for social action all depend on research and development. Further, all are required to meet the demands of various pressure groups: customers, employees, stockholders, the government.

Like other organizational components, R and D will vary membership according to the problem at hand. Experts will be pulled in for R and D on a temporary basis, returning to their primary activity upon project completion. Research and development will thus become incorporated into ongoing business life and structure.

Continuing Evolution of Information Technology

We have already gone through four generations of computers, and no one knows how many more there will be. Without question, computers will become more sophisticated and more capable of handling the most complex well-structured problems as well as ill-structured problems. Time-sharing on computers and development of the mini-computer open up market potentials in small business and the home.

Processing ever-increasing amounts of data in less and less time, working through complex mathematical and statistical models, and doing simulations of problems that could be done no other way, the computer, as an integral part of information technology will have, and already has had, profound impacts on organizational life.

Numerous predictions about the impact of computers have been made: the rapid, comprehensive availability of information to top management will provoke a trend to recentralization; top management will do all planning, leaving routine operational details to middle management; the ability to disburse masses of information rapidly will provoke a trend toward decentralization; organizational levels will be more sharply differentiated; organization level distinctions will be more blurred; and middle managers will have more responsibility than ever before.

In fact, it is difficult to gain any agreement on what will happen to organizations as a result of advancing information technology. This difficulty is understandable, since there are so many phenomena that do and will affect organizations—public pressure, for example. The author personally feels that there will continue to be diverse organizational forms and managerial styles, although with a detectable trend toward the organic, collaborative type.

Multinational Companies

Since World War II, the multinational company (MNC) has moved from a relatively minor position in world trade to one of major importance. The MNC roster includes such familiar names as General Motors, IBM, Shell (Royal Dutch), Standard Oil, and Unilever. Historical extrapolation suggests that the MNC will continue to be an important organizational structure in business, and as such, it deserves our attention. But what, exactly, is a multinational corporation? William Dymsza distinguishes between the international firm and the MNC in his definition of the latter:

The "international company" is a generic term that comprises enterprises with various degrees of world orientation in their business; on the other hand, the "multinational firm" is one type of international company. The international company engages in any activity or combination of activities from exporting-importing and licensing to full-scale manufacturing in a number of countries. The international involvement of such a company varies from the point at which overseas sales and profits take on importance and top management begins to devote some attention to them to the stage when the company is globally oriented in its marketing, production, investments, and other decisions and considers alternative opportunities around the world.

When a company reaches the latter stage, it becomes multinational. Thus, the multinational company is one type of international company. It is a highly developed international company with a deep worldwide involvement and a global perspective in its management and decision making.

More specifically, the multinational company in manufacturing does business in a number of countries; it has a substantial commitment of its resources in international business; it engages in international production in a number of countries; and it has a worldwide perspective in its management. Our definition of the multinational company is primarily for the industrial firm, but it also applies to other types of enterprises.[18]

Key characteristics of the MNC include a willingness to consider opportunities throughout the world and a substantial portion of its assets, perhaps one-third and more, invested in countries around the world. Being truly multinational also means that organizational structure, policy, planning, and control are different from nationally-oriented organizations. Some reasons for these differences will be apparent shortly, when we discuss comparative management. We predict that more companies will be developing the differences as they change from national and international companies to multinational companies.

The MNC is no more exempt from criticism than the domestic company. For example, MNCs do not invest enough in emerging countries. Rebuttal: emerging countries resent the presence of MNCs because of perceived exploitation. The MNCs leave behind depleted resources, underpaid workers, a polluted environment, and a damaged social and cultural fabric. To avoid conflict, Peter Gabriel suggests that MNCs no longer invest directly in emerging countries but that they supply managerial, administrative, and technological services on a contractual basis instead: ". . . under such arrangements, management of the overseas venture will no longer be a permanent right vested in ownership, but rather an obligation assumed by agreement for a specified period. And the managing corporation's reward will no longer be an entrepreneurial one for risks taken, but a managerial one for services rendered."[19]

Another criticism: in the case of the United States at least, MNC operations cause loss of jobs for United States workers through the location of plants in other countries, which then ship products to the United States. Various studies show, however, that while particular industries may be hard hit at times, MNCs operating under a liberal trade policy actually produce more jobs for United States workers than they destroy.

The multinational company is still evolving, more so in the United States than in Europe, where a longer history of multinational operations grants a larger degree of sophistication and maturity. While multinational companies may not be the answer to world peace through trade, there seems little doubt the MNC is here to stay. And not only stay, for as the MNC evolves in the United States, MNCs will have increasingly important impacts on the companies themselves and on trade, investment, and development throughout the world.

Comparative Management

Directly applicable to the operations of a multinational company, comparative management studies differences and similarities in management practice throughout the world. Given educational, cultural, social, legal, political, and economic differences among the countries of the world, comparative management in the United States has tried to determine the extent to which United States management principles, practices, and knowledge can be transferred and applied in other countries.

Comparative management explicitly recognizes that management practice does not occur in a vacuum; that the organization is an open system; and that organizational activities very likely will have to be adjusted to local constraints. Some observers, however, believe that differences in the external environments of countries are so great and management practice in the United States is so closely tied to United States culture that transfer of management theory and practice from the United States to other countries is impossible.

Unquestionably there are vast differences at present. Workers in Europe and Japan, for example, usually have far greater job security than workers in the United States. When an individual accepts a job with a Japanese firm, he generally regards it as a lifelong association. In Japan, decisions traditionally have required a consensus of all persons involved, though we can note in the United States an increasing emphasis on participation and individual influence. Attitudes towards profits, wealth, status, work, and a host of other factors differ from country to country.

Nearly everyone agrees that there are differences among countries. But some challenge the "myths" that demand great differences in operations between multinational and purely national companies.[20] David Sirota says:

The core of the multinational management mythology is simply this: there are fundamental differences between the methods of management appropriate to a company that operates within a single nation and one that cuts across national boundaries. While some differences are indisputable—for example, the need to take into account national variations in trade regulations, labor laws—I suggest that many of the proclaimed contrasts between the two kinds of organizations are either nonexistent or inconsequential. Specifically, I dispute the severity of the "human" problems assumed to be inherent in an organization whose membership is multinational. I will propose that these problems differ little in kind and intensity from the difficulties commonly experienced by single-nation firms.[21]

In his study of a large multinational firm, Sirota found that "employees in all countries rated as most important to them those goals concerned with what might be called 'individual achievement.' These were goals such as challenging work, high earnings, training opportunities, and advancement opportunities."[22] Types of occupation and occupational levels appeared to make a bigger difference in goal orientation than did country of origin.

In addition, differences in effectiveness of communication and performance were found to be more a matter of organizational and managerial competence rather than a matter of differences between countries. And a majority of employees in one sampling from a foreign country felt that when managerial appointments are made, the best person should get the job—regardless of nationality.

One of the dangers in naively applying assumed differences among countries to management practice is that practice is often based on stereotypes. Germans are stereotyped as authoritarian; hence, management may assume they need highly directive control. Latins are stereotyped as procrastinators, so management may impose tight controls on any organization in a Latin country.

Stereotyping, then, tends to become a self-fulfilling prophecy.

Another danger is the use of cultural differences to excuse failure. Sirota states that in every case he looked into where a subsidiary was experiencing serious difficulties and was managed by a foreigner, "the problems stemmed not from nationality differences but rather from the incompetence of the manager."[23] In other words, the manager probably would have failed whether he was managing in his own country or in a foreign country.

The multinational firm is still evolving; we will not know its fully mature form for some time. Comparative management is also developing, and as empirical evidence accumulates, we will be able to say with greater surety how important national differences are for the multinational company. The study of comparative management will become increasingly important to the overall study of management.

The Challenge to Management

The future holds several challenges to the theory and practice of management. In the later 1960s, for example, the United States enjoyed what it felt was a comfortable lead in technology over the rest of the world. Today there are some who claim that not just the United States lead has melted away, but that the United States has actually fallen behind. Harvey Brooks combines prediction with assessment as he describes the situation:

I believe that the United States is experiencing only a few years earlier some of the forces and trends that will become worldwide among industrialized countries: saturation of the population able to undertake science and technology, competition of social welfare and other public expenditures for the government budget, increased public preoccupation with the side effects of technology, disenchantment with science on both the right and the left of the political spectrum, and increased preoccupation of society with equality rather than excellence.

Furthermore, the scientific system is increasingly international, so that the very concept of national superiority in science or technology is obsolescent. It will be harder and harder to tell who is "ahead" or "behind" as frontier science is conducted in multinational institutions . . . and as technology is introduced and diffused by international corporations that will become truly multinational and identify less with particular home countries.

The United States will never again enjoy its enormous superiority of the first half of the 1960s, but neither is it about to be overtaken dramatically by Europe or Japan. Rather, we are all approaching a common asymptote, which will probably represent a condition of slower growth, both in science and in the economy at large, than we have been accustomed to in the recent past.[24]

One of the challenges facing United States business, therefore, will be not only to progress in technology but to forecast technological progress in the United States and around the world. Forecasting in general will become more important as business strives to be competitive and to foresee and avoid those problems, such as pollution, that turn away public approval and force costly turnabouts in policy.

The managerial job in the future will require more knowledge and sophistication as organizations grow even more complex. Job requirements will call for a more intellectual approach and great skill in applying the manager's store of knowledge, which will comprise technical and scientific knowledge as well as knowledge of organization theory and behavior. Middle and upper-level managers will continue to work relatively long hours, while others enjoy more leisure (under the four-day week, for example). Compensation will continue to be in various combinations of salary and bonus.

H. Igor Ansoff and R. G. Brandenburg suggest that the manager of the future will have to play multiple roles; that is, he will need "simultaneous competence as a leader, administrator, entrepreneur, statesman, planner, and system architect"[25] (figure 16–2). They also suggest that management education today concentrates on the administrative and leadership roles, with little emphasis given to roles of the entrepreneur, statesman, or system architect.

In the past, one particular type of manager was needed in each stage of growth. The growth model we discussed in chapter 14 also indicated this need, and the histories of many organizations offer verification. In the case of General Motors, Durant provided the charismatic, creative leadership during the early phase of rapid growth while Sloan introduced GM to rational administration during an extended period of steady growth and consolidation.

Our overall prediction, then, includes the following: (1) business firms will increasingly take on a share of the responsibility for such social issues as pollution, discrimination against members of minority groups, and urban redevelopment; (2) business will strive to build higher quality, safer products at reasonable prices; (3) organizations will be more collaborative, with emphasis on people, open communication, innovation, and flexible structure; (4) there will be continued emphasis on research, development, and information technology; (5) multinational companies will become more mature and more common; and (6) the challenge to management will become ever more complex, requiring more team effort and new approaches to management education and training.

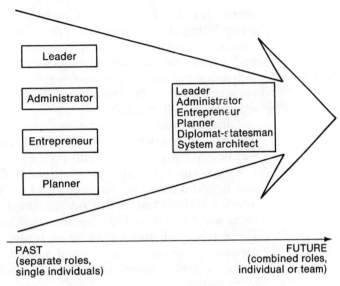

Figure 16–2 Change in managerial roles

There are some who say the type of organization we envision, and particularly its associated management, represents a soft approach. Similarly Douglas McGregor's theory Y approach, which provides a good deal of the basis for our projections, has been criticized as soft as opposed to the so-called hard approach of theory X. We believe these labels, "hard" and "soft," to be extremely misleading.

There will be nothing soft or easy about managing tomorrow's organization. To maintain a behavioral system, to sustain technological advances and scientific inputs, to meet external environmental demands, to perform against more precise measurements of results, and to do the multitude of other things we have discussed will require nothing short of managerial excellence. As a matter of fact, a good case could be made that managing in a traditional hierarchical structure with tight direction and control is considerably easier than managing in the type of organization we envision. Tomorrow's manager faces a tough job, one that will require the best efforts of anyone aspiring to the managerial role.

Summary

Management today confronts a number of social issues at the same time that the organization continues to evolve in form and substance. Business is increasingly willing to take a share of the responsibility for social action in areas such as pollution, minority-group hiring and training, and urban redevelopment. In addition to accepting social responsibility as one of its goals, business must find ways to measure the results of social action, to satisfy itself as well as the public that business is making a contribution. Reasons for social involvement include an ethical, moral commitment, and enlightened self-interest.

Although there will be a continuing need for a variety of organizational designs in the future, the trend will be toward an organic collaborative organization with primary emphasis on people, innovation, and flexibility. The multinational company will grow in numbers and maturity. The challenge to management will be even tougher in the future as the individual manager or team management will be required to play several roles rather than just one. These roles will include those of leader, administrator, entrepreneur, statesman, planner, and system architect. At the same time, we predict increasing opportunities for those interested in management.

In this book, we have tried to present that knowledge essential to managerial decision making in a complex organization operating in a complex, dynamic environment. In addition, we have tried to indicate the range and nature of decisions ordinarily charged to management and how management does and in certain cases should handle those decisions. In a book of this nature it is not possible to provide all of the answers, but we hope this introduction will help the student to find challenges and opportunities in management and, perhaps most important of all, to know the right questions to ask when faced with the challenge of opportunity or the need to resolve a managerial problem. Figure 16–3 illustrates the scope of our studies in organizational management.

Management Profile

Joseph Wharton

Business has long recognized the importance of professional education in management. It is fitting, then, that we conclude our series of management profiles with a profile of the man who funded the first business school in the United States—Joseph Wharton.[26] In 1881 Wharton, a Philadelphia financier and iron manufacturer, gave $100,000 to the University of Pennsylvania to set up a department of finance and economy. That year thirteen

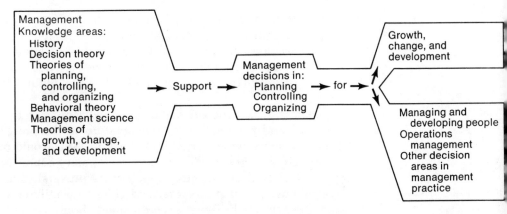

Figure 16–3 Scope of our study of organizational management

students marked an historic occasion in education by being the first ever to enroll in a business curriculum.

Wharton estimated that his $100,000 would yield an annual income of $6,000. This, plus tuition, would provide enough money to pay a $3,000 salary to the dean and $1,500 to each of five professors. As it turned out, the department started with one and one-half professors—one full-time in political economy and one part-time in accounting—and no dean. Not until 1912 did the university recognize the department as a separate school and appoint a dean. In the meantime, eighteen other universities had set up business schools; and from 1912 through 1925, 164 more were born.

Wharton stipulated that the name of the school should be the Wharton School of Finance and Economy, and it was so called for some years, later being changed to the Wharton School of Finance and Commerce. For many years the school awarded a B. S. degree in economics and was staffed predominantly by economists. Nonetheless, students in other fields scoffed at business students during the early years of the school. In 1883, editors of the college yearbook carefully explained, "It is a 'School of Finance and Economy.' If you know what that means, good for you—we don't." In 1885, the liberal arts students commented, "From the Wharton School no one is dropped. All that is required is a regular attendance upon chapel and the lunch counter."[27] The Wharton School has matured considerably in the past ninety-some years, and today is recognized as one of the finest business schools in the country.

Wharton wanted to give students a liberal business education. To his mind, this goal included not only such subjects as mathematics and history, but ". . . the phenomena and causes of panics and money crises; the nature of pawn establishments and of lotteries; the nature of stocks and bonds." In addition there would be emphasis on the problem of strikes, the need for cooperation, business law, elocution, and athletics "within moderate limits."[28]

Needless to say, the curriculum changed rapidly in the following years and has continued to change up to the present time. Joseph Wharton, who started it all, back in 1881, would probably be amazed if he were to survey the contemporary education scene: approximately 1,000 business schools at the university and college level; thousands of professors; and close to a million students, studying subjects he never even dreamed about.

Discussion Questions

1. To what extent should business organizations accept responsibility for social improvement? Is it true that the cost of corporate social goals is tantamount to a hidden tax on workers, customers, and shareholders? Explain your answer.

2. Do you think attitudes toward business are changing now—becoming more favorable or more unfavorable? What are the reasons for the change you perceive?

3. Is it essential for a business to continue growing in order to be successful? In other words, can a stable organization be successful?

4. If you were the owner of a business firm, would you act to promote the public welfare in a positive way on the basis of enlightened self-interest? Is it fair to ask all businesses, no matter what kind or how small or large, to act on the basis of enlightened self-interest? Why or why not?

5. Some multinational companies are very powerful, even more powerful than some small nations. Is it necessary to carefully control these companies? If so, how could this control be accomplished?

6. There are conflicting opinions about the importance of differences among nations with respect to the success of international companies. What is your view? Can differences among nations be more or less ignored in terms of managerial style? Or should companies operating in several nations vary their managerial approaches depending upon the particular national cultures involved?

7. What do you see in the future of organizational management—more collaborative organizations, more opportunities, and more challenge;

or a lessening of interest in management and a return to more traditional types of organizations? Are there any possibilities that you feel have not been fully considered? What are they?

References

1. "America's growing antibusiness mood," *Business Week*, no. 2233 (1972): 100–103.

2. *Ibid.*, p. 101.

3. A. C. Filley, "Today's College Graduate and Small Business," in J. H. Turner, A. C. Filley, and R. J. House, eds., *Studies in Managerial Process and Organizational Behavior* (Glenview, Ill.: Scott, Foresman, 1972), pp. 461–465.

4. "The World's Smokiest Factory," *Business Week*, no. 2162 (1971): 54.

5. "How Business Tackles Social Problems," *Business Week*, no. 2229 (1972): 95–103.

6. J. S. Pillsbury, Jr., "Management's Stake in Core City Survival," *Advanced Management Journal*, 35 (1970): 41.

7. W. F. Mueller, "The Merger's Impact on the Community," *The American Federationist*, 78 (1971): 14–18.

8. *Ibid.*, p. 18.

9. A. F. Southwick, Jr., "The Disenchanted Consumer—Liability for Harmful Products," in J. H. Bearden, ed., *The Environment of Business* (New York: Holt, Rinehart and Winston, 1969), p. 513.

10. F. Luthans and R. M. Hodgetts, *Social Issues in Business* (New York: Macmillan, 1972), pp. 265–266.

11. "How Business Tackles Social Problems," pp. 95–103.

12. "How Business Tackles Social Problems," p. 95.

13. "Changing Times," *The Wall Street Journal*, 52 (1971): 1.

14. J. Cohn, *The Conscience of the Corporation* (Baltimore: Johns Hopkins Press), as reported in *Business Week*, no. 2182 (1971): 16.

15. *Ibid.*

16. "Business Week's manual for social action," *Business Week*, no. 2229 (1972): 104–108. The commandments are summarized and not quoted in their entirety.

17. *Social Responsibilities of Business Corporations* (New York: Committee for Economic Development, 1971), p. 27.

18. W. A. Dymsza, *Multinational Business Strategy* (New York: McGraw-Hill, 1972), pp. 4–5.

19. P. G. Gabriel, "MNCs in the Third World: Is Conflict Unavoidable?" *Harvard Business Review*, 50 (1972): 93–102.

20. D. Sirota, "Management Myths in Multinational Corporations," in R. B. Higgins, P. V. Croke, and J. F. Veiga, eds., *Proceedings of the Thirty-first Annual Meeting of the Academy of Management* (Atlanta: Academy of Management, 1972), pp. 130–135.

21. *Ibid.*, p. 130.

22. *Ibid.*, p. 131.

23. *Ibid.*, p. 132.

24. H. Brooks, "What's Happening to the U. S. Lead in Technology?" *Harvard Business Review*, 50 (1972): 118.

25. H. I. Ansoff and R. G. Brandenburg, "The General Manager of the Future," in J. H. Turner, A. C. Filley, and R. J. House, eds., *Studies in Managerial Process and Organizational Behavior* (Glenview, Ill.: Scott, Foresman, 1972), p. 475.

26. Adapted from "Famous Firsts: How Business Schools Began," *Business Week*, no. 1781 (1963): 114–116.

27. *Ibid.*, p. 116.

28. *Ibid.*, p. 114.

Suggested Readings

Ansoff, H. Igor, and Brandenburg, R. G. "The General Manager of the Future," in J. H. Turner, A. C. Filley, and R. J. House, eds. *Studies in Managerial Process and Organizational Behavior*. Glenview, Ill.: Scott, Foresman, 1972. Pp. 466–477.

Dymsza, W. A. *Multinational Business Strategy*. New York: McGraw-Hill, 1972.

Luthans, F., and Hodgetts, R. M. *Social Issues in Business*. New York: Macmillan, 1972.

Robinson, R. D. *International Business Management: A Guide to Decision Making*. New York: Holt, Rinehart and Winston, 1973.

Zaltman, G., Kotler, P., and Kaufman, I., eds. *Creating Social Change*. New York: Holt, Rinehart and Winston, 1972.

Danger! Deadly Gas*

In 1955 the Bleach Clean Company opened a small single-story plant in West Atlanta, Georgia, a suburb of Atlanta, located about 12 miles west of the metropolitan core. Some years before, the West Atlanta City Council zoned approximately 70 acres for exclusive industrial use in the vicinity of the Southern Railroad tracks. Subsequently, several small light manufacturing plants were constructed in the area.

From 1955 to 1969, the population of the city expanded rapidly. This created a need for more residentially zoned land and caused real estate values to soar. The scarcity of vacant land for residential development resulted in rezonings, and gradually the industrial area was reduced in size and surrounded by single-family homes, business property, and apartment houses. An elementary school was located a block and one half beyond the industrial fringe.**

The Bleach Clean Company used liquid- and gas-phase chlorine in the production of its product, a nationally-marketed cleaning aid. The company also sold chlorine to industry. In 1968, the average annual employment of the West Atlanta cleanser plant was about 180 people. During the first week of August of that year, trouble arose when chlorine fumes leaked from a hole in a 3/4-inch rubber tube that was being used to transfer chlorine from a railroad tank car to a storage cylinder inside the plant. These chlorine fumes incapacitated more than 30 persons working and living nearby. Employees of the cleanser plant were quickly evacuated, but a light southeast breeze carried the fumes into adjacent industrial establishments and residential neighborhoods. People working nearby were the chief victims. The four most serious cases remained hospitalized for three days; 26 other persons were given emergency treatment and released. One of the victims described the effect of the gas, "You get a burning in your throat and feel like

---

*Reprinted with permission from M. M. Hargrove, K. M. Crites, L. C. Megginson, and B. H. Sord, *Cases in Administrative Policies and Contemporary Issues* (Homewood, Ill.: Richard D. Irwin, 1973), pp. 426–428.

**The Bleach Clean plant was bounded two blocks on the north by low-density acre-size residential property; four blocks on the south by high-density multifamily apartment houses; on the east by the Southern railroad, and across the tracks by a major highway with residential and business property; one-half block on the west by an off-street parking lot, and beyond this area by residential property and the elementary school.

you are going to pass out. You're sick and dizzy and then you're throwing up ''*

An aroused West Atlanta City Council ordered an around-the-clock watch at the cleanser plant. The city's director of sanitation stated, "My department has had several complaints this year about gas leaks at this plant. I asked the Zoning Board to order the plant to move, but never received a reply. I'd like to see them stay in our community, but in an area where they won't be a hazard to residents." After an extensive investigation, the West Atlanta Fire Department and the County Health Department issued statements that the Bleach Clean plant was being properly operated and was equipped with adequate safeguards against gas leaks.

A second chlorine gas leak occurred at the cleanser plant approximately one week after the report was made public. There were no deaths, but 20 persons required hospitalization. Five remained hospitalized for about one week, and the remaining 15 were released after initial oxygen treatment. All of these people were local residents or employees of local business establishments.

The next incident occurred in December 1968, when Bleach Clean workmen accidently spilled muriatic acid while cleaning a nearly empty 10,000 gallon container. About 35 gallons vaporized and floated across the railroad tracks to another plant where 14 persons were overcome. Three of these people had to be hospitalized overnight, but none was seriously injured. A Bleach Clean vice president described the incident as not serious and stated, "Our men worked in the middle of it for 45 minutes without ill effects."

After the muriatic acid incident, two West Atlanta councilmen indicated that they were considering a vote to suspend the firm's operation license; however, they pointed out:

1. The Bleach Clean Company was invited to locate its plant within the city and subsequent rezonings were not the responsibility of the company.

---

*According to the Chlorine Institute, a nonprofit trade association dedicated to the promotion of safety in all aspects of chlorine production, handling, and use, chlorine gas is primarily a respiratory irritant. It is so intensely irritating that concentrations above five parts per million (by volume) of air are readily detectable by the average person. When exposed to normal atmospheric pressure and temperature, liquid chlorine vaporizes into a greenish yellow gas about two and one-half times heavier than air. A moderate exposure to chlorine gas causes irritation of the eyes, coughing, and labored breathing. A prolonged exposure results in a general excitement of the nervous system, copious salivation, retching, and difficulty of breathing which may increase to the point where death can occur from suffocation.

2. The city of West Atlanta benefited economically from the firm's employment of local people.
3. Forcing the company to leave town could have undesirable repercussions, particularly since the city was not completely blameless.
4. It was the joint responsibility of the company and the city to provide adequate safeguards for the local residents, local industry employees, local elementary school children, and in fact anyone visiting or living in the city.

If this could not be accomplished, the council indicated that they would recommend the passage of an ordinance outlawing the transference of dangerous gases.

The West Atlanta residents were content to be considered ordinary citizens so long as they could determine the desirability of local industry. Any councilman who failed to put this need ahead of his own views faced crushing public disapproval and could have certainly expected his political reputation to be endangered and involved in continuous controversy.

Additional Information

Residential land values in the West Atlanta area had doubled in value since 1955.

Although serious chlorine gas leaks were rare in establishments handling chlorine, they did occur. On July 13, 1958, a rupture in a chlorine gas line at a paper company's plant in Mobile, Alabama, poisoned 37 workers and killed Walter Jordan, 34, brother of Lee Roy Jordan, former All-American football lineman at the University of Alabama. None of the aforementioned 37 employees were listed in critical condition, and all were released within two days from Mobile hospitals.

According to Bleach Clean management there had been no critical chlorine leaks in their other southern plants.

Bleach Clean Company officials expressed the thinking of management in stating: "We had not reached a decision regarding this operation. There were alternatives of action that could be taken. The company was fully aware of this reponsibility for conducting a safe operation and continued to work with the city and county officials to insure every safeguard in the transference of chlorine gas in our plant."

Index

Quantitative analysis (continued)
  linear programming, 101–103
  minimax technique, 107–109
  Monte Carlo technique, 98–100
  network techniques, 104–106
  simulation, 98–100
  statistical decision theory, 106–107
Queuing theory, use of in maintenance,
    384–385

Rationality and structure, 215–216
Raven, Bertram, 330
Reiley, Alan C., 37
Research and development, 375–376, 438–439
  future and, 438–439
  operations management and, 375–376
Research methods, 45–47
  case study, 45
  field survey, 46
  laboratory experiment, 46
Rockefeller, John D., 9
Roethlisberger, Fritz, 50

Satisfaction, group size and, 313–315
Sayles, Leonard, 312
Scalar process, 35, 196
Scientific management, 31–34
  efficiency experts and, 34
  principles of, 33
  shoveling experiment, 32
Scientific method in decision making, 96–98
Sensitivity training, 130, 263–264, 418
  organizational development and, 418
Shelden, Oliver, 267–268
Simon, Herbert A., 39
Simulation, 98
Single-use plan, 148
Skinner, B. F., positive reinforcement and,
    289–290. See also Operant conditioning
Slavery, effects of, on manufacturing, 29–30
Sloan, Alfred P., Jr., 9, 221–222
Smith, Adam, 394–395
Social action, 436
Social issues, management and, 429–437
  consumerism, 432
  doctrine of enlightened self-interest, 436–437
  evaluation of results, 433–434
  growth and stability, 431
  minority groups, 430
  pollution, 429–430
  recommendations, 436–437
  results, 434–435
  urban redevelopment, 430–431

Span of control, 37, 197
Staff assistance, 201–203
  functional authority and, 202–203
  types of, 201
Staff-line conflict, 226–227
Staff-line organization, 200–201
Standing plan, 148
Statistical decision theory, 106–107
Stereotypes, 277
Strategic planning, 147
Structure, group, 316–318
Structure, informal organization and, 235–236
Structure, organization, 195–219
  board of directors, 217–218
  committees, 212
  coordination, 203–204
  decentralization, 205–206
  departmentation, 199
  determinants of, 212–216
  free-form, 211–212
  functional authority, 202–203
  functional organization, 206–207
  line, 200–201
  line and staff, 201–203
  matrix type, 207–210
  modified traditional, 197–206
  organic type, 211–212
  project type, 208
  size and, 218–219
  team-at-the-top, 216
Supportive leadership, 336–337
Synergy, 6
System, 4, 12
  closed, 12
  open, 12
  organization as a, 4
Systems, 13–15
  classification of, 14
  entropy in, 13
  feedback and, 15
  homeostasis and, 14
Systems approach, 61–62
  organizational linking processes and, 62

Taylor, Frederick W., 31–34, 206–207
  functional organization and, 206–207
  scientific management and, 31–34
Technology, 213–215, 235–236, 238–241,
    443–444
  future and, 443–444
  informal organization and, 235–236, 238–241
  organizations and, 214–215
  structure and, 213–215, 238–241